SONIC THEOLOGY

Hinduism and Sacred Sound

GUY L. BECK

MOTILAL BANARSIDASS PUBLISHERS
PRIVATE LIMITED • DELHI

First Indian Edition: Delhi, 1995

ISBN: 8120812611

For sale in India only

Also available at:

MOTILAL BANARSIDASS

41 U.A. Bungalow Road, Jawahar Nagar, Delhi 110 007
120 Royapettah High Road, Mylapore, Madras 600 004
16 St. Mark's Road, Bangalore 560 001
Ashok Rajpath, Patna 800 004
Chowk, Varanasi 221 001

PRINTED IN INDIA

BY JAINENDRA PRAKASH JAIN AT SHRI JAINENDRA PRESS,
A-45 NARAINA, PHASE I, NEW DELHI 110 028
AND PUBLISHED BY NARENDRA PRAKASH JAIN FOR
MOTILAL BANARSIDASS PUBLISHERS PVT. LTD.
BUNGALOW ROAD, DELHI 110 007

To my Teachers
and to my Parents

Contents

Series Editor's Preface ix
Foreword xi
Preface xiii
Introduction 1
  Approach and Design 9

PART 1: BASIC SOURCES FOR SONIC THEOLOGY IN HINDUISM

Chapter 1: Vedic Sound 23
  The Principle of Vāk 25
  Vedic Ritual Language: Mantra 30
  Śabda-Brahman in the Upaniṣads 42

Chapter 2: Indian Philosophies of Language 50
  External Śabda-Brahman: Mīmāṁsā and Varṇavāda 55
  Internal Śabda-Brahman: Grammar and Sphoṭavāda 62
  Rejection of the Sphoṭa Doctrine 77

Chapter 3: Nāda-Yoga: Sacred Sound as Nāda-Brahman 81
  Patañjali and the Yoga-Sūtra 83
  The Yoga-Upaniṣads 92
  Gorakhnāth and the Nāth Yogīs 97
  Three Haṭha-Yoga Treatises 102
  Nāda-Yoga and Indian Music 107
  Current Trends in Nāda-Yoga 111

PART 2: THEISTIC HINDUISM: NĀDA-BRAHMAN AS FEMALE ENERGY

Chapter 4: Śākta-Tantra: Sacred Sound as the Goddess 121
  Śrī-Vidyā 136
  Goddess Kālī 144

Chapter 5: Śaivism: Sacred Sound as the Energy of Śiva 148
  Śaiva-Āgama 150
  Śaiva-Siddhānta 156
  Kashmiri Śaivism 160

Chapter 6: Vaiṣṇavism: Sacred Sound as the Energy of Viṣṇu 172
  Vaiṣṇava-Āgama: Pāñcarātra 173
  Bhāgavata-Purāṇa and the Sectarian Movements 183

Conclusion: Sonic Theology, the Study of
  Religion, and Hermeneutics 204

Notes 220
Glossary 246
Bibliography 253
Index 274

Series Editor's Preface

Several years ago a student in advanced string performance in our College of Music enrolled in my graduate seminar on religious meanings of space and time. After reading Mircea Eliade's *The Sacred and the Profane* for the first time, she observed that it was a very illuminating experience in all ways but one: there was no music, no sound, no sense of acoustic space. It is generally true that Western studies of religion have privileged, first, written texts, and second, visual images and descriptions. The phenomenology of sound has been largely neglected, much to the detriment of attempts to understand and appreciate spiritual traditions—both Western and Eastern—that have bases, at least in part, in sacred sound as well as in narratives (whether oral or written) and imaginal and iconographic modalities.

Creation as a speech event is part of the Abrahamic traditions, although theological developments of this foundational assertion have tended toward abstract and intellectual formulations, thus depriving them of their sonic quality, their "noise." As the Qur'ān relates: "Allah creates what He wills. When He decrees something, He simply says to it, 'Be!,' and it is." (Surah 3:47) The Qur'ān is more widely known and loved across the Muslim world through chanted performance than by literal comprehension. Sacred sound in Judaism has ancient roots in the Psalms, as in this early example: "The voice of the Lord is upon the waters; the God of glory thunders, the Lord, upon many waters. The voice of the Lord is powerful, the voice of the Lord is full of majesty." (Psalm 29:3–4)

Guy Beck has provided a welcome corrective, even a reorientation in the phenomenological study of religion by focusing on the traditions of sacred cosmic sound (*Nāda-Brahman*) in Hinduism. Probably no religion has had as central a place for sacred sound as Hinduism, which according to Beck is a *mysterium magnum* of the tradition, by which its multifarious sectarian varieties of devotionalism and theological discourse can be correlated in meaningful ways. *Sonic Theology* is both a focused technical analysis of the classical Sanskrit-based traditions of sacred sound in Hinduism and an essay in comparative hermeneutics of sound in religion. By delving deeply into the enduring acoustical mysteries of Hinduism, Beck simultaneously invites consideration of other traditions' sonic dimensions, which, in the West particularly, have languished in quests that privilege rational and visual approaches to knowledge and understanding.

Frederick Mathewson Denny

Foreword

This is an unusual and important book. It makes available in English for the first time an exposition of the Hindu notion of Nāda-Brahman, which Beck translates as "Sonic Theology." Although recent books by myself and others have opened the door to Hindu philosophies of language such as Bhartṛhari's *Vākyapadīya,* in which the divine is described as Śabdabrahman (God as "Word-Consciousness"), the closely allied notion of Nāda-Brahman (God as "Sound-Consciousness") has awaited Guy Beck's presentation. As is the case with Bhartṛhari where a "Yoga of the Word" is prescribed as spiritual discipline through word-use (including mantra chanting) until the final goal of *mokṣa* is realized, Beck unfolds the esoteric practice of Nāda-Yoga, "the Yoga of Sacred Sound," as a most effective means of reaching spiritual release (*mokṣa*).

The first two chapters set the stage for an understanding of sacred sound through a consideration of sound in the Vedas and in the Indian philosophies of language. Then the concept of Nāda-Brahman, God as divine sound, is introduced as well as the various techniques of Nāda-Yoga as found in Patañjali's *Yoga Sūtras,* the Yoga-Upaniṣads, the Nāth Yogis, Hatha Yoga, Indian Music, Sākta Tantra, Śaivism, and Vaiṣṇavism. This is a considerable tour de force, but one that Guy Beck brings off with style and sensitivity. Undoubtedly it is his background in both Western and Indian classical music that provided Beck the necessary sensitivity to hear sound as a yoga or means for knowing the divine—thus the apt title *Sonic Theology.*

A special quality throughout this, at times, very technical volume is Beck's facility in referencing the Indian experience of Nāda-Brahman to Western parallels. This makes the book accessible to readers unfamiliar with Indian philosophy and religion, as well as drawing the attention of Indian specialists to comparative Western phenomena. Beck's writing will evoke in both Eastern and Western readers a sense of the sonic dimension of the sacred—a sense that seems universal.

As an oral tradition, Hinduism has "tuned" itself with great care to the sonic experience of the divine. Contemporary Westerners can benefit from exposure to this Indian experience. It can sensitize us to aspects of reality that in modern secular society we often lose touch with, and to aspects of other religious traditions such as Christianity and Judaism that we have not fully appreciated. But over and above these important side benefits, Guy Beck's signal accomplishment is that he has provided us with a more complete understanding of the Hindu tradition—namely, its soteriological experience of the divine through sound.

Harold Coward

PREFACE

This book is the consequence of a long journey that began with childhood piano lessons and study of Western classical music. Having a professional musician for a father, I was surrounded by music history books and recordings of the major composers. Through years of listening and painstaking practice at the piano, I grew to recognize and appreciate certain recurring melodic phrases and intervals—often neatly camouflaged—which gave many of the masterworks of the great composers a certain "exotic," or "oriental," flavor. These were found especially in some orchestral works of Tchaikovsky, Mussorgsky, Rimsky-Korsakov, and Saint-Saëns and in piano works of Liszt, Satie, Debussy, and Ravel.

My college years during the late 1960s exposed me to the curious yet remarkable music of the Indian sitar and sarod of Pandit Ravi Shankar and Ustad Ali Akbar Khan. At first these sounds were unfamiliar, a kind of "purple haze" from a distant land. Closer listening, however, allowed me to recognize many of the same exotic phrases and intervals that I had earlier noted in Western music. Not surprisingly, a fascination developed regarding the theory and structure of Indian classical music, one that was to prompt some kind of formal training.

Combined with an interest in Hinduism invoked by undergraduate courses at the University of Denver in religion and Eastern philosophy, the desire for training in Indian music provided the impetus for a trip to India in the early spring of 1976. Having a reasonably good singing voice, at least from a Western perspective, I decided to take up Hindustani vocal music in Calcutta. I had also read that vocal music was the foundation for all other Indian music.

Shopping around for music teachers in India is perplexing, indeed, yet fate seemed to bring me to the Tansen Music College in Bhowanipur, a southern suburb of Calcutta. There I met my teacher and guru, Sri Sailen Banerjee, a reputable master, who was steeped in tradition yet could communicate well in English. He was even a *guru-bhai* of Ali Akbar Khan, having studied with one of his teachers, Ustad Dabir Khan.

Having obtained a one-year visa, I was naively confident that I could "learn the basics" during that period. I came to realize, however, that music training in India moves at an excruciatingly slow pace. Between weekly lessons the practice of vocal exercises, scales, and "rāgas" requires concentrated attention until sufficient mastery is achieved to warrant advancement. Thus, the first year went by very quickly, with only the initial training completed. Further visa extensions became necessary on a year-to-year basis. Professor Banerjee very kindly obliged to help in this regard by writing letters to the visa authorities, both affirming my continued progress in Indian singing and requesting my extension to continue the course of study. Being the major organizer of an annual musical conference in Calcutta, the Tansen Sangīt Sammelan, he personally groomed me for three public performances. In fact, under his patient care and guidance I was able to remain in India for nearly five years until the late fall of 1980.

During the course of Indian music instruction I would repeatedly come into contact with the concept of sacred cosmic sound known in Indian languages as "Nāda-Brahman." Though it was something I had not encountered in my introductory studies in Hinduism, my mentor had insisted that Nāda-Brahman was the zenith of Hindu religious and aesthetic experience, and the highest stage of musical perfection. The ancient singers and musicians were said to have experienced the universe as sound, and these experiences were recorded in the oldest Hindu literatures. Thus, Indian music seemed to have a primary religious origin and function, unlike certain segments of Western music. Perhaps it was this "religious" dimension of Indian music which accounted for my attraction to its unique phrasing and nuance, echoes of which seem to be encoded in Western music.

I was suddenly in the midst of a new quandary, namely, the question of the relationship between Hindu religion and Indian music as well as that between religion and music in general. Being puzzled by these issues, and having finally exhausted my visa extensions, I returned to America to enroll in graduate study in religion at the University of South Florida. Under the tutelage of George Artola (retired from the University of Toronto, Department of Indian Languages) I endeavored to consult multitudes of Sanskrit texts in search of hidden connections between Indian music and the Hindu tradition. This was then followed by doctoral study at Syracuse University under the expert guidance of H. Daniel Smith and Swami Agehananda Bharati of the program in South Asian religions. After two years of further preparation in the study of religion, with an additional M.A.

in Musicology, I was finally encouraged to undertake a project in "sonic theology" as a doctoral dissertation. As graduate seminars were already being offered in Hindu "visual theology," this enterprise seemed doubly justified. A small travel grant allowed me to spend four months of targeted research in India during 1988, at which time I was able to corroborate my thesis with new evidence. Needless to say, I found several connections between Indian music and Hinduism and was subsequently able to articulate in part the presence and little-known significance of sacred sound as Nāda-Brahman in Hindu religious thought and practice.

At this time I would like to take the opportunity to express my warmest appreciation to those individuals and institutional channels that made this project possible at its various stages: George Artola (Sanskrit), James F. Strange, William Shea, Daniel Bassuk (Hinduism and mythology), and Pat Waterman (ethnomusicology), all of the University of South Florida; Syracuse University—H. Daniel Smith (South Asian religions), Swami Agehananda Bharati (Tantrism and Hindu traditions), Richard Pilgrim (comparative religion), Charles H. Long (history of religions), Robert I. Crane (Indian history) as well as James Wiggins, David L. Miller, Patricia C. Miller, Amanda Porterfield, Alan Berger, and Charles Winquist of the Department of Religion; my music teachers at Syracuse University, including Howard Boatwright, Ellen Koskoff, Eric Jensen, Frank Macomber, and George Nugent; and the Senate Research Grant committee at Syracuse University, which provided funding for additional research in India during 1988. I would also like to thank Harold G. Coward of the University of Calgary for his timely help and kind encouragement.

Next I wish to thank my mentors and teachers in India, namely Sri Sailen Banerjee of the Tansen Music College, Vijay Kichlu and the Sangeet Research Academy, Gaurinath Sastri, Govinda Gopal Mukhopadhyaya, M. R. Gautam, N. Ramanathan, M. Narasimhacari, Smt. S. S. Janaki, S. D. Joshi, C. R. Sankaran, P. P. Apte, G. U. Thite, Smt. Vimala Musalagaonkar, Ritwik Sanyal, and N. N. Bhattacharya. I also want to thank my colleagues in Religious Studies at Louisiana State University, Baton Rouge, for their help and guidance in seeking a publisher—John H. Whittaker, Robert A. Segal, Stuart Irvine, and John B. Henderson. The persons associated with the University of South Carolina Press—Kenneth Scott, Frederick M. Denny, and David Caffry—are especially thanked for their generous encouragement of the project and their patience during the period of revision. In addition, and along with my parents who were always behind me, the abiding presence of my wife Kajal furnished untold sustenance.

In addition, this book commemorates my respected teacher Swami Agehananda Bharati and my father-in-law Sri S. K. Das, both of whom were called home before publication.

SONIC THEOLOGY

INTRODUCTION

> Very well, I shall describe to you the supreme character of the *mantras,* their key letters and the way to use them. This is however a secret. . . . It is by *mantra* that God is drawn to you. It is by *mantra* that He is released. By secret utterance these are *mantras,* and therefore these are not to be published. Their form is not to be written and their features not to be described.
>
> —*Parama-Saṁhitā* 6.2–4

The above message from medieval Hindu literature reminds us of a prevailing attitude among traditional cultures toward the written word: the transmission of sacred power and authority being primarily vested in the oral word, the written form by itself is often seen as typically worthless and even prohibited.

The quotation also points to a growing impasse in the current study of human culture, a deadlock brought on by an overdependence on visual sources leading to a virtual neglect of what may be "undescribed" or "unseen." Grappling with the seemingly Western obsession with the notion of empirical evidence, concerned writers have indicated that the emphasis on "visualism" in Western thought reflects a deeper "ideological bias toward vision as the 'noblest sense' and toward geometry *qua* graphic-spatial conceptualization as the most exact way of communicating knowledge . . . inherited . . . from rationalist thought [Descartes] and from the empiricists [Hobbes and Locke]."[1] Indeed, John Locke's famous dictum "The perception of the mind is most aptly explained by words relating to the sight" has proven to be one of the most stubborn tenets of the empiricists. The situation continues today as "anthropologists of all persuasions have been in overwhelming agreement that their knowledge is based upon, and validated by, observation."[2]

This imbalance in the world of ideas, represented by an overreliance on visual and written manifestations at the expense of the sonic or oral, is said to reflect an acute phenomenon in Western culture itself: the overwhelming triumph of images and the visual dimension of life in every sphere. The social critic Jacques Ellul has sounded the alarm in one of his recent works, claiming that the West has become an extremely visually oriented culture, with the consequent devaluation of the sonic or verbal dimension: "The invasion of the verbal realm by images results in role reversal and domination, leading us to another characteristic of our modern reality; the humiliation of the word."[3] It is even more unsettling when one considers his remarks on the deeper truth value of the oral dimension of language as opposed to the more surface-oriented realm of the visual, material universe of everyday reality: "The Word [spoken language] is related only to Truth. The image is related only to reality."[4]

Yet the comparable significance of the oral word and its ontological dimension had already been stressed by Western philosophy: "Indeed, it is the word, it is language, that really reveals to man that world which is closer to him than any world of natural objects and touches his weal and woe more directly than physical nature."[5] Accordingly, theologian Walter J. Ong has called attention to the inherent power of the spoken word: "Sound signals the present use of power, since sound must be in active production in order to exist at all.... Words are powerful. We take them in tiny doses, a syllable at a time.... Being powered projections, spoken words themselves have an aura of power." In Western modernity the absence of such oral "word power" has marked effects, such that "the shift of focus from the spoken word and habits of auditory synthesis to the alphabetized written word and visual synthesis devitalizes the universe, weakens the sense of presence in man's life-world, and in doing so tends to render this world profane."[6]

The above concerns are now influencing the academic study of religion in important ways. The oral dimension of scriptures and their recitation is currently recognized by scholarship in religious studies: "Recitation or reading aloud of scripture is a common feature of piety in virtually every scriptural tradition."[7] We are even severely cautioned regarding an avoidance of a sense of the "power" or mystery of the spoken dimension of scriptures: "The scholarly study of scriptures of the various religions will remain seriously limited and one-sided if it does not become more sensitive to the fundamental oral character of scriptures such as the Veda, the Qur'an, and even the Gospels."[8]

To be sure, the oral dimension of language and scripture in religion is truly significant. In the West one has only to recall the Gregorian chant of the Roman Catholic church, the "Jesus Prayer" chant of the Eastern Orthodox church, the role of hymns in Protestantism, and the general emphasis on rhetoric in the ancient world.

Yet, in order to climb less familiar peaks, the present study will focus on the broader sonic realm—including both linguistic and nonlinguistic sound—in religion as a vital and sacred category expressive of the numinous. Appropriately, it strives to fill, in part, a lacuna in religious studies. While historians of religion have routinely conducted research into sacred space and sacred time, they have curiously overlooked or "overheard" the dimension of sacred sound. "The classic, and invaluable, accounts of religious history have most of them been brought to a kind of head in the work of Mircea Eliade, who has shown quite beautifully the roots of religion in special attitudes to time and space. . . . This kind of study cannot be replaced, but it can be supplemented by another which sees religion in terms of man's relation to sound."[9] Consequently, this book generates a partial answer to this appeal by examining the integral sonic realm of the Hindu tradition.

Within the numerous subfields in the study of religion remarkably limited attention has been given to the nature and function of sound as a religious phenomenon. The sonic dimension of a number of religious traditions, as well as the textual and ritual sources reflecting it, are thereby done a disservice. While not aiming to devalue the written word or the visual dimension of religion, this study seeks to provide a partial corrective to this larger imbalance by focusing on the dimension of sacred sound in the Hindu tradition as an exemplary case. After examining a number of important traditions in India we have found that sacred sound, in theory and practice, indeed forms a "central mystery" of the Hindu tradition and functions as a common thread connecting a number of outwardly different sectors within it. As the Hindu experience of the divine is shown to be fundamentally sonic, or oral/aural, the theological position of sacred sound constitutes a kind of *mysterium magnum* of Hinduism. Conceivably, "Hindu theology" contains a necessary sonic realm built into its structure and substance. The concept of "sonic theology" which includes several important linguistic and theological issues, will become clear as we proceed, both as central to Hinduism and as a useful hermeneutic for the broader study of religion and theology. Thus, while recognizing and understanding the linguistic dichotomies of holy word / holy writ and oral/written, our enterprise embodies a more distinct emphasis on the sonic realm over and against the visual.

Through the years the visual dimension of Hinduism has received competent attention by Western art historians, iconographers, mythographers, and anthropologists. The concept of "seeing" the divine image or icon has been particularly stressed in modern scholarship. For example, "To a Hindu, image-worship is the air he breathes; the food of his soul and the fountainhead of his hopes, both for this world and for the other."[10] More recently, "*Darśana*, seeing the divine image, is the single most common and significant element of Hindu worship."[11] And scholarship in Hindu architecture has duly showcased the role of the temple wherein the visual icon is housed: "The temple is the most characteristic artistic expression of Hinduism, . . . imbued with a complex system of symbolism by which it embodies the most elevated notions of Hindu philosophy while still serving the requirements of everyday religious life."[12] Much of the work with visual images, icons, and temples is praiseworthy, as, indeed, Hindu traditional thinkers guarantee the sustaining value of the visible realm. Yet, without complementary studies in the audible or sonic realm of Hinduism—which are in fact proportionately absent—an important aspect of Hinduism becomes unduly obfuscated. The eminent status of sacred sound within Hinduism activates us to extend the clarion pronouncements of Ellul and Ong for non-Western traditions and beckons us to further explore the Hindu sonic world.

In order to discuss the sonic dimension of Hinduism as a "central mystery" it is helpful to make some prefatory remarks about the role of mystery in religion generally. Rudolf Otto had already validated the essentially numinous character of religious experience: "There is no religion in which it does not live as the innermost core." And the numinous necessarily includes—along with *tremendum*, or "awe"—the hidden yet positive quality of *mysterium*: "Conceptually *mysterium* denotes . . . that which is hidden and esoteric, . . . extraordinary and unfamiliar. . . . But though what is enunciated in the word is negative, what is meant is something absolutely and intensely positive."[13]

Thus, a major characteristic of the study of religion is its preoccupation with terms or concepts that seem to elude precise definition: *God, revelation, faith, salvation, mokṣa*. The fact that such words have remained equivocal throughout history is not necessarily, however, a defect of religion but, rather, a signal that something about religion, its core or center, is always ineffable and inexplicable and, therefore, mysterious: "Any religion has its central . . . *mysterium magnum*." Kees W. Bolle further explains the notion of central mystery as a kind of centripetal force which attracts and empowers other aspects of religion. "The ability to fertilize minds and hearts with a central mystery is probably the clearest mark of a religious tradition.

Whatever the fertilization leads to—socially, politically, logically, emotionally—it seeks its original center again and renews the very power that impelled it." And this force or power is unitive in thrust despite apparent disunity: "The central mystery . . . presents a unity in spite of doubts, manifoldness, confusion."[14]

Among the myriad elements or senses associated with the religious or numinous experience, sound (namely, sacred sound) most fully characterizes or represents the ineffable and irreducible character of the divine, as noted by Walter Ong: "The mystery of sound is not the only mystery among the senses. There is boundless mystery, of another sort, in vision, too, and further mystery in touch, as well as in taste and smell. But the mystery of sound is the one which . . . is the most productive of understanding and unity, the most personally human, and in this sense closest to the divine."[15] Rudolf Otto had even associated sound directly with the numinous, for "it is evident that the numinous feeling also, in its first outbreak in consciousness, must have found sounds for its expression."[16]

Consequently, the present book explores the terrain of Hinduism in order to corroborate the argument that sacred sound, in both its speculative and practical aspects, constitutes a *centralis arcanum* of the Hindu tradition. This central mystery, the domain of sacred sound which remains mysterious or undefinable despite continuous revelation and interpretation, provides the motivating and unifying power behind a religion that not only has proved resilient over centuries of invasion and desecration but also persists to this day in being recognized as a living, "universal" truth.

The audible, or sonic, dimension of Hinduism has only recently begun to receive attention in the West. Selected works of Madeleine Biardeau, Lilian Silburn, André Padoux, Harold Coward, and Frits Staal, among others, have contributed in various ways to the study of sacred sound in Hindu ritual and philosophy, some of which will be woven into our discussion. Since the field of religious studies and its methods is just beginning to gain acceptance in India, the focus of Indian scholarship on sacred sound has hitherto remained largely within specialized Indological disciplines such as Sanskrit linguistics, philosophy, aesthetics, and musicology. Some of these studies will also be cited to indicate the range and extent of Indian interest in this topic.

Theoretically speaking, the rudimentary assumption that equates language with consciousness underlies nearly all of the discussions of language in Hinduism. For example, "The existence of parallel structures of language, consciousness (or the Self) and the world is an insight of traditional Indian ontology."[17] Indeed, even among the earliest linguistic speculations of the Hindus "language was examined in relation to consciousness—consciousness not constricted even to human consciousness—and all aspects of the world and human experience were thought of as illuminated by language."[18] Not too surprisingly, this notion has parallels in the Western ancient world: "In Greek philosophy, the very term 'logos' always suggested and supported the idea of a fundamental identity between the act of speech and the act of thought."[19]

Accordingly, the oral dimension of language has been highlighted recently by Western scholars of Hinduism: "Holy words have been operative in human history. . . . The way that they have found their way into human lives is not through the eye, but through the ear; Hindus have affirmed that the holiness of the Word is intrinsic, and that one participates in it, not by understanding, but by hearing and reciting it."[20] Another states: "In the Hindu tradition, language is thought to be truly and most fully experienced only in its oral form."[21] And, even more emphatically: "Recitation of sacred texts forms the indispensable core of Hindu ritual life."[22] Such being the case regarding oral recitation, the element of sound and the sonic realm in Hinduism warrants proportionate emphasis.

Unlike some Indian traditions that accent the ideal of silence and quietism—for example, Buddhism, Jainism, and modern synthetic movements such as the Ramakrishna Mission, Brahmo Samaj, and Sri Aurobindo Ashram—Hinduism has sacred sound as its heart and soul. As such, the ambiance of the traditional Hindu is consistently saturated with an astounding variety of different sounds. Drums, bells, gongs, cymbals, conch shells, flutes, lutes, and a wide assortment of vocalizations are often heard simultaneously, blending together to create a vibrant sonic atmosphere within the Hindu temple, home, or sacred space. The initial impression to an outsider, or non-Hindu, is one of cacophony and profane chaos, an irrational ensemble of noise without order, rhyme, or reason. On closer inspection, however, one finds that what are being heard are specific sets of "prescribed sound" backed by an arsenal of oral and written sacred tradition. Consequently, whole categories of "proscribed sound" are restricted from holy enclosures.

Glancing at the textual sources in Sanskrit, the traditional language of orthodox Hinduism, one finds an underlying religious foundation for the element of sound in general, along with discussions of the kinds of sound considered efficacious in Hindu worship and soteriology. Particular texts reveal a concern with the divine origin of sound, including speech, language, and music. Among the many varieties of sonic discourse some describe the universe as an emanation from cosmic sound, others prescribe methods of individual salvation through the use of sonic techniques, while still others dilate upon the nature of sound as an eternal substance in itself. These and other topics often overlap within the same text, eliciting careful examination. The subject of the interrelationship between the Hindu theories of sound, language, and oral word, on the one hand, and their practical application is, indeed, an intriguing one and constitutes part of the motivation for this study. Furthermore, it can be reiterated that my present concern is not simply with the oral versus written dimension of sacred texts but with the entire "sacred" sonic realm—including both linguistic and nonlinguistic sound—in the Hindu tradition. The term *nonlinguistic sound* refers here mainly to the sounds of objects employed in worship, interior sounds heard in meditation, and especially to musical sounds in both categories.

Let us begin. From the Vedic and Upaniṣadic period up to the present certain issues, structures, and nomenclature persist which allow us to assemble a firm case for sacred sound as a common thread in Hinduism. These include the following: speculation on a primal vocalic syllable such as Om or AUM; sonic cosmogonies involving Vāk, Śabda-Brahman, or Nāda-Brahman; sacred sound—mostly Vāk or Nāda-Brahman—as the feminine energy of either a neuter Brahman or a specific male deity; the division of language into three levels corresponding to levels of consciousness or awareness (namely, Paśyantī, Madhyamā, and Vaikharī); positing physiological centers (Cakras) or arteries (Nāḍīs) in the human body which correspond to either letters of the Sanskrit alphabet or musical notes; the importance given to mantra utterance and the vocal repetition (*japa*) of divinely bestowed names, syllables, and phrases; and the philosophical confrontation between schools of linguistic thought such as Varṇavāda and Sphoṭavāda. Before proceeding, however, some of these terms will be briefly introduced below.

The exact Sanskrit counterpart to the English term *sacred sound* does not exist. As such, it tentatively includes a number of different Sanskrit expressions, some of which have been used to denote "sound" or "word" in a general sense and others that are encumbered with additional theological baggage.

The most widespread term for sound in general is *śabda,* according to the lexicon a masculine word denoting "sound, noise, voice, tone, note, word, speech, language, the sacred syllable Om, verbal communication or testimony, oral tradition, verbal authority or evidence."[23] Although it is used profusely in many diverse areas of Indian thought, *śabda* is the best single word for "linguistic sound" mostly connoting vocal sound to which meaning is attached, either in the form of an object or a thought: "In India all the schools of thought have assumed a direct relationship between *śabda* (word) and *artha* (meaning)."[24] In other words, if the word *śabda* is mentioned, the corresponding *artha* is assumed to accompany it. This *śabda* normally has two parts: unlettered sound, or *dhvani;* and lettered sound, or *varṇa*. Whereas the Indian Grammarians selected the word *śabda* to signify a meaning-bearing sound, the early phoneticians used the term *nāda* to signify only the "voiced" sound of vowels, as opposed to the "unvoiced" sound of most consonants.

The ancient Vedic sound includes the terms *vāk,* or *Vāk* (personified as a Goddess), and *mantra*. *Mantra* is a kind of "applied Vāk" as it refers to the utterance of Vedic verses in the ritual context. Parallel with the rise of Brahman as a theological or philosophical concept during the later Vedic period, the term *Śabda-Brahman* is introduced in the Upaniṣads. It chiefly refers to the "Sonic Absolute," which continues to operate within the sphere of linguistic meaning yet, in terms of gender, is basically neuter. *Śabda-Brahman* continues to be developed along with *śabda, dhvani,* and *sphoṭa* in the grammatical and philosophical traditions. *Sphoṭa* refers to the interior apprehension of meaning in language and forms part of our discussion.

In Yoga, Indian music (Saṅgīta), Śākta-Tantra, Śaivism, and the Vaiṣṇava traditions the most commonly used term for sacred sound is *Nāda-Brahman*. This rather ubiquitous compound, joining the Vedic phonetic term for voiced sound (*Nāda*) with the Upaniṣadic term for the Absolute (*Brahman*), generally denotes the feminine "sonic" energy of the divine. Though absent as a compound word in the ancient Vedic and Upaniṣadic literature, *Nāda-Brahman* nonetheless receives a broader and deeper exegetical treatment in the succeeding Sanskrit literature than any of the other terms and becomes the classical Hindu notion of sacred sound par excellence.

Śabda-Brahman as the term for sacred sound commonly found in the Upaniṣads and the philosophical literature still retains its connection with meaning (*artha*) in a linguistic sense, albeit on a metaphysical level. As *Śabda-Brahman* is gradually superseded by *Nāda-Brahman* during the rise of the Tantric and theistic traditions (after 500 A.D.), it tends to lose that strict connection and is more accurately identified with the notion of a primordial sound or vibration existing before the creation of the universe and simultaneously residing within the human body. As *Nāda-Brahman* includes the realm of possible "nonlinguistic" sound, the relatively consistent association of musical sound with *Nāda-Brahman*—a meaning rarely ascribed to *Śabda-Brahman*—becomes more understandable.

Praṇava, or *Om,* is the most prevalent vocalic "symbol" of sacred sound as word or syllable (*akṣara*) throughout the entire Vedic, Yoga, and Hindu (and Tibetan Buddhist) traditions and has been the cynosure of religious chant up to the present day. More than an ordinary sign or symbol, *Om* is often designated as the personal name of Śiva or Viṣṇu in the theistic traditions, given to the devotee by divine benefaction.

All of the above terms have been variously related to Brahman, the unifying Absolute, or God, of Hinduism, such that sacred sound, in whichever form or name, is almost always involved in the salvific process to attain final liberation, or release, known as *mokṣa,* or *mukti*—interpreted monistically as union with Brahman itself or theistically as communion with a chosen deity who is identified theologically with Brahman. As will be shown, these terms also take on additional nuances of meaning according to their context.

Although a full-scale explication of the structures and semantics of sacred, or prescribed, sound within Hindu religious thought and practice vis-à-vis tradition and textual sources remains to be written, it is hoped that this work will pave the way for further inquiries and studies leading to a more complete project.

Approach and Design

The implications of the above statements and critiques form the initial impetus for the present study, which seeks to articulate the integral sonic realm within Hinduism and, as already indicated, contribute to the general "recovery" of the sonic experience of religion, both as a means for transforming human lives and as a locus for an authentic hermeneutic.

Insofar as a phenomenological study of sacred sound in Hinduism is being attempted, we are prone to observe that the school of phenomenology itself has been recently expanding beyond its original "visualist bias" in order to include an approach to the "phenomemon of sound," as evidenced in the work of F. J. Smith: "phenomenology is not merely a standpoint or a perspective but a radical attempt to let reality speak (or sound) for itself. . . . It is a question of letting 'reality' speak in and to us. . . . That is why the truly phenomenological attitude is one of listening. . . . For the heart of phenomenological philosophy is sound and hearing."[25]

Yet, in the course of acquiring the myriad expressions of sacred sound given by the Indian texts and informants, the author has been prompted to redress certain kinds of methodological weaknesses. Inductive, "fact-finding" methodologies based on strict literary, chronological, or geographical partitioning fall short and are often irrelevant, contributory only to what is sometimes labeled as mere "surface phenomenology." They reflect biases in favor of "visualism," and may also exhibit Western positivist prejudices toward the study of non-Western mysticisms (or cultures) unnecessarily deemed "irrational." Indeed, if "India has no tradition of irrationalism,"[26] as stated by Frits Staal, then descriptive methodologies meant to rationalize so-called irrational data or phenomena would be found wanting with regard to Indian traditions, which seem to have their own uniquely "rational" structures and categories. Bolle made this observation regarding the study of mysticism in general: "The fact remains that we have too many mystical statements that are coherent, the obvious products of sound minds, that speak of real experience (not hallucinations), and that are not deviations of an individual. That means we are dealing with claims to truth in the face of which the erudition of objective facts is a mere escape-mechanism."[27]

To be sure, reason, or rational thinking, in the Western sense has an important and unique place in Indian thought. Yet it runs second place to revelation. The Vedas—revealed texts and thus "nonrational," or numinous, from a certain outlook—are the basis of all truth for the Hindu. Hinduism may even be defined, according to Brian K. Smith, as "the religion of those humans who create, perpetuate, and transform traditions with legitimizing reference to the authority of the Veda."[28] The use of reason in Indian thought (namely,

Indian philosophy in the strict sense) is thereby limited to the attempt to reconcile these revelations with human experience and empirical observation. Indian scholarship has duly recognized the "satellite" status of reason in Indian traditions: "It is surprising that reason has continued to remain in this subordinate position throughout the development of Indian religious and philosophical thought almost to our own days. . . . Reason was never trusted as the only true and safe guide."[29]

In order to penetrate beyond visual and rational surface data, then, and to accommodate a perspective that lets reality "sound" for itself, a more deductive approach was required. Such a method involved hypotheses that were set up and then tested according to the data received from texts and informants. In this regard, certain names, structures, and categories of sacred sound (i.e., Vāk, Śabda-Brahman, Nāda-Brahman, Om or AUM, Paśyantī-Madhyamā-Vaikharī, Nāda, Bindu, Cakra, etc.) which had been hitherto assumed to belong to only specific branches of Hinduism were first identified then searched for in a larger number of sectarian contexts. Rather than being a "visual analysis" of texts and artifacts, the methodology proceeded as a kind of "sonic synthesis" of common themes throughout the practicing Hindu tradition. After the above terms were sounded out and a significant number of different traditions were audited, as it were, the results were affirmative; that is, the necessary textual and confessional support was garnered through both research and fieldwork.

Thus, the present work is not intended to be an exercise in textual study, nor simply a survey of sacred sound in Hinduism. Formally, it is a case argument for the central significance of something that has not yet been sufficiently expounded in the field of religious studies. Briefly recapitulated, the central thesis is that sacred sound, under the guise of several different identifiable terms, operates in a mysterious way that networks a large number of Hindu sectarian traditions and creates new points of intersection between otherwise distinct religious communities. In a word, the nexus of otherwise diverse theories and practices is discovered to be a *mysterium magnum* in the form of a sonic theology.

The most authentic evaluation of what is happening religiously or theologically in the encounter with sacred sound in India necessarily entails a perusal of the traditions on their own terms. Paradoxically, yet true to the Kantian approach, it is in this interest that particularly

Western terminology such as *sonic* and *theology* is also being employed, both to broaden these terms, and to generate new forms of interpretive tension in academia. Though several attempts at comparative theology or comparative liturgy have been made in the last hundred years, the intention was largely to prove the superiority of Christianity. While the present purpose is not to demonstrate the superiority of either Christianity or Hinduism, these terms are used in combination with a careful reading of what Indian scholars and practitioners have to say about their own tradition to arrive at justifiable outcomes. The risk of intellectual colonialism, so characteristic of the West since the ancient Greeks, must be averted through the proper understanding and usage of Indian expressions. At the other extreme an attempt has been made to avoid the overapologetic tone arising from extensive use of internal or emic vocabulary, so delicately termed as "Eastern wisdom chatter" by Swami Agehananda Bharati. Consequently, Western vocabulary is used here with discretion, not in the interest of establishing a universal theory of sonic theology but, rather, in the pursuit of genuine hermeneutical paradigms that may in turn be applicable to other religious traditions.

The use of the term *theology,* however, needs some clarification here. Recently, Christian theologian Wilfred Cantwell Smith has placed theology on a level above sectarian affiliation by stating it simply as "speaking the truth about God."[30] Furthermore, the root word *theos* has been broadened by a postmodern theologian: "Theos, not in the classical sense of 'God,' but with regard to the archaic Greek meaning of the term as 'divinity,' that which 'shines' or 'reveals' itself from beyond the horizon of intelligible representations."[31] *Theos* may then be expanded to include that which sounds or resonates from behind or above, as this is closer to the overall Hindu concept of God, which is found to contain the element of sacred sound both as a structural part and as a hermeneutic that may uncover or disclose the divinity. Much as the term *cosmology* signifies the structure and workings of the cosmos, *theology* is thus taken here to mean the structure, substance, or nature of "Supreme Reality."

In further response to possible objections to the use of the terms *theology* and *soteriology* in the Indian context, some additional reminders are appropriate. As indicated above, the entire Hindu tradition is based on revelations that are considered to be transhuman and hence authoritative. Hindu traditions are thus much more theological than philosophical. The term *philosophy* has often been erroneously applied to Indian traditions, when, if strictly understood, it refers to inquiry determined by human reason without the influence of supposed revelation. The commentarial traditions of exegesis in the various schools of Hinduism conform in spirit to the content of the revelations and are thus "theological." Even the schools of Vedānta, which are so often considered the zenith of Indian "philosophy," are basically theological or soteriological in nature, as noted by John B. Carman: "the whole of Vedanta is, in Western terms, theology."[32] This statement basically agrees with J. A. B. Van Buitenen's earlier observation that "the soteriology of Vedanta is not philosophic in purpose, but religious, inspired and borne out by scripture and revelation."[33]

As pointed out by a recent study, the confusion in the terms *theology* and *philosophy* with regard to Indian traditions may be due to semantic misunderstandings: "The difference between theology and philosophy is a Western one, and not part of the Indian tradition; many Hindus prefer to speak of philosophy rather than theology, feeling that 'theology' implies uncritical acceptance of tradition."[34] Recognizing that all Hindus accept Vedic authority in some form or another, the use of the term *theology* for Indian traditions is legitimized.

Hinduism indeed provides ample substance for theology and, especially, sonic theology. The Vedas are considered self-revealed, and the sectarian traditions each claim their chosen divinity as the verbal source of revelation—Vaiṣṇavas claim Viṣṇu (including Rāma or Krishna) as supreme, Śaivas claim Śiva as supreme, and Śāktas claim the Goddess as supreme. Most all of the groups within these divisions evidence sonic theology—similar structures of the divine vis-à-vis sacred sound and similar traditions of interpretation of sonic themes which are fundamental to their identity as a division of Hinduism and cannot be dismissed as peripheral.

Furthermore, sonic theology as an academic enterprise is theology in that it searches for a consistent dimension (sonic) within a variety of Hindu revelations—Vedic, Śaiva, Vaiṣṇava, or Śākta—making connections between them and showing the relationships between sacred sound and the God, or divinity. While avoiding reading into the texts and traditions things that are not there, we have tried to "read out" meanings that are there but have not been previously brought to light, or "given voice."

Soteriology is expressly pertinent to Hinduism, as the majority of philosophies and religious traditions of India teach the necessity of *mokṣa*, or release of the individual human soul from temporal worldly existence, and are thus soteriological. As noted by an Indian scholar, "with the exception of Cārvāka, all other Vedic and non-Vedic philosophies of India accept rebirth and *mokṣa* in one form or the other."[35] And the preoccupation with *mokṣa* is based on the Indian view of the alienated human condition: "Both the myths and the philosophies portray the person as in need of salvation—as being in a condition that is not yet the ultimate one, as being estranged from the true self."[36] The present world is either depicted as *māyā* and *avidyā*, full of illusion and ignorance, or else reeling with evil forces and demons from which redemption is required.

All of the different divisions and sects that will be examined in this work reflect this basic concern for deliverance from an evil or nescient world, employing sonic themes in their theologies and advocating sonic techniques in their soteriologies. The Vedic practitioners and Mīmāṁsā thinkers achieve a kind of corporate salvation through the ritual performance of sacrifice and correct utterance of the mantras. The Grammarians claim to reach salvation through correct grammar and, thus, never transcend language, since Ultimate Reality is Śabda-Brahman itself. Similarly, although for different reasons, the theistic sects of Hinduism almost never advocate a transcendence of sacred sound or language resulting solely in a quiet beatific vision of their chief deity: mantras and corresponding Nāda-Brahman meditation are never really given up, even after liberation, since the deity is always elusively "Nādānta," or at the climax of the energy of Nāda-Brahman. Of the traditions covered it is only in Kashmiri Śaivism (perhaps under Buddhist influence) that language and sound are ultimately consumed by silence, though a silence pregnant with all sonic possibilities.

If, as this study maintains, traditional Hindu theology depicts the Ultimate Reality as including either Śabda-Brahman or Nāda-Brahman in some form, it may be questioned how this idea squares with the Christian notion of the "Word of God," or the Greek concept of Logos as timeless Word. Though basic differences exist, some comparative perspectives can be entertained. The strategic move, for example, of extracting the word *theology* from its Christian dominion can be reduplicated with regard to Word of God, or "Verbum Dei." Since the Protestant theologian Gerhard Ebeling had defined the subject of theological hermeneutics as "the theory or doctrine of the Word of God,"[37] then one could apply the term to mean the apprehension and interpretation of the Hindu eternal Word (Śabda-Brahman or Nāda-Brahman) through or by means of ordinary word event, language, tone—that is, sound. This is more precisely termed here as *sonic theology*. Moreover, for the Hindu sonic theology as a theological hermeneutic can be considered a kind of intellectual "brush-clearing" activity which discloses or draws one closer to the Eternal Truth by sonic or verbal means. There will be more discussion of hermeneutics in the concluding chapter.

Yet, in making comparisons between the notion of Word of God for Christianity and for Hinduism, a few points of distinction need to be made. Whereas in Hinduism language and sacred sound are intimately bound up with the divine, in Christianity any special kind of sacred language or sacred sound is ultimately suspect, since only the person of Jesus Christ is defined precisely as the Word of God: "Not the words of Jesus but he himself is the 'Word of God.' His words are one of several expressions of his being, which is the bearer of the Word, the principle of the divine self-manifestation."[38] The striving to reach an ultimate truth beyond language is an implicit factor of Christian practice, which separates it from most Hindu aspirations wherein language or the name of the deity as a verbal formula, or mantra, being identical with the deity itself, is never "shaken off" or discarded. Though the deity in Hinduism is Nādānta, "at the end of sacred sound," the devotee remains enveloped in sacred sound and the deity's holy name. Recent comparative studies in this area have suggested this difference. For example, "The nearest thing in Christian experience to the use of *mantras* is perhaps the invocation of the Name of Jesus, so essential to Hesychastic spirituality but practiced ardently by Western mystics as well; there is also the "prayer in tongues" or "prayer of jubilation," in which phrases, syllables, even a single vowel sound, without concrete signification for the one who utters them, lifts prayer upward beyond the limits of language and conceptual thought."[39] Contrary to the Vedic revelation, in which the language itself is revealed and thus divine, or Hindu theism, in which sound or language is the revealed feminine energy of God, in Christianity something "wholly other" which is nonlinguistic or non-sonic appears to quicken ordinary language at will in order to *make it* sacred.

But the more general notion of "God-language as mystery" is shared by both Hinduism and modern Protestantism. As explained by Karl Barth, "the Language of God is and remains God's mystery.

Mysterium signifies not only the hiddenness of God, but rather his becoming manifest in a hidden, i.e., in a non-apparent way, which gives information not directly but indirectly."[40] Paul Tillich expands this notion with regard to revelation: "Language as a medium of revelation . . . has the 'sound' and 'voice' of the divine mystery in and through the sound and voice of human expression and denotation. Language with this power is the 'Word of God.' . . . The Word of God as the word of revelation is transparent language. Something shines (more precisely, sounds) through ordinary language which is the self-manifestation of being and meaning."[41]

The evaluation of sacred sound in Hindu religious traditions is most productive by investigation into the following areas: Vedic sound, Indian philosophies of language, Nāda-Yoga, Śākta-Tantra, Śaivism, and Vaiṣṇavism. Grouped under different parts, each of these areas will form a separate chapter in the present work, with their subcategorization and general subject matter being clarified there. While reflecting neither chronological nor geographical categories, they represent cognate territories that have engaged scholars in the past and which include rich textual corpora and identifiable praxes.

Part 1, following this introduction, includes three chapters that attempt to present the Vedic and Yogic sources for sacred sound in Hinduism, sources that agree on the ultimacy of sacred sound, though in different forms. Chapter 1 begins by highlighting some of the important texts and traditions of the revealed Vedic canon, including especially the *Ṛg-Veda*, some of the Brāhmaṇa texts, and the principal Upaniṣads. As these are important sources for the linkage between sound and the divine in Hinduism, selected verses will be cited. After an explication of the principle of Vāk in the Veda, the role of sound in Vedic ritual language will be explored, it being inextricably bound up with notions of cosmic creation, mythology, poetic intuition, and performative verbal art. Accordingly, the relevancy of Vedic phonetics (speech production) and poetic meter will be stressed and incorporated into the discussion. The notions of *vāk* and Vāk, the goddess of speech, are seen to form the substance of what is to become transformed into the Upaniṣadic Śabda-Brahman. A major dictum in the Upaniṣads, *Vāg vai Brahman* ("Speech is Brahman"), informs the entire thrust of the emerging theological assumptions. As a compact form or symbol of Śabda-Brahman, the sacred syllable Om in the Upaniṣads will be studied in order to highlight features that determine in large part the evolution of this important aspect in the Hindu tradition, especially its axial role in the recitation of mantras both Vedic and post-Vedic. In the concepts of Vāk and Śabda-Brahman sacred sound is mainly linguistic sound; that is, it denotes a relation between word and meaning. Since the Vedas are themselves viewed as the revealed Ultimate Truth, and the Upaniṣadic seers and Grammarians view the Absolute as Śabda-Brahman, sacred sound here is construed as identical or nearly identical with Ultimate Reality itself.

Chapter 2 will discuss two philosophical positions—positions developed out of the application of human reason to revelation—representing the two major linguistic viewpoints that evolved directly from the Vedic tradition, the Varṇavāda and Sphoṭavāda theories. The confrontation between the Mīmāṁsā school (Varṇavāda) and the Grammarians (Sphoṭavāda) informs the underlying linguistic substructure of many of the post-Vedic, Yogic, and sectarian theories and practices of sacred sound encountered in the forthcoming chapters.

Though for different reasons, each of these schools holds sacred sound as the Ultimate Reality itself. While for the Mīmāṁsā school Ultimate Reality is limited to the eternal and "external" Vedic corpus, the Grammarians represented by Bhartṛhari posit Ultimate Reality as "internal" Sphoṭa or Śabda-Brahman, the very substance of all language, consciousness, and the universe. Yet, as will be seen, both views differ from the theistic traditions that view sacred sound (Nāda-Brahman) not as the primary Ultimate Reality but, rather, as its female power or energy. The chapter concludes with a discussion of the anti-Sphoṭavāda positions of the Sāṁkhya and Advaita-Vedānta schools, since it will be shown later that many of the Hindu theistic traditions overtly reject Sphoṭavāda yet adopt various Bhartṛharian terminologies according to their own theological designs.

Chapter 3 will examine the Yoga tradition as a primary source for the study of sacred sound by focusing on the developing theory and practice of Nāda-Yoga, including the principal sonic meditational techniques shared by most Yoga traditions and theistic sects. After introducing and defining key terms such as *Nāda-Brahman, Nāda,* and *Bindu,* the discussion begins with Patañjali and the Yoga-Sūtra tradition and proceeds with consultation of the principal commentaries. Then specific Yoga-Upaniṣads that highlight speculation on and application of sacred sound in the form of Nāda-Brahman will be targeted, followed by the Gorakhnāth tradition, the largest and most important Yoga sect and lineage. The above texts and traditions, along with three major Haṭha-Yoga texts—*Śiva-Saṁhitā, Gheraṇḍa-Saṁhitā,* and *Haṭha-Yoga-Pradīpikā*—reflect an extensive, and previously unrecognized, concern for sacred sound as Nāda-Brahman by practitioners of Yoga, and, in fact, inform the orthopraxy as well as many of the modern practices of Nāda-Yoga. This will be followed by a brief discussion of Nāda-Brahman in the tradition of Indian classical music, a tradition often viewed as a form of Nāda-Yoga and which itself views Nāda-Brahman as the highest reality. The chapter will conclude with some of the current trends in Nāda-Yoga.

Part 2 includes three chapters (4, 5, and 6) that provide an overview of the major sectarian developments of Hinduism, both Tantric and theistic. They, as a group, generally view sacred sound not as the highest reality but, rather, as the female energy of either a neuter Brahman or a male personal divinity such as Śiva or Viṣṇu. It is understood that in all these traditions the chief divinity is identified with Brahman, as argued by their respective Vedānta schools of theology, Brahman being designated both with and without gender and attributes. Chapter 4, covering the tradition of Śāktism (otherwise known as Śākta-Tantra or simply Tantra), will include the two major traditions of Śrī-Vidyā and Kālī Śākta-Tantra. In Śākta-Tantra the Ultimate Reality, though often conceived as the Goddess, is, in fact, a neuter Brahman that polarizes itself into male and female, with the male portion playing the minor "passive" role. Somewhat like the Vedic and Brāhmaṇic Vāk, yet unlike the Upaniṣadic and Grammarian Śabda-Brahman, Nāda-Brahman is viewed in this section as the feminine energy of an otherwise neuter Brahman Absolute. Though often referring directly to the Goddess herself, sacred sound as Nāda-Brahman in Śākta-Tantra is sometimes identified with the coital energy between the male Śiva and the female Śakti, the creative "vibration" resonating from their cosmic orgasm. The *Śāradā-tilaka-Tantra* is perhaps the most significant text for the study of Nāda-Brahman in the Śākta tradition and is freely drawn upon by most Śākta cults as well as other sectarian traditions. The Śrī-Vidyā sectaries, in their worship of the benign form of Tripurasundarī, offer some unique interpretations of Om and Nāda-Brahman, along with their special mantras. In Bengali Tantrism, Kālī reigns supreme as the terrifying Goddess who stands above her prone husband Śiva. Some of the key Kālī Śākta-Tantra texts and practices reveal some interesting applications of Nāda, *varṇa,* mantra, and *bīja.*

Chapters 5 and 6 cover the two major theistic divisions of Hinduism: Śaivism and Vaiṣṇavism. Though sacred sound is also primarily represented here as Nāda-Brahman, it is depicted as the feminine energy of a male deity, namely Śiva or Viṣṇu (Krishna).

In chapter 5 the Śaiva-Āgama, Śaiva-Siddhānta, and Kashmiri Śaiva traditions are discussed. The south Indian Śaiva-Āgama texts, insofar as they are available, offer some early sources for theories of Nāda and Bindu in dualistic Śaivism, generally viewing Śiva as Nāda and Śakti as Bindu. Conversely, Śaiva-Siddhānta posits Śiva as Bindu and Śakti as Nāda, in conformity with the emerging theistic tendency of placing Nāda as power, or Śakti. It also develops its own linguistic position regarding Nāda and Sphoṭa in a text known as the *Nāda-Kārikā*. Kashmiri Śaivism is monistic with its ultimate repose as silence yet borrows and modifies terminologies from both the Āgamas and Bhartṛhari. This tradition is unique for its "vowel mysticism" and the theory of cosmic pulsation known as *Spanda*.

Lastly, chapter 6 discusses sacred sound in the largest sectarian division in Hinduism known as Vaiṣṇavism. Selected Pāñcarātra texts will be cited first for early evidence of Nāda-Brahman and mantra in the Vaiṣṇava-Āgamas, followed by a discussion of the *Bhāgavata-Purāṇa* and some of the major sectarian movements. The later Vaiṣṇava Sampradāyas (Śrī, Madhva, Nimbārka, Vallabha, and Gauḍīya), along with some of their particular outlooks and practices regarding sacred sound, are examined so as to underscore previously unrecognized continuities with the other branches of Hinduism. Throughout these traditions references are cited to demonstrate the singular importance of sonic themes: theoretical conceptions of Nāda-Brahman, Praṇava divisions, linguistic levels (Paśyantī, for example), Varṇavāda/Sphoṭavāda dichotomies, and sonic creation sequences. While most of the theistic traditions exhibit all of these features, "the whole is greater than the sum of its parts." That is, the distinguishing factor in Hindu theism, which is especially visible in Vaiṣṇavism, is the presence of a male Supreme Being (Viṣṇu, Nārāyaṇa, Krishna, Rāma, Śiva, etc.) who empowers and monitors the functioning of these features to wield a uniquely personal sonic theology.

The Conclusion includes remarks regarding the ascendancy of Nāda-Brahman in Indian traditions, the relevancy of sonic theology for the study of religion, and a short discourse on the growing field of hermeneutics vis-à-vis the sonic realm.

The main desideratum in our investigation is to disclose a central network, or infrastructure, of sacred sound in the Hindu tradition, based on an underlying unity of correspondences which is theologically significant for the devout Hindu and based on the proviso that the investigation of Vedic, grammatical, Yogic, and theistic textual materials can illuminate both individual and group use of religious language and sound. As such, the concepts of Vāk, Śabda-Brahman, Om, Nāda-Brahman, and mantra are being specifically targeted in the contexts of both theoretical discussion and practical application. While an exploration of the many Indic vernacular sources would no doubt prove fruitful, the primary sources that are consulted throughout this work consist of texts in the Sanskrit language. As can be surmised already, this subject is extremely vast and cannot be exhausted in a single work. Thus, efforts will be made toward brevity and conciseness so as not to belabor the unfamiliar reader.

And, for the benefit of the reader, it should be said that the arguments and discussions herein are corroborated by a variety of sources, including both learned scholars of Indology and apologetic informants. Because sometimes these categories overlap in the same person, it should be realized that the purpose of the present research is hermeneutical—that is, it seeks to understand the practicing Hindu tradition on its own terms, to let it sound forth.

Part 1

Basic Sources for Sonic Theology in Hinduism

Chapter 1

VEDIC SOUND

The function of oral language as an agent of transformation from the human realm to the divine has been a perennial concern of Indian theological speculation, since language in Hinduism is nearly always identified with both human consciousness and the divine. This transformative aspect of language finds a firm foundation in the ancient Vedic tradition of ritual recitation. While sonic speculation was to be further developed by many heterogeneous groups in Hinduism, the earliest attempts in India to understand the mysteries of speech and language were contained within the circle of Vedic poets, ritualists, Sanskrit Grammarians, and philosophers. "The Brāhmaṇas [Vedic priests and seers] succeeded in impressing upon the minds of every subsequent generation a need to study the influence of sound phenomena on human consciousness and physiology by orienting the perceptual centers toward the inner acoustic space of the unseen." And the sonic effects of language upon human consciousness which were introduced in the Vedic period continued to inform the theories and practices of Hinduism, "for Hindus still believe that such precision in the repetition of exact intervals, over and over again, permits sound to act upon the internal personality, transform sensibility, way of thinking, state of soul, and even moral character."[1] This initial chapter on Vedic sound focuses on divine speech as Vāk; Vedic ritual language as mantra (applied Vāk), including phonetics and meter; and, lastly, the sonic developments of the principal Upaniṣads wherein the absolute principle of Śabda-Brahman fully emerges. An examination of these topics will subsequently provide insights into the theories and practices of Yoga and sectarian Hinduism.

The concepts and structures of language as sacred speech or sound are already present in the Vedic revelation itself, consisting of the four Vedas (*Ṛg, Yajur, Sāma,* and *Atharva*), Brāhmaṇas (texts of ritual elaboration and speculation), Āraṇyakas (forest treatises), thirteen principal Upaniṣads (wisdom texts), and the six Vedāṅgas (appendixes). The term *Veda* denotes "that which is known," from the Sanskrit root *vid,* "to know." The ancient Vedic poets, from a very high level of poetic intuition, are said to have "heard" or "seen" the original Veda through a kind of internal television. Interestingly, this root is a cognate of the Latin *vid,* "to see," as in the word *video.* Although visual metaphors are sometimes appropriate, the Vedas are most often characterized as *śruti,* or "that which is heard." *Śruti* as a concept features both the auditory character of Vedic truth and its transcendent, revealed nature. Being that which was seen and heard by those in closest touch with Supreme Reality, the Veda "sounded forth" as eternal truth. This contrasts with the later religious literature known as *smṛti* ("that which is remembered"), consisting of law books, histories, and commentaries.

On a comparative note, the oral nature of the Vedic revelation and its transmission has a corollary in both Judaism and Islam. Besides the commonly known written form of the Torah, Jews recognize an "oral Torah" that is equally authentic: "According to the rabbis the oral Torah is both the authoritative interpretation of the written Torah and a separate Mosaic tradition." This oral tradition, though originally in fixed form, continues to evolve up to the present day: "In this oral transmission, the oral Torah is understood as both fixed and evolving from generation to generation."[2]

The Koran in Islam functions as a similar kind of oral revelation but does not seem to evolve like the oral Torah: "The Koran is believed by Muslims to have been orally delivered to mankind by the Prophet [Mohammed] exactly as it had been orally delivered to him by the angel [Gabriel].... In like manner Muslims have transmitted the Koran orally down through the ages exactly as they received it from the Prophet. Accordingly, the teaching of the Koran has always been oral."[3] Though the Koran has, in effect, "punctured" temporal human history by its direct manifestation, Muslims acknowledge the nature of the Koran as a reflection of an eternal, unchanging "heavenly book" beyond the limits of time: "But the Message itself claimed to be from a 'heavenly book' preserved in the presence of God."[4] As we shall see, the Vedic revelation displays both a fixed and evolving nature depending on the particular school or tradition.

The dating of the ancient Vedic culture in India has been controversial. The nineteenth-century theories of Max Müller and his successors regarding a late Aryan invasion of India (ca. 2000 B.C.E.) are not supported by current scholarship. Based on a scrutiny of available scientific sources, a modern Indian scholar has pointed out that "the hypothesis that the Aryans first arrived in India around

2000 B.C. is in contradiction with literary and archaeological evidence."[5] The traditional theory of a much earlier, possibly indigenous Vedic civilization now appears to be vindicated, as concluded by current anthropology: "The Vedic literature reflects, then, not a foreign human invasion, but a radical alteration in the social, political, and economic organizations of the indigenous culture."[6] As Indian historiography is currently undergoing renewal, we are safer to assume that the Vedic culture represents a much longer occupancy of India than is generally assumed.

The Principle of Vāk

The *Ṛg-Veda* is believed to be impregnated with sacred speech, or Vāk, a concept traditionally interpreted as being mysterious and extraordinary: "The Indian conception of Vāk is not exactly the same as that of speech in its ordinary application. To the spiritual vision of the Hindus Vāk is more sacred than speech [ordinary] and carries with it a far deeper significance. The rishis (sages) are said to have visualized the mystic form of Vāk which is subtle, eternal or imperishable and incomprehensible by ordinary sense organs."[7]

According to the lexicon, *vāk* is a feminine noun meaning "speech, voice, talk, language (also of animals), sound (also of inanimate objects as of the stones used for pressing, of a drum), a word, saying, phrase, sentence, statement, and speech personified."[8] In trying to thematize the position of *vāk* in the *Ṛg-Veda* we find three kinds of references which are useful for us and not totally distinct from each other: the Goddess Vāk as the revealing Word, *vāk* as speech in general, and *vāk* in the symbolism of cows.[9] Due to the obscure nature of many of the passages on *vāk* and the paucity of historical information regarding the origin of language in India, most scholars have refrained from speculation beyond the accessible texts.

The various references to *vāk* in the *Ṛg-Veda* are, indeed, couched in mysterious poetical expression. The *ṛṣis,* or poets, who "heard" the original verses are said to be responsible for revealing the divine nature of human speech. It also appears that *vāk* referred to an underlying "language" of nature in which the sounds of cows, animals, birds, frogs, drums, and even inanimate objects participated: "Every sound is a kind of speech; this is so even in the case of animals and birds. . . . The extent of Vāk is said to be as wide as the earth and fire."[10]

This language of nature and earth extended beyond the visible realm and into the nonvisible heavens. The sound of thunder, included under the name *abhriya vāk* (*Ṛg-Veda* 1.168.8), represented the voice of Vāk from above and symbolized the divine afflatus that overcame the Vedic poets and seers. Vāk is said to reside in the "upper-half of heaven," with only a portion of herself known to mortals. The most famous verse in the *Ṛg-Veda* which describes Vāk (1.164.45) provides us with the clue to her mysterious and composite nature: "Vāk was divided in four parts [*catvāri vāk*]. These those Brahmans [wise priests] with insight know. Three parts, which are hidden, mortals do not activate; the fourth part they speak."[11]

In order to understand the significance of this text it is useful to examine the importance of thunder for poetic inspiration and also the rain god Indra, who provides it: "If the lightning is Indra's weapon (*vajra*), the sound that accompanies the lightning might also be regarded as having a magic potency";[12] and "The imagination of the Vedic *ṛṣis* (poets) was very early inspired by the sound of thunder, which formed a very important element in the Indra-Vṛtra myth. . . . The *vāk* (sound) produced by the thunderbolt of Indra is alluded to in innumerable passages in the *Ṛg-Veda*" (i.e., 6.27.4).[13] Indra thus plays a vital role in the production, albeit manifestation, of human speech, acting as the courier of Vāk.

Indeed, the description of Indra's role as the first Grammarian enunciated in the Brāhmaṇas is in fact an interpretation of the *catvāri vāk* verse quoted above. The mythological narrative contained in the *Śatapatha-Brāhmaṇa* (4.1.3.1–16) is as follows:

> Indra having hurled his thunderbolt at Vṛtra hid himself together with the gods. They did not know whether Vṛtra was killed. So they requested Vāyu, the swiftest of them, to go and report whether Vṛtra had died or not. Vāyu asked for a reward and was promised the first share in the Soma-draught. Then Vāyu brought the happy news that Vṛtra was killed. Now Indra became jealous of Vāyu and asked for a share of Soma for himself together with Vāyu. Indra, being asked what would be gained by giving him a share with Vāyu in the same cup, replied that by giving him a share the speech would speak distinctly. The gods granted Indra's request, but then a quarrel started between Indra and Vāyu about the division of their shares. Indra insisted that he should have one half of the cup and Vāyu should be

given only one fourth of it, while Vāyu made the same claim for himself. They went to Prajāpati for decision. Prajāpati divided the cup in two equal parts and allotted the first half to Vāyu. Thus Indra received only one-fourth of the cup. At this Indra said that his share being only one-fourth of the cup, that much [one-fourth] of speech would speak distinctly. Now the Brāhmaṇa concludes by stating hence only that fourth part of speech is intelligible, which men speak, but that fourth part of speech which beasts speak is unintelligible; and that fourth part of speech which birds speak is unintelligible; and that fourth part of speech which small vermin here speak is unintelligible.[14]

It is said that, before Indra took part in this contestation, Vāk spoke in only one fashion, which was more of a plangent sound without articulation: "It was just a sound and did not have distinctive sound units, which constitute human speech.... When Indra received a share, he separated sound from sound (*vācaiva vācaṁ vyāvartayat*) and thus this Vāk speaks, being made distinct by the force of Indra."[15] As the word for "grammar," *vyākaraṇa* signifies this same kind of separation and classification, the identification of Indra with grammar is not surprising. Moreover, we are reminded of passages in the Upaniṣads. The *Chāndogya-Upaniṣad* (2.22.3, 5) says, "All vowels are embodiments of Indra.... All the vowels should be pronounced strong and sonant, with the thought: 'To Indra let me give strength.'" The *Kauśītaki-Upaniṣad* (4.6) states: "As the soul of Sound... I reverence him [Indra]. He then who reverences him thus, becomes the soul of sound."[16]

In the only hymn spoken by the Goddess Vāk in the *Ṛg-Veda* (10.125) we find her boldly proclaiming her divine qualities and for the first time asserting power and autonomy in her own terms:

1 I move with the Rudras, with the Vasus, with the Ādityas and all the gods. I carry both Varuṇa and Mitra, both Indra and Agni, and both of the Aśvins.

2 I carry the swelling Soma, and Tvashtṛ, and Pūshaṇ and Bhaga. I bestow wealth on the pious sacrificer who presses the Soma juice and offers the oblation.

3 I am the Queen, the confluence of riches, the skillful one who is first among those worthy of sacrifice. The gods divided me up into various parts, for I dwell in many places and enter into many forms.

4 The one who eats food, who truly sees, who breathes, who hears what is said, does so through me. Though they do not realize it, they dwell in me. Listen, you whom they have heard: what I tell you should be heeded.

5 I am the one who says, by myself, what gives joy to gods and men. Whom I love I make awesome; I make him a sage, a wise man, a Brahmin.

6 I stretch the bow for Rudra so that his arrow will strike down the hater of prayer. I incite the contest among the people. I have pervaded sky and earth.

7 I gave birth to the father on the head of this world. My womb is in the waters, within the ocean. From there I spread out over all creatures and touch the very sky with the crown of my head.

8 I am the one who blows like the wind, embracing all creatures. Beyond the sky, beyond this earth, so much have I become in my greatness.[17]

This hymn, which also appears in the *Atharva-Veda* (4.30.1–8) in nearly the same form,[18] is "the earliest document of the personification of speech as a productive principle of energy."[19] Vāk is clearly conceived in this hymn as a powerful female potency who solely pervades and sustains all aspects of life, exhibiting a tendency of the later Ṛg-Vedic poets to consolidate various natural and cosmic entities. As Vāk is given a feminine personification as the goddess of speech in the Vedas and Brāhmaṇas, it serves as a precursor for the Hindu theistic and Tantric speculations on the divine female power of language known as "Śakti."

The parameters of Vāk gradually expand in the Brāhmaṇa literature, best exemplified by the following passage from the *Taittirīya-Brāhmaṇa* (2.8.8.4–5): "Vāk is endless; Vāk is more than the end of all creation; she is great; all the gods, Gandharvas, men and animals live upon Vāk; Vāk is *akṣara* (the immutable); the first-born of Ṛta, the mother of the Vedas, the navel of immortality."[20]

As many of the male characteristics were being gathered under the Vedic Purusha and ultimately the Brāhmaṇic Prajāpati, the various female energies, or *śaktis,* including the metrical powers of the mantras, came to be associated with the name of Vāk. It is then no surprise that, by the time of the Brāhmaṇa literature, Vāk has become the wifely spouse, or Śakti, of the principal male demiurge: "It is not until we come to the period of the Brāhmaṇas that we find her position as the Śakti of Father Prajāpati definitely established.... As Suparṇī she becomes the mother of Vedic meters and serves as the source of all living beings.... In the Brāhmaṇas the relation of Prajāpati to Vāk is becoming a hieratic symbol of that of the Absolute to Logos." Furthermore, the union with Prajāpati, who is also conceived as mind, ensures the promulgation of intelligible speech: "The intimate relationship of Vāk with Prajāpati (mind)... becomes more explicit only when suggested by the analogy of the interdependence of Mind and Speech commonly perceived in the phenomenon of language.... Vāk in the Brāhmaṇas is not only the personification of incoherent external speech but a complete entity of creative speech energy holding together her subjective and objective aspects in a perfect synthesis."[21] Vāk became identified with the evolving concept of Brahman (*vāg vai brahman*), the power of speech in the Vedic ritual, such that the earliest meaning of the word *Brahman* is "sacred word" or "sacred formula" (*Ṛg-Veda* 10.125) and, thus, by extension the Veda in general.

The sacred syllable "Om" (*praṇava*) was believed to be the offspring of the creator god Brahmā (Prajāpati). In the *Gopatha-Brāhmaṇa* (1.1.16–30), the Brāhmaṇa text attached to the *Atharva-Veda*, there is a section that has been subtitled the "Praṇava-Upaniṣad." After a number of Om cosmogonies are recounted, the text presents a mythological narrative concerning the ascendancy of Om as the necessary accompaniment to any Vedic mantra, as summarized by Maurice Bloomfield: "In Brāhmaṇa manner a conflict of the gods and Asuras [demons] about the city (*aindra-nagaram*) of the Vasudharas is narrated; the Asuras are victorious until the gods turn victors under the leadership of Om, the oldest son of Brahmā. The reward of the Om is that no holy text shall be chanted without Om."[22] After this, the etymology, pronunciation, and use of Om are described in great detail, betraying a later date for this portion of the Brāhmaṇa.

The presence of eternal Vāk in the *Ṛg-Veda* thus contributed to its unique status as an orally revealed text and provided a beginning theme for our elucidation of sacred sound. As a feminine personification of speech or sacred sound, Vāk was represented and applied practically in Vedic ritual in the form of mantra, or "applied Vāk."

Vedic Ritual Language: Mantra

The Vedic culture includes the oral Vedas and their application in ritual. As the Vedic verses are still accepted by orthodoxy to be authorless and eternal, their early use in ritual signals an important locus for study. Vedic ritual is one of the oldest surviving rituals of humankind, and the best documented, as pointed out by Frits Staal: "Vedic ritual offers the most promising source material. Not only is it the richest, most elaborate and most complete among the rituals of mankind. It is also the ritual for which we possess the richest, most elaborate and most complete descriptions."[23]

In ancient Vedic India (ca. 3000–800 B.C.E.), the center of religious life was the *yajña,* or ritual sacrifice, and two of the central features of Vedic ritual were, and still are, the sacrificial fire and the oral recitation of ritual language, or mantra: "Sound had, like fire, a central place in the sacrifice from early times. . . . The fires, the sacrificial plot, ritual actions, and offerings of various kinds were woven together into an elaborate structure that was heavily dependent on the *mantras* which established the basic identities and correspondences."[24]

J. A. B. Van Buitenen has stressed how the sacred word or syllable of the mantra is radically tied to the ritual fire itself: "The ultimate measure of the word is the syllable from which all formulae start and to which their power can be reduced. . . . For speech to be effective at all, it must be spoken in conjunction with the ritually powerful fire of the sacrifice. . . . The interdependence, the biunity, of Word and Fire . . . [is such that] Fire is contained in the germ of speech which is the syllable. . . . *Mantra* bears the fire . . . [and] fire begets the *mantra.*"[25]

Indeed, before any ritual act is performed the intonation of sacred sound in the form of mantra is necessary, as noted carefully by Jan Gonda: "If ritual acts and ceremonies are to be performed successfully the consecretory word is an indispensable requirement."[26] The ritual utterance is consequently performative in that the act is accomplished only if the prayer formulas are first released in sonic form: "In any sacrificial performance the ritual *mantra* has to be recited first before an offering is poured in the sacrificial fire. The offering is voiced in the formula and then given to a particular deity with the word *svāhā.*"[27]

Mantra (m. "instrument of thought, speech, sacred text") is a chant formula composed of words and syllables in the Sanskrit language (*saṁskṛta,* "well-formed," considered the reproduction in sound of the structure of reality). Mantras are considered in most cases equivalent to ritual acts themselves and carry a unique form of meaning: "Sanskrit words were not just arbitrary labels assigned to phenomena; they were the sound forms of objects, actions, and attributes, related to the corresponding reality in the same way as visual forms, and different only in being perceived by the ear and not by the eye."[28] The importance of speech for the execution of the ritual acts as well as the nature of the Sanskrit language itself leads us to an examination of Vedic ritual language, not only as an important part of Vedic ritual but also as an important precursor to the concept of Śabda-Brahman found in the Upaniṣads and Indian philosophy.

The language used in ritual generally differs from ordinary language, as noted by linguistics scholar George Steiner: "Priests and initiates use a vocabulary and formulaic repertoire distinct from everyday language."[29] An anthropologist says it stronger: "In ritual, language appears to be used in ways that violate the communication function."[30] This concept, which may be substantiated in the Indian context from various angles, needs some additional clarification.

The verses of the *Ṛg-Veda,* as found in the written tradition, betray mostly normal features of grammatical form and meaning yet in their ritual application exhibit an altogether different set of structural and performative elements. As prayers, they are by themselves reminiscent of the Book of Psalms. But, as mantras in ritual context, they seem to have their own rule system, which departs from that of ordinary language and encompasses other nonsemantic and nonlinguistic features included under the aegis of sonic theology: "The ritual meaning or function of such *mantras* does not lie in their language or even in their poetic or metrical structure, but in the sounds with their themes and variations, repetitions, inversions, interpolations, and the particular distribution of their elements."[31] In fact, the rituals associated with the chanting of the Veda eventuated into complex choreographies of mantras that were chanted, sung, and sometimes accompanied by musical instruments.

But just what are mantras, and why do they have such an important function as embodiments of sacred sound? These questions direct us back to one of the fundamental Indian assumptions regarding Vedic language: the eternal relationship between word (*śabda*) and meaning (*artha*), between signifier and signified. As was indicated above by Hopkins, the Vedic word has an intrinsic connection with the object signified and, thus, with reality. The entire infrastructure of Vedic sacred sound rests on the validity or nonvalidity of this relation, and the school of Indian philosophy known as Mīmāṁsā, or Pūrva-Mīmāṁsā, is founded on defending it. The philosophical ramifications implicit in the word-meaning relationship are, thus, of paramount importance as we first assess what is "at stake" for the believing Hindu in his or her sonic quest.

Modern scholars have advanced theories regarding the nature and function of Vedic ritual language. Frits Staal has argued, for example, that the syntax of the ritual action formed the basis for the development of ordinary language and that the original language of the Vedic ritual was meaningless and not actually language at all. Staal first distinguishes between ordinary language and ritual language. Much like James Frazer had attached myths to primal ritual acts, Staal suggested that mantras began as phrases or sentences attached to ritual acts, and these mantra/ritual action units formed the raw material out of which ordinary language arose. The entire oral Vedic corpus consisted of mantras, or "locution units": "The main reason that a *mantra* is a single unit is its ritual function and character. In Vedic ritual, one mantra corresponds to one ritual act."[32] Since the structure, or syntax, of ordinary language bears a close resemblance to ritual (Vedic) structure, language was originally used in that context before it became conventionalized. The example given is the manner in which phrases of ideas are embedded in ordinary sentence structure resembles the way in which smaller ritual acts are "embedded" in larger sacrifices, regardless of their intrinsic meaning. Thus, "linguistics originated in India because of the requirements of ritual."[33]

Since the requirements of ritual reflect activity, or "doing," language was primarily performative in the early stages and secondarily communicative. Ritual is claimed by Staal to be prelinguistic (cf. animals have ritual but no language) and ultimately meaningless, since it is performed for its own sake.[34] The original use of language, if involved in ritual, as he says, would then also be meaningless and "alinguistic." Semantics—the system of meanings that are attached to words, signs, and expressions—represents for Staal a stage posterior to the use of language in ritual, while nonsemantic chant, music, gesture, and perhaps dance represent an earlier stage. "The simplest hypothesis which makes sense of these various puzzling expressions is the assumption that a structured domain of ritual preceded the origin of language. . . . In simple terms this means that men already sang, danced and performed rites before they spoke."[35] Thus, language would appear to be derived from mantras, which derived from ritual: first ritual, then mantras, then language. As sacred sound was ritually available before meanings were attached to words, it would be prior to language.

By implication, this suggests that the *Ṛg-Veda,* which is not meaningless since it displays normal features of language construction, must have been composed around the needs of an already existing ritual. This cannot be justified, as noted by Jan Gonda: "The thesis that all Ṛg-Vedic hymns were . . . primarily written for definite sacrifices is not only hazardous but also untenable."[36] It is feasible with regard to the *Yajur-Veda,* which is a ritual "reworking" of the *Ṛg-Veda* into prose, but not when the latter is subsumed under a "meaningless" ritual structure. Wade Wheelock has shown that even the mantras in ritual context are not meaningless: "The vast majority of mantras in the New- and Full-Moon Sacrifices are completely intelligible and translatable."[37] Yet the translatability of mantras does not convey their entire import within a ritual context.

C. Kunhan Raja had argued that the Vedic authors were primarily poets, not priests, and that poetic intuition preceded ritual priestcraft: "The *ṛṣis* (who composed the Veda) were normal citizens in their private life, who lived . . . with their family; the only factor that distinguished (them) from the general citizens was their special poetic gift." Moreover, "in the texts of the *Ṛg-Veda* and the *Atharva-Veda,* we see only insufficient evidence of the exact nature of the religious rituals current at that time. They are not ritualistic texts. They are poetry."[38] Contrary to Staal, this seems to place linguistic activity prior to ritual and reveals an important polemic that has occupied scholars over recent years. Since there is no firm evidence that the Vedic ritual preceded the Vedic hymns or vice versa, this polemic cannot be resolved here.

The traditional view, however, that the Vedas are "authorless" (*apauruṣeya*) is what propels their power and force in Vedic ritual. And the injunctions in the Veda are persuasive precisely because they are not the poetry of this or that sage but something other. And what is Vedic ritual without the Vedic injunctions? The orthodox viewpoint on Vedic injunctions is clarified by John Taber with reference to speech acts theory: "For the Veda, the act of getting someone to do something usually attributed to the utterer of injunctions instead belongs to the injunctions [themselves]. In other words, Vedic language manifests intentions without anyone ever having spoken them; Vedic injunctions are speech acts without anyone ever having enacted them; Vedic language has inherent illocutionary force."[39] Indeed, mantras somehow generate their own "intention" as they are uttered and are curiously reflective of the much more recent Heideggerian maxim of "language speaks."

Accordingly, the historian of religion Gerardus Van der Leeuw sheds light on the power and self-generating capacity of sacred language by his reference to the numinous and mysterious character of sacred sound itself:

> The word . . . is a decisive power: whoever utters words sets power in motion. . . . Raising the voice, emphasis, connection by rhythm or rhyme—all this endows the word with heightened energy . . . [such that] singing, rejoicing and mourning generate greater potency than mere speaking. . . . More important still is the vast power which always emanated from such cult terms as Hallelujah, Kyrie eleison, Amen, Om; a mystical tone-color is attached to them, while their very incomprehensibility enhances their numinous power. . . . Words possess the greatest power when they combine into some formula, some phrase definite in the sound of its terms, their timbre and their rhythm.[40]

The philosopher Ernst Cassirer attested to the oral power of the name of a deity by citing an example from ancient Egypt: "As the Word is first in origin, it is also supreme in power. Often it is the name of the deity, rather than the god himself, that seems to be the real source of efficacy. Knowledge of the name gives him who knows it mastery even over the being and will of the god. Thus the familiar Egyptian legend tells how Isis, the great sorceress, craftily persuaded the sun-god Ra to disclose his name to her, and how through possession of the name she gained power over him and over all the other gods."[41]

In addition, the underlying linguistic philosophy behind traditional Western magic also appears to be in line with the Vedic understanding. "In magical theory the 'real' name of a god or an idea contains the essence of that god or idea, and therefore enshrines its power. Using the name turns on this power automatically, in the same way that pressing the light switch turns on the light. . . . In the ancient world there was a widespread belief in the existence of a secret name of infinite power which automatically controlled everything in the universe."[42]

Despite some arguments to the contrary, Vedic Vāk and ritual language as mantra are never meaningless or "nonsense," since each word of the Veda (*śabda*) has its corresponding meaning (*artha*) in the form of its object. Even as Vedic sound becomes unified and congealed in the Upaniṣads as Śabda-Brahman and developed further in the Grammarian theories of Sphoṭa and Paśyantī, *artha* is still present because all language is attached to human consciousness. It is only in the Yoga, Tantra, and music traditions wherein Śabda-Brahman is recast as Nāda-Brahman that the idea of "pure cosmic sound" detached from linguistic meaning emerges, as will be shown.

The scholastic definition of *mantra* given by Jan Gonda reflects the above concerns and foreshadows the complexity of the evolving concept of sacred sound from the Vedas to Hindu theism and Tantrism. He says that mantras are "word(s) believed to be of 'superhuman origin,' received, fashioned and spoken by the 'inspired' seers, poets and reciters in order to invoke divine power(s) and especially conceived as means of creating, conveying, concentrating and realizing intentional and efficient thought, and of coming into touch or identifying oneself with the essence of the divinity which is present in the *mantra*."[43] As the role of sound in Vedic ritual is inextricably bound up with culturally specific notions of cosmic creation, mythology, poetic intuition, and performative verbal art, accordingly, the complexities and "mystery" of mantras suggested by Gonda are evidenced when additional aspects of phonetics (speech production) and poetic meter are considered.

The correct pronunciation of the sacrificial formulas, or mantras, proved to be crucial to the proper execution of the Vedic sacrifice. From within the context of the Vedic ritual, which utilized these highly charged "magazines of sound" to facilitate the ritual action, the notion of "properly pronounced" language as power, or Śakti (Vāk, the goddess of speech), emerged during the Vedic period.

The first branch of Indian linguistics to attain independent status was the study of phonetics, since the attempt to preserve the sacred text in a strictly oral tradition with the correct pronunciation was the immediate practical concern of linguists. The Indian phoneticians sought primarily to preserve the Vedic canon for priestly use by developing a rigid system of phonetics, or Śikṣā ("the study"). The categories of this "new science" were fundamental for all further linguistic and philosophical studies of sound, since the primary interest was sounds and not written letters. The regulation of the production of Vedic speech sounds thus became a kind of quality control system for the preservation of Vedic ritual. The other branches of linguistics—namely, etymology and grammar—were based on the system of sounds which had already been developed by Vedic phonologists. Also, these studies reflected the need for serious inquiry into the nature and production of speech sounds themselves.

The seeds of the interest in phonetics and speech production may actually be traced to the *Ṛg-Veda* itself, which dedicates two entire hymns to speech (10.125 and 10.71). The former, given above in the subsection on Vāk, personifies speech as a powerful goddess and author of the hymn. The latter, which is given in full below, speaks of the origins of the sacred word, or language.

> 1 Bṛhaspati! When they set in motion the first beginning of speech, giving names, their most pure and perfectly guarded secret was revealed through love.
>
> 2 When the wise ones fashioned speech with their thought, sifting it as grain is sifted through a sieve, then friends recognized their friendships. A good sign was placed on their speech.
>
> 3 Through the sacrifice they traced the path of speech and found it inside the sages. They held it and portioned it out to many; together the seven singers praised it.
>
> 4 One who looked did not see speech, and another who listens does not hear it. It reveals itself to someone as a loving wife, beautifully dressed, reveals her body to her husband.
>
> 5 One person, they said, has grown awkward and heavy in this friendship; they no longer urge him forward in contests. He lives with falsehood like a milkless cow, for the speech that he has heard has no fruit no flower.
>
> 6 A man that abandons a friend who has learned with him no longer has a share in speech. What he does hear he hears in vain, for he does not know the path of good action.
>
> 7 Friends have eyes and ears, but their flashes of insight are not equal. Some are like ponds that reach only to the mouth or shoulder; others are like ponds that one could bathe in.
>
> 8 When the intuitions of the mind are shaped in the heart,

when Brahmins perform sacrifices together as friends, some are left behind for lack of knowledge, while others surpass them with the power to praise.

9 Those who move neither near nor far, who are not real Brahmins nor pressers of the Soma; using speech in a bad way, they weave on a weft of rags, without understanding.

10 All his friends rejoice in the friend who emerges with fame and victory in the contest. He saves them from error and gives them food. He is worthy to be pushed forward to win the prize.

11 One sits bringing to blossom the flower of the verses. Another sings a song in the Śakvarī meter. One, the Brahmin, proclaims the knowledge of the ancient ways. Another lays out the measure of the sacrifice.[44]

This important reference evinces three stages in the development of language: (1) inarticulate speech, (2) primitive articulate speech, and (3) language proper. The first is said to include the sounds of snakes, insects, birds, and beasts, while the second, which is mentioned in the first stanza of this quotation, points out that men in the early stage imparted names to objects. The third stage, as in the second stanza, most likely suggests that language was apprehended and polished (*saṁskṛta*, "refined") from an already existing substratum of sound by the sages, poets, or seers while under the divine afflatus. This appears to coincide with Staal's interpretation when he says that, "when language came into being, sound was already available."[45] It can also be understood, however, to explain the revelatory character of the Veda as it was received by the sages in various stages. It clearly supports the view that sound, whether articulate or inarticulate, was seen as an all-pervading and mysterious feature of the Hindu cosmos.

This brings us to a major issue in the understanding of the Vedic, and later theistic, notion of sound, and hence of all oral language: the concept of "speech production," especially in the Indian context of the eternity of sound.

First, the Vedic and Hindu theistic notion of the eternity of sound rests on the following three philosophic axioms, which have been enumerated by P. Chakravarti: "(1) Sound is eternal like space, since both are imperceptible to touch. . . . (2) Sound is eternal and not liable to perish immediately after its utterance, inasmuch as it is capable of being given to others, as in the case of a teacher communicating words to his pupil.... (3) Sound is eternal, as there is no cognition of the cause that might destroy it."[46] Although many counterarguments were advanced by rival philosophical schools, the force of these propositions (namely, the eternality of sound and language) continued to inform the religious practices of later Hinduism.

Regarding "speech production," the following question arises: Do the vocal organs actually create sounds when someone speaks or simply manifest them from some other plane? The issue of the eternality or noneternality of words revolves around this moot question—whether articulate speech, the subject or content of phonetics, manifests inarticulate sound that is already existent or creates sound out of nothing in each specific utterance. The orthodox Vedic position, as exemplified in the Mīmāṁsā school of philosophy, strongly upholds the former view, while the Indian logicians subscribing to Nyāya doctrines as well as various conventionalist approaches (namely, Buddhist, Jain, Vaiśeṣika, etc.) support the latter.

Mīmāṁsā argues that all sounds, even the beating of a drum, are already existent but only require some exciting causes for their manifestation—namely, the conjunction and disjunction of air. Though it is generally accepted that speech is a modification of the act of breathing, the chief proponent of the early Mīmāṁsā view, Śabara, has described the physical process required for the human utterance of a sound in terms of "internal air": "The internal air, he says, first rises from the naval region, receives expansion in the heart and undergoes changes in the throat; Then it strikes the head (palate) and comes back and finally gives rise to different kinds of sounds in the mouth which acts as a 'resonance-chamber.'"[47]

This Mīmāṁsā view seems to be based on an earlier position found in a phonetic text. According to the *Pāṇinīya-Śikṣā* (3), "having intellectually determined the object to be communicated to others, the soul urges the mind in order to give expression, i.e., to vocalize the thought rising within. The mind so stimulated acts upon the physical fire which in its turn brings about a movement in the region of internal air. The internal air thus moved gets upward till it reaches the vocal apparatus."[48]

A parallel to this view appears in the *Chāndogya-Upaniṣad* (1.3.3), which has described speech as the result of internal air, or "diffused breath," which is the same as *vāk*: "When one breathes in—that is the in-breath (*prāṇa*). When one breathes out—that is the out-breath (*apāna*). The junction of the in-breath and the out-breath is the diffused breath. Speech is the diffused breath [*vyāna*]. Therefore one utters speech without in-breathing, without out-breathing."[49]

There is, thus, a difference between ordinary breathing and the internal air and diffused breath being discussed in the above passages. Most Indian descriptions of the process of speech formation include the influence of bodily fire (*agni*) to "activate," or create, a movement of internal air (*prāṇa*) such that, when the act of breathing is connected with internal physical heat, audible sound is manifested: "It is fire that pushes air upwards or sets the internal air in motion and represents the energy that is required for the utterance of a sound."[50] This view is again corroborated by the *Chāndogya-Upaniṣad* (3.18.3), which says that, "speech, truly, is a fourth part of Brahman. It shines and glows with Agni [fire] as its light."[51] This concept of the cooperation of air and fire in the formation of speech sounds in the phonetic texts is precursory for some of the later Tantric theories of sacred sound and, especially, the theory in Indian classical music treatises that musical sound as Nāda-Brahman is created from the friction between Prāṇa (life air) and Agni (fire) in the body of the singer.

In the early phonetic texts some information is also given regarding the classification of speech sounds. The role of breath is clearly distinguished from voice in the act of speaking: "Breath is emitted in the case of the voiceless consonants, and voice in the case of the voiced consonants and vowels." All vowels, semivowels, and "voiced" consonants contain descending degrees of "voice," or what is called "glottal resonance" (*nāda*) by the phoneticians: "The air which obtains *nāda* 'voice, resonance' on account of the closure in the glottis is basically viewed by this tradition as constituting the pure *ghoṣa* 'voice, resounding, reverberating' and is represented by the sound *a*."[52] As each consonant also contains the letter *a* in combination with either a voiced or unvoiced consonantal prefix, the various letters of the alphabet are distinguished and categorized according to "voiceness," with the vowels at the forefront.

In explication of the above chapter 2 of one of these texts known as the *Taittirīya-Prātiśākhya* (2.1–10) begins with an inquiry into the origin of sound then propounds some of the main tenets of classical phonetic theory: "By the setting in motion of air by the body, at the junction of throat and breast [*body* here means Agni, or "body heat," according to the commentator]. The parts that give it audible quality are breast, throat, head, mouth, and nostrils. When the throat is closed tone is produced [*nādaḥ kriyate,* said by the commentator to be a definition of *nāda*]. When it is opened breath is produced."[53] A tendency throughout this text, and in the commentary by Somācārya, is to highlight the importance of voiced sound, or *nāda*—and this is perhaps the oldest reference to *nāda* as voice in Sanskrit literature—which, as we have seen, combines internal fire with breath (Agni and Prāṇa) and, as we shall find, points to the prodigious rise of the metaphysical concept of *nāda* as Nāda-Brahman in Yoga, Indian music, Śākta-Tantra, and Hindu theism.

The notion of human beings controlling the gods or spirits with various rhythmic meters deepens our discussion of oral language in relation to power. In the Western world the practitioner of magic developed his power by loud incantation with close attention to the rhythm or meter of the chant: "The magician works himself up into a state of frenzy by intoning words which roar and beat and swell and reverberate. The words must never be said flatly, but rhythmically chanted."[54]

The Indian tradition of meter known as Chandas, though receiving scant attention from Indologists, contributes to our study of the power of mantras. Except for prose formulas such as those found in the *Yajur-Veda,* the power of the Vedic mantra was almost always associated with its respective meter, which was identified with any number of gods or goddesses in the Vedic pantheon.

The notion of the power and energy of metrical locution finds its fullest expression in the Brāhmaṇa literature. Besides the mention in the *Taittirīya-Brāhmaṇa* (5.1, 7, 2) of the meters as the "wives of the gods," the authors of the Brāhmaṇas realized the potency of the particular "rhythmic combination" of syllables in the mantras. To them "Gāyatrī, Triṣṭubh, Jagati and such other Vedic meters were not mere mechanical arrangements of syllables but represented 'living creative forces.' . . . They are regarded in these treatises as having a certain potency in them by virtue of which they yield the secret power of *yajña* [sacrifice], which enables the gods to defeat the Asuras [demons] and gain supremacy over them."[56] The significance of Triṣṭubh meter, four lines of eleven syllables each, is its association with Indra: "Triṣṭubh is described as the thunderbolt of Indra. . . . Indra killed Vṛtra [demon] by means of Śakvarī, Satpada, Anuṣṭubh and Triṣṭubh having gathered them together."[57] The *Śatapatha-Brāhmaṇa* (1.7, 3, 23–25) describes "how by the eight-, eleven- and twelve-syllabled meters,

Gāyatrī, Triṣṭubh, and Jagati, the gods can 'go aloft' to heaven." The Gāyatrī meter, three lines of eight syllables each, which is also the name of a famous prayer (*Ṛg-Veda* 3.62.10) that is also considered the most important Vedic mantra, is regarded as "the special meter of Agni [the god of fire], who is produced with her from Prajāpati's mouth (*Śatapatha-Brāhmaṇa* 2.3, 5, 4).... [She has] the power of carrying the fruit of sacrifice to the gods (*Śatapatha-Brāhmaṇa* 1.3, 4, 6)."[58] The Anuṣṭubh meter is closely connected to Prajāpati, the chief god of the Brāhmaṇa period: "For sacrifice is identical with Prajāpati and Anuṣṭubh is Prajāpati's own meter."[59] Among the numerous meters found in the Vedic literature,[60] the Anuṣṭubh meter has become the most common in later Indian literature. It has four lines of eight syllables each and is the most prominent syllabic division found in the *Bhagavad-Gītā*, the *Mahābhārata*, most of the Purāṇas, and a large percentage of the Tantric literature.

A close analysis of meters in the Veda reveals an incredibly complex network of correspondences between them and every conceivable aspect of ritual life: "Wherever there is the sacrifice, there are the meters and wherever the meters, there the sacrifice.... The origin of meters is said to be from sacrifice [*Ṛg-Veda* 10.90.9]."[61] The meters came to be associated with gods, goddesses, wives, priests, bricks, utensils, soma pressings, cattle, animals, birds, chariots, Saman chants, heaven, castes, seasons, and the planets—a multilevel concatenation mediated and manipulated by ordered sonic utterance empowered by Vāk.

The connection of the Vedic meters with Vāk is also very clear during the Brāhmaṇa period: "Meters are speech; *chandāṁsi vai vāk*.... Meters are identical with the whole speech; *chandāṁsi vai sarva vāk*." The connection of Vāk with each of the well-known meters is also repeatedly mentioned throughout the Brāhmaṇa texts: "Gāyatrī is said to be identical with speech; *vāg vai gāyatrī*.... Anuṣṭubh is specifically connected with speech; *vāg anuṣṭubh*."[62] The power of speech is characterized as not only the female meters but even as the "thousand-fold progeny of Vāk."[63]

Following the already apparent merging of the notions of meter, Prajāpati, Vāk, and Brahman in the Brāhmaṇa texts, further identification of Brahman and Om—and the concomitant rise of the concept of Śabda-Brahman—will become apparent in the division of Vedic literature known as the Upaniṣads.

Śabda-Brahman in the Upaniṣads

The notions of sacred sound which emerge during the time of the Upaniṣads (ca. 1000 B.C.E.–A.D. 200) reflect an ongoing concern with the transformation of the Vedic mythological notion of Vāk into an ontological reality in itself known as Śabda-Brahman. As we have seen, the concept of Vāk was taking on increasingly larger proportions even during the Brāhmaṇa period. In general, various speculations on the Supreme Reality find coalescence under the term *Brahman*, which continues to expand its dimensions up until the absolute monism of Śaṅkara around A.D. 800.

The *Chāndogya-Upaniṣad*, attached to the *Sāma-Veda*, furnishes early examples of the kind of speculation which tends to combine notions of speech (Om) and singing or chant (*udgītha*) with revelation and Brahman. In the very first section (1.1.1–5) various correspondences are advanced: "Om! One should reverence the *udgītha* (loud chant) as this syllable [*akṣara*], for one sings the loud chant (beginning) with 'Om.'. . . The essence of a person is speech [*puruṣasya vāg rasaḥ*]. The essence of speech is the Ṛg (hymn) [*vāca ṛg rasaḥ*]. The essence of the Ṛg is the Sāman (chant). The essence of the Sāman is the *udgītha* (loud singing). . . . The *udgītha* is this syllable Om [which joins together the pair of speech and breath]."[64]

The origin of the syllable *Om* is also described in the *Chāndogya-Upaniṣad* (2.23.2–3): "Prajāpati brooded upon the worlds. From them, when they had been brooded upon, issued forth the threefold knowledge [the three Vedas]. He brooded upon this. From it, when it had been brooded upon, issued forth these syllables: *bhūr, bhuvaḥ, svar.* He brooded upon them. From them, when they had been brooded upon, issued forth the syllable Om. As leaves are held together by a spike, so all speech is held together by Om [*oṁkāreṇa sarva vāk*]. Verily, Om is the world-all. Verily, Om is this world-all [*oṁkāra evedaṁ sarvam*]." This latter concept is echoed by the *Taittirīya-Upaniṣad* (1.8), which contains a short glorification of the sacred word *Om*: "Om is Brahman. Om is the whole world [*om iti brahma, om itīdaṁ sarvam*]."[65]

The *Kaṭha-Upaniṣad* (2.15–17) talks about *Om* as the supreme syllable as well as an aid to salvation: "The word which all the Vedas rehearse, and which all austerities proclaim, desiring which men live the life of religious studentship—That word to thee I briefly declare. That is Om! That syllable, truly, indeed, is Brahma! [*akṣaraṁ brahma . . . akṣaraṁ param*] That syllable indeed is the supreme!

Knowing that syllable, truly, indeed, whatever one desires is his! That is the best support. That is the supreme support. Knowing that support, one becomes happy in the Brahma-world."[66]

The *Muṇḍaka-Upaniṣad* (2.2.3–4) describes the process of sonic meditation with the metaphor of an archer: "Taking the bow as the great weapon of the Upaniṣad, one should put upon it an arrow sharpened by meditation. Stretching it with a thought directed to the essence of That, penetrate that Imperishable [Brahman] as the mark, my friend. The mystic syllable Om (*praṇava*) is the bow. The arrow is the soul (*ātman*). Brahman is said to be the mark (*lakṣya*). By the undistracted man is It to be penetrated [also to be known]. One should come to be in It, as the arrow (in the mark)."[67]

In the *Praśna-Upaniṣad* (5.1–5) Śaibya Satyakāma inquires from Pippalāda about the value of meditation on Om, or "AUM." *Om* is by now commonly broken into the three elements *A U M*, which are referred to as *mātras* (the rule in Sanskrit known as *sandhi* allows for the combination of *A* and *U* to form *O*). The equation of *Om* with Brahman is made here, resulting in the formulation of the concept of Śabda-Brahman. Pippalāda replies:

> Verily, O Satyakāma, that which is the syllable Om is both the higher and the lower Brahman [*param* and *aparam*, said also to refer to *nirguṇa*, "unqualified," and *saguṇa*, "qualified" Brahman, respectively]. Therefore with this support . . . a knower reaches one or the other. If he meditates on one element (namely A), having been instructed by that alone he quickly comes into the earth (after death). The Rig verses lead him to the world of men. There, united with austerity, chastity, and faith, he experiences greatness. Now, if he is united in mind with two elements (namely A+U), he is led by the Yajus formulas to the intermediate space, to the world of the moon. Having experienced greatness in the world of the moon, he returns hither again. Again, he who meditates on the highest Person (*puruṣa*) with the three elements of the syllable Om (namely A+U+M) is united with brilliance (*tejas*) in the sun. As a snake is freed from its skin, even, so, verily, is he freed from sin (*pāpman*). He is led by the Sāman chants to the world of Brahman. He beholds the Person that dwells in the body and that is higher than the highest living complex.[68]

It is significant that the analysis of AUM in the principal Upaniṣads is always in triplicate, with the concluding substantive element as *M*. In these symbolizations of sacred sound there is no mention of a fourth element, or "degree," elsewhere to be understood as Nāda-Brahman and broken down into the *anusvāra* (nasalization point) and *ardha-chandra* (half-moon) features, as will be shown, that grow to prominence in the Yoga and Tantric traditions. Accordingly, the *Maitri-Upaniṣad* (6.5) enlarges on the correspondences between the three parts of Om and various Vedic triadic phenomena:

> This, namely, A, U, and M (= Om), is the sound-form of this (*ātman*, Soul). Feminine, Masculine, and neuter: this is the sex-form. Fire, wind, and sun: this is the light-form. Brahmā, Rudra, and Vishnu: this is the lordship-form. The Gārhapātya sacrificial fire, the Dakṣiṇāgni sacrificial fire, and the Āhavanīya sacrificial fire: this is the mouth-form. The *Ṛg-Veda*, the *Yajur-Veda*, and the *Sāma-Veda*: this is the understanding-form. Earth (*bhūr*), atmosphere (*bhuvas*), and sky (*svar*): this is the world-form. Past, present, and future: this is the time-form. Breath, fire, and sun: this is the heat-form. Food, water, and moon: this is the swelling-form. Intellect (*buddhi*), mind (*manas*), and egoism (*ahaṅkāra*): this is the intelligence-form. The Prāṇa breath, the Apāna breath, and the Vyāna breath: this is the breath form. Hence these are praised, honored, and included by saying Om. For thus it has been said [*Praśna-Upaniṣad* 5.2]: "This syllable Om, verily, O Satyakāma, is both the higher [*para*] and lower [*apara*] Brahman."[69]

The words *para* and *apara* used here are also used to signify higher and lower knowledge of Brahman, as in *Muṇḍaka-Upaniṣad* I.1.4., which states that "two kinds of knowledge are to be known, as, indeed, the knowers of Brahman declare—the higher as well as the lower. . . . Of these, the lower is the *Ṛg-Veda*, the *Yajur-Veda*, the *Sāma-Veda*, the *Atharva-Veda*. Phonetics, Grammar, Etymology, Metrics and Astrology. And the ḥigher is that by which the Undecaying [*akṣaram*] is apprehended."[70] The lower is by no means mundane or "false," but is construed as a support that leads to the higher Brahman.

The entire *Māṇḍūkya-Upaniṣad* (1–12) purports to be a quaternary explanation of Om broken down into four elements (in fact, *A U M* plus a "nonelement"), corresponding to the four stages of sleep and the self: "The past, the present, the future—everything is just the word Om. And whatever else that transcends threefold time—

that, too, is just the word Om. For truly, everything here is Brahman; this self (*ātman*) is Brahman. This same self has four fourths.... The waking state...is the letter A....The sleeping state...is the letter U....The deep-sleep state...is the letter M....The fourth is without element [*amātra*]....Thus Om is the self (*ātman*)."[71] This text is extremely important for the school of Advaita-Vedānta, which posits a numerical identity between the self (*ātman*) and Brahman. There is further discussion of this Upaniṣad in connection with Advaita-Vedānta in chapter 3.

The *Maitri-Upaniṣad* (6.22) explains the different types of Brahman in relation to sound and also introduces us to Śabda-Brahman:

> Verily, there are two Brahmans to be meditated upon: sound [*śabda*] and non-sound [*aśabda*]. Now, non-sound is revealed only by sound. Now, in this case the Sound-Brahman is Om. Ascending by it, one comes to an end in the non-sound.... This is immortality....As a spider mounting up by means of his thread (*tantu*) obtains free space, thus, assuredly, indeed, does that meditator, mounting up by means of Om, obtain independence (*svātantrya*)....Passing beyond this variously characterized Sound-Brahman, men disappear in the supreme, the non-sound, the unmanifest Brahman. There they are unqualified, indistinguishable, like the various juices which have reached the condition of honey. For thus it has been said:—There are two Brahmans to be known: Sound-Brahman, and what higher is. Those people who Sound-Brahman know, unto the higher Brahman go.[72]

Here we find the division between "Sound" and "non-Sound" Brahman, a characteristic that carries over into Hindu theism, wherein a personal deity is identified with the "Higher," non-Sound Brahman. Yet the Sound-Brahman as Śabda-Brahman becomes refashioned into Nāda-Brahman and becomes the female power of a personal male God. In this case sacred sound (Om) becomes both an effective hermeneutic for understanding, or "knowing," Ultimate Reality and a vehicle for the salvific quest. Already in the *Maitri-Upaniṣad* (6.23) there is the identification of the Higher Brahman with the god Viṣṇu as well as an enumeration of the qualities of that which lies beyond sound, or Śabda-Brahman:

> The Sound Brahman is the syllable Om. That which is its acme

is tranquil [*śāntam*], soundless [*aśabdam*], fearless [*abhayam*], sorrowless [*aśokam*], blissful [*ānandam*], satisfied [*tṛptam*], steadfast [*sthiram*], immovable [*acalam*], immortal [*amṛtam*], unshaken [*acyutam*], enduring [*dhruvam*], named Viṣṇu (the Pervader) [*viṣṇu-saṁjñitam*]. So for paramountcy one should reverence both these. For thus it has been said:—Who is both higher and lower, that god, known by the name of Om. Soundless [*niḥ-śabda*] and void of being [*śūnya-bhūta*], too—thereon concentrate in the head!"[73]

The Vedic and Upaniṣadic notions of sound are also forerunners of the many esoteric notions prevalent in the Yoga and Tantric methods for meditation on sacred sound, methods wherein Nāda-Brahman has largely replaced Śabda-Brahman and the Vedic Vāk as the essence of sound both in the cosmos, *ākāśa*, and within the human heart, *hṛdayākāśa*. In the *Maitri-Upaniṣad:* "Having crossed over with the raft of the syllable Om [*oṁkāra-plavena*] to the other side of the space in the heart [*antar-hṛdayākāśa*], in the inner space which gradually becomes manifest one should enter the hall of Brahman [*brahma-śālam*]" (6.28); "Verily, the nature of the ether within the space of the heart is the same as the syllable Om. With this syllable [*akṣaram*], indeed, that bright power is raised up from the depths, goes upwards, and is breathed forth. Verily, therein is a perpetual support for meditation upon Brahman" (7.11); "There is a channel called the Suṣumnā, leading upward, conveying the breath, piercing through the palate. Through it, by joining the breath, the syllable Om, and the mind, one may go aloft. By causing the tip of the tongue to turn back against the palate and by binding together the senses, one may, as greatness, perceive greatness. Thence he goes to selflessness. . . . [Those who adhere to the doctrine of Sound-Brahman, *śabda-vādinaḥ*, maintain:] By closing the ears with the thumbs they hear the sound of the space within the heart [*antar-hṛdayākāśa-śabdam*]. Of it there is this sevenfold comparison: like rivers [*nadyaḥ*], a bell [*kiṅkiṇī*], a brazen vessel [*kāṁsya*], a wheel [*cakra*], the croaking of frogs [*bheka*], rain [*vṛṣṭi*], as when one speaks in a sheltered place [*nivate vaditi*]" (6.21–22).[74] It is precisely these kinds of nonlinguistic, "auditory phenomena" which are heard during the practice of Nāda-Yoga outlined in the *Yoga-Upaniṣads* and the texts associated with the Haṭha-Yoga tradition, as will be demonstrated in chapter 3.

The *Śvetāśvatara-Upaniṣad* (1.13–14) contains one of the most significant passages about sonic meditation and demonstrates the primacy of sound for the Hindu apprehension of the deity or divine presence:

> As the material form (*mūrti*) of fire when latent in its source [i.e., the firewood] is not perceived—and yet there is no evanishment of its subtle form (*liṅga*)—but may be caught again by means of the drill in its source, so, verily, both the universal and the individual Brahman are to be found in the body by the use of Om. By making one's own body the lower friction-stick and the syllable Om the upper friction-stick, by practicing the friction of meditation (*dhyāna*) one may see the God (*deva*) who is hidden, as it were.[75]

Thomas J. Hopkins has remarked on the above verses and underscored several salient points regarding the early formative stages of Hindu theistic worship. As we know, the Vedic religion was basically aniconic, with little or no visual representation of the gods or divine powers; hence, "distinctions between both gods and powers were related to variations in the meters and sounds of *mantras*; the sound-form was all-important, since from it everything else could be produced."[76] In contrast, the indigenous "popular" religions were strongly iconic, worshipping various anthropomorphic or theriomorphic images. The synthesis suggested in the *Śvetāśvatara-Upaniṣad,* a synthesis that had great importance for later theistic Hinduism, involves the juxtaposition of the Vedic syllable *Om* with the perception of a non-Vedic form (*mūrti*) of God. Hopkins explains that "meditation enables one to see God's *mūrti,* His physical form, which is hidden within man's self. The procedure . . . may involve Vedic *mantras,* but the goal is a mental image, the internal *mūrti* of God. . . . As the Āraṇyakas and early Upaniṣads had internalized the fire sacrifice [i.e., "Inner Agnihotra," *Kauśītaki-Upaniṣad* 2.5] by emphasizing its mental performance, so the late Upaniṣads now internalized images." It must therefore be understood that the evocation of sacred sound is critical in the late Upaniṣadic, and Hindu, visual apprehension (*darśana*) and adoration of deities in and out of temples. Though the particular god Śiva (Rudra) is stressed in the *Śvetāśvatara-Upaniṣad,* the principle could be—and was—applied to any personal god: "What was essential was not the specific identity of the Lord but his accessibility through meditation [on Om or mantra]."[77] Thus, the application of the "friction-stick" of sacred sound is a prerequisite for the proper "visualization," internal or external, of the chosen deity. This form of meditation remained from this point forward as a central feature of Brahmanical theism.

Although there are few conclusive statements about the use of *Om* in the Veda proper (the four Vedas), the speculation on Om found in the Upaniṣads clearly connects it to Brahman, thus forming the concept of Śabda-Brahman. There continues to be an abundant use of *Om* in the Śaiva, Śākta, and Vaiṣṇava texts and traditions. While the speculation on the nature and function of sacred sound vis-à-vis Om or Praṇava seems to have originated primarily in the Brāhmaṇa and Upaniṣadic texts, the subsequent incorporation of several extra-Vedic traditions, including "ancient Yoga," Nāda-Brahman meditation, and Āgamic ritual, contributed significantly.

In summary, the prevailing terms denoting sacred sound in the Vedic canon are *Vāk, Śabda-Brahman, Om* (in three divisions of *A + U + M*), *Praṇava,* and *Udgītha* (loud chant). They have slightly different shades of meaning yet are often used interchangeably in the texts. Contrary to the assumptions of many pious Hindus and proponents of Indian classical music, the term *Nāda-Brahman* does not appear anywhere in the Vedic canon, including the *Sāma-Veda* and the principal Upaniṣads: *nāda* only appears in the phonetic texts as a word to denote "voiced sound." The notion of sacred sound as Nāda-Brahman assumes a primary position in later Hindu theistic and Tantric traditions (including classical music treatises), however, and seems to garner its own metaphysical status independently of the normative tradition of Vedic sound outlined in this chapter. The Upaniṣadic Śabda-Brahman signifies the merging of Brahman with Om, such that Om in triplicate as AUM is Śabda-Brahman, or the Sound Brahman. It generally denotes a kind of linguistic Absolute in which a meaning, albeit transcendent, is attached. The extra-Vedic *Nāda-Brahman*—AUM including a fourth (*turīya*) stage of Nāda-Bindu as Sound Brahman—gradually supersedes *Śabda-Brahman* and becomes the most consistent cosmological and psychological characterization of sacred sound in the Hindu tradition: connected with either Śiva or Viṣṇu as female energy or cast as the goddess portion of an otherwise neuter Brahman. This term also contains a number of nonlinguistic sonic features, as will be shown in chapter 3.

In the next chapter, however, we will discuss the linguistic philosophies of word (*śabda*) and meaning (*artha*) which emerged out of the Vedic tradition—the Mīmāṁsā doctrine of Varṇavāda and the Grammarian theory of Sphoṭavāda. Interpreting the Upaniṣadic Śabda-Brahman as either external or internal, they form the substructure of the Indian philosophy of language.

Chapter 2

Indian Philosophies of Language

Indian sages have been studying language since the beginning of their own oral and written history, while Western scholars of religion have only recently turned to the study of religious language in the wake of biblical hermeneutics and literary criticism. The current Western focus on language in religious studies, being motivated by the discovery that what is crucial or important for the study of religion is contained in the subtle structures and tensions of language (speech and writing) itself, has been anticipated by a long tradition on the Indian soil. As will be seen, the Vedic ritual language formed the basis of early linguistic debates in India about the nature of language and its relationship to human consciousness.

Surprisingly, many of the ancient Indian ideas about language concur with the modern axiom of phenomenology and hermeneutics that "all thought has linguistic form." The first chapter of Edmund Husserl's *Formal and Transcendental Logic* pointed to his refusal to separate the analysis of speaking from thinking, of language from thought: "Thinking is always done in language and is entirely bound up with speech. Thinking, as distinct from other modalities of consciousness, is thus always linguistic, always some use of language."[1] And among more recent phenomenologists of note Maurice Merleau-Ponty "insists that thought does not exist independently of words."[2]

The impetus for the serious study of language and phonetics in the West seems to have come initially from India, as noted by W. Sidney Allen: "The impact of Sir William Jones's 'discovery' of Sanskrit is well known"; and "Our [Western] phonetic categories and terminology owe more than is perhaps generally realized to the influence of the Sanskrit phoneticians."[3] J. R. Firth of the English school of phonetics made the following observation: "Without the Indian grammarians whom he [Jones] introduced and recommended to us, it is difficult to imagine our nineteenth century school of phonetics."[4]

Many philologists in the West had previously believed that the human language most closely representing the original speech of God and the first man was Hebrew, though other languages were thought to contain remnants as well. "God's actual speech, the idiom of immediacy known to Adam and common to men until Babel, can still be decoded, partially at least, in the inner layers of Hebrew and perhaps, in other languages of the original scattering."[5] The original eighteenth-century notion that Hebrew was the divine language par excellence was seriously challenged, however, with the discovery of Sanskrit, which played a major role in the development of the new disciplines of comparative philology and comparative religion.

The results of Western Indological study in the nineteenth century are by no means exhausted. In fact, many of the ancient insights discovered then regarding language and meaning are finding an increasing audience in today's linguistic circles. Allen remarked: "These early (Indian) phoneticians speak in fact to the twentieth century rather than to the Middle Ages or even the mid-nineteenth century, and many a statement which the commentators and even Whitney or Max Müller have failed to comprehend makes immediate sense to the phonetician today."[6] Indeed, many of the insights that frequent the work of Ferdinand de Saussure, the French founder of modern structuralism and linguistics, very likely emerged out of his tenure as professor of Sanskrit at the University of Geneva during the 1880s. Though there is no scope for discussion here, it is arguable that his notion of *différance,* the sequencing factor in all language, was inspired by the theories of Bhartṛhari and the early Buddhist theory of Apohavāda. The implications arising out of the juxtaposition of ancient Indian grammatical theory with modern linguistics and hermeneutics are only beginning to be discussed in the academies today.[7]

Above and beyond the ritual application of the Vedic verses, various philosophies of language sprang out of the Vedic period in Indian history. In order to discover the underlying role of sacred sound, the present chapter attempts to explicate some of the major philosophical issues at stake in the perception of meaning in language.

As discussed in the last chapter, the Vedic view of language and sacred sound was inextricably bound to ritual activity and coincided with the metrical and mythological permutations of the Goddess Vāk. Vedic mantras, or applied Vāk, providing a locus of power beyond ordinary speech and governed, as they were, by rigid rules of grammar and phonetics, invited access to the unseen world of supernatural forces and energies. Language was never meaningless for the ancient

Hindus, unless they were in a state of ignorance, or noninitiation. Language was not simply taken for granted but, rather, was fused with the innermost workings of the tradition itself.

Vedic Vāk as Śabda-Brahman became the object of philosophical debate regarding the locus of comprehension. The Mīmāṁsā school (Varṇavāda) posited the individual word or letter (*varṇa*) as the prime substance of Vāk, whereas the Grammarians (Sphoṭavāda) developed the notion of *sphoṭa* to explain the mysterious manner by which meaning is conveyed in sentences; a process of cognition which culminates in the intuitive perception of the Absolute as Śabda-Brahman. These two positions form the polemical substructure for the discussion of the Indian philosophy of language and later serve to inform the Yoga, Śaiva, Śākta, and Vaiṣṇava traditions, nearly all of which share in common much of the nomenclature as well as the anticipatory expectations about sacred sound.

According to T. R. V. Murti, "Two principal schools, the Mīmāṁsā and the philosophy of grammar [Bhartṛhari], made massive and the most significant contributions to the philosophy of language."[8] Indeed, among all of the Indian philosophical schools, the Mīmāṁsā and the Grammarian tradition devoted the most energy to investigation and discussion of issues related to *śabda* and its meaning: "The Mīmāṁsakas and the Vaiyākaraṇas [Grammarians] were particularly interested in *śabda*."[9] Though both claim allegiance to the orthodox Vedic outlook on speech production, which holds that *śabda* is eternal and "manifests" itself rather than is created or produced, they display fundamental and irreconcilable differences regarding the relation of sound to *artha*, or meaning, being engaged in debate for centuries.

The specific arguments between the Grammarians, Mīmāṁsakas, and even the Nyāyas, which have extended up to the present, have been well rehearsed elsewhere.[10] Yet an explication of their platforms in relation to theological and soteriological questions vis-à-vis sacred sound has never, to my knowledge, been attempted. These specific issues are taken up in this section.

No doubt, the ideas of *śabda* and Śabda-Brahman find a polemical context in all of the six philosophical schools or Darśanas: Pūrva-Mīmāṁsā, Yoga, Sāṁkhya, Nyāya, Vaiśeṣika, and Vedānta. The status of *śabda-pramāṇa* (verbal testimony or authority) in the epistemology of these respective schools is a main point of contention among all Indian philosophers, including Buddhist and Jain. Though the traditions that accept the Vedas as revelatory tend to concede to the eternity of sound, or language, the different Indian philosophical schools reflect a variety of subtle responses to this issue. The Buddhist and Jain schools, for example, having rejected the revelatory status of the Vedic canon, view all language as conventional and temporal, with no epistemological functions regarding Ultimate Reality. Hence, for them the relationship between word and meaning is purely arbitrary and ephemeral, individual utterances being created from nothing rather than from an eternal sonic substratum. Similar issues were discussed in Plato's *Cratylus.* The Nyāya and Vaiśeṣika thinkers are close to this conventionalist view yet posit that the conventions were established by a Creater god rather than by human beings. By contrast, the Mīmāṁsās hold that the bond between word and meaning in all language is solidified by the presence of the Vedas as eternal word, uncreated and not established by any Supreme or human author.

But, among the schools who do subscribe to the eternal Word as Śabda-Brahman, a major division exists between those who conceive of Ultimate Reality itself as Absolute Sound (Sphoṭavāda) and those who conceive of sacred sound as embodied only in a text, the Veda, without the addition of any other Ultimate Reality (Varṇavāda). Though they both claim to be strictly in line with Vedic tradition, there are major differences that are reflected both on the cosmic level and on the human level of semantics with regard to sentence and word meaning. The semantic problem of the relationship between sound and meaning in language is thus at the forecourt of our inquiry, since "all Indian systems deal more or less with problems of the nature of language, the relation of sound to sense."[11] Indeed, though this topic has been mooted by nearly all branches of Indian thought for centuries, it is within the Mīmāṁsā and Grammarian traditions that it finds the most dogged articulation.

The Sphoṭavāda of the Grammarians, as we will explain further, holds that the meaning of a sentence is conveyed in a "flash" or "burst" of cognition known as *sphoṭa,* which is objectively real, eternal, and said to operate over and above the individual words themselves. The whole is greater than the sum of its parts. By extension, the universal categories of meaning inhere in a Universal Sonic Absolute (Śabda-Brahman or Sabda-Tattva), which is both material and efficient cause of creation. The Grammarians—Patañjali, Bhartṛhari, Maṇḍana Miśra, Nāgeśa, etc.—members of the Yoga schools and, to some degree, the Kashmiri Śaivas generally subscribe to this view.

The Varṇavāda doctrine maintains that the meaning of a sentence is conveyed by the sum total of the meanings of the individual letters (*varṇa*). The whole results from the sum of its parts. That is, the main unit of language is the phoneme, or meaning-bearing syllable, which is real and eternal. The Mīmāṁsā school is the arch defender of this view, with Advaita-Vedānta, Sāṁkhya, Nyāya, and Vaiśeṣika philosophical schools following suit. Furthermore, the nonmonistic Pāñcarātra texts, Śrī-Vaiṣṇavism, Dvaitādvaita-Vedānta, Gauḍīya-Vaiṣṇavism, Śaiva-Siddhānta, and some varieties of Kashmiri Śaiva and Śākta-Tantra have all, more or less, refuted the Sphoṭavāda position and embraced Varṇavāda.

The Sphoṭavāda and Varṇavāda viewpoints should not be completely foreign to Western readers, as there are some analogies in Greek and Hebraic traditions. In the Stoic philosophy of language the meaning of sentences, known as *lecta,* was construed to be separate from mere verbal sounds: "As Diogenes tells us, speech is very different from mere utterance, for only sounds are uttered, but matters of discourse are spoken of, and these are . . . *lecta.*"[12] Jewish mystics probed the meaning of the letters of the Hebrew alphabet such that the ultimate unit of signification for the Hebrew tradition, as in the Sanskrit Mīmāṁsā and Varṇavāda, is the individual letter or syllable: "There is a philology and gnosis of the individual Hebrew letter as there is of the word and grammatical unit. In Merkabah mysticism [the earliest form of Jewish mystical exegesis and forerunner of Kabbalah], each written character may be regarded as embodying a fragment of the universal design of creation; all human experience, no less than all human discourse unto the end of time, is graphically latent in the letters of the alphabet."[13]

At first glance at the two sides of Sphoṭavāda and Varṇavāda, it seems like a linguistic or religious duel between monism and nonmonism, or dualism. Yet the matter becomes much more complex. Advaita-Vedānta, for example, the role model for Indian monistic thought, refutes the inherently monistic Sphoṭavāda and agrees with the Varṇavāda accepted by the dualistic traditions. The more basic issue seems to be that the eternal Śabda-Brahman is Janus-faced with regard to its strategic location in living Hinduism—whether external in the form of the Veda or internal in the form of Sphoṭa within human consciousness. The two-sidedness of its very nature contributes to its inherence and persistence as a centralized *mysterium*. This issue, indeed, forms a new paradigm for the study of Hinduism, as it forces us to reclassify groups in ways other than standard sectarian rubric or nomenclature.

External Śabda-Brahman: Mīmāṁsā and Varṇavāda

The Mīmāṁsā, or Pūrva-Mīmāṁsā, school developed as a kind of exegesis of the Vedic text and ritual. The aim of Mīmāṁsā philosophy is to establish the authority of the Veda as dharma, divine law, on rational grounds, as the word *mīmāṁsā* means "profound thought or reflection or consideration, investigation, examination, discussion."[14] Though its origins coincide with the Vedic period itself, the first systematic treatise by Jaimini, along with the commentary, is said to follow somewhat later: "Jaimini's *Mīmāṁsā-Sūtras* were probably written about 200 B.C.E. and are now the groundwork of the Mīmāṁsā System. . . . The famous commentary known as the *Śābara-Bhāṣya* [by Śabara at approximately 57 B.C.E.] is the basis of the later Mīmāṁsā works."[15] The work of Śabara has been explained by the two chief exponents of Mīmāṁsā philosophy, Prabhākara (A.D. 650) and Kumārila Bhaṭṭa (A.D. 700).

Ganganath Jha, a renowned Mīmāṁsā scholar of recent times and the translator of *Śābara-Bhāṣya* as well as the Sūtras of Jaimini, has summarized the position of the Mīmāṁsā as follows: "The Mīmāṁsaka's main thesis is that Dharma can be known only from the Vedic injunction; and in order to establish the infallibility and utter reliability of the Vedic injunction, he has had to prove that—(1) words are eternal, (2) the denotation of words are eternal, (3) the relationship between words and their denotations is eternal, (4) the meaning of the sentence is comprehended only on the comprehension of the meanings of the component words, and the sentence has no meaning apart by itself."[16] This last applies only to sentences composed by human beings, as Vedic sentences or injunctions are held to be eternal, self-determined, and valid.

In the first chapter of the *Mīmāṁsā-Sūtra* (1.1.6–11) six objections are raised which must be addressed before the above assertions can hold any conviction.[17] The first one claims that words cannot be eternal because they are produced by effort and, therefore, the result of temporary action. The second says that, in addition, the words have no stability because they vanish immediately after they are spoken. The third one points out that the use of the words *to make* (*karoti*) in the descriptions of speech indicate that words are made or created and are, therefore, not eternal. In the fourth objection the opponent argues that, since words are heard simultaneously in many diverse places, they cannot be one and eternal. The fifth one insists that words become modified through usage and, therefore, exhibit change, while the sixth states that the increase and decrease in the sound of words by different numbers of speakers reveals their ephemeral character.

In response to these six objections Jaimini offers (*Mīmāṁsā-Sūtra* 1.1.12-17) logical rebuttals, which are developed by Śabara in his commentary.[18] The first answer states that, if the word did not exist before, it could not be pronounced. Sound is a quality of ether, which is eternal and, thus, does not need to be continuously present to prove its eternality. The third response explains that the making of words actually refers to the "using of words," since the pronunciation, instead of creating words, only makes them audible. Just as sunlight is received by many people from the same sun, various sounds that are heard are actually located in the ether, which is one and eternal like the sun. In the fifth response Jaimini states that the changes of letters in words are not modifications of the root word itself and, thus, do not disprove the eternity of words.

The sixth and final response by Jaimini is especially significant with regard to its implications for sonic meditation practices: "The increase [and decrease] is with reference to the increase [and decrease] of the tone [not the increase or decrease of the Word, *śabda*] [*nāda-vṛddhi para* 1.1.17]."[19] The explication by Śabara is quoted as follows:

> Sound has no parts, as is shown by the fact that we cannot perceive any component parts of sound; and as it is without parts, no augmentation of it is possible. Hence there can be no augmentation of the Word (sound). What happens is that when the Word is pronounced by one man, its sound is soft; but when it is pronounced by several persons, those same letters (which had sounded soft), on account of being taken up continuously by such conjunctions and disjunctions (ripples [resonances or reverberation]) as fill all the space in the ear-cavity, come to be heard as "augmented," and hence as having parts. As a matter of fact, however, when the conjunctions and disjunctions continuously set up render the (same) Word manifest, they come to be called by the name "noise" [or tone, according to Sandal's translation of the word *nāda*]. Hence the "augmentation" (spoken of by the opponent) is of the noise [*nāda*, or tone], not of the Word [*śabda*].[20]

This notion of *nāda* agrees with Bhartṛhari, as we shall see.

The cornerstone of the Mīmāṁsā method is the acceptance of all knowledge, excepting memory, or *smṛti*, as valid in itself (*svataḥ-prāmāṇya*). This theory of knowledge is realistic, since there is no knowledge that does not correspond to an object in reality. The validity of cognition depends on the validity of language, which is said to be not only eternal and natural but also interwoven with reality, which is also eternal. The self-validity of the Veda does not rest on its being the creation of God or man but, rather, on the fact that it consists of words, which are eternal. The Mīmāṁsā holds that "the Veda is eternal, uncreated, without beginning or end, and of absolute authority. . . . Vedic commands [injunctions, *codana*] constitute the whole duty of man [dharma], and it is the aim of the Mīmāṁsā to interpret these commands systematically."[21] The Vedic injunctions to action constitute the target and substance of the Mīmāṁsā interpretive position and also point beyond the visible world to the dimension of reality which is unseen (*adṛṣṭa*). Since our point in trying to understand the Mīmāṁsā philosophy and theory of meaning is a prerequisite for examining the later theories of mantra recitation, further clarification is needed here.

The Mīmāṁsā idea of the self-existence and authority of the Veda is supported by the theory of language which maintains the following consideration as stated by Mysore Hiriyanna: "The relation between a word and its meaning is natural and therefore necessary and eternal. We ought not to think that things were there already before they were named. The word and the thing it names go together and it is impossible to think of either as having had a beginning in time."[22] In agreement, Surendranath Dasgupta has explained the Mīmāṁsā position by stating that "all words have natural denotative powers by which they themselves out of their own nature refer to certain objects irrespective of their comprehension or non-comprehension by the hearer. . . . Mīmāṁsā does not think that the association of a particular meaning with a word is due to conventions among people who introduce and give meaning to words. . . . Words are thus acknowledged to be denotative of themselves [and] all words are believed to be eternally existent."[23]

To further illustrate this concept, a note concerning the Hebraic understanding of the relationship between language and reality is helpful, for comparison: "The Hebrew word was not just an arbitrary designation, but an aspect of the continuous divine creative force itself. Each word . . . was the inner specific character or essence of its respective reality. Names are not conventional, but intrinsically connected to their referents; the name indeed, is the real referent of the thing, its essential character."[24]

According to Western occult traditions, the biblical Adam is said to have been able to know the intrinsic nature of things so as to give them names that were also translations of the divine eternal Word. After the Fall of Babel, however, these names were corrupted so that only "signatures" remained, partially recoverable in our ordinary language. The names Adam gave to animals and to creation before the Fall—that is, the Adamic language—are said to be translations of the divine Word, signatures. For Adam, knowing the virtues of all beings, gave them their correct names. This correctness was perverted, however, by the Fall, "but the Adamic signatures can still be partially read in the words we use for things. For the language of nature—the Word in creation—also exists, and letters, words, and syllables reflect its secrets and significations. Since man is created in God's image and his spirit partakes immediately of the divine spirit, letters, and so on, are figurations of this divine centrum."[25]

Similarly, although Hinduism does not accept creation ex nihilo, the unity of all language was affirmed by the Mīmāṁsā tradition. Śabara had stated in his *Bhāṣya* (1.3.30) that "the words in the Veda are the same as those in common speech" and stressed that all statements, whether Vedic or non-Vedic, are meaningful.[26] Language is here primarily meaningful in essence, since all words have a definitive aprioristic "meaning"—and all objects have an a priori "name"—as exemplified by the Veda and vouchsafed by tradition.

The question then arises that, if all words are eternal and the language of the Veda is the same as ordinary language, why is the Veda unique over other types of literature? Mysore Hiriyanna, a modern scholar of Indian philosophy, has responded to this question by arguing that the permanence of the relation between a word and its meaning does not establish the eternity of the Veda. The Veda consists of words, and so far it is like any other literary work that may or may not be considered eternal. "If the Veda alone is eternal and not other works as well, it should be traced to some unique feature it possesses; and such a feature, it is said, is the particular order (*anupūrvī*) in which the several words occur in it. When the Mīmāṁsaka states that the Veda is eternal, it is this permanence of the text that he means."[27] The specific word order of the Veda is, thus, what makes it unique as a "composition," which is self-determined rather than created by any outside agent, human or divine. Thus, it is known as *apauruṣeya,* meaning "uncreated by any person."

The assertion that there is only one kind of language is important for the Mīmāṁsā school. Rather than demonstrating the existence of two sets of languages, one eternal and one temporary, it thus affirms that all language is part of the one eternal universal order. Yāska (ca. before 500 B.C.E.), in his refutation of Kautsa, who claimed that *mantras* are meaningless, was the earliest thinker to posit the equality of Vedic and ordinary language: "*Mantras* have meaning, since the words [of the Veda and ordinary speech] are the same [*Nirukta* 1.16]." The Mīmāṁsā went a step beyond Yāska, however, and said that "the words of the Veda and ordinary usage have the same meanings. Yāska appears prepared to say only that both are meaningful."[28]

This notion of "one language" is characterized in the Mīmāṁsā as *śabda* and is even more important for the following reason. The Veda is said to be the purest form of *śabda,* as it is the most reliable source for knowledge, both of the visible world (*dṛṣṭa*) and the invisible world (*adṛṣṭa*) mentioned above, since "language [*śabda*] encompasses both dimensions of reality, *dṛṣṭa* and *adṛṣṭa*. The fact that *śabda* is directly related to both these dimensions is of crucial importance for Śabara in understanding reality."[29] The locus for the mediation between these two dimensions is the Vedic sacrifice or, more specifically, the Vedic injunctions and the action they engender within the ritual context. It is axiomatic here that there exists a link between human beings, sacrifice, and heaven and that "all men desire heaven." Language, or *śabda* (Vedic injunction), is the only link, since it prescribes particular actions for the sacrificer, whose own efficient force (*bhāvanā*) causes unseen merit to accrue, known as *apūrva*. This merit is the direct result of actions commanded by Vedic injunctions in the form of verbs and gains the aspirant entrance into *svarga* (heaven). Verbs or verbal phrases, not nouns or names, are more directly connected to the unseen, or *adṛṣṭa,* dimension of reality because they produce ritual activity, which creates *apūrva*. An act in the visible realm, according to Vedic injunction, inevitably (i.e., only after death) leads to an unseen result—namely, heaven—in the invisible or inaudible realm. And for Śabara *svarga* "is not experienced by man on the basis of sense perception.... [It] has to be realized..., and this is made possible only by being involved in sacrificial acts."[30]

Another comparative note can be inserted here regarding the

continuing effort of Christian theologians to come to terms with the precise nature of Holy Scripture or language. Paul Tillich reflects the general Christian position of ambivalence regarding biblical language itself: "The Biblical language is neither a divine language nor a divinely dictated human language. The Biblical language is the human expression of the state of revelatory ecstasy which the Biblical writers have experienced. . . . But these words are at the same time 'Word of God' in so far as they are received by men as the divine self-manifestation."[31] The actual distinction between sacred language and ordinary language does not seem to have a clear resolution here.

The assertion of "one language" appears to assuage the case of ambivalence for the Mīmāṁsā school and brings us back to Ellul's general distinction between the realm of Reality which is visual and the realm of Truth which is nonvisual and only mediated by language or the Word: "Anything concerned with the ultimate destination of a human being belongs to the domain of Truth. . . . The word must always remain a door opening to the Wholly Other [and] an indicator of ultimate answers."[32] Like the Mīmāṁsā, all language for Ellul is ambivalent, encompassing both realms of the seen and the unseen—or unheard.

In order to defend the infallibility of the Vedic "sentences" as containing meaning both Prabhākara and Kumārila of the Mīmāṁsā school have elucidated their theories regarding the power (*śakti*) of letters, which forms the basis of the doctrine of Varṇavāda. They both agree that, "as the potency of the word originates from the separate potencies of the letters, it has to be admitted that the latter is the direct cause of verbal cognition."[33] Since words are held to be eternal and mutually exclusive, meaning must inhere in the separate building blocks, or corpuscular syllables, rather than in something internal and intangible like *sphoṭa*.

Unlike the Sphoṭavāda, the Varṇavāda posits no separate meaning-bearing entity over and above the words themselves. The term *varṇa* (m. "letter, sound, vowel, or syllable")[34] is best expressed for our purposes by *phoneme*, an "oral meaning-bearing syllable." The *varṇa* is, in fact, the fundamental unit for all Mīmāṁsā philosophy and the sole meaning-carrying agent. The meaning inherent in the *varṇa* is directly related to the inherent meaning in the thing signified rather than in a separate mental cognition as in Sphoṭavāda. This realist—as opposed to idealist—position of Mīmāṁsā sheds light on such phenomena as word magic, spells, and incantations, the underlying assumption being that there is a one-to-one connection between words and physical things whereby the things can be brought under control by the oral words themselves. This also helps in understanding the rules governing Vedic ritual.

The most zealous protagonist of the Varṇavāda doctrine was Kumārila, who argued it extensively in his work *Śloka-Vārttika.* The theory itself is one of the earliest in Indian history regarding the nature of sentence meaning and seems to be based on the view—words denote universals, which combine to form sentence meaning—advocated by the ancient Grammarian Vājapyāyana (mentioned by Kātyāyana, a contemporary of Pāṇini). Kumārila, however, traces this conception directly to Śabara (*Bhāṣya* on Sūtra 1.1.25), who says, "In a sentence the words express their own meanings, and stop with that; the meanings of the words thus known convey the meaning of the sentence."[35]

To the question of what is a word, or *śabda,* Śabara refers to Upavarṣa,[36] who explains that the word is nothing more than the syllables themselves: "The word *gauḥ* (cow) is nothing more than the three phonemes which are found in it, namely *g, au,* and *h.*... It is also these very phonemes which cause the understanding of the meaning of the word."[37] The human process of comprehension is therein said to result from the mysterious accumulation of individual letter potencies (*śakti*), each of which leaves an impression or trace (*saṁskāra*), which carries over onto the next letter or syllable. Each syllable of a word, and thus of a sentence, appears at a separate moment in time and, consequently, disappears, leaving behind its unique impression onto the next letter, until the accumulated meaning is finally deposited in the mind of the hearer.

To clarify this Gaurinath Sastri has posited that the process of language comprehension in Mīmāṁsā is analogous to the unseen (*apūrva*) effect of the Vedic fire sacrifice:

> Let us suppose that the final letter together with the impressions left by the preceding letters is the word and let this word deliver the meaning..., [which] is a different entity [from memory impressions] endowed with a different capacity like the unseen result left behind by the different operations of a religious act, e.g., sacrifice....The after-effect which is left by the different letters upon the subject is analogous to such religious

> leaven. . . . So the final letter leavened by the impression of the previous letters gives out the meaning.[38]

Noted Grammarian scholar K. A. Subramania Iyer agrees with this analogy when he says that "the impression left by the cognition of a phoneme is very much like this *apūrva*."[39] Indeed, the whole linguistic theory of Mīmāṁsā relies on this notion of *apūrva* to knit the letter sounds and their traces into a whole word; otherwise, the memory traces of each letter would remain separate and discrete like the letters themselves. If this analogy with *apūrva* is valid, and it is arguably so, then it helps us to envision the soteriological effect of mantras or sacred sound, in later Hindu theism—in the operation of mysterious forces in both ordinary language comprehension and in the accumulation of spiritual merit through sacrifice and worship.

So far some of the major tenets of the Mīmāṁsā philosophy have been advanced. Yet the above issue of the unique "word order" of the Veda as opposed to other forms of literature, and to the sequence in the Vedic ritual, has reemerged. If the meaning of all sentences for Mīmāṁsā is determined solely by the combination of the meanings of the individual words, which by definition have no particular or fixed sequence, what is it that accounts for the unique sequence, much less the meaning, of the Vedic sentences? The same question applies to the need for sequence in the sacrificial ritual. Unless the need for sequence is proved, there is no reason why we should accept it. The Veda prescribes the order of events in the ritual so that *apūrva* is attained—but why a particular sequence of acts in a ritual or words in a sentence? As to the condition that the phonemes have to be uttered in a definite sequence and that the ritual acts have to be done in a certain order, "the Mīmāṁsaka has not been able to show [their] necessity considering that, for him, they are eternal and cannot have any inner sequence."[40]

These particular weaknesses of the Mīmāṁsā school were recognized and taken up by the Grammarians, who developed their refutation of Varṇavāda by positing the doctrine of Sphoṭavāda.

Internal Śabda-Brahman: Grammar and Sphoṭavāda

Notions of inerrancy coupled with the unquestionable position of the written Bible had delayed the critical study of "religious language" in the West. Furthermore, the biblical idea that language itself arose from the act of naming (Genesis 2.19–20) perpetuated the notion that grammar was something imposed from outside and, hence, not worthy of serious consideration or study by religionists. In India, by contrast, grammar as well as all language were almost never separated from religious or soteriological concerns.[41] Indeed, the earliest name given to Sanskrit grammar was *vedānām vedaḥ*, the "Veda of the Vedas," such that "the origin of grammar is organically and most intimately connected with the study of the Vedas."[42]

The Indian grammatical tradition, narrowly conceived, refers to the work of Pāṇini, Kātyāyana, Patañjali, and Bhartṛhari. While Pāṇini and Kātyāyana limit their discussion to semantics and linguistic methodologies related to common everyday speech, it is Patañjali and his *Mahābhāṣya* (second or first century B.C.E.) that provide the terminus a quo for the systematic philosophical approach to language in the grammatical tradition: "Patañjali's *Mahābhāṣya* occupies a position that is unique in Sanskrit literature. . . . It embodies within its limits information of a varied kind relating to every conceivable field of human enquiry."[43] After this text no other important grammatical works are available until the *Vākyapadīya* of Bhartṛhari. Despite the time difference (nearly six hundred years), there is an amazing continuity regarding the role of sound and speech in the destiny of human life. Though the cause of Bhartṛhari was taken up in the ninth century by Maṇḍana Miśra (*Sphoṭa-Siddhi*), wider concepts concerning the philosophy of grammar in India draw most heavily from Patañjali and Bhartṛhari.

The two schools, Mīmāṁsā and Grammarian, part company as to the nature and locus of Śabda-Brahman. For the Grammarians Śabda-Brahman exists both in the cosmos and within human consciousness. The Eternal Verbum manifests itself in the form of *sphoṭa*, a kind of meaning-bearing sound revelation within normal human consciousness. According to Mīmāṁsā, the Eternal Word exists only as the external text of the Veda and does not manifest in any other form apart from the specific linguistic constructions found there.

As in the Mīmāṁsā, the relation of word (*śabda*) and meaning (*artha*) is aprioristic for the Grammarians. The *Vākyapadīya* (1.23) of Bhartṛhari states that "words, meanings, and their relations are described in it [the grammatical tradition] as timeless by the sages."[44] For the Grammarians, however, meaning (*artha*) is always something mental, which does not depend on objective existence. A distinction is made between the existence of an object in the external world and its being in the form of mental cognition (*artha*). It is this relation between the word and its mental cognition that Bhartṛhari argues is eternal, whereas the Mīmāṁsaka accepts the eternity of the relation between words and their direct physical referent. Or, to put it another way, for Mīmāṁsā meaning, which is inherent in things themselves and by nature manifold, has an eternal relation with words or syllables exemplified by the Veda. For the Grammarian all meaning resides not in things but only in human consciousness, where it is eternally related to sound on various distinct levels, aspires toward ultimate unity as Śabda-Brahman, and is epitomized by Praṇava (the syllable *Om*), the "essence" of the Veda.

The nature of the relation between word and cognition for the Grammarian is explained further by Subramania Iyer: "Human beings cannot create this relation between the word and its meaning, whether we look upon the latter as eternal or transitory. . . . What is noteworthy is that the meaning is understood as identical to the word. Both the word and the object meant are designated by the same word. . . . Therefore, the things denoted by the nouns and the verb have an existence only in the mind. This kind of Being which consists in something figuring in our mind is the basis of the use of all words."[45]

For Indian thinkers like Patañjali language was considered to be the spoken word. Patañjali, at the very beginning of the *Mahābhāṣya*, raises the question of what constitutes a word by using the example of the word for cow (*gauḥ*). He defines the word as "that which, when uttered, gives rise to the knowledge of objects possessed of dewlap, tails, humps, hoofs, and horns. Or, in other words, word is that sound from which there arises the knowledge of things in the affairs of the world. . . . Word means sound or utterance of letters also."[46] He explains that a knowledge of words (*śabda*) and grammar (*śabdānuśāsana*) is necessary to preserve the Vedas, since a modification of gender, case, etc., in the mantras will be required in the performance of sacrifices.

Among all the other reasons for the study of grammar (to maintain caste status, to avoid corrupt speech, etc.) Patañjali stresses the salvific intention: "He who is an adept in details and employs words properly in communication, he who knows the secrets of speech, obtains eternal victory in the next world (*svarga*), while he who does not is contaminated by corrupt words. . . . That man who knows the secret of words [*vāg-yogavid*] attains unending happiness in the next world. . . . The great God is Sound (*mahan devaḥ śabdaḥ*). . . . We should study grammar so that we may be like the great God."[47]

Although the exact meaning is not clear, the concept of *vāg-yoga* (Yoga of the Word), as mentioned here by Patañjali, forms the basis for Bhartṛhari's notion of *śabdapūrva-yoga*.

The grammatical and philosophical work of Bhartṛhari (fifth century A.D.) represents the conjunction of several Indian traditions yet, like the Mīmāṁsa, purports to be firmly rooted in the Vedic tradition: "Agreeing with Patañjali, Bhartṛhari regards grammar as the most important Vedāṅga [branch of the Vedas]; for him, its value is . . . in its revelation of Brahman (through meditation exercises centered on language: *vāg-yoga* or *śabdapūrva-yoga*). Speech is Brahman. This central role of speech goes back to early Vedic tradition and was stressed again in Tantric systems, with which Bhartṛhari shares a few key terms (*śakti, sādhana*)."[48] Bhartṛhari's employment of the word *nāda* in the context of audible sounds probably derives from either the *Mīmāṁsā-Sūtra* (1.1.17) or the Pratiśākhya phonetic literature, yet the possibility of it reflecting another Āgamic or Tantric influence should not be ruled out.[49] Bhartṛhari was more or less forgotten for centuries after the triumph of Advaita-Vedānta philosophy in intellectual circles, but he is gradually receiving the attention he deserves. A. L. Herman recently observed that "the Grammarian's [Bhartṛhari's] arguments are more appealing philosophically, based as they are on common experience and memory, while Śaṅkara comes out second best as a philosopher."[50]

The uniqueness of Bhartṛhari as a philosopher rests on his assertion of the existence of a universal linguistic Absolute:

> The Supreme Reality in the philosophy of Sanskrit grammar has been called the Eternal Verbum (Śabda-Tattva or Śabda-Brahman) or the Supreme Word, which . . . lies beyond time and space, . . . and eludes all description by means of positive and negative predicates. . . . In the system of Bhartṛhari consciousness and word are interchangeable terms. This makes for his difference from the Vedānta, though both of them are at one with regard to the unitary character of the Absolute.[51]

Bhartṛhari seems to have qualified this apparently monistic conception further in order to avoid confusion with rival doctrines. It provides no small confusion, however, that Śaṅkara rejects Bhartṛhari and subscribes to the Mīmāṁsā theory of language, especially in that Bhartṛhari's later commentators had read Śaṅkara into the text of the *Vākyapadīya*. As we shall see, many of the later theistic traditions reject the ultimacy of Śabda-Brahman in favor of a more qualified Brahman with attributes, one of which is the female energy of Nāda-Brahman.

In contrast to the ultimate non-Sound Brahman of the *Maitri-Upaniṣad* (namely, *aśabda*) Bhartṛhari boldly asserts in the very beginning of the *Vākyapadīya* (1.1) that this Ultimate Truth, known as Śabda-Brahman, is the acme of sound and word: "That beginningless and endless One, the imperishable Brahman of which the essential nature is the Word [*śabda*], which manifests itself into objects and from which is the creation of the Universe [*anādi-nidhanaṁ brahma śabda-tattvaṁ yad-akṣaram / vivartate 'rtha-bhāvena prakriyā jagato yataḥ*]."[52] Gopinath Kaviraj explains that, to the Grammarian, "the difference between Śabda-Brahman and Para-Brahman [that is, the non-Sound Brahman of *Maitri-Upaniṣad*] is in reality a difference without any distinction. To him the two represent the two aspects of the same Supreme Śabda."[53] Thus, Śabda-Brahman for the Grammarian is not a "secondary reality," as in some Upaniṣadic thought and Advaita-Vedānta, but is always coeval with the highest level of Being. The perception of a distinction between these two modes of thought—i.e., Brahman as Śabda versus Brahman as beyond Śabda—important as it is philosophically, becomes somewhat reconciled in the concept of Nāda-Brahman, which becomes the energy of a deity who is identified with the highest Brahman. Yet for now these two positions remain significant in the development of sonic theology, as both claim Vedic, albeit Upaniṣadic, authority.

In summarizing the contents of the first section (1.1–9) of the *Vākyapadīya* Pillai states that "the Vedas reflect this Brahman. They are also the means of knowing it. . . . The true significance of the Veda is contained in the syllable 'om'—The Oṁkāra [Praṇava]."[54] Thus, the Vedic conception of the Praṇava "seems to have provided the model upon which the later Grammarian philosophers based their conception of *sphoṭa*. In fact, *sphoṭa* is often identified with Praṇava."[55] Chakravarti was convinced that "*sphoṭa*, taken as an imperishable unit of Vāk . . . which finally accounts for the evolution of speech, is analogous to Praṇava."[56]

The lexical definition of the term *sphoṭa* will serve to illuminate its function: "m. bursting, opening, expansion, disclosure, the eternal and imperceptible element of sounds and words and the real vehicle of the idea which bursts or flashes on the mind when a sound is uttered."[57] Betty Heimann further explores the nature of the root word from which *sphoṭa* derives and its relation to natural processes of ebullition:

> *Sphuṭ*, to burst into view, to rent [*sic*] asunder, pictures in its very onomatopoetical form the suddenness, abruptness and forcefulness of the process. It is no accident that other terms derived from the very same root *sphuṭ* all indicate the same dynamic explosive function. *Sphoṭa* means the "whipped out" hood of a snake in the moment of irritation; *sphuṭi* means the cracking of the skin of the foot by bursting blisters [also a swelling, boil, or tumor].[58]

Probably the simplest and clearest image for the meaning of *sphoṭa* is that of a light bulb flashing on when one understands ("gets") an idea.

The metaphors suggested here lead us to reflect on issues similar to what the German philosopher J. G. Herder was suggesting in his "Essay on the Origin of Language" (1772): Whether in Sanskrit or German, "the name in itself is an onomatopoetical image of the essence of the thing which it designates; and whether the articulation of its sounds produces a psychological reaction which suggests the essential meaning."[59] Furthermore, we are reminded of the Tantric initiation where the teacher (guru) imparts a mantra, the sound of which is said to be the "essence" of a particular deity or supernatural power.

In explication of the doctrine of Sphoṭavāda it is first necessary to clarify its relationship with the concept of *śabda*, as outlined by Patañjali: "To the meaning-bearing element which Patañjali calls *śabda*, Bhartṛhari applies the word *sphoṭa*,"[60] yet, "Bhartṛhari, like Patañjali, starts from the observation that the word can be considered under two aspects, as sound, or as meaning-bearer."[61] Patañjali had differentiated two aspects of *śabda—sphoṭa* and *dhvani*: "*Sphoṭa* represents what is *śabda* proper, whereas sound [*dhvani*] is only a quality, that is to say, it serves only to manifest *sphoṭa*. . . . It is sound that seems to be either long or short, but what is manifested by sound, i.e., *sphoṭa*, is not at all affected by the variations of sound."[62] *Dhvani* and *sphoṭa* are intimately connected with each other through natural fitness (*yogyatā*), yet the former acts as an outer garment over the latter, which, though otherwise incomprehensible, is manifest through a physical exertion of the vocal organs. Thus, the vocal apparatus is not the source of the sound that we hear but merely the instrument through which the eternal *sphoṭa* emerges, "bursts forth," into the sensate world.

As was said previously, the concept of *sphoṭa* developed as a foil to the views of Mīmāṁsā and other philosophies. Like the Mīmāṁsā, however, it represents a serious attempt to explain the rather mysterious process by which a word or sentence conveys meaning to the hearer. But, rather than postulating that the individual words or letters contain meaning themselves or "leave impressions which accumulate," Bhartṛhari sets forth the meaning-bearing aspect of language as something over and above the actual sounds or words. The British linguist John Brough describes this succinctly, as follows:

> The *sphoṭa* is not a "hypostatization of sound." Its fundamental attachment is to the other side of the linguistic function, namely, the meaning [*vācya*]. . . . The *sphoṭa* then is simply the linguistic sign in its aspect of meaning-bearer [vācaka]. . . . The sounds by themselves have clearly no capacity to attach themselves directly to meaning, otherwise the collection of the first three sounds [or letters] of the word "manage" would present to the mind the word "man"; and this, in fact, does not happen. To deal with the situation adequately, it is necessary to postulate a meaning-bearer which is not identical with the collection of sounds, but is related to this collection in such a way as to be capable of being revealed by it.[63]

Bhartṛhari's view, contrary to the Mīmāṁsā, holds that "the primary linguistic fact is the undivided sentence-*sphoṭa*. Just as a bare root has no meaning in the world, so also the meanings of individual words are merely hints or stepping stones to the meaning of the sentence [*vākya*]." To Bhartṛhari and his school individual words and letters were no more than "artificial constructions of the grammarian, and, looked on from the point of view of language functioning in the world, they were unreal (*asatya*)."[64] This seems to trivialize the position of the Vedic god Indra who, as the divine Grammarian, partitions the unified Vāk into segregated human language.

Śabara makes it clear in his comments on *Mīmāṁsā-Sūtra* 1.1.5 that the Sphoṭavāda theory has been thoroughly rejected by Mīmāṁsā because it threatens one of the very roots of Mīmāṁsā doctrine, namely, the reality of Vedic words. Brough goes on to emphasize that "one should realize that this theory [the unreal nature of words] is not derived from *a priori* speculation, but is the result of careful examination of what happens when we speak or listen in ordinary conversation." Regarding the way in which the meaning of a sentence is conveyed, however, "the utmost that can be said... is that it is grasped by an instantaneous flash of insight (*pratibhā*). The same word is used in later times with reference to the insight of a great poet, and in such contexts may be reasonably translated as poetic genius."[65] Thus, while words are unreal, intuition, or *pratibhā*, is real.

Gopinath Kaviraj has described *pratibhā* as "a flash of light, a revelation, usually found in literature in the sense of wisdom characterized by immediacy and freshness. It might be called the supersensuous and supra-rational apperception, grasping truth directly." The concept of revelation, however, does not find general acceptance in all branches of Indian thought: "The doctrine of *pratibhā*, in some form or other, has ever been an article of universal acceptance in this country [India]. It is an anomaly... that we find the Mīmāṁsakas alone maintaining an attitude of bitter opposition to this doctrine. They deny the possibility of omniscience of any kind, eternal as of God or what is due to contemplation as in the case of the Yogins."[66] Thus, while Mīmāṁsā does not accept interior intuitive revelation as a source of knowledge within the human mind, the Grammarian posits *pratibhā* as both the "higher intuition" of Śabda-Brahman and the essence of the Vedas, which has already been said to be identical with the syllable *Om*.

With regard to the nature of *sphoṭa*, it is said by Sastri that it has an external as well as an internal aspect: "The grammarian declares that a sentence does not admit of division into terms, syllables and letters. This is in fine the view of those who regard the sentence or *sphoṭa* as an external entity with an individuality of its own." He continues: "*Sphoṭa* is [also] an internal entity, purely spiritual and assuming externality only when it is revealed by sounds. [It] is indivisible and partless, consciousness in essence, and, therefore, luminous... [and] inseparably linked to *pratibhā*."[67] Accordingly, Chakravarti has remarked that "*Praṇava* has two... aspects—external and internal—corresponding to those of *sphoṭa*."[68]

These two features of *sphoṭa* (external and internal) have been recently accommodated to Western linguistic theory, first by way of Saussure, the founder of modern linguistics: "The *sphoṭa* as explained by Bhartṛhari is something analogous to the linguistic sign, which in the terminology of Saussure has two facets: the signifier [phonic or acoustic] and the signified [semantic or mental], that which means and that which is meant."[69] Hjelmslev and the School of Glossematics also recognized the dual nature of the linguistic sign: "The sign is a two-sided entity, with a Janus-like perspective in two directions, and with effect in two respects: 'outwards' toward the expression substance and 'inwards' toward the content substance."[70] The fact that this inward "content substance" attained ontological and even transcendental status for Bhartṛhari does not detract from the appropriateness of these basic linguistic observations.

In addition to the terms *sphoṭa* and *dhvani* taken from Patañjali, Bhartṛhari introduces the word *nāda* into the Grammarian tradition, as it does not appear in Pāṇini or Patañjali.[71] It signifies here the gross sound which results from an ensemble of very subtle *dhvanis*. To the *sphoṭa*, which conveys the meaning, the *dhvani* and the *nāda* are opposed. The commentary on *Vākyapadīya* 1.47 related to *nāda* explains, as follows:

> The *dhvanis* are conceived of as something atomic, all-pervasive and imperceptible. When amassed by the movements of the articulatory organs, they become gross and perceptible and are then called *nāda*. It is they which suggest the word. The word is first conceived as a unity in the mind of the speaker. In order to utter it, he makes movements of his articulatory organs which have the effect of progressively collecting the subtle, atomic, all-pervading *dhvanis* and bringing into being the *nādas* which are gross and audible. These have divisions and sequence and so the word, suggested by them, though changeless and sequenceless, also seems to have them.[72]

The term *nāda* is without metaphysical connotation in the *Vākyapadīya,* though it appears in several passages (1.48, 49, 84, 97, 101, 105, and 2.30). Yet an interesting notion appears in verse 1.105, where *nāda* is said to be "the sounds which modify diction arising after the cessation of the movements of the organs"[73] or "sounds produced after the cessation of the vibrations [of long and protracted vowels which] bring about variations in the speed of utterance."[74] As we have seen, the word *nāda* was used in the *Mīmāṃsā-Sūtra* (1.1.17) to denote the variance of speech sounds, loud or soft. Althought *nāda* does not have metaphysical or cosmic significance for either the Mīmāṃsā or Bhartṛhari, its use therein can at most be a precursor for—or, at least, a parallel to—the mystical resonance caused by the utterance of sacred syllables (i.e., vowel sounds), mantras, in varying degrees of speed and volume in later Yoga texts and practice. On the other hand, it does seem rather remarkable that a term denoting "external content substance," rather than one denoting "internal content substance" such as *artha* or *sphoṭa,* should ascend to such singular importance as the concept of Nāda or Nāda-Brahman surely has done.

This brings us to the function of the theory of Sphoṭavāda for the supposed efficacy of mantra recitation. The explanation has been offered in the *Vākyapadīya* 1.82–84:

> Just as a Vedic passage or a verse [*mantra*] is well-fixed in the mind after the (last) repetition and not fully grasped in each repetition, in the same way, through previous cognitions, unnameable, but favorable to the final clear cognition, the form of the word, manifested by the last sound, is perceived. The word is grasped in the (final) cognition the seeds [*bīja*] of which have been sown by the sounds [*nāda*] including the final one and which has gradually attained maturity.

The commentary advances the explanation further: "The sounds, while they manifest the word, leave impression-seeds [*bīja*] progressively clearer and conducive to the clear perception (of the word). Then, the final sound brings to the mind which has now attained maturity or a certain fitness by the awakening of the impressions of the previous cognitions, the form of the word as colored by itself."[75]

It is made clear that the three terms that denote the somewhat vague cognitions received in the mind from language—in the present life or from previous lifetimes—are interchangeable for the Grammarian: *saṁskāra* (trace), *bhāvanā* (form of consciousness), and *bīja* (seed). There is, however, an important difference between the Mīmāṁsā theory and Bhartṛhari with regard to the locus of the traces, or seeds. For Mīmāṁsā the traces reside in the syllables or letters themselves and are transferred to the mind of the hearer in a fixed sequence. They remain distinct and virtually autonomous. For the Sphoṭavādin the traces of cognition, which are already latent in the human mind, are gradually perceived, by repeated utterance of the mantra, as parts of the universal *sphoṭa,* or Śabda-Brahman, and ultimately without necessary sequence:

> Repetition of the uttered sounds of the *mantra,* especially if spoken clearly and correctly, will evoke fresh the *sphoṭa* each time, until finally the obscuring ignorance is purged and the

> meaning-whole of the *mantra* is seen (*pratibhā*). . . . The psychological mechanism involved is described by Bhartṛhari as holding the *sphoṭa* in place by continued chanting. Just as from a distance or in semidarkness, it takes repeated cognitions of an object to see it correctly, so also concentrated attention on the *sphoṭa*, by repeated chanting of the *mantra*, results in *sphoṭa* finally being perceived in all its fullness. (*Vākyapadīya* 1.89)[76]

Thus, meaning is transferred, "not by the summation of phonemes/*padas* or their special *apūrva*-like powers, but by the progressive revelation of the inherent *vākya-sphoṭa* [sentence-*sphoṭa*] as the phonemes/*padas* are uttered."[77] Maṇḍana Miśra, a contemporary of Śaṅkarācārya, in his *Sphoṭa Siddhi* (Karika 19–20) describes the process of cognition as a chain of successively lucid impressions that culminate in a sharp and correct apprehension.[78]

In his explanation of how mantras act as instruments of power Harold Coward reveals the function of grammar in the recitation of mantras. He states that, "from Bhartṛhari's perspective, the special role of grammar is to control and purify the use of *mantra* so that its powers will not be wasted or misused."[79] The *Vākyapadīya* (1.14) provides support for this: "It (grammar) is the door to salvation, the remedy for all impurities of speech, the purifier of all the sciences, and shines in every branch of knowledge."[80] The inherent meaning, the power, of all mantras is realized in the inner self only when they are grammatically and phonetically correct. Though the ultimate meaning is indeed "grammar-less," the function of grammar is doubly significant, leading as it does to both worldly success and liberation (*mokṣa*).

Suffice it to say here that, as for the Mīmāṁsā, there is no such thing as a "meaningless mantra" for the Sphoṭavāda, since all language is related to the unitary meaningful cognition of Śabda-Brahman. "A meaningless *mantra* would imply a piece of consciousness without a word-meaning attached and, according to the *Vākyapadīya*, that is impossible."[81] The only reason given for what may appear to be meaninglessness in language is the ignorance (*avidyā*) of the person which obstructs the clear cognition of the *sphoṭa*. This is remedied through initiation by a qualified teacher (guru) and instruction in the Sphoṭavāda doctrine of the various levels of human consciousness, as outlined by Bhartṛhari.

According to Bhartṛhari and the Grammarians, consciousness

itself is permeated by language on three distinct levels, which are introduced in the *Vākyapadīya* 1.142: "This science of grammar is the supreme and wonderful source of the knowledge of the three-fold word, comprising many paths [levels of realization], of the Vaikharī [the "elaborated" level of ordinary speech, where word and meaning are fully differentiated], the Madhyamā [the middle level, where word and meaning are mentally differentiated yet still a unity], and the Paśyantī [the "higher" premental level, where word and meaning are totally undifferentiated]."[82] These levels represent both degrees of linguistic comprehension and stages of advancement of consciousness. They are said to be presaged by the verse from the *Ṛg-Veda* (1.164.45) which describes four levels of speech. Out of these four, three remain hidden in the cave of the inner self, while the fourth is spoken by humans in their outward language. Since this Vedic verse is quoted in the commentary on *Vākyapadīya* 1.142, scholars have speculated about the possibility of a fourth level known as Parā-Vāk, or *parā-prakṛti*. Gonda has described them:

> According to the Indian philosophers of grammar the sound of a word is only the outward manifestation of that word (Vaikharī form); it presupposes a subtle form (Madhyamā), in which the words are not articulated as aerial vibrations, but are articulated as mental processes. This state presupposes the still subtler form (Paśyantī), in which the word and the concept for which it stands lie inseparable as a potency like the seed of a tree before sprouting. Behind the potential state is the state called *parā,* i.e., the . . . highest state.[83]

Nevertheless, these various levels are concomitant to the more complex processes of sonic meditation outlined in Yoga.

Soteriology, for Bhartṛhari and the Grammarians, involves a progression through correct grammatical usage, upward to the level where word and meaning are nondifferentiated and finally to the region of pure unalloyed cosmic sound, as Śabda-Brahman, or Vāk: "As creation consists of the inherent power of this Vāk to become manifold . . . , salvation consists in the equally inherent power of man as partaker of Vāk to return to this state of oneness."[84] The text of the *Vākyapadīya,* after stating that grammar is the "gateway to liberation" (*tad dvāram apavargasya*) in 1.14, goes on to say in 1.22 that the Supreme Brahman is attained by having recourse to grammar (*tad vyākaraṇam āgamya paraṁ brahmādhigamyate*).[85] The actual technique of attaining this Oneness, or Brahman, was referred to as *vāg-yoga* (Yoga of the Word) in Patañjali's *Mahābhāṣya* and provided the impetus for Bhartṛhari's concept of *śabdapūrva-yoga*. Since the *Vākyapadīya* seems to assume the reader's familiarity with the practice of *śabdapūrva-yoga*, however, there are only scattered references in the text. Moreover, as we also do not possess grammatical works of the Pāṇinian school between the time of Patañjali and Bhartṛhari, the precise technique of "Grammatical Yoga" within the textual tradition remains somewhat obscure.

In a personal interview Gaurinath Sastri has succinctly explained the process and goal of the study of grammar:

> You must in the beginning study grammar to acquaint yourself with chaste or correct forms, and to dissociate yourself from the habit of using incorrect expressions. Now as a result of your contact with correct forms you are expected to develop some moral power within yourself. And as this moral power develops more and more you are in a position to move in the direction of the goal of life. A rigorous and disciplined progress enables you to acquire intuition (*pratibhā*), and with its acquisition, you become confident to obtain the vision of the transcendent One or the Summum Bonum of mortal existence. The study of grammar is meant for this. This is the goal and main objective of the study of grammar. Vyākaraṇa gives you the power of reaching the goal described in the Vedas, which is the attainment of the highest principle of life [*mokṣa*].[86]

In further clarification of the process K. A. Subramania Iyer has explained that correct grammatical usage, being closer to Patañjali's *vāg-yoga*, is not quite the same as Bhartṛhari's *śabdapūrva-yoga*, which is conceived in four stages with grammar as only the beginning:

> For Bhartṛhari, grammar is the first step in the ladder of ascent. Knowledge of the correct form of words as taught in grammar and its use in real life is then the first stage. That produces spiritual merit [*dharma*, "moral power" for Sastri] in the aspirant and he goes beyond the senses and the mind, that is, he reaches *vaikāraṇya* [second stage]. . . . In the next stage [third], the aspirant sees the Word as free from all distinctions and reaches *pratibhā*, the sources of all differentiation, though itself free from it. It is also the source of all manifested words and

their meanings. It is also called *paśyantī*. . . . Reaching *pratibhā* or *paśyantī* or *prakṛti* is the third stage. The next and the last stage consists in going from *prakṛti* to *parā-prakṛti*.[87]

In a separate article Subramania Iyer stresses further the distinction between using correct forms of grammar and *śabdapūrva-yoga:* "Mere acquisition of spiritual merit [dharma, or "moral power"] by the use of correct forms of words is not enough for the attainment of *prakṛti* or *parā-prakṛti*. That may be enough for obtaining *abhyudaya* [*svarga*, or "heaven" for Patañjali, otherwise "well-being"], but for the attainment of *pratibhā* or *parā-prakṛti*, the aspirant has to practice *śabdapūrva-yoga*."[88]

The process of *śabdapūrva-yoga* is referred to in the commentary on *Vākyapadīya* (1.131) as a kind of meditation whereby consciousness is raised to the level of nondifferentiation by the breaking of various "knots" of nescience and ego sense:

> The "bonds" or "knots" referred to are the *saṁskāras* or memory traces and their tainted motivations left by egocentric activity—in either spoken words (Vaikharī-Vāk) or inner thoughts (Madhyamā-Vāk). These ego bonds are removed by meditating on the Divine Word (Śabda-Brahman) so that the purified forms of language are clearly reflected. The amount of such meditation required will be equal to the strength needed to negate the egocentric *saṁskāras* stored up within the mind.[89]

The ego sense is related to the literalization of language, the words of the Veda, and is a serious pitfall for the *mokṣa*-seeking Grammarian. It follows that the technique of *śabdapūrva-yoga* focuses on a "deliteralizing" of language, whereby attachment to the letter, or sequence of letters, is broken or severed.[90] The Grammarian would view any sequenced language, whether denoted as the Word of God or inspired revelation in the form of sentences, to be an obstacle which must be overcome in order to perceive or "hear" the Śabda-Brahman, which has no fixed sequence, or grammar.

In other words, for Bhartṛhari and his school, grammar is a kind of fictionalized discipline whereby words and sentences are analyzed for the purpose of attaining moral power. Once this moral power, or dharma, is achieved the aspirant proceeds to contemplate the Sonic Absolute, Śabda-Brahman, which is beyond grammar: "*Śabdapūrva-yoga* takes us beyond the planes of Vaikharī and Madhyamā to the plane of Paśyantī. The modus operandi in *śabdapūrva-yoga* is *krama-saṁhāra*, 'withdrawal of sequence.' According to the Grammarians, there is sequence in articulate speech (Vaikharī), there is a trace of sequence in mental discourse (Madhyamā); but the Eternal Verbum or Paśyantī is destitute of all sequence."[91] The logic employed by Bhartṛhari is, thus, that "the whole is greater than the sum of its parts," in contrast to the Mīmāṁsā view, which adopts the logic that "the whole results from the sum of its parts."

In a variety of sources on the study of Sphoṭavāda the definition of the highest stage to be attained in the practice of *śabdapūrva-yoga* increases our understanding of the original postulation of the word *theology* in the first chapter of our work. Sastri, for example, describes the highest stage as follows, which reminds us of the notion of *theos*, or God, as that which "sounds through" or, metaphorically, "shines through": "Paśyantī is the purest state which is completely free from every kind of mixture.... Unlike the other two, Paśyantī does not follow the movement of vital breath, and so, it is not influenced by it in any manner. It is immune from division and divested of all attributes of priority and posteriority. As the name suggests, Paśyantī is the shining one, the purest of all lights, eternal and ever resplendent."[92]

A major contribution of Bhartṛhari lies first in his providing fresh insight into the Vedic revelation of Diving Vāk as an all-pervading feature of both human consciousness and the divine. In addition, "the chanting of Om and other *mantras*, which has come to occupy such a central position in Indian religion, is placed on a firm foundation by Bhartṛhari."[93] He not only reestablished the Brahmanical roots of sacred sound but also opened the door for many varieties of esoteric word mysticism prevalent in medieval Yoga and Tantric traditions. Sastri has demonstrated the marked influence of Bhartṛhari on the Kashmiri Śaiva philosophy, and Coward has shown how Bhartṛhari's notion of *dhvani* informed the entire school of Indian aesthetics. The fact remains, however, that Sphoṭavāda has been summarily rejected by most of the Indian intellectual tradition: "All the orthodox systems of Hindu philosophy, the Pūrva-Mīmāṁsā, the Nyāya, the Vedānta and the Sāṁkhya have spared no pains in criticizing the theory and finally rejecting it. It is only the Yoga system of Patañjali which has lent support to the Grammarian's theory of *sphoṭa*."[94] We now turn to a brief examination of this issue.

Rejection of the Sphoṭa Doctrine

Before proceeding to the next chapter on Yoga it will be useful to say a few words about the viewpoints of certain philosophical schools toward *sphoṭa* and to *śabda-pramāṇa* in general. Having already mentioned the positions of Pūrva-Mīmāṁsā and Nyāya, the Sāṁkhya and Advaita-Vedānta standpoints can be summarized briefly.

In spite of their relation with the Yoga school the teachers of the Sāṁkhya doctrine, with a few exceptions, have rejected the *sphoṭa* theory of language: "The *Sāṁkhya-Sūtra* (5.57) distinctly rejects *sphoṭa* as practically incomprehensible. . . . As no other element apart from letters comes to our notice in the cognition of a word, it is absolutely useless to assume the existence of *sphoṭa* (which passes our vision and comprehension) as distinct from letters. . . . It is letters alone, no matter if they are perishable, that constitute words in the real sense of the term." This is perhaps needless to say, since the very next verse of the text (5.58) rejects the eternality of *śabda* and, therefore, the Vedas (*na śabda-nityatvaṁ kāryatā-pratīte*). Thus, although the Sāṁkhya appears to agree with Mīmāṁsā regarding the meaning-bearing aspect of letters, they cannot concur about the nature of sound, or *śabda*, itself. For practical purposes the Sāṁkhya philosophy has neglected the internal aspects of speech and consciousness and instead has focused purely on the external and "perishable" dimension of language. Though they claim to be rationalists [meaning at the very least an acceptance of "innate ideas" in the Cartesian sense], "their main difficulty is that they ascribe significance to so transient a thing as letters, but do not strive further to find out the permanent source of *śabda*, as is manifested by sound."[95]

In the epistemology of Sāṁkhya, although the Vedas are not generally accepted as eternal, verbal testimony is accepted as an "independent means of knowledge in addition to perception and inference. . . . [It] requires an understanding of the meaning conveyed by words without which there is no possibility of communication."[96] Though the authority of the Veda is accepted by Sāṁkhya, the lack of satisfactory treatment of the question of its authorship precludes a clear understanding of Sāṁkhya linguistic doctrines. One has to assume that the teachers of this school did not develop a consistent body of thought.

The school of Advaita-Vedānta seems to founder as well when these same linguistic issues are pressed. As mentioned earlier, Śaṅkara rejected the theory of *sphoṭa,* yet in order to do that he took the help of a Mīmāṁsaka, the philosophy of which he loathed: "In his commentary on the *Brahma-Sūtra* 1.3.28 [1.3.28 proclaims the creation of the world from the word, while 1.3.29 asserts the eternity of the Veda], Śaṅkara has caused some confusion by his use of the arguments of Upavarṣa, the Mīmāṁsaka, against the pro-Sphoṭa grammarians."[97] In this rather lengthy commentary Śaṅkara faces the same dilemma as Kumārila in his need to explain the "order" of words, though at first he appears less vehement toward Sphoṭavāda: "The letters of which a word consists—assisted by a certain order and number—have, through traditional use, entered into a connection with a definite sense. . . . This hypothesis is certainly simpler than the complicated hypothesis of the grammarians who teach that the *sphoṭa* is the word. For they have to disregard what is given by perception, and to assume something which is never perceived."[98] There is an elliptical argument here, as what is perceived is already illusory (*māyā*), by definition. If one is arguing the illusory nature of the world, it is, of course, simpler, if not more convenient strategically, to accept the "conventional" theory of the relation between word and meaning, where nothing is at stake. In fact, Śaṅkara is hesitant to accept the reality of *sphoṭa* because that would posit another reality besides that of Brahman, which for him is the only reality.

In light of Śaṅkara's basic philosophy it is easier to recognize the dilemma. For Śaṅkara the world is perceived as false, as "illusion" (*māyā*). Language, being also false, has no inherent connection with Ultimate Reality, since "Brahman cannot be directly designated by any word."[99] Even *Om* is a convention for Śaṅkara.

Perhaps a reference to Greek philosophy will further illustrate the position of Śaṅkara and Advaita-Vedānta philosophy toward language. Platonic ontology, from Plato's *Cratylus,* advises us that true Being "must be known not from language but 'from itself,' and the object of thought is not words but 'ideas.' Language, like the inferior sensible appearance of things, must be transcended." Aristotle also views discourse and Being as not coterminous: "Like Plato, for Aristotle the central act of knowing is a movement beyond discourse, beyond talking." This faculty of silent knowing in Greek metaphysics is known as the "Nous," as opposed to the Logos (discourse): "*Nous,* . . . is the activity, power, or 'place of forms' and the real human intellectual power capable of knowing truth, and of transcending the limits of particulars to attain direct intellectual vision of things as they are [i.e., to recognize universals]."[100] Similarly, for

Śaṅkara, to know Brahman is ultimately a cognitive move beyond language and sonic elements.

Śaṅkara's overall view of language is, however, more ambivalent. On the one hand, he is "suspicious of language—it is the instrument of ignorance. . . . But on the other hand, he finds the mechanism of liberation ultimately in an act that requires speech." The so-called Mahā-Vākyas, or great sentences (i.e., *tat tvam asi*, etc.), though they are false and imperfect indications of Brahman, can still lead to liberation, as "one can be killed by being frightened by an illusory snake."[101] The school of Śaṅkara holds that the Veda is revealed at the beginning of each creation cycle and hence is not eternal: "To the Advaitins, as against the Mīmāṁsakas, the Veda is not eternal, since it has an origin, and whatever has an origin must have an end. The letters, words, and sentences are as much the products of creation as ether, etc., are, and the Veda is composed of these words and sentences only. It comes into being at the time of creation and comes to an end at the time of dissolution."[102]

Śaṅkara claims that Brahman is the material cause of the world, while *śabda* is merely an efficient cause: "Śaṅkara points out that the origination of the world from the word [as stated in the *Vedānta-Sūtra* 1.3.28] is not to be understood to mean that *śabda* is the material cause of creation of the world as Brahman is. . . . The Creator first gets the Veda revealed to Him and He then proceeds to create things corresponding to those words."[103] As to the question of what motivates the operation of *śabda* as an efficient cause, Śaṅkara can only say that "it is the mysterious desire of Brahman to get into diversity from unity [1.1.5]."[104]

Śaṅkara argues that liberation, or *mokṣa,* is not something to be achieved through any process of action or meditation. Knowledge (*jñāna*) of Brahman is the keystone of the system, and this is received often in a sudden, radical shift in experience. It entails a single, epiphanic, sometimes momentary overthrow of the false (*māyā*) in realization of the Truth, which is Brahman, a truth that for Advaita-Vedānta is fully apprehended only in silence. The Advaita process is distinguished from the slow and gradual focusing of the Grammarian on the eternal *sphoṭa:* "For Śaṅkara the process is a single all or nothing inferential negation; for Bhartṛhari it is a series of perceptions with an increasingly positive approximation to the real."[105]

The current interest in Bhartṛhari has perhaps helped our understanding of the philosophy of Śaṅkara. In fact, since Bhartṛhari lived several centuries before Śaṅkara, there is every reason to assume that Śaṅkara knew Bhartṛhari's work. Beside the fact that Śaṅkara took great pains to refute the Sphoṭavāda doctrine and that one of his favorite disciples, Padmapāda, read Bhartṛhari's ideas into his own commentary on the master's teachings, it has been suggested that Śaṅkara was, nonetheless, influenced by it: "Śaṅkara conceives of *māyā* as a limiting condition (*upādhi*) of Brahman in a way that bears marked similarity to Bhartṛhari's conception of time (*kāla*) as a limiting function of Śabda-Brahman."[106]

For the sake of convenience as well as summation, a tentative grouping of the pro-Sphoṭavāda and anti-Sphoṭavāda adherents are offered for comparison. The pro-Sphoṭavādins include Yāska, Patañjali, some Yoga commentators, the later Grammarians, Bhartṛhari, Maṇḍana Miśra, Nāgeśa, and some of the Kashmiri Śaivas. The anti-Sphoṭavādins include Upavarṣa, Prabhākara, and Kumārila Bhatta of the Mīmāṁsā school, Sāṁkhya and Nyāya-Vaiśeṣika schools, Śaṅkara, Śaiva-Siddhānta theorists, some Kashmiri Śaivas, Rāmānuja, Madhva, Jīva Goswami, and most Vaiṣṇava schools. As most doctrines and philosophies of Hinduism fall in line with one or the other position when examined closely, this tautology becomes extremely useful when approaching diverse religious groups and practitioners. Without taking sides, a clarification of the positions is useful so that we may now move on to the sectarian divisions of Hinduism with a particular mode of scholarly apparatus in hand.

But, first, as the concept and terminology of Nāda-Brahman largely succeeds that of Vāk and Śabda-Brahman in the Hindu theistic traditions, it is necessary to trace the development of sacred sound as Nāda-Brahman as it appears within the Yoga and musical traditions.

Chapter 3

NĀDA-YOGA
Sacred Sound as Nāda-Brahman

Although the Yoga tradition falls within the six orthodox systems of Indian philosophy, it differs in several ways from the Vedic tradition regarding its discussion of sacred sound. Introducing a number of new elements into the conversation, this chapter will examine the Yoga tradition with the intention of disclosing the central importance it gives to meditation on sacred sound in the form of *Nāda-Brahman*, a term that largely supplants the linguistic *Śabda-Brahman* of the orthodox Vedic tradition with a more encompassing concept that also includes the non-linguistic dimension of sacred sound (musical sounds, etc.). The sonic aspect of Yoga has been frequently referred to as Nāda-Yoga in India and elsewhere, yet a full-scale exposition of this rather elusive subject has never been undertaken. In partial answer to this challenge, this chapter attempts to assemble and evaluate the following classical sources: the *Yoga-Sūtra* of Patañjali and its commentators, the *Yoga-Upaniṣads*, the Gorakhnāth Yoga tradition, and three major Haṭha-Yoga treatises. This will be followed by a concise exposition of the role of Nāda-Brahman in Indian classical music and a brief sampling of current trends in Nāda-Yoga practice.

Before discussing the Yoga tradition and its subsequent connection with the notion of Nāda-Brahman, forming what became known as Nāda-Yoga, the term *nāda* itself needs clarification as well as *bindu* and its accepted symbol, known as the *anusvāra*. According to the lexicon, *nāda* is: "m. a loud sound, roaring, bellowing, crying; any sound or tone; (in the Yoga) the nasal sound represented by a semicircle and used as an abbreviation in mystical words." The words *sonant*, *resonance*, and *reverberation* are also associated with the generic term *nāda*. *Bindu* is almost always associated with *nāda* when it is discussed in terms of Śiva-Sakti metaphysics. It means simply: "m. a detached particle, drop, globule, dot, spot; the dot over a letter representing *anusvāra* (supposed to be connected with Śiva and of great mystical importance)." *Candra-bindu* ँ refers to the symbolic combination of *nāda* as semicircle (*candra*, or half-moon) with *bindu*, as dot. As for the *anusvāra*, with which *nāda* is most commonly related, the meaning given is: "m. after-sound, the nasal sound which is marked by a dot above the line, and which always belongs to a preceding vowel."[1] In Nāda-Yoga, as well as in related Tantric traditions, the word *nāda* signifies the reverberating tone of vocal sound, especially the buzzing nasal sound with which the word *AUM* fades away. The *nāda* sound fades away into the point of *bindu*, which means the nasal point of the *anusvāra*, especially in its position as the dot above the *ardha-mātra*, half-syllable, or half-moon, within the total three and one-half morae—sometimes four morae—of metrical time in the pronunciation of *AUM*. Thus, we have the configuration A + U + M + *nāda-bindu* repeated throughout the pertinent traditions. The *Dhyānabindu-Upaniṣad* (2), one of the *Yoga-Upaniṣads*, furnishes a succinct account: "The *praṇava*, 'AUM' is the superb seed-letter, with the *bindu* (dot) and the *nāda* (nasal sound indicated by the *ardha-mātra*, the semicircle)."[2]

Unlike Mīmāṁsā, Sāṁkhya, and the Grammarians, the Yoga tradition has continually affirmed the existence of a personal Supreme Being, Īśvara. This Being, closer to a paradigmatic role model for other Yogīs to emulate, is signified by the syllable *Om*, and responds to devotion, or *bhakti*. "Īśvara can, in fact, bring about *samādhi* [final emancipation], on the condition that the Yogī practice Īśvara-pranidhāna—that is, devotion to Īśvara. . . . Patañjali introduces a God, to whom . . . he accords but a minor role."[3]

The Yoga tradition did not begin with Patañjali. He is said to have been more of a systematizer of Yoga practices that were already long existent: "Vācaspati and Vijñāna Bhikṣu, the two great commentators on the *Vyāsa-Bhāṣya*, agree with us in holding that Patañjali was not the founder of Yoga, but an editor. Analytic study of the *sūtras* [Patañjali's *Yoga-Sūtra*] also brings the conviction that the *sūtras* do not show any original attempt, but a masterly and systematic compilation which was also supplemented by fitting contributions."[4] There are ongoing debates about the relative antiquity of Yoga practices in pre-Vedic times, in the *Atharva-Veda*, and in the Harappan civilization of yore. The origins of Yoga are thus very obscure and probably will remain as such.[5] Yet its importance is underscored by the current popular understanding that there is virtually no Hinduism without Yoga and no Yoga without Hinduism.

The academic study of the Yoga tradition has been recently revived with the work of Mircea Eliade (1958).[6] Earlier Surendranath Dasgupta, author of the renowned five-volume *History of Indian Philosophy* (1952-55) and Eliade's teacher in Calcutta, was deeply interested in Yoga philosophy throughout his life. Dasgupta's first book, *The Study of Patañjali* (1920), was followed by several more thematic studies along similar lines. Although the precise details are not evident in his published works, Dasgupta summarized what was to be his position regarding sacred sound in the Yoga process in the forementioned first work: "Devotion to God and meditation of his name the Praṇava (Om) is . . . the shortest and easiest way of attaining the Yoga salvation."[7] Unfortunately, the final volume in the above series, which was to include the philosophy of Sanskrit grammar and Tantra, was not completed.

Rama Prasada, a Theosophist,[8] produced perhaps the first complete English translation of the *Yoga-Sūtra* of Patañjali, with the commentaries of Vyāsa and Vācaspati, in the early part of this century (1910), while T. S. Rukmani has recently published an English translation of Vijñāna Bhikṣu's commentary, the *Yoga-Vārttika* (1980). Among earlier Western scholars James H. Woods had translated the *Yoga-Sūtra* of Patañjali into English (1914). The plethora of modern "popular" books on Yoga is seldom rewarding to the serious student of Yoga philosophy, as such books rarely expound beyond the classical texts themselves. Moreover, though many of the modern trends in Yoga practice still emphasize the tradition of mantra and Nāda meditation, they are often found in modified forms. Nevertheless, the Yoga tradition has a rich history and has engaged some of the finest academic minds in the field of religion and philosophy.

Patañjali and the Yoga-Sūtra

The classical Yoga tradition appears to be aligned with the linguistic speculations of the early Grammarians. This becomes recognizable initially in the work of Patañjali and secondarily in the life of Bhartṛhari, the famous Grammarian who was also believed to be a great Yogī of the Gorakhnāth tradition. Patañjali, a Grammarian who wrote the most authoritative commentary on the work of Pāṇini, the *Mahābhāṣya,* has been reputed to be the author of the first systematic treatise on Yoga, the *Yoga-Sūtra* (second century B.C.E.). Scholars have been divided on the issue of their mutual identity and were at loggerheads at the time of Eliade's work: "The identity of the two Patañjalis . . . has been accepted by B. Liebich, Garbe, and Dasgupta and denied by J. H. Woods, Jacobi, and Keith."[9] Modern scholarship, however, has not accepted their identity: "The traditional identification of Patañjali with his namesake the grammarian, first made by Bhoja in his *Rāja-Mārtaṇḍa* (Introduction, stanza 5), is generally rejected by modern scholars."[10] Without taking sides the evidence concerning the doctrine of Sphoṭa will focus our attention.

Dasgupta's acceptance of the identity of the two Patañjalis hinges on the concurrence of the Sphoṭa theory in each of their works, as reflected in his own statement: "The most important point in favor of this identification seems to be that both Patañjalis as against the other Indian systems admitted the doctrine of *sphoṭa* which was denied even by Sāṁkhya."[11] Furthermore, Eliade has noted a textual reason behind Dasgupta's conclusion: "Both begin alike (*Yoga-Sūtra: atha yogānuśāsanam* [Now begins the instruction on Yoga]; and *Mahābhāṣya: atha śabdānuśāsanam* [Now begins the instruction on words])."[12] As this question is important for our inquiry, here it will be examined more closely, with the help of modern scholarship.

In sorting out the issue of the two Patañjalis some modern critical discussion indeed focuses on whether the text of the *Yoga-Sūtra* espouses the Sphoṭa doctrine or not. The particular sutra that is targeted, though not mentioning the word *Sphoṭa*, discusses a theory of language with marked similarities to the Grammarian doctrine. Chapter 3 verse 17, says, "The word [*śabda*], the object [*artha*] and the idea [*pratyaya*] appear as one [in ordinary discourse], because each coincides with the other; by *saṁyama* [meditation] over their distinctions comes the knowledge of the sounds of all living beings."[13]

Georg Feuerstein, in attempting to reinforce the notion that Yoga stands on its own as a branch of Indian philosophy—not terribly mixed up with Sāṁkhya, as Eliade claims—seriously doubts the connection of this passage with the Sphoṭa doctrine. He recognizes that, if a definite reference to Sphoṭa could be found in the *Yoga-Sūtra*, "that would be a significant factor in the support of the traditional claim that the author of the *Yoga-Sūtra* is identical with his namesake the grammarian. However, this does not seem to be the case. Patañjali [in the *Yoga-Sūtra*] . . . nowhere mentions the word Sphoṭa. . . . [This passage] probably merely relates to the very practical matter of reading another person's mind, which is a generally recognized Yogic feat."[14] In addition, there is no mention of Sphoṭa in the commentary attributed to Vyāsa entitled *Yoga-Bhāṣya.*

The commentary by Vācaspati, however, is said to refer to Sphoṭa and, indeed, provides a long discussion on the meaning of *Sphoṭa* below verse 3.17 of the *Yoga-Sūtra.*[15] He states: "A verbal sign is single and partless. The letters are taken to be its parts by virtue of the difference of the contiguity of similar letters in different words. The difference of words being thus due to the conception of there being constituted by letters conceived as such a single and partless sonorous image (Sphoṭa). . . . It is the sentence alone that conveys the meaning not the separate words."[16] The gloss on Vācaspati by Vijñāna Bhikṣu further elaborates the Sphoṭa doctrine.

Moreover, a well-known Indian practitioner of Yoga in the West, Rammurti Misra, supports the tradition of the latter commentators. Regarding the above verse, he claims that this aphorism actually presents the doctrine of Sphoṭa:

> Ordinarily letters, sense, and idea are all so intimately fused as not to be separable. . . . [They] are [actually] separate from one another but, due to conventional use, people find the distinction difficult to believe. . . . Word is one thing, meaning is another, and idea is another. . . . In a deeper state of *samādhi,* one is in direct communication with Sphoṭa which is the source of all knowledge. . . . So when a Yogī reaches the state of Sphoṭa he understands the sounds of all living beings.[17]

Thus, since both the Yoga and the Grammarian traditions themselves seem to accept the doctrine of Sphoṭa, we will proceed on the basis of a unique contiguity of the traditions themselves, if not of the original authors.

The practice of Yoga as outlined in the *Yoga-Sūtra,* with the commentaries by Vyāsa (*Yoga-Bhāṣya,* ca. A.D. 600), Vācaspati (*Tattva-Vaiśāradī,* A.D. 900), and Vijñana Bhikṣu (*Yoga-Vārttika,* A.D. 1500), reflects an ongoing concern with the use of sacred sound and linguistic symbols as fundamental aids in meditation. Indeed, the Patañjalian process of reciting and meditating on the sacred syllable *Om* is of seminal importance for our understanding of the various techniques of meditation on sacred sound which emerge after the Vedic and Upaniṣadic period. The relevant verses from the *Yoga-Sūtra* in this connection are in the first section entitled "Samādhipāda" (1.27–

28): "The sacred word [*Om*] connotes him [Īśvara] [*tasya vācakaḥ praṇavaḥ*]; Its repetition [*japa*] and the understanding of its meaning [should be done] [*taj-japas tad-artha-bhāvanam*]."[18]

The first commentator on the *Yoga-Sūtra,* Vyāsa, stresses in this regard the inherent "fixed" relationship between the sign (Om) and the thing signified (Īśvara): "The relation [of the sign, *vācaka,* with the signified, *vācya*] is inherent [*sthitaḥ*] and thus ever-present."[19] He uses the analogy of father and son to explain what sometimes appears to be "convention" in the relationship: "The actual relation of father and son is permanent, but the verbal statement that that man is this man's father is suggested [to the mind] by usage. . . . The authoritative sages maintain that the relation between a word and an intended object is eternal so far as the consensus [of successive generations of speakers] is eternal."[20] In other words, the basic relation is inherent by divine convention, but the particular usage may vary by human convention; Om is the symbol or sign of Īśvara as established and maintained by Īśvara.

With regard to Vyāsa's comments on this verse (*Yoga-Sūtra* 1.27) Feuerstein explains further using a Western analogy:

> Om is an experience rather than an arbitrary verbal label. It is a true symbol charged with numinous power. Experienceable in deep meditation, it is a sign of the omnipresence of Īśvara as manifest on the level of sound. . . . In other words, the human voice is employed to reproduce a "sound" which is continually "recited" by the universe itself—an idea which in the Pythagorean school came to be known as the "harmony of the spheres." On the Indian side it led to the development of the Yoga of sound (Nāda-Yoga).[21]

Vyāsa comments on the second verse (28) and stresses the need for the practice of mantra meditation: "The Yogī who has come to know well the relation between word and meaning must constantly repeat it, and habituate the mind to the manifestation therein of its meaning. The constant repetition is to be of the *praṇava* (A U M), and the habitual mental manifestation is to be what it signifies, Īśvara. The mind of the Yogī who constantly repeats *praṇava,* and habituates the mind to the constant manifestation of the idea it carries, becomes one-pointed [*ekāgra*]." After this Vyāsa quotes a verse about the benefits of study: "Let the Yoga be practiced through study [*svādhyāya,* or "self-study"], and let study be effected through Yoga. By

Yoga and study together the Highest Self shines [*paramātmā prakāśate*]."[22] Here we have another example of the notion of the divinity as self-revealing, self-manifesting.

Vācaspati, roughly three hundred years later, comments on these two verses (27-28) with the intention of qualifying the arguments of the conventionalists, such that divine convention is established over and above human convention: "All words have the capability of meaning objects of all forms. Their relation with objects of all forms must, therefore, be inherent. And the convention of Īśvara is the determining factor and shower thereof. The division of the sign signifying and not-signifying something is also made by Īśvara's convention or non-convention."[23]

As Vācaspati was influenced by Sāṁkhya philosophy, he seems particularly vexed concerning the Sāṁkhya objection to the eternity of words and qualifies the meaning of the term *eternity* (*nityatā*). Since sound, as part of material energy, *prakṛti*, disappears into it at the time of universal dissolution, the "eternal" relation between word and meaning appears problematic to the Yoga philosopher (Vācaspati). He responds, however, with the following argument:

> Although a word does become one with the *prakṛti* along with the power, it comes back into manifestation along with the power; as earth-born creatures becoming one with the earth on the cessation of the rains, come back to life on being wetted by showers of rain water. Thus God makes a convention similar to the convention which indicated the former relation. Hence on account of the eternity of the succession of similar usage, due to simultaneous knowledge, the relation of word and meaning is eternal. Independent etern ty is not meant.[24]

His point here is that, without the help of the Vedas, it is impossible to assert that the usage was exactly the same in previous creations.

Vācaspati generally follows Vyāsa in his acceptance of the necessity of mantra repetition in the worship of Īśvara. Furthermore, he says that "repeated understanding (*bhāvana*) means making it enter the mind over and over again until it becomes the very substance of the mental existence. [Regarding attainment,] The mind of the Yogī who constantly repeats the Praṇava . . . feels bliss in the One Lord alone."[25]

There are another two verses in the *Yoga-Sūtra* (3.35, 40) which shed light on the auditory dimension of meditation. In the third section entitled "Vibhūtipāda" verse 35 reads: "Thence proceed prescience, higher hearing [*śravaṇa*], touch, vision, taste, and smell." Vyāsa says, "By higher hearing comes the hearing of divine sounds [*divya-śabda-śravaṇam*]."[26] Vācaspati remarks that the word *śravaṇa* is a technical term used to denote the hearing of divine sounds. Verse 40 reads: "By *saṁyama* [meditation] over the relation between *ākāśa* [ether] and the power-of-hearing, comes the higher power-of-hearing [*divyaṁ śrotram*]." Vyāsa says in this regard: "In *ākāśa* abide all powers of hearing and all sounds. . . . The power of hearing is the means of perceiving sound. . . . Therefore, the power of hearing only is the sphere for the action of sound. Whoever performs *saṁyama* with reference to the relation between the power of hearing and *ākāśa* [where there is absence of obstruction], evolves the power of higher audition." Vācaspati adds: "All powers of hearing, even though they have their origin in the principle of egoism, reside in the *ākāśa*, placed in the hollow of the ear. . . . That which is the substratum of the auditory power (*śruti*) which manifests as sound of the same class, is *ākāśa*. Such a manifestation of sound cannot be without auditory power."[27] Since the ether is all-pervading and timeless, and sound fundamentally resides in it, it logically follows that sound is also universal and nontemporal. This realization by the Yogī accords him perception of sound as *dīvyam*, or sacred by his higher power of audition acquired by *saṁyama*. The "celestial" nature of the Absolute is exemplified again as "shining" or "bright," since the word *divya* has this same meaning in its root formation of *div* or *dī*.

Though tradition identifies Vyāsa as the legendary author of the Mahābhārata and the Purāṇas, very little is known about him. Despite a plethora of scholarship, the date of the Mahābhārata itself remains remarkably vague: "The actual composition of the epic seems to have been carried out between about 500 B.C.E. to 400 C.E."[28] If the terminus ad quem for Vyāsa is indeed 400 C.E., then it is unlikely that he is the same "Vyāsa" who composed the *Bhāṣya*. While Feuerstein and H. Jacobi date this Vyāsa in the fifth century A.D., Eliade places him in the seventh to eighth century A.D. Other scholars, such as Hajime Nakamura, place the Yogī Vyāsa in the fifth to sixth century A.D.

Nevertheless, the Vyāsa of the *Bhāṣya* was a Yogī of considerable attainment, since he furnishes us with useful clues to an understanding of the more enigmatic sutras of Patañjali. The only drawback seems to be that "he belonged to a school which had not retained all the original tenets and the terminology of the school of Patañjali."[29]

The commentary of Vācaspati is invaluable for deciphering the rather cryptic language of Vyāsa. Vācaspati himself was a renowned scholar who lived in the tenth century A.D. and wrote commentaries on all six of the philosophical systems, or *darśanas*. An extremely important section of his commentary on *Yoga-Sūtra* 1.36 will be quoted in full below, as it provides us with an important "missing link" in the gradual evolution of a distinctively Yogic meditation on sacred sound. Not only is this the earliest appearance of Nāda-Brahman in the classical Yoga tradition, it represents the first incidence of *nāda* within the six systems of Indian philosophy as meaning anything more than the physical voiced sound found in the phonetic, Mīmāṁsā, and Grammarian traditions. Underneath the verse *viśoka vā jyotiṣmatī*, which means "Or, the state of painless lucidity," Vācaspati has explained a Yogic technique of interior apprehension of Nāda-Brahman. He says:

> Painless lucidity means that which is devoid of pain. The state of lucidity is the light shining in the lotus of the heart. Let the mind be concentrated upon the lotus which is located between the chest and abdomen. It has eight petals and is placed with its face downwards. Its face has first to be turned upwards by the process of the expirative control of breath. In the middle thereof is the sphere [*maṇḍala*] of the sun, the place of waking consciousness, and is called A. Above that is the sphere of the moon, the place of dreaming consciousness, the U. Above that is the sphere of fire, the place of dreamless sleep, the M. Above that is the higher space, the Sound of Brahman itself [*paraṁ brahma vyomātmakaṁ nādas turīya-sthānam*], the fourth state of ultra-consciousness, which the knowers of Brahman call the half-measure (the *ardha-mātra*).[30]

This passage is best understood in juxtaposition with *Maitri-Upaniṣad* 6.22, as well as with the entire *Māṇḍūkya-Upaniṣad*. As noted in chapter 1, the former describes the two Brahmans to be meditated upon, Sound (lower) and non-Sound (higher). The latter enumerates the four elements, or "degrees,"[31] of Om: A U M as three elements plus the nonelement (*amātra*) as the fourth (*turīya*) stage, or degree. The above passage not only posits a Higher Brahman which is "sound-ful" (*paraṁ brahma = nādaḥ*) but also redefines the fourth stage (*turīya-sthānam*) of AUM as being of half-measure or half-syllable (*ardha-mātra*) rather than of no-measure (*amātra*) as found in the *Māṇḍūkya-Upaniṣad*. This is very significant, as it allows us to observe the way in which the theory of sacred sound develops a distinctive profile in Yogic meditation, in stark contrast to monistic Vedānta. At this point it becomes necessary to articulate this disparity a bit further in detail.

As also mentioned in chapter 1, the *Māṇḍūkya-Upaniṣad* became a central text in the philosophy of Śaṅkara known as Advaita-Vedānta. Śaṅkara's grand-preceptor, Gauḍapāda, had written a commentary in 215 verses known as his *Kārikā* on this Upaniṣad, describing in precise detail the Advaita-Vedānta position relative to the "analysis" of the syllable *Om*, or A U M. Śaṅkara subsequently wrote a commentary on these verses.

The Advaita position seems to assume that *amātra*, or boundlessness, can be directly identified with *aśabda*, or soundlessness. Though the *Maitri-Upaniṣad* 6.22 describes the Higher Brahman as *aśabda*, or "soundless," there is no obvious equation there with the word *amātra*. But, since the fourth degree of AUM is referred to as *amātra*, or "beyond measure," in the *Māṇḍūkya-Upaniṣad* (v. 12, *amātras caturthaḥ*, etc.), the Advaita commentators have used this concept to signify the idea of "beyond sound," or simply the absence of sound in the *turīya*, or fourth degree. Gauḍapāda says, "The sound (letter) A helps its worshipper to attain to *viśva* [waking state], U to *taijasa* [dream state], and M to *prājña* [dreamless sleep]. In the 'Soundless' there is no attainment." Śaṅkara says, "AUM [in all four degrees] is both the lower Brahman and the supreme *turīya*. When from the highest standpoint, the sounds and quarters disappear (in the soundless AUM) it is verily the same as the Supreme Brahman. . . . *Amātra* or soundless AUM signifies *turīya*."[32]

Accordingly, Swami Nikhilānanda has given what appears to be a faithful Advaita-Vedāntic reading of these passages. The process of Advaitic meditation involves the gradual merging of one stage into the succeeding one by identification until soundlessness is reached. He says, "*Viśva* merges in *taijasa*, *taijasa* in *prājña*, and finally *prājña* which is looked upon as the cause of the two preceding states merges in *turīya-ātman* [the fourth degree of pure Self]. Similarly the three sounds. A, U, and M ultimately merge in the soundless AUM. In the soundless AUM, the three sounds become identical with it as the three states are identical with *turīya* from the absolute standpoint. Therefore *turīya-ātman* is the same as soundless AUM." He then explains the state of soundlessness: "Soundless—It is because *amātra* AUM cannot be expressed by any sound. It is relationless and therefore it cannot be described as the substratum of three other sounds. Sound points out, by contrast, the soundless AUM. All sounds must, at some time or other, merge in soundlessness. This *amātra* AUM is identical with *turīya-ātman* as described in the previous text."[33]

The process of Yoga as outlined further above by Vācaspati, being at variance with the basic Advaita philosophy, is thereby distinguished by its attention to the Higher Sound Brahman as Nāda-Brahman. This highest degree, or stage, is said to be attainable through Yogic meditation on the syllable *AUM* in its sequential stages, beginning with concentration on the eight-petaled lotus flower situated in the heart and ending with the apprehension of Nāda-Brahman itself. Eliade has explained the significance of this description by Vācaspati in relation to its "mystical physiology": "It introduces us to a 'mystical' or 'subtle physiology,' concerned with organs that reveal their existence only in the course of Yogic exercises in concentration and meditation."[34] Recently, Paul Muller-Ortega quoted this passage of Vācaspati, from Eliade, as being a precursor for the Kashmiri Śaivite "heart" meditation of Abhinavagupta.[35] Both, however, have overlooked the importance of Vācaspati's use of the term *nāda* in describing the highest state of Yogic meditation. This is by no means unusual for Indic scholarship. While many Indian scholars employ the word *nāda* or Nāda-Brahman with the assumption that the reader automatically understands what is being talked about, both the term *nāda* and the concept of Nāda-Brahman are conspicuously absent in nearly all Western studies of Yoga and Hindu esoteric practices. The actual importance of Nāda-Brahman for Indian thought and Hinduism may by now be coming more explicit as we continue to proceed along our present course in this work.

Though the respective commentaries by Vyāsa, Vācaspati, and Vijñāna Bhikṣu shed light on Patañjali, they still cannot be said to represent the Yoga philosophy in extenso nor reflect the practicing traditions. The fact that Vācaspati was more disposed toward Sāṁkhya philosophy and Vijñāna Bhikṣu partial to Advaita-Vedānta contributed toward the obscuration of Patañjali's original intentions. In order to approach the practicing tradition of Nāda-Yoga we must at this point focus on the *Yoga-Upaniṣads*, which provide ample details regarding the role of sacred sound in Yoga. After this the Yoga orthopraxy of the Gorakhnāth tradition along with the Haṭha-Yoga texts will be examined.

The *Maitri-Upaniṣad*, being one of the principal Upaniṣads as well as a philosophic source for Advaita-Vedānta, has been singularly cited as being of a formative nature with regard to the subject of Nāda-Yoga, or the Yoga technique of meditation on sacred sound: "This scripture brings detailed information about Yoga techniques, particularly on the employment of the sacred syllable Om. This led to the later Yoga of sound (Nāda-Yoga)."[36] Indeed, by taking a possible cue from verse 6.22 of this text, the "hearing of divine sounds" has been emphasized in the *Yoga-Upaniṣads*, the principal Haṭha-Yoga texts, and by the Nāth Yogīs (followers of Gorakhnāth). The common sharing of "mystical audition" among these traditions indicates a fertile area for investigation. In fact, the perusal of these texts and traditions has revealed an underlying theology and epistemology of sound as Nāda-Brahman. While not explicitly occurring in either the four Vedas, the Brāhmaṇas, the Āraṇyakas, or the classical Upaniṣads, the theology of Nāda-Brahman begins to enter into dialogue with the classical Yoga, Mīmāṁsā, Advaita, and Sphoṭa standpoints. By articulating some of the structural subtleties and thematic nuances of Nāda-Brahman in this chapter, we will be in a more suitable position for evaluating the theistic practices of mantra, *japa*, and other forms of sonic meditation in the following chapters.

The Yoga-Upaniṣads

The twenty-one available *Yoga-Upaniṣads*,[37] though often understood to be of late origin, are attested to reflect practices of a much earlier period: "Although the first Tantras and the *Yoga-Upaniṣads* date from the 8th century after Christ, we may and should assume as a certainty that their contents were formulated at least ten centuries earlier, then continuously elaborated upon and renewed before being finally fixed in the texts we possess."[38] This statement is more realistic than the estimation of Eliade, who says that these texts were "contemporary with the didactic portions of the *Mahābhārata* and probably very little earlier than the *Vedānta-Sūtras* and the *Yoga-Sūtras*."[39]

The esteem accorded to *nāda* or Nāda-Brahman in this tradition is indicated by a statement in the *Yogaśikha-Upaniṣad* (2.20–21): "There is no *mantra* higher than the *nāda:* there is no god higher than one's own Ātman; there is no worship higher than investigation of the *nāda* and there is no higher satisfaction."[40] Moreover, whether concerned with meditation on *nāda, bindu,* AUM, Praṇava, *japa, ajapa,* mantra, or *bīja* ("seed" phonemes), attention to the soteriological dimension of Nāda-Brahman pervades the entire spectrum of the *Yoga-Upaniṣads.*

The *Nādabindu-Upaniṣad,* attached to the *Ṛg-Veda,* spearheads our investigation into this text group, as it reflects the most one-pointed effort to advance the speculation on sacred sound and is possibly the oldest document on the "Yoga of Sound," since it "probably belongs to the pre-Christian era."[41] As the name suggests, it is of initial interest for the study of Nāda-Brahman: "The most interesting part of this Upaniṣad is its description of the auditory phenomena that accompany certain Yogic exercises." Suggesting its "experimental origin," Eliade posits that it was "composed in a Yogic circle that specialized in 'mystical auditions'—that is, in obtaining 'ecstasy' through concentration on sounds.... Such concentration is acquired only by the application of a Yogic technique (*āsana* [sitting postures], *prāṇāyāma* [breathing exercises], etc.).... Its final objective is to transform the whole cosmos into a vast sonorous theophany."[42]

The *Nādabindu-Upaniṣad* (31–41) describes a process of Yogic meditation wherein the aspirant listens to eleven different internal sounds in successive degrees of subtlety:

> The Yogī should always listen to the sound [*nāda*] in the interior of his right ear. This sound, when constantly practiced, will drown every sound [*dhvani*] from outside.... By persisting... the sound will be heard subtler and subtler. At first, it will be like what is produced by the ocean [*jaladhi*], the cloud [*jīmūta*], the kettle-drum [*bherī*], and the water-fall [*nirjhara*].... A little later it will be like the sound produced by a tabor [*mardala,* or small drum], a big bell [*ghaṇṭā*], and a military drum [*kāhala*]; and finally like the sound of the tinkling bell [*kiṅkiṇī*], the bamboo-flute [*vaṁśa*], the harp [*vīṇā*], and the bee [*bhramara*].

As the mind of the Yogī is fully lost in the sound (*nāda*), he becomes indifferent to everything in the world: "Leaving all thoughts and devoid of actions, he should meditate upon *nāda* alone. This mind will then merge completely in the *nāda*." Not only are past actions (*karma*) obliterated by this practice, but it leads to the ultimate goal of all religious endeavors: "All of them [religious actions, including concentration on the *bindu*] find their last resting place in the *nāda* of the

Praṇava, wherein is manifest the Brahman which is no other than the innermost *ātman* [self]."[43]

The *Haṁsa-Upaniṣad* (16) contains a similar sequence of ten "mystical sounds":

> That *nāda* is produced in ten different ways (in the right ear of the seeker). The first is of the character of the "*ciṇi*" sound. The second is of the character of the "*ciṇi-ciṇi*" sound. The third is like the sound of a bell [*ghaṇṭā*]. The fourth is distinctly like the blast of a conch [*śaṅkha*]. The fifth is like the note produced by the wire of a harp [*vīṇā-tantrī*]. The sixth is like the sound of cymbals (made of bellmetal) [*tāla*]. The seventh is like the sweet note of the flute [*veṇu*]. The eighth is like the sound of a kettle-drum [*bherī*]. The ninth is like the sound of a tabor [*mṛdaṅga*, or drum]. The tenth is like the sound of a thunder-cloud [*megha*].[44]

Out of all these the text highly recommends concentration on the tenth alone. The connection between the sound of the thundercloud, the Param Brahman, and the Parā-Vāk (Supreme Vāk) in these verses reminds us of the Vedic god Indra, his thunderbolt, and the birth of speech sounds. Eliade mentions Indra in relation to the Yogic source of sound, the Mūlādhāra-Cakra: "The Mūlādhāra-Cakra is related to the cohesive power of matter, to inertia, the birth of sound [*nāda*], the sense of smell, the *apāna* breath, the gods Indra, Brahmā, Ḍākinī, Śakti etc." In the Grammarian tradition the power of Sphoṭa to "burst through" is referred to as *kratu*, which is also said to be connected to Indra: "The Indian word *kratu* . . . began by meaning the energy of the ardent warrior, especially Indra."[45] As we proceed through these and other Hindu texts, it may be useful to pay attention to such references (i.e., the sound of thunder, drums, Indra, Vāk, *nāda*, etc.) in order to provide cohesiveness in viewing the presence of sacred sound as a continuum of Indian thought.

The *Yogaśikha-Upaniṣad* (1.168–178) contains one of the earlier descriptions of the system of energy centers known as *cakra*, along with the placement of *nāda* therein:

> The Mūlādhāra, which is triangular in shape, is situated in the interspace between the anus and the genitals. That is said to be the seat of Śiva in the form of the *jīva* [living being], wherein

is established the exquisite power known as the *kuṇḍalinī*; wherefrom the vital air has its origin; whence arises the fire; whence the *bindu* takes its origin; whence is generated the *nāda;* whence is produced the *manas* or introspecting mind.... At the root of the genitals and with six corners is situated the *cakra* known as Svādhiṣṭhāna. In the region of the navel is situated the ten-petalled Maṇipūra-Cakra. In the heart region is the great Cakra Anāhata with twelve petals.... In the well of the throat is situated what is known as Viśuddhi, the sixteen-petalled plexus.... The superior plexus known as Ājñā is situated with the two petals in the middle of the eyebrows.... The region of the *manas* or mind in the middle of the eyebrows they know to be of the form of *nāda* [*nāda-rūpam*].[46]

Moreover, the Praṇava is stated (2.9) to originate in the lowest *cakra,* the Mūlādhāra, and is equivalent to *nāda:* "All speech is vitalized by the Oṁkāra... and on account of its originating from the Mūlādhāra, and being the symbol of the form of the basic entity (the Brahman), it is known as the *mūla-mantra*.... (2.5) That *mantra,* made up of Śiva and Śakti, taking its rise from the Mūlādhāra is fit to be the *praṇava* or the *nāda*." The text coins the term *nāda-liṅga* to express the symbolic nature of this mantra (2.10): "On account of its subtle and causal nature, on account of its state of repose and mobility and its being symbolic of the transcendent Īśvara [God], it is known as *liṅga* (symbol)."[47]

The *Darśana-Upaniṣad* (6.36.-38) describes the perception of sounds in the highest position, or *cakra,* in the body known as the Brahma-randhra, located in the region of the head:

When air [*prāṇa*] enters the Brahma-randhra, *nāda* (sound) is also produced there, resembling at first the sound of a conch-blast [śaṅkha-dhvani] and like the thunder-clap [*megha-dhvani*] in the middle; and when the air has reached the middle of the head, like the roaring of a mountain cataract [*giri-prasravaṇa*]. Thereafter, O great wise one! the Ātman, mightily pleased, will actually appear in front of thee. Then there will be the ripeness of the knowledge of Ātman from Yoga and the disowning by the Yogī of worldly existence.[48]

With regard to the appearance of *nāda* in the heart of the Yogī the *Yogacūḍāmaṇi-Upaniṣad* (115) says, "When the vital air [*prāṇa*] has reached the ... *ākāśa* of the heart, a great sound is produced, as of bells [*ghaṇṭā*] and other musical instruments. That is known as the accomplishment of the *nāda* [*nāda-siddhi*]." Besides, the *Maṇḍalabrāhmaṇa-Upaniṣad* (5.4–5) says, "Of the sound [*śabda*] produced in the *anāhata* of the heart, there is the reverberation [*nāda* or *dhvani*] of that sound; there is radiance [*jyoti*] penetrating the interior of that reverberation. There is the mind penetrating the interior of that radiance: which mind is the doer of the deed of creating, sustaining and destroying the three worlds. Wherein that mind meets with dissolution, that is the supreme state of Viṣṇu (the Brahman) [*tad viṣṇo paramaṁ padam*]."[49]

Four forms of Nāda-Brahman, corresponding in part to the three levels of Sphoṭa in Bhartṛhari (Paśyantī, Madhyamā, and Vaikharī) plus Parā, are also enumerated in the *Yogaśikha-Upaniṣad* (3.2–5):

> [*akṣaraṁ paramo nādaḥ śabda-brahmeti kathyate,* Śabda-Brahman is said to be imperishable, supreme, and consisting of *nāda*]. "There is the *parā* power [*śakti*] ... inherent in the Mūlādhāra of the indistinct form, known as *bindu* and having *nāda* as its support. From that alone arises *nāda,* even as the sprout out of the subtle seed [clearly analogous to the idea of *sphoṭa*]. That, by means of which the Yogīs see the universe, they know it as *paśyantī* (also known as *anāhata* [or "unstruck"]). ... In the heart (wherein is the *anāhata*) is placed this sound [*ghoṣa*], which resembles that of a thunder-cloud [*garja,* the roaring of the elephant, or the rumbling of clouds]. It is known as *madhyamā*. ... That alone is again known as *vaikharī,* when, in conjunction with the *prāṇa* vital air, it goes by the name of *svara* (when it takes the form of articulate expression).[50]

As we have seen, or heard, the sounds of musical instruments are included in the mystical auditions of Nāda-Yoga. There has indeed been a close continuity between Indian classical music and the Yoga and Tantric traditions. Furthermore, for the pious Hindu, the sounding of the flute (*vaṁśa, veṇu*) may suggest Krishna and Krishna worship, while that of the *vīṇā* (harp or fretted zither) is reminiscent of Sarasvatī, goddess of learning and music. As the sound of Krishna's flute is sometimes termed *nāda* in the Bhakti poetry and Sarasvatī is a later evolute of the Goddess Vāk, there are some obvious correspondences here which need to be attended to in future research.

In assessing the overall importance of Nāda-Yoga in this group of texts we are directed to several statements in the *Varāha-Upaniṣad* which accent Nāda-Brahman and Nāda-Yoga. "Giving up all worries, with a composed mind the *nāda* (the Brahman) alone should be meditated upon by one who aspires to hold sway over the Yogasāmrājya (Yoga empire) [2.83]." Three types of Yoga are said to culminate in *nāda*: "Of the three, the soft (Laya), the middle (Haṭha) and the mystic (Mantra), one should know in order, the Mantra (meditation on the *nāda* [*nādānusandhāna*, according to the commentary of Śrī Upaniṣad Brahmayogin]), then the Laya (the repose in the *nāda*), and then the Haṭha (the means to attain the Laya). Thus the Yogas are threefold, Laya, Mantra, and Haṭha [5.10]."[51]

The kinship of these texts with Patañjali's Yoga is quite clear. Most of them expound and dilate upon the practice of Praṇava-Japa, the repetition of AUM, and employ terminology from the classical system. As to their overall value, Jean Varenne, a French scholar of Yoga, says, "The evidence of the *Yoga-Upaniṣads'* relationship to the theory and practice of classical Yoga remains irreplaceable, not merely quantitatively but also on account of the mystic exaltation they succeed in conveying."[52] Though some of the texts have been influenced by Vedāntic thinking, they by-and-large subscribe to the Hindu theistic pattern of Īśvara worship outlined by Patañjali.

In retrospect, it appears that the post-Vedic concept of Nāda-Brahman has become so totally fused with the traditional Vedic and Upaniṣadic notions of Vāk, Śabda-Brahman, and Om that it is almost indistinguishable from them. By now, in fact, Nāda-Brahman has largely succeeded Śabda-Brahman in most discussions of sacred sound in Hinduism. In addition, Nāda-Brahman has become part of Tantric conversations regarding both the Cakras, or energy stations, in the human body and the three-four levels of speech manifestation introduced by the Grammarians. An esoteric physiology of sound has been clearly developed which denotes advancement along the path of salvation for the Yogī. Sound as reverberation beckons the aspirant toward deeper penetration of himself, as he awakens toward higher and higher levels of sonic perception.

Gorakhnāth and the Nāth Yogīs

While the classical texts of the Yoga system disclose many valuable theoretical concerns, the historical development of Yoga practice as a formal initiatory discipline gravitated around the Nāth Yogīs,[53] the largest Yoga sect, or lineage, in India. This group claims to have received transmission of Yogic revelation from the God Śiva via Matsyendranāth and Gorakhnāth: "Matsyendranāth and Gorakhnāth brought a new 'revelation,' which they declared that they had received directly from Śiva."[54] The dates and legends ascribed to each of these "human" founders vary with the particular locale, such that a considerable amount of folklore has accumulated around both the founders and the tradition itself: "Traditions and legends concerning Gorakhnāth are widespread and extensive. Nepal, the United Provinces, Bengal, Western India, Sind and the Punjab each has a large collection."[55]

Despite the jumble of data, however, scholars have generally accepted the conclusions first proferred by G. W. Briggs and followed by Eliade, which were based on a close scrutiny of literary records: "Gorakhnāth lived not later than A.D. 1200, probably early in the eleventh century, and . . . came originally from Eastern Bengal."[56] In describing their religious beliefs, Eliade has said: "As for the theology of the Gorakhnāthīs [Nāth Yogīs], it is extremely elementary: Śiva is their supreme god, and salvation consists in union with the divinity through Yoga."[57] Without rehearsing the various legends and myths associated with the Nāth Yogīs, we will briefly highlight the central role of sacred sound (Nāda-Brahman and Praṇava meditation) in the achievement of immortality or union with Śiva.

The Nāth Yogīs, named after Śiva as Ādināth, developed into twelve subsects of Haṭha-Yoga practitioners, striving after *mokṣa* by renouncing the world and worshipping Śiva as the greatest Yogī (Mahā-Yogī). "The final aim of the Nāth Siddhas [Yogīs] was the attainment of Śivahood in and through the attainment of immortality, and the means of attaining was primarily Haṭha-Yoga. . . . The emphasis of Haṭha-Yoga seems to be primarily on the physical or physiological practices which remove disease, decay, and death."[58] In addition, they split their ears (*kānphaṭa*) and, being generally celibate, wear the characteristic "ochre robe," and live by collecting alms. Overall, the Gorakhnāthīs "constitute the principal group and the better class of Yogīs. . . . [They] are found everywhere in India."[59]

There is a text ascribed to Matsyendranāth, the traditional preceptor of Gorakhnāth. The *Kaulajñāna-Nirṇaya,* also considered the earliest reference to Matsyendranāth himself (eleventh-century manuscript), describes a practice of Yoga which appears to be a further development of that contained in the *Yoga-Upaniṣads.* In fact, within the long description of the bodily Cakras, Śiva as Bhairava, in response to Devī's question, accents the meditation on Nāda-Brahman when contemplating the petals of the interior lotuses (5.31): "After meditating on each Cakra separately as consisting of *bindu, nāda,* and *śakti,* one obtains *dharma, artha, kāma,* and *mokṣa*—with *aṇimā* and the rest of the eight *siddhis*."[60] In a state of deep meditation the *jīva* (living being) is again depicted as an aural recipient of mystical sounds (14.85–86): "When the *jīva* is dissolved in this state, he hears inner sounds, such as that of a kettle-drum [*bherī*], a conch [*śaṅkha*], a *mṛdaṅga* [drum], a *vīṇā* [string instrument], or a flute [*vaṁśa*]. One should always meditate on this, which is the highest state of all. One becomes imperishable, immortal."[61] These five sounds appear to be reduplicated from the "earlier" ten or eleven sounds found in the *Yoga-Upaniṣads.*

Among the several writings attributed to Gorakhnāth, the *Gorakṣa-Śataka* has been declared "a fundamental text of the [Nāth] sect.... There seems to be unanimous agreement that Gorakhnāth is the author of the *Śataka* [One Hundred Verses]; and, in that case, the work must be as old as the twelfth century." After a prolonged discussion of Cakra meditation the text prescribes the repetition of the sacred syllable *Om* (83): "Having taken the lotus posture, holding the body and neck steady, fixing the sight on the tip of the nose, in a secluded place, one should repeat the imperishable Om [*japed oṁkāram avyayam*]." Verse 87 serves to include the *bindu* among the elements: "That Om, in which these three letters A, and likewise U and M, which has the *bindu* as its mark, exist, is the supreme light [*param jyoti*]."[62]

After the Śiva (*bindu* = moon) and Śakti (*rajas* = sun) metaphysics are fully explained in relation to the rising of the *kuṇḍalinī-śakti,* the *Gorakṣa-Śataka* concludes with a verse concerning the manifestation of Nāda-Brahman (101): "By cleansing the *nāḍīs* [esoteric channels in the body] the *prāṇa* (is) restrained as desired, the digestive fire (is) kindled, internal sound [*nāda*] is heard (becomes manifest) [*abhivyaktir*] (and) one becomes diseaseless [*arogyam*]."[63]

The above verse has (already) appeared verbatim in two of the *Yoga-Upaniṣads,* the *Yogacūḍāmaṇi-Upaniṣad* (99) and the *Śāṇḍilya-Upaniṣad* (7.8), and is destined to appear in the *Haṭha-Yoga-Pradīpikā* (2.20), thus demonstrating again the widely disseminated nature of Nāda-Brahman meditation. Furthermore, the verses of the *Nāda-bindu-Upaniṣad* which enumerate the sounds heard in *nāda* meditation (31, 33–36) correspond, with slight modification, with verses 141 and 144–47 of the *Gorakṣa-Vacana-Saṁgraha,*[64] an important "anonymous" text of the Gorakhnāth school, as well as with verses 4.82–85 of the later *Haṭha-Yoga-Pradīpikā*. It thus becomes clear that the *Yoga-Upaniṣads*, the Nāth tradition, and the Haṭha-Yoga treatises are threaded with the theory and practice of Nāda-Brahman meditation.

A. K. Banerjea, drawing upon a recently edited Nāth text known as the *Siddha-Siddhānta-Paddhati*, describes a characteristic type of auditory meditation:

> Gorakhnāth instructs a Yogī to practice concentration upon what he calls "Dhuṁ-Dhuṁ-kāra Nāda" within the head (*śiro-madhye*). For the practice of listening to this internal sound, he advises the Yogī in the initial stage to close firmly both the ears with the forefingers, so that no external sound may distract the attention. He would then hear a continuous sound like *dhuṁ-dhuṁ* within some center of his brain. He should fix his attention upon this internal sound and become absorbed with it. The sound would gradually take the monotonous form of Om. His mind will then be filled with ecstatic joy, and he would not like to attend to the various kinds of sounds outside. When concentration will be sufficiently deep, there will be realization of the Spirit in the *nāda*. It has already been mentioned that *nāda* is the pure self-revelation of Śiva-Śakti in sound-form.[65]

An intriguing aspect of the Nāth contribution to Indian linguistics is the addition of a fifth stage of language apprehension. This notion appears to bridge the "gap" between the Varṇavāda and Sphoṭavāda theories of language, as outlined in the previous chapter. According to Gorakhnāth and his school, Vāk, or divine speech, has five stages instead of the four of the Grammarians—namely, *parā, paśyantī, madhyamā, vaikharī,* and *mātṛkā*. As the fifth level,

> *mātṛkā* refers to the ultimate phonetic constituents of *vaikharī-vāk*. All words (*pada*) and sentences (*vākya*) . . . are found on analysis and reflection to be constituted of a certain number of ultimate verbal sounds, which are represented by *varṇa* or *akṣara* (letters). These are the units of vocal speech. They cannot be further analyzed or divided. . . . They are the seeds (*bīja*) of all languages, of all forms of articulate speech. They are accordingly called *mātṛkā* [f. "mother, source, origin, womb"] from which all kinds of words and sentences of the apparently diverse forms of languages in the world are evolved. Though they are the roots

of all vocal speech, they usually appear unrecognizably intermingled with words and sentences evolved from them.[66]

The school of Gorakhnāth is apparently closely related to the "genderized" Tantric theory of mantra meditation and recitation. Although the use of mantra becomes much more prominent and diverse in the sectarian traditions, the Nāth tradition is still accepted as an important precursor: "Nāthism is an especially important source for that 'sonic mysticism' central to the Tantric understanding and use of mantras."[67] As explained further by Banerjea, members of the Nāth Yoga and Tantric schools

> have by dint of the deepest reflection and meditation, entered into the inner spirit of these letters and discovered that each letter is a particularized sound-embodiment of Śiva-Śakti, and is associated with and manifested from a particular center within the living physical body [*cakra*]. Each letter is accordingly surcharged with a vital force and a spiritual meaning. In order to exhibit distinctly the Śiva-aspect and the Śakti-aspect in these root-letters, each letter is pronounced with a *bindu* . . . attached to it. . . . *Bindu* denotes Śiva [also male "sperm"] and *bīja* denotes Śakti [also "receptacle," source—that is, *mātṛkā*]. *Nāda* evolves from the mutual communion between them. . . . Thus the adepts in Yoga perceive the communion of Śiva and Śakti in every elemental sound (*nāda*) and in every letter representing it. Śiva is the common unchanged soul of all sounds and letters, and this is indicated by the *bindu* attached to every letter. Śakti assumes the diversified forms of sounds and letters (*nāda* and *varṇa*). All forms of articulate speech, all forms of verbal expressions of mental ideas, all kinds of words and sentences uttered apparently by human tongues (and recorded in various written forms), are complex manifestations of original *nāda* and *varṇa*. Yogīs therefore perceive the self-manifestation of Śiva-Śakti in all of them.[68]

Regarding the Nāth theory of mantra recitation, the upshot here is that power is generated as in the Vedic sense, with an additional emphasis on the internal experience of the binary Absolute of Śiva-Śakti. In the practices of the Nāth Yogīs these root letters and root sounds are developed into mantra and have deep spiritual significance. These mantras are not mere symbols conveying some spiritual concepts but are charged with great potency. "Repetition of the *mantras* according to prescribed methods reveals the powers inherent in them, and it leads to the development of various psychical and spiritual capacities in the *sādhakas* [adepts], as well as the attainment of many occult experiences. An adept can work wonders and perform miracles by activating the mysterious powers of the *bīja-mantras.* Among all *bīja-mantras,* Om (Praṇava) is universally regarded as having a unique pattern. It is the perfect embodiment of Śiva-Śakti."[69]

As seen in chapter 2, the theories advanced by Bhartṛhari and Mīmāṁsā appear to be quite at loggerheads. Sphoṭavāda with its disregard for the "reality" of letters and words does not pass muster with the Varṇavāda emphasis on the Absolute Reality of letters and syllables. The bipolar genderization of language which was accomplished by the Nāth and Śākta-Tantric schools, however, seems to fuse these two positions into an enormously intricate system of "occult linguistics." In Bhartṛhari and Mīmāṁsā the conception of *nāda* was limited to audible speech sounds. In the Yoga and Nāth traditions *nāda* is not only elevated to parity with the Absolute (as Nāda-Brahman) but becomes a powerful dynamic in itself, exemplifying the tension and communion between the masculine Śiva and the feminine Śakti. Neither *sphoṭa* nor *varṇa* is denied, since they are now more or less replaced by the metaphysical opposites of *bindu* (masculine, "soul," "burst-full" and "*sphoṭa*-like") and *bīja* (feminine, "body," "container," and "*varṇa*-like"). The *nāda* as Nāda-Brahman has permanent cosmic dimension, since the vibration, the resonance, accompanying the conjugal dyadism of Śiva-Śakti is said to permeate the entire universe. Om, instead of being a symbol of the Absolute Brahman, or Īśvara, as in the earlier traditions, is now the exemplification of a dynamic, bipolar universe.

Three Haṭha-Yoga Treatises

The *Gheraṇḍa-Saṁhitā, Śiva-Saṁhitā,* and *Haṭha-Yoga-Pradīpikā* are three of the most important Haṭha-Yoga texts and are intimately connected with the practice of Nāda-Yoga as propounded by Gorakhnāth and his school: "The connections between Gorakhnāth, the Kānphaṭas [Nāth Yogīs], and Haṭha-Yoga are beyond question."[70] While there are often prescriptions pertaining to the cleansing of the physical body, the ultimate goal of all purification, as proclaimed in these texts, is the meditation and auditory perception of Nāda-Brahman—hence, their importance for the study of Nāda-Yoga.

The *Gheraṇḍa-Saṁhitā,* composed by a Bengali Vaiṣṇava named Gheraṇḍa in perhaps the fifteenth century A.D., enumerates thirty-two sitting postures (*āsana*), twenty-five hand positions (*mudrā*), and eight kinds of breathing exercises (*prāṇāyāma*) involved in Haṭha-Yoga yet lists no less than twelve internal sounds that are heard by the Yogī. The text (5.79–80) reads: "He will hear then various internal sounds in his right ear [*karṇe nādam*]. The first sound will be like that of crickets [*jhiñjhī*], then that of a flute [*vaṁśī*], then that of thunder [*megha*], then that of a drum [*jharjhara*], then that of a bee [*bhramarī*], then that of bells [*ghaṇṭā*], then those of gongs of bell-metal [*kāṁsya*], trumpets [*turī*], kettle-drums [*bherī*], *mṛdaṅga* [drums], military drums [*ānaka*], and *dundubhi* [different kind of kettledrums]." Then he apprehends the primordial, or "unstruck," Nāda-Brahman (*anāhata-nāda*) in the heart (5.81–82): "Thus various sounds [*nāda*] are cognized by daily practice of this *kumbhaka* [breathing exercise]. Last of all is heard the *anāhata* sound rising from the heart; of this sound there is resonance, in that resonance there is a light. In that light the mind should be immersed. When the mind is absorbed, then it reaches the Highest seat of Viṣṇu [*paramaṁ padam*]."[71] The Vaiṣṇava penchant of this text is, of course, obvious.

The *Śiva-Saṁhitā,* the longest of the three treatises, is more philosophical in content. The description of five sounds (5.27) that are heard by the Yogī borrows from the standard vocabulary yet places them in slightly different order from the others—namely, from subtle to gross:

> Let him close the ears with his thumbs. . . . This is my most beloved Yoga. From practicing this gradually, the Yogi begins to hear mystic sounds (*nādas*). The first sound is like the hum of the honey-intoxicated bee [*matta-bhṛṅga*], next that of a flute [*veṇu*], then of a harp [*vīṇā*]; after this, by the gradual practice of Yoga, the destroyer of the darkness of the world, he hears the sounds of ringing bells [*ghaṇṭā*]; then sounds like roar of thunder [*megha*]. When one fixes his full attention on this sound, being free from fear, he gets absorption [*laya*]. . . . When the mind of the Yogī is exceedingly engaged in this sound, he forgets all external things, and is absorbed in this sound [*nāda*]. . . . There is no posture like that of *siddhāsana,* no power like that of *kumbha,* no *mudrā* like the *khecarī,* and no absorption like that of *nāda* (the mystic sound).[72]

The *Śiva-Saṁhitā* (5.56–131) also contains a lengthy description of the Cakras with their respective lotus petals and *bīja* letters. This digression reflects the Śākta-Tantric system, whereby the entire Sanskrit alphabet of fifty letters is homologized into these six or seven physiological centers of the human body. Each center contains a lotus (*padma*) with a specific number of petals. Each petal contains a letter, which represents the place of the union of Śiva and Śakti, of male and female divinities and forces. Furthermore, each letter (*bīja*) contains the symbol of the crescent (*nāda*) and the dot (*bindu*) and is often drawn with symbolic use of color and mythical animal forms.

The *Haṭha-Yoga-Pradīpikā* (4.64–67) is a very well-known Yoga text among Haṭha-Yoga practitioners and explains Nāda-Brahman meditation as Nāda-Upāsana, the "Worship of Nāda-Brahman," as the foremost practice:

> I will now describe the practice of Anāhata-Nāda [*nādopāsana*] as propounded by Gorakhnāth. . . . Ādināth [Śiva] propounded ¼ crore methods of trance, and they are all extant. Of these, the hearing of the Anāhata-Nāda is the only one, the chief, in my opinion. . . . The Yogī should hear the sound inside his right ear, with collected mind. The ears, the eyes, the nose, and the mouth should be closed, and then the clear sound is heard in the passage of the Suṣumnā which has been cleansed of all its impurities.[73]

The various knots (*granthis*), or obstacles, along the route of the bodily centers (*Cakra*) are connected to the various *nāda* auditions:

> When the Brahma-Granthi (in the heart) is pierced through by *prāṇāyāma*, then a sort of happiness is experienced in the vacuum of the heart, and the Anāhata sounds, like various tinkling sounds of ornaments, are heard in the body [4.69]; . . . By this means the Viṣṇu knot (in the throat) is pierced which is indicated by highest pleasure experienced, and then the *bherī* sound (like the beating of a kettle-drum) is evolved in the vacuum of the throat [4.72]; In the third stage, the sound of a drum [*mardala*] is known to arise in the *śūnya* [space] between the eyebrows [4.73]; When the Rudra-Granthi is pierced and the air enters the seat of the Lord (the space between the eyebrows), then the perfect sound like that of the flute is produced [4.75].[74]

Verse 2.20 of the *Haṭha-Yoga-Pradīpikā,* which describes the manifestation of *nāda* (*nādābhivyakti*) after the purification of the bodily channels (nāḍī), is the same verse that has already appeared in the twelfth-century *Gorakṣa-Śataka* (101) of Gorakhnāth. Furthermore, the listing of ten sounds (4.82–85) heard by the Yogī are exactly the same as those enumerated in the *Nādabindu-Upaniṣad* (33–36), giving support to Eliade's claim that the *Haṭha-Yoga-Pradīpikā* is the oldest of the three Haṭha-Yoga treatises.

Slightly different terminology is used at the end of the second chapter (*Haṭha-Yoga-Pradīpikā* 2.78), when describing the manifestation of Nāda-Brahman (*nāda-sphuṭa*) at the conclusion of the Yoga exercises. The similarity of this word (*sphuṭa*) with *sphoṭa* suggests a close correspondence between the Grammarian and Yoga schools with regard to the notion of eternal sound,[75] bursting forth within an advanced state of human consciousness. Vimala Musalagaonkar supports their direct correlation when she states that "what is understood as *sphoṭa* in grammar, *dhvani* in poetics, is called *nāda* in Yoga."[76]

The union of *bindu* and *rajas* is the "mechanical" aim of the Haṭha-Yoga ascetics and parallels the process of Nāda-Upāsana discussed above. The *bindu,* sometimes called "soma" and representing the male semen, is believed to fall in pale white drops from the moon itself: "It is the product of the moon and is distilled to the left of the space between the eyebrows. Its seat is in the hollow above the throat, . . . also described as the hole at the upper end of the Suṣumnā [spinal cord]. Thence it naturally proceeds down through the Suṣumnā to the place of fire, in the Mūlādhāra . . . where it is consumed. For this reason the *khecarī-mudrā* is performed to hold the *bindu* in its native station. . . . It [the *bindu*] is Śiva."[77]

The conservation and control of the *bindu* is of great importance for all Haṭha-Yoga practice, since it is directly linked to the protection and preservation of the body: "The quintessence of the visible body is distilled in the form of Soma [*bindu*] in the moon; this Soma rejuvenates the body and makes it immortal."[78]

Though both *bindu* and *rajas,* the menstrual fluid, are crucial to the production of the human body, their union must be enacted under the characteristic Yoga methods. The source of *rajas* is the place, or circle, of the sun situated in the naval region and is described in its function as "devourer": "It [*rajas*] is Śakti. It is *rajas* that drinks the Soma (= *bindu*) falling from the moon."[79] It is the drying or burning up of the soma that brings decay and death to human beings, such that the soma must be somehow "saved," or consumed, by the aspirant, effecting an "inner union" of physical opposites.

While the *bindu* remains suspended in the body, the body is said to remain immortal and undisturbed while embracing a woman. Celibacy, however, is strongly encouraged in the Nāth Yoga tradition: "The Nāth Siddhas [Yogīs] were strict celibates, and it appears from the Nāth literature in all the vernaculars that women are regarded as the greatest danger in the path of Yoga and they are given no status higher than that of ferocious tigresses always bent on sucking the blood of the prey."[80]

The prescribed Yogic method for bringing the correct union into place is known as the Khecarī-Mudrā. The Khecarī-Mudrā, the chief *mudrā*, or position, in Haṭha-Yoga, involves the rolling back of the tongue into the hollow (*khe*) above the throat for the purpose of restraining the *bindu*, which trickles down from the moon and is normally "eaten up" by the sun situated in the naval: "The tongue thus extended backwards shuts up the tenth door [*daśama-dvāra*] and the nectar, thus saved, is drunk by the Yogī himself."[81] When this *mudrā* is practiced by gradually cutting the skin below the tongue, either physically or metaphorically, the mind goes (*carī*) to *ākāśa* (*khe*) and ecstasy or liberation is achieved.

While the philosophy of Gorakhnāth has many correlations with the Śākta-Tantric texts and practices, the points of difference emerge when discussing the role of the feminine, or Śakti, in the overall worldview and *sādhana*. While the Nāth Yogīs were, in principle, celibate and life-denying, the adherents of Śākta-Tantra, as we shall see, were less so, and they organized their theory and practice around the principle of the bipolar manifestation of the sacred—male and female. The practice of Kuṇḍalinī-Yoga is more common among the Śākta-Tantrics, wherein the internal Śakti is aroused and merged with Śiva at the top of the skull, appearing to be more congruent with the Śākta-Tantra view of universal bipolarity and the pervasiveness of Śakti. Since the Śakti is in all the letters, Kuṇḍalinī as Śakti enjoys Śiva in each Cakra in her form peculiar to that lotus and finally reaches the Supreme Śiva in the Sahasrāra, or "thousand-petalled Lotus." While there are some parallels with the basic Nāda-Yoga discussed above, more of the linguistic subtleties of Kuṇḍalinī-Yoga will be discussed in the next three chapters.

Nāda-Yoga and Indian Music

The tradition of Indian classical music and dance known as Saṅgīta is fundamentally rooted in the sonic and musical dimensions of the Vedas (*Sāma-Veda*), Upaniṣads, and the Āgamas, such that Indian music has been nearly always religious in character. The recital of sacred verses in a melodious voice to the accompaniment of musical instruments has been one of the hallmarks of Indian religion from the earliest times. The connection between musical sound and Śabda-Brahman or Nāda-Brahman appears to be very close and long-standing, especially since the principal and medieval texts and traditions of Indian classical music view music as a manifestation of Nāda-Brahman. As noted in chapter 1, however, the terminology of Nāda-Brahman is foreign to the Vedic and Upaniṣadic canon, appearing as it does only in Yogic and Āgamic (Tantric) sources. There is, thus, a need to be cautious of misleading statements found in musical scholarship such as the following: "The importance of sound (nāda) as a primeval organizing principle has its roots in the Vedic texts and the chanting of the Sāma Veda."[82] The metaphysical concept of *nāda* as Nāda-Brahman has not been discussed in the literature associated with the *Sāma-Veda* or its recitation.

Aside from the question of Nāda-Brahman, however, it is generally agreed that Indian music indeed owes its beginnings to the chanting of the *Sāma-Veda*, the vast collection of verses (Sāma), many from the *Ṛg-Veda* itself, set to melody and sung by singer-priests known as *udgātā*. As noted by V. Raghavan, "Our music tradition [Indian] in the North as well as in the South, remembers and cherishes its origin in the *Sāma-Veda*, . . . the musical version of the *Ṛg-Veda*."[83] And this point seems evident from a perusal of the textual sources themselves: "The fact that Sāma chanting is the basis for Indian music has been mentioned by all musicologists dealing with the history of Indian music."[84]

A unique feature of the *Sāma-Veda* chanting was the insertion of a number of meaningless words or syllables (*stobha*) for musical and lyrical effect:[85] *a, e, o, au, ha, ho, uha,* and *tayo*.[86] The method of reciting the Sāmans varied since the earliest time from one school to another. Three major traditions, the Kauthumas, Rāṇāyanīyas, and the Jaiminīyas, have maintained their individuality through the centuries with regard to the musical style of their singing: vowel prolongation, interpolation and repetition of syllables (*stobha*), the number of notes in their scales, phonetics, and meter.

Besides the singing or chanting of the *Sāma-Veda*, instrumental music formed part of the Vedic sacrifices as well, the most important instrument being the *vīṇā*, or lute, which was often played by the wife of the sacrificer. A recent study of the *vīṇā* has found it compared to the human body in the *Aitareya-Āraṇyaka*.[87] Other instruments mentioned in Vedic literature include various types of flutes, drums, and cymbals. All the rules and strictures regarding singing and playing instruments were gradually collected and codified in a number of texts which came to be known collectively as the Gandharva-Veda, said to be an Upaveda attached to the *Sāma-Veda*.

The mystical and esoteric significance of Sāman singing was propounded in the Upaniṣads, specifically the *Chāndogya-Upaniṣad* (1.1.2), which is the Upaniṣad attached to the *Sāma-Veda*. Therein, the role of Udgītha (loud singing) is eulogized as a highly religious act: "The essence of the *Ṛg-Veda* is the *Sāma-Veda*, the essence of the *Sāma-Veda* is the Udgītha (loud singing). This is the quintessence of the essences, the highest, the supreme, . . . namely the Udgītha."[88] Thus musical sound has a deep theological importance throughout the Vedic literature, an importance that gives rise to its ultimate equation with Nāda-Brahman in the tradition of Saṅgīta.

The overall significance of Nāda-Brahman in Indian music has been noted by a recent scholar: "This integral relation of music and Nāda is essential to Indian views of the soteriological significance of music, for music, as a manifestation of Nāda, is seen as a mode of access to the highest reality."[89] The Āgamic or Yogic notion of Nāda-Brahman actually emerged in the context of music as late as the eighth century A.D., wherein it appears in a text known as the *Bṛhaddeśī* by Mataṅga:

> The word *śabda* of the *Nāṭya-Śāstra* [seminal text on music and drama by Bhārata Muni, before fourth century A.D., in which there is no mention of *nāda* or Nāda-Brahman] has been replaced by Nāda in the *Bṛhaddeśī* of Mataṅga. The musicians enjoyed the full benefits of the special significance hidden in the word *nāda* which the Yogīs enunciated or expounded. In the field of music right from Mataṅga the word *nāda* has been used with special significance.[90]

Verses 17–18 of Mataṅga's *Bṛhaddeśī* provide us with perhaps the earliest formal connection between Nāda-Brahman, music, and the Hindu deities: "Without Nāda-Brahman, there is no song, no musical notes, no dance; the entire universe consists of Nāda-Brahman [*na nādena vinā gītam na nādena vinā svaraḥ / na nādena vinā nṛttam tasmād nādātmakaṁ jagat*]. Nāda-Brahman is remembered as the form of Brahmā, Janārdana (Viṣṇu), the Supreme Śakti (Goddess) as well as Śiva [*nāda-rūpaḥ smṛto brahmā nāda-rūpo janārdana / nāda-rūpā parā-śaktir nāda-rūpo maheśvaraḥ*].''[91] These verses appear in nearly the same form within later Vaiṣṇava works of the Bhakti period; cf., the fifteenth-century Vaiṣṇava musical text, *Saṅgīta-Dāmodara* (2) by Śubhaṅkara,[92] and the eighteenth-century Gauḍīya-Vaiṣṇava compendium known as *Bhakti-Ratnākara* (5.2505–6) by Narahari Cakravartī.[93] The importance of Mataṅga in relation to Nāda-Brahman and other features of Yoga and Tantra has elicited attention in recent scholarship in musicology: there is "a clear indication of the Tantric influence on Mataṅga and in extant literature he is the first author to introduce these details."[94]

Influenced by Mataṅga, subsequent musicological authors discussed Nāda-Brahman in relation to musical sound production, both in the cosmos and in the human body. The *Saṅgīta-Ratnākara* of Śārṅgadeva (ca. A.D. 1200–1500), for example, probably the most important musicological treatise of India,[95] contains an entire section (3A) on Nāda-Brahman, which opens with the following salutation: "We worship Nāda-Brahman, that incomparable bliss which is immanent in all the creatures as intelligence and is manifest in the phenomena of this universe (1). Indeed, through the worship of Nāda-Brahman are worshipped gods (like) Brahmā, Viṣṇu, and Śiva, since they essentially are one with it (2)."[96]

Speculation on Nāda-Brahman in the *Saṅgīta-Ratnākara* begins with the statement about it being the source of all kinds of musical sound as well as dance: "Nāda is the very essence of vocal music. Instrumental music is enjoyable, as it manifests Nāda. Nṛtta follows both (i.e., vocal and instrumental music); therefore, all the three together depend on Nāda." The esoteric dimension of Nāda-Yoga is coupled with music theory in that the twenty-two microtones, or Śrutis, of Indian music are paired with the twenty-two Nāḍīs, or subtle arteries, in the body perceived in Yoga meditation: "Nāda is differentiated into 22 grades which, because of their audibility, are known as Śrutis. It is believed that, closely associated with the two upward Nāḍīs in the heart there are 22 Nāḍīs placed obliquely, and 22 Śrutis successively higher and higher in pitch, are produced by the force of wind acting upon them."[97] Thus, in distinction from Śabda-Brahman,

Nāda-Brahman is both the external source of musical sound in the cosmos as well as its internal manifestation within the human body, originating in the lower Cakra of Kuṇḍalinī Yoga and gradually revealing itself through a kind of "sympathetic string" correspondence. This interior manifestation gives rise to a traditional etymology that identifies *Nāda* as the result of a kind of interior ignition, much like the Upaniṣadic (*Śvetāśvatara*) notion of Om recitation compared to a friction-stick: "It is understood that the syllable Nā (of Nāda) represents the vital force and Da represents fire; thus being produced by the interaction of the vital force and fire it is called Nāda."[98] This conjunction of Agni (fire) with Prāṇa (vital breath or force) to produce speech sound was already found in the phonetic and grammatical texts discussed in chapter 1.

While most traditions of Hindu theism engage in some sort of music making, an interesting parallel emerges between the particular musical practices of certain groups and the Yoga texts that describe musical sounds heard during meditation. The divine sounds of the drum, cymbal, *vīṇā,* and flute which were enumerated in texts such as *Nādabindu-Upaniṣad* and *Haṭha-Yoga-Pradīpikā* exhibit marked correspondences with the instruments employed in devotional music. In some styles of standing *kīrtana,* for example, there is a strong emphasis on the loud playing of the *mṛdaṅga* drum and the *karatāla* hand cymbals, as if to reflect externally what the advanced Yogī should be perceiving internally. In many of the seated *bhajans* optimum attention is given to the subtle sounds of the stringed instruments (*vīṇā*), almost as if each sound brought one closer to the region of the gods. A serious study of the Indian musical instruments and how they correspond to the sounds heard in deep Nāda-Yoga meditation is a desideratum.

The relationship between sacred sound and music is, of course, familiar to students of Pythagoras and his "Harmony of the Spheres." The Pythagorean school, however, based the sacrality of music on the sacredness of numbers instead of words, as explained by a modern scholar conversant in both traditions: "Words are the Vedic Yoga: they unite mind and matter. Pure, ecstatic contemplation of phonetic sound reverberating on the ether in the sacred chant may be compared to the contemplation of geometrical forms and mathematical laws by the Pythagoreans. The Word is God, Number is God—both concepts result in a kind of intoxication. Only the Pythagorean Master can hear the music of the spheres: only the perfected Hindu sage can hear the primordial sound—Nāda."[99]

Current musical instruction in India continues to emphasize the implicit connection between Nāda-Brahman, including Nāda-Yoga techniques of breathing and voice production, and the performance of Indian classical music, both northern Hindustani and southern Carnatic. M. R. Gautam, noted singer and musicologist, stated in an interview that, "regarding the mystical side of our Hindustani vocal music, when the singer has produced the various notes (*svaras*) to perfection, then that outward audible vibration is capable of producing a corresponding inner, 'sympathetic' vibration, which in our terminology is known as Nāda-Brahman."[100]

Sri Sailen Banerjee, noted vocal instructor and founder of the Tansen Music College, has confirmed the unitary nature of musical sound and its identification with Nāda-Brahman: "When your voice is perfectly trained, you will find that all of the notes of our classical music, *sa, re, ga, ma, pa, dha, ni,* [cf. *do re mi fa so la ti* in Western solmization], are actually variations of one note which is Nāda-Brahman or Om."[101] Regarding the classical tradition of south India known as Carnatic, N. Ramanathan of the University of Madras explained in an interview that "the music of our Carnatic musicians reflects an underlying preoccupation with the extra-linguistic features of the divine and universal Nāda-Brahman."[102] In a variety of ways Indian musicians proclaim Nāda-Brahman as the basis of their music, testifying to the growing importance of the sonic dimension of Hindu culture.

Current Trends in Nāda-Yoga

Before moving on it is appropriate to mention the present-day use of Nāda-Yoga techniques of meditation, techniques that have mostly come to the West since 1965. The current usage of these techniques among Westerners, as well as Indians, has been partly due to the efforts of the following practitioners cited in this section: Usharbudh Arya, Swami Śivānanda, Swami Nādabrahmānanda, the Rādhā Soami sect, and Bhagwan Rajneesh. Meanwhile, scientifically inclined Indian scholars have been conducting research into the nature and effects of Nāda-Brahman meditation.

In an audiotape entitled *Nāda Yoga Meditation* Usharbudh Arya of the Himalayan Institute instructs a process of meditation somewhat based on the Yoga texts we have discussed yet creating new metaphors for contemporary parlance. While stressing the male (inhalation) and female (exhalation) division of breaths, attention is directed to non-linguistic sounds and their reverberation. The first example is the sound of a bell: "Observe how long you can hear the resonance of the bell. . . . Even when the actual sound resonance is gone, continue to be aware of the very fine subtle note in your ear."[103] Then the seven notes of the major scale, ascending and descending, are played on the cello, wherein attention is given to resonances perceived in the various Cakra centers of the body with regard to intervals.

A similar process is applied to the recitation of Om, with special emphasis on the hearing of "after-sounds":

> You will close the ears with the thumbs. . . . You will recite Om reverberating in your skull three times, then you will stop reciting. When you recite once, you stop and continue to listen to the reverberations. Then you recite the second time, reverberating in your skull as though the sound rises from the base of your spine upwards into the skull. When you have completed the second recitation, you will keep listening to it with ears closed. Again the third time; then, you will remove your thumbs and you will continue to listen to the same reverberations, especially in the right-half, from the base of the skull to the eyebrow center in the right half of the skull inside the right ear.[104]

Indeed, in accordance with the *Yoga-Upaniṣads* and the Haṭha-Yoga texts, the Yogī is told to concentrate on his right ear: "Let the mind remember the *mantra,* and let the inside of the inner ear hear it together with all the inner sounds as though you are listening to your *mantra* with inner right ear, in the spaces between the base of the skull and the eyebrow center, in the right half of the dome of the skull-cathedral." Further, "relax, bring your mind's attention to the cave of bees inside your skull. Let the *mantra* appear, listen to the *mantra* against the *vīṇā* sound and you will sit as long as you wish."[105]

Swami Śivānanda Sarasvatī (1887–1963), formerly Kuppuswami Iyer of Tamil Nadu, founded the Divine Life Society in 1937. It was just before this time that Mircea Eliade had studied Yoga under him in Rishikesh. At present, under the direction of Swami Cidānanda, the society sustains thousands of disciples around the world. Though his teachings reflect Advaita-Vedānta philosophy, Śivānanda has propagated the recitation of *japa*, or Om, throughout his over three hundred written works, but especially in books like *Japa Yoga* (1986, 9th ed.), *Philosophy and Meditation on Om* (1941), and *Tantra Yoga, Nāda Yoga, and Kriyā Yoga* (1955). Defining *japa* as the repetition of any mantra whatsoever, he explains that, "in this Kali Yuga or Iron Age when the physique of the vast majority of persons is not good, rigid Haṭha-Yoga practices are very difficult. *Japa* is an easy way to God-realization. . . . *Japa* checks the force of the thought-current moving towards objects. It forces the mind to move towards God, towards the attainment of eternal bliss."[106]

Śivānanda has composed several prayers in praise of Om and Nāda-Brahman. The "Oṁkāra-Smaraṇa-Stotra" begins, for example, with: "The Supreme Brahman is attained by contemplation, hearing, *japa*, and *saṅkīrtana* [singing] of Om always."[107] Regarding Nāda-Brahman, which he equates with the powerful vibration of *japa*, the "Nāda-Śloka" begins with: "In this world there are 125,000 *sādhanas* [spiritual practices], all told by Sadāśiva. We consider *nādānusandhāna* [worship of Nāda-Brahman] as the best."[108]

Swami Nādabrahmānanda, a disciple of Swami Śivānanda, based his teachings on the musical Nāda-Brahman, which he demonstrates through particular vocalization techniques (the science of *tāna*).[109] Since *nāda* has the meaning of "re-sonance," the performance of Indian devotional music is especially effective in the illustration of Nāda-Brahman. His singing and other demonstrations have attracted many disciples in the United States, especially California.

A prominent organization today which practices meditation on the "sound current," or Nāda-Brahman, is the Rādhā Soami sect, founded in the 1850s by a Hindu banker in Agra (Uttar Pradesh). According to an early Western practitioner, the goal of their *sādhana* (practice) is reconnection of the aspirant by a recognized master to the eternal sound current: "Without a Master there is no contact with the Sound Current, and without the Sound Current there is no salvation. This is the sum of the entire philosophy of the saints."[110] This statement sounds very much like something which could encompass the majority of Hindu traditions with regard to the role of sacred sound.

The Rādhā Soami Satsaṅg (organization), which is the more popular branch of the original parent group and is currently under the supervision of Maharaj Charan Singh, has its headquarters in Beas

(Punjab) and teaches a "Yoga of Sound" entitled Surat Śabda Yoga. Claiming this Yoga to be the simplest and most original method for attaining liberation, the practitioners say that it "involves neither physical exercises nor the rising of the Kuṇḍalinī. It consists in connecting the soul (Surat) with the sound current (Śabda)."[111]

There is a close parallel with the Sikh tradition also prevalent in the Punjab area. The Sikhs, followers of their founder Guru Nanak (1469–1539), stress meditation on the Word or sound current in the form of prayer and song. "For the Sikh, as for the Hindu, participation in the divine word has power to transform and unify one's consciousness."[112]

The Rādhā Soami sect has been studied by modern scholarship. The explanations of Lawrence A. Babb provide more indications of the sect's close ties with the practices of Nāda-Yoga outlined in this chapter. After reaffirming that Surat Śabda Yoga is the very essence of their spiritual practice Babb explains the sonic journey of the initiated devotee of this tradition:

> The devotee is said to take his or her seat at the third eye [Ājñā-Cakra]. There the devotee has a vision of the guru and/or a brilliant flame, and hears the sound of a conch and bell. The devotee then ascends to *sahas dal kanval,* the "thousand-petalled lotus." Sounds come from the left and the right. The devotee rejects the sound from the left and concentrates on that from the right. Then, in the company of the guru he or she is pulled further upward. The ascending devotee sees marvelous sights—suns, moons, skies beyond the sky—and hears the sounds of bells, thunder, musical instruments, and sounds quite unlike anything we know in this world. The devotee has visions of the deity presiding over each of these celestial levels. At the end of the journey—that is, if the end is reached—the devotee has a vision of the Supreme Being himself [i.e., Rādhā Soami, "Lord of the Sound Current"], who is the object of this vertical pilgrimage.[113]

A sect that became popular in the United States in the early 1970s, and whose teachings are based in part on those of Rādhā Soami is the Divine Light Mission. In addition to the perception of "divine light," the leader, Balyogeshvar, or Guru Maharaj Ji, taught techniques for the hearing of divine sounds and the Word:

> The technique of hearing the music or the sound is simple. One is asked to block his ears with the thumbs so that one does not hear any external sounds. When one listens long enough to his inner silence he can eventually hear some noises. To some people this sounds like celestial music whereas others think they are hearing their favorite tune played on some heavenly instrument.... Hearing the Word is the main meditation. In fact it is often regarded as "the knowledge." It is simply a breathing exercise, in which one sits in a lotus position (if possible), with both hands on the knees, and concentrates on the breath going up and down, up and down. Through concentrating on one's breathing, one supposedly tunes into that "primordial vibration," the Word or Logos, which has created the universe and sustains it.

A particular exercise is also advised which seems to be taken from Haṭha-Yoga (Khecarī-Mudrā): "One has to try and curl his tongue to come up to the back of the throat and then has to swallow the tongue in such a way that it points upwards. Here the tongue is supposed to hit a point and make contact with the nectar [*bindu*?] that is constantly flowing through one's body. It is claimed that this nectar is indescribably tasty and it is the 'living water' of which Jesus spoke."[114] The eclectic nature of the Rādhā Soami sect has obviously influenced the Divine Light Mission as well.

During the 1970s and 1980s other Indian imports and so-called New Age groups have also drawn upon this tradition of sound, such as Self-Realization Fellowship and Transcendental Meditation. While many of the methods used by these groups are at least founded on traditional Hindu sources, a rather innovative technique of Nāda-Brahman meditation has been advocated by Bhagwan Shree Rajneesh of Oregon repute and is described as follows:

> First Stage: For a minimum of thirty minutes, sit in a relaxed position with the eyes closed. With lips together, begin to hum, loudly enough to create a vibration throughout your entire body. The humming should be loud enough so that people around will be able to hear it. You can alter the pitch as you like, humming, then inhaling, at your own pace. If the body wants to move, allow it, but the movement should be very slow, very graceful. Visualize your body as a hollow tube, an empty vessel filled only with the vibrations of the humming. After a while a point

will come where you are just the listener: the humming will be happening by itself. This activates the brain, cleansing every fiber. It is also particularly helpful in healing.

Second Stage: With your eyes still closed, begin to move your hands (palms up) outward in a circular motion—the right hand moving to the right and the left hand moving to the left. Make the circles large and move as slowly as possible, the slower the better. You may even feel sometimes that they are not moving at all. If your body wants to move, allow it, but, again, keep the movement slow, soft, and graceful. After seven and a half minutes, move the hands in the opposite directions: palms down and hands moving, circularly, inward toward your body. Move your hands in this direction for another seven and a half minutes. As your hands move inward, imagine that you are taking energy in. As they move outward again, away from the body, imagine energy going out.

Third Stage: Stop your hand movements and sit silently for fifteen minutes, with no movement anywhere in the body.[115]

Shree Rajneesh has fashioned a Nāda-Yoga technique for couples involving "sexual" elements rarely found in the classical Yoga texts:

Sit facing one another, with your hands crossed, and holding your partner's two hands. Cover yourself with a bedsheet so that the two bodies are completely covered. It is best if no clothing be worn at all. The room should be fairly dark, with four small candles providing the only light. Burn incense. The same incense should be burning every night, and this particular incense should be used only when this technique is being practiced. Facing one another, with your hands crossed and clasped, close your eyes and begin humming. Continue your humming for a minimum of thirty minutes. The humming should be done together. After a minute or two, your breathing will begin to be in unison and the humming in unison. As you hum, feel your energies merging with one another, uniting.[116]

Emphasizing the use of sacred sound for Tibetan Buddhist meditation, the well-known Western initiate Lama Govinda has indicated subtle connections between *Om* and the syllable *Hūṁ* in a recent exposition: "Om is the ascent toward universality, Hūṁ the descent of the state of universality into the depth of the human heart.... Om is the infinite; but Hūṁ is the infinite in the finite, ... In other words, we must have passed through the experience of Om in order to reach and to understand the still deeper experience of Hūṁ."[117] Though any actual connection between Rajneesh's "humming" and reciting the syllable *Hūṁ* in Tibetan Yoga is probably unlikely, the linguistic resemblance is arresting.

A "scientific" venture to uncover the secrets of primal speech as Nāda-Brahman resulted in the formation of the Nāda Brahma Institute in Poona, India, during the early 1980s. C. R. Sankaran, founder and former scholar of the Phonetics Laboratory of Deccan College, expressed the purpose of the institute: "We are seeking knowledge, in conjunction with the disciplines of phonetics and music, about the ultimate unit of speech. An investigation into the 'gap' between where consonants end and vowels begin will reveal the dimension of Nāda-Brahman which is perceivable in the four stages or Parā, Paśyantī, Madhyamā, and Vaikharī. This 'hiatus' or interval is also related to perception of objects and brain motor activity."[118] Unfortunately, this project has not garnered sufficient support to warrant continuation of the institute, which had to close a few years ago.

A group of Indian scientists, with assistance from the government of India, have attempted to monitor the effect of Nāda-Brahman meditation on human consciousness by experimentation. The initial assumption regarding the effect of Om recitation, based on a study of the appropriate religious texts, was as follows: "The continuous muttering of Om releases the spiritual energy from the central part of the [cerebral] cortex and the continuous echoing in this region creates the feeling of expansion in and around the regions of the brain and subsides in the brain so that ego-feeling gets merged in the Divine consciousness. When we allow our mind to relax completely our scattered vital energy has a tendency to go to its original source."[119] In the subsequent experiments several groups of "subjects" were subjected to a variety of tests. The conclusion of one study involving motor performance before and after the hearing of Om in different pitches was as follows: "The recitation of Om, in low-pitch gives rise to decreased psycho-motor function while high-pitch Om increases the psycho-motor performance as judged by the capacity to mark dots on the McDougall-Schuster Spot Dotting apparatus."[120] When asked to report their "inner feelings" after Nāda-Yoga meditation another group responded with the following results: "8 out of 10 subjects (i.e., 80%) from the experimental group on Nādānusandhāna reported inner experiences in the form of vibrations felt all over the body or travelling from one part of the body to another part, a feeling 'as if floating in the sky without contact with the earth' which was an unique experience for the first time in their life."[121]

The above examples of modern-day Nāda-Yoga meditation are given only to underscore the continuity and complexity of the tradition of sacred sound as Nāda-Brahman in the Yoga tradition. Due to certain limitations of space, we were able to offer here only a smattering of the more distinctive persons and societies. Many more examples could be included. Indeed, as there are thousands of Yoga teachers and practitioners in India and abroad, a comprehensive head count and categorization remains to be done.

Having laid some of the basic foundations of Nāda-Yoga in the orthodox sense by discussing Patañjali's Yoga, the *Yoga-Upaniṣads*, the Gorakhnāth tradition, the Haṭha-Yoga texts, and some of the musicological literature, we may now discuss the sectarian divisions of theistic Hinduism and their relation to sacred sound. As noted earlier, there have been parallel developments of both linguistic and nonlinguistic sounds in the Nāda-Yoga tradition, accenting the Om recitation and Nāda-Brahman meditation, as well as the divine hearing of various interior sounds of a nonlinguistic nature (namely, musical sounds). As the Hindu sectarian developments regarding sound were built initially upon the Upaniṣadic speculations on Om and Brahman as Śabda-Brahman, yet gradually reshaped by the implicitly Yogic and Āgamic traditions of Nāda-Brahman and Kuṇḍalinī-Yoga, the traditions examined in the following chapters will display these aspects in varying degrees of modification.

Part 2

Theistic Hinduism
Nāda-Brahman as Female Energy

Chapter 4

Śākta-Tantra
Sacred Sound as the Goddess

Nearly all of the sectarian schools of Hinduism have elements of the feminine blended with their teachings, so much so that any discussion of sacred sound in sectarian Hinduism must include an explication of Śākta-Tantra, the esoteric tradition of goddess or female worship. As sacred sound conceived as feminine power constitutes a common denominator in all three major divisions of Hinduism (Vaiṣṇava, Śaiva, Śākta), part 2 will begin with Śākta-Tantra, which focuses primarily on the Goddess (Śakti) as the central image of its worship.

Although traces of goddess worship have been found in the Harappan civilization and the oldest layers of Indian culture, Śākta-Tantra as an isolated group, or in cultic form, is considered to be later than Śaivism and Vaiṣṇavism. Yet the larger portion of what is known as Śāktism is closely related to Śiva and Śaivism, as explained by Teun Goudriaan: "Śāktism, the belief in and worship of the Supreme Principle as a female force or Śakti (accompanied by a male partner, usually Śiva or one of his manifestations) which creates, regulates and destroys the cosmos, as it were grew into maturity under the cover of Śaivism where Śiva holds a similar position."[1]

While there are many subsects devoted to the Goddess and goddess worship, this chapter draws primarily from Śri-Vidyā and Kālī Śākta-Tantra, the two dominant Śākta, or Tantric, traditions in India. Śrī-Vidyā includes the traditions surrounding the Goddess in her benign form of Tripurasundarī, worshipped from Kashmir in the North to Tamil Nadu in the South. The Kālī tradition represents the major Śākta vein in northeast India (Bengal) and depicts the goddess Kālī as terrifying. In each of these two Śākta divisions the reliance on the philosophy and practice of sacred sound as Nāda-Brahman is paramount. Before discussing Śrī-Vidyā and Kālī Śākta-Tantra traditions in detail, however, some general issues related to Śākta-Tantra need to be clarified.

The term *tantra* (n. "loom, warp, system, framework"; from *tan,* "to stretch or to weave") can refer to basically any kind of tradition or textual continuity, yet for most purposes it signifies an emphasis on the female dimension of the divine. Thus, Śaktism as a basic term is generally assumed to be "Tantric": "There are no Śākta texts that are not Tantric. . . . Śākta ideology is . . . fundamentally inherent to Tantrism."[2]

Tantrism, as a field of study, has received unfavorable reception due to prejudice and misunderstanding both in India and the West, especially since it was often associated with licentious and amoral practices. The current status of Tantric studies has been steadily improving, however, since the pioneering work of Arthur Avalon, otherwise known as Sir John Woodroffe (1865–1936). His collaboration with Bengali pandits such as Swami Pratyagātmānanda Sarasvatī and Atul Behari Ghosh provided the scholarly world with a series of edited Sanskrit texts of the Tantras known simply as *Tāntrik Texts* (Calcutta, 1933). The study of the Tantras became grudgingly respectable, rising above the previous stigma of being an endless desert of "nonsense, lust, and superstition." "Thanks chiefly to the enlightened and fruitful labors of the Agama Anusandhana Samiti, of which Sir John Woodroffe and Atul Behari Ghosh were the leading lights, the investigation of the philosophy, religion, and practice of the Tantra-Śāstra is no longer under a ban."[3] Several of Woodroffe's books and articles are among the first English explanations—the first by a non-Asian—of the Tantric theories of sacred sound (see bibliography). Having access to important texts such as the *Śāradā-tilaka-Tantra, Kulārṇava-Tantra,* and *Mahānirvāṇa-Tantra,* he provided the academic world with unique descriptions of the cosmic processes of sound, the origin of the Sanskrit alphabet, and the yogic methods of mantra meditation which are sacrosanct to many of the Tantric sects.

The study of Tantrism has increased in recent times.[4] Beside the works of Sir John Woodroffe in the early part of this century, the Bengali savant Gopinath Kaviraj has produced numerous studies on Tantrism, including some on sacred sound. Under his guidance several new Indian scholars began working in the field. Umesha Mishra, for example, wrote an early exposition in English on the Tantric theory of sound. The Navabharat Publishers in Calcutta have begun a series of Tantric works in Bengali script, and several authors have produced new surveys and studies of the literature in English. Other notable Bengali scholars of Tantric traditions are P. C. Bagchi, Chintaharan Chakravarti, Swami Pratyagātmānanda Sarasvatī, Govinda Gopal Mukhopadhyaya, and Ajit Mookerjee. Tantric studies in the West, mostly piloted by Swami Agehananda Bharati, have increased as indicated by the rise of persons associated with the newly formed Society for Tantric Studies. While pursuing the area of Tantrism, however, one must keep in mind that there are still thousands of unpublished manuscripts in libraries in Benares, Gaya, Patna, and Calcutta which require attention before we can accurately assess the depth and extent of the so-called Tantric tradition.

From the creation of the universe to the production of sound in the human body Tantrism stresses the importance of sound as a divine substance and vehicle for salvation, as firmly noted by Dasgupta: "The phenomena of the production of the sound occupy an extremely important position in the development the Tantric ideals." Indeed, Śākta-Tantra assumes that the same movement that has produced the world as macrocosm is represented within the human body in miniature as microcosm in the production of the sound: "Tantra [has]... the assumption that man and the universe correspond as microcosm and macrocosm and that both are subject to the mysterious power of words and letters."[5] The process of human sound production is, thus, a replica of the cosmic process of creation. Accordingly, the realization of the all-pervading cosmic sound is one of the cardinal points of Śākta-Tantra theology, since humankind is intimately related to the universe at large. The goal in Śākta-Tantra is to bring about a sonically unified consciousness of divine reality, a state wherein language and sound are apprehended for their own sake. That is why a special emphasis is placed upon mantra recitation and the consequent generation of sonic power within the human body or microcosm:

> An infallible means to liberation [,] *mantra* is concentrated thought of great power. It is built upon *śabda* (sound), *nāda* (sound), and *prāṇa* (breath), synonymous of cosmic energy. In gross form *nāda* supports the things of the universe as their soul, in subtle it is represented by the Absolute Goddess. The subtle form is realized in the gross one. So, *mantra*, breathing, *japa*, generate vibrations of *nāda* as soul of the universe. *Nāda-sādhana* (practice of *nāda*) all efficient, is the invaluable discovery of the Tantras. *Nāda* (vibration) and *jñāna* (illumination) are two parallel manifestations of Śakti. One leads to and awakens the other.[6]

Most Śākta, or Tantric, schools view Ultimate Reality as a neuter Brahman. During creation it divides and genderizes itself into male

(Śiva) and female (Śakti). Indeed, Śākta-Tantra conceives of the cosmos as a vast movement toward the polarization of genders, as noted by André Padoux: "All practices and notions constituting the Tantric way correspond to a particular conception of the deity, polarized as masculine and feminine, and of the universe and man, both imbued with this divine power."[7]

Swami Agehananda Bharati further clarifies the Tantric binary universe and stresses the role of the Ultimate neuter Brahman in the entire worldview:

> The Tantric seeker . . . conceptualizes Brahman as the union of the male and female principles; namely, Śiva (benign) and Śakti (energy). In this initial polarity the male stands for the quiescent, for cognition, and for wisdom. The female represents action, conation, and energetic elan. While Śiva and Śakti belong to the general pantheon, they are here transmuted into the cosmic principles of cognition and action. . . . The successful practitioner, while identifying with Śiva if he is male and with Śakti if female, eventually transcends this partial, albeit divine quality to be the Absolute [Brahman].[8]

The homology between the human and the cosmic is especially visible, or audible, in the domain of sacred sound and the divine Word. "The cosmic process and the human process of word, sound, or speech are parallel and homologous. From this central idea ensues the entire impressive development of the metaphysics of the Word, of the phonic and phonetic cosmogonies, and of the practices which are achieved through the use of speech or word, and more specifically through its most efficacious and usable form, the *mantras* and *bījas*. This is essential to Tantrism."[9]

The creation of the universe in Śākta-Tantra is analogous to the process of human reproduction. "Although the Ultimate transcends all duality, the Godhead is conceived as having two aspects, masculine and feminine, whose conjunction, described as a sexual union, is the first and necessary step, within God, toward cosmic evolution, the active principle being the feminine."[10]

Several Tantric cosmogonies describe Nāda-Brahman (cosmic sound) as being the vibration resulting from the sexual act of Śiva and his consort Śakti, a kind of "rumble in the cosmic mattress," as it were. Similar to the primordial vibration, or "pulsation" which is discussed by the Kashmiri Śaiva tradition as "Spanda," this "Nāda vibration" filters down into human speech and activity. In fact, Tantrism views the material universe as an immensely complex web of vibrations and resonances which all originate from a single self-originated point of sound, the "Nāda-Bindu." The assortment of vibrational patterns which make up our world of experience derive from its basic modifications. In spiritual practice these vibrations are to be reversed in order to rediscover and consequently to return to the primordial vibration itself.

Given the pervasiveness of resonances in the world, it follows that the oral, in contrast to the written, nature of language in Śākta-Tantra is of paramount importance. The Tantrics have always considered oral instruction by the guru as indispensable for the aspirant toward mystical realities. In fact, the initiation by a guru, which is mandatory for the performance of Hindu as well as Tantric ritual, involves the granting of one or more oral sound formulas (*mantras*) to the disciple: "No one can perform an orthodox Hindu ritual unless qualified by initiation (*dīkṣā*); and the core of every initiation is the imparting of a *mantra*. . . . Tantrics are admitted by initiation to sects in which each individual strives for salvation and for the acquisition of occult powers by an indissoluble combination of ritual and meditation, in both of which *mantras* are central."[11] Initiation by a guru is duly conceived as a kind of induction into the "world of sound," insofar as the candidate is personally escorted into the sonic dimension of reality.

The entire Tantric worldview is permeated by sonic utterance, or mantra, according to Padoux, and the cornerstone of all Tantric practice is said to be comprised of sacred sound:

> The most characteristic practices are those associated with the use of sacred and ritual formulas, *mantras* and *bījas* (phonic "germs"). These linguistic or phonetic elements—sentences, words, letters, sounds—symbolize spritual entities and are believed to embody the very power of the main deity. Such formulas are used at all times and in all types of Tantric practice, initiatic and religious rites as well as usual duties or activities. There is no life for a Tantric adept . . . without *mantras*. Indeed, Mantra-Śāstra, the teaching of *mantras* is often taken as meaning Tantra-Śāstra, the teaching of the Tantras.[12]

The Śākta-Tantra position regarding language conforms closer to the Varṇavāda scheme of the Mīmāṁsā branch of philosophy, wherein the power, or Śakti, of all linguistic meaning inheres in the separate syllables from which words and sentences are constructed: "Tantric linguistic or metalinguistic speculations depend on those of the Mīmāṁsā."[13] The eternality of language (including signifiers and their particular signifieds) is assumed here as well: "The Tantra agreed with the Mīmāṁsakas that the Śabda as well as its denotation was eternal." Rather than on the sentence meaning as in Sphoṭavāda, the primary focus of Śākta-Tantra is on the letters of the alphabet and their various permutations in terms of mantric utterance: "The Tantra agreed with Mīmāṁsā in holding the Śabda to be of the nature of *varṇas*. They, therefore, naturally thought that the creative force presiding over the Śabda must be held to be the totality of the fifty *varṇas* from *a* to *ha*."[14]

The importance of the human body and its physiological centers is also reflected in this linguistic approach: "These *varṇas* therefore being parts of the creative power were associated with particular conative, cognitive and feeling tendencies and were naturally also connected with corresponding physiological centers which formed the physiological data of these psychological functions." Furthermore, the power of letters is believed to be the same as the power of nature and the world order: "The creative force [the unity of Śiva and Śakti] forming the reality of the *varṇas* is the same as the creative force forming the reality of the world order."[15]

An extremely important primary text for the general discussion of sacred sound as Nāda-Brahman in Śākta-Tantra is the *Śāradā-tilaka-Tantra,* written in the eleventh century A.D. by Lakṣmaṇa Deśika, a Kashmiri Tantric of the Śrī-Vidyā tradition. The text is replete with over ten commentaries, the most famous of which was written by Rāghavabhaṭṭa in A.D. 1494. Lakṣmaṇa Deśika is sometimes said to have been the disciple of Vidyāraṇya, a renowned teacher in Śaṅkara's line during the Vijayanagara empire (ca. A.D. 1336), which would place him in the fourteenth century. Most accounts, however, render him a student of Utpala, the tenth-century Kashmiri Śaivite theoretician. There does not seem to be firm resolution on this issue. Nonetheless, the *Śāradā-tilaka-Tantra* remains a seminal work for the Śākta-Tantra tradition, providing a source and precedent for the ritual portions of such well-known compendiums of Śākta mythology as the *Devī-Bhāgavatam.*[16]

The opening verses of the *Śāradā-tilaka-Tantra* (1.7–8) describe the process of cosmic creation as a kind of sequential "unpacking" of Nāda,[17] Bindu, and Bīja:

> The starting point is the Sat-cit-ānanda attribute-possessing (*saguṇa*) Parameśvara. From Parameśvara Śakti is produced. . . . From Śakti comes Nāda, i.e., the nasal sound represented by a semicircle and here put apparently for unmanifested sound. From Nāda comes Bindu, i.e., the dot representing *anusvāra*. This Bindu possesses the qualities of the highest Śakti and is itself made up of three parts, viz., Bindu, Nāda, and Bīja. From the division of this highest Bindu, sound is produced. Sound which is thus created takes shape in letters and words. Letters and words form *mantras;* hence *mantras* incarnate, as it were, the power of Śakti, which is the power of Parameśvara.[18]

The next verse (1.9) reveals to us the role of Nāda-Brahman as the link between the two genders: "Bindu is the part in which the Śiva-aspect is predominant, while in Bīja Śakti prevails. In Nāda, however, the elements of Śiva and Śakti are of equal strength [*tayor mithaḥ*]."[19] The terms *tayor mithaḥ,* "the linking of the two"—namely, the male Śiva with the female Śakti—express the vibration resulting from the sexual coition of Śiva and Śakti. This may be roughly compared to the role of the Logos in Neoplatonism, wherein Plotinus (A.D. 205-270), the chief architect of Neoplatonism, regarded the Logos as an intermediate force or activity that connected all the elements of the cosmos, especially soul and nous.

Umesha Mishra has explained the manifestation of Nāda within the human body according to the Śākta-Tantra view. His description is in general agreement with most of the schools of thought thus far examined:

> Though this Nāda is all-pervading (*sarvagata*), it is manifested only in the Mūlādhāra—a mystic center of spiritual energy supposed to be located at the base of the spinal column—by a peculiar type of rarified air (*saṁskṛta-pavana*) generated on the spot. . . . This Nāda, in course of further manifestation, rises up to the navel and assumes a distinct character when it is known as Paśyantī. . . . When the same rarified air rises up and reaches the heart, there is another manifestation of the Śabda-Brahman, known as Madhyamā. . . . When the Vāyu [air], passing through

the Suṣumnā, reaches the cranium (*mūrdhana*), as the way to the above is generally closed for lack of intuitive knowledge, it turns back and finds a way out, through our mouth. In the mouth there are various places, such as larynx (*kaṇṭha*), palate, tooth, etc., which the air touches in passing and where it gives rise to ordinary sound called Vaikharī.[20]

Nāda-Brahman, as feminine Śakti, manifests within the bodies of the syllables (*varṇa*) and is understood to be present there in her form of "Little Mothers," or *mātṛkās*: "The creative force of the universe, which, . . . was identified with the *varṇas* or letters, was placed in diverse parts of the body. This creative power, the mother of the universe, in its aspect as being identified with the *varṇas* or letters was called *mātṛkā*. Her self was formed of the fifty letters from *a* to *ha*."[21] As explained in chapter 2, the energy centers (Cakras) within the body are repositories for the various letters of the alphabet and, thus, harbor the accumulated *mātṛkās* on their respective lotus petals.

The way in which the adept utilizes the creative forces of language is through the science of mantra, which has its unique status within Tantrism. In Tantrism a fundamental mantra is a single syllable, which commonly ends in a nasal M, or sometimes K or Ṭ. A complex mantra is made up of a series of syllables to form a phrase, which often has meaning. The syllables are pure sounds in their own right, the best known of course being the ancient Vedic Om. Other important syllables are the first syllables of the names of a deity. A Tantric mantra in the form of a syllable is, thus, a very compact form of the god or power that it "is" in essence. A single mantra may focus the energy of a deity into a grosser or more bodily representation. The heart mantra, for example, is known as HRĪṀ and is based on the Sanskrit word *hṛdaya* for heart, used when the heart energy of a deity is to be evoked. RAṀ is the mantra of fire. The syllable KLĪṀ denotes the energy of sexual union. In other words, "just as Bindu is the compact form of Nāda, a *mantra* is the condensed form of a deity or force."[22]

In further clarification Agehananda Bharati offers a strict linguistic definition of the Tantric idea of mantra and stresses the esoteric nature of its structure and transmission: "A *mantra* is a quasi-morpheme or a series of quasi-morphemes, or a series of mixed genuine and quasi-morphemes arranged in conventional patterns, based on codified esoteric traditions, and passed on from one preceptor to one disciple in the course of a prescribed initiation ritual."[23]

The creation of resonances by the utterance of mantra is an important oral feature of language which is exploited to the fullest extent within the Śākta-Tantra tradition. Mantras are believed to create their own special kind of resonance in space, in the realm of subtle sound or vibration, called Nāda. Since everything in the creation is held to be a complex web of resonances, the mantra user is aware of the immense power at his or her disposal. And the feminine quality of resonance or sound is coterminous with the deeper recesses of a person's being as Śakti.

The multiplication of the cosmic root vibration (Nāda-Brahman) constitutes the string, or garland, of letters that make up the Sanskrit alphabet, itself an object of extreme reverence due to its being intertwined "warp and woof" with all of creation. The notion of the garland of letters (*varṇa-mālā*) appears in the *Śāradā-tilaka-Tantra* possibly for the first time. Near the end of the first chapter, wherein the cosmogonic features of sound are proclaimed, the gradual extension of the original cosmic sound is termed *varṇa-mālā*, or the "necklace of letters," and is analogous to the goddess Kuṇḍalī residing at the base of the spine in the Mūlādhāra-Cakra. This concept formed the title of Sir John Woodroffe's (Arthur Avalon) well-known book on the study of Mantra-Sastra, in which he translates this passage (1.104–5).

Though the *Śāradā-tilaka-Tantra* is believed to be a text celebrating the goddess Tripurasundarī, Woodroffe also identifies the garland of letters with the garland of severed heads surrounding the head of the goddess Kālī.[24] This is understandable in that Kālī and Tripurasundarī share the common identification of each being one of the ten Mahā-Vidyās, or "Great Śaktis." The textual sources, however, do not provide a clear picture of when and how either of these two goddesses took up the role of being a wearer of the garland of letters. Though some additional discussion is given to this in the following section on Kālī, it remains a task for scholars to determine an accurate genealogy of this notion.

The fifty letters making up the garland are said to be distributed over the six Cakra energy centers located along the spinal column. The *Ṣaṭcakra-Nirūpaṇa* (v. 4–32), a definitive text on Kuṇḍalinī-Yoga written by Pūrṇānanda Swami in A.D. 1577, describes each Cakra in terms of a specific number of lotus petals with their corresponding Sanskrit letters.[25]

The distribution of the Sanskrit letters over these energy centers forms the substance of a number of esoteric initiations known as *dīkṣā*. The *Śāradā-tilaka-Tantra* (5.121–32) describes a *dīkṣā*, which is said to be the highest type, and which incorporates all the elements of *varṇa,* Nāda, and Bindu: "The highest form of *dīkṣā* is the Vedhamayī, the *dīkṣā* of the penetration (*vedha*). It liberates the pupil from the *saṁsāra* [material world] and gives divine awakening and understanding of all things." The guru first meditates on the pupil's Mūlādhāra-Cakra then gathers the corresponding four letters from there and unites him with the Svādhiṣṭhāna-Cakra. Thereafter, the guru takes the letters BHA through LA and unites the disciple to the next Cakra, and so on. After each Cakra is penetrated and all the letters are gathered up "the guru takes these . . . letters together in the Bindu (Śiva) and unites him with the Kalā. . . . The guru unites the Kalā with the Nāda. The guru unites the Nāda with the Nādānta (having the Nāda as end) [*taṁ nāde 'nantaraṁ nādam nādānte yojayed guruḥ*]. The guru unites the Nādānta with the Unmanī, the supreme transcendent energy, one with Śiva and quasi-identical with him."[26]

A slightly similar process of Nāda initiation is found in Abhinavagupta's *Tantrāloka* (29.240–44), wherein the guru first penetrates the disciple's Anāhata-Cakra (Heart-Lotus). This has been translated by Lilian Silburn:

> The master first meditates on the eight-spoked center (that of the heart) . . . , dazzled with light. Then, through it, he penetrates into the heart wheel of his disciple. Such is penetration by means of *mantra*. . . . Known as Nāda-Vedha is the piercing brought about by the upward push of the resonance according to the process of creation . . . ; through this spontaneous resonance, let the master enter the disciple's consciousness. This is what is called piercing through mystic resonance.[27]

In other words, after the guru releases the Śakti, or Kuṇḍalinī energy, in the disciple's heart via mantra this female energy in the form of Nāda pierces each succeeding Cakra until the pupil attains the supreme state.

On a macrocosmic level the *Śārada-tilaka-Tantra* (7.9–14) describes the world as a cosmic tree (body) consisting of a complex network, or "intricate mesh," of Sanskrit letters, which are said to be the "root vibrations" of the material creation, maintenance, and destruction of the universe. Madhu Khanna offers a partial translation as follows:

> The entire physical universe, composed of the five elements (earth, water, fire, air, ether), is represented by a set of sound combinations on the various parts of the world-tree. Its seed is the self-creating original principle; its tap roots are cosmic "location" and vibration (Bindu and Nāda) that spring from the eternal male and female principles; its branches are composed of letters that denote the earth element; its leaves that spread over the three worlds are made up of letters that stand for the water element; its shoots, bright as "gems," are made up of the letter combinations that denote the element fire; the flowers of the tree are represented by the letters of the air element and the fruits of the tree by the letters representing ether. . . . Virtually every aspect of the physical world, including the solar system with its planets and stars, is symbolically represented by mantric equations.[28]

The practice of mantra meditation, often called Puraścaraṇa in Śākta-Tantra, is conceived as a gradual regressive process whereby the aspirant attempts to "merge" back with the original cosmic Sound, or vibration, and thus into the unified Brahman. "The point at which consciousness touches the ultimate through sound comes at the end of the long-drawn, skull-penetrating vocalization of this seed-*mantra* of the cosmos [Om], the sharpest vibration of the nasal hum with which Om concludes, written in the Sanskrit alphabet as a dot. Here merges the points of sound and light, indescribably fine and small, but also comprehending the whole world of manifested things in cosmic history."[29]

Govinda Gopal Mukhopadhyaya described in a recent interview the process that takes place in the meditative practice of *japa,* wherein this cosmic sound (Nāda) gets released within the heart or mind of the aspirant due to the "melting" of the concrete letters themselves:

> Generally the guru gives you a *mantra* consisting of a few words or syllables. The words which we get from the lips of an ordinary person, and which are heard by us through our ears, are looked upon as words in the most crude form, and are termed *vaikharī.*

They are generated through the sense apparatus. However, they can help us to realize the supreme spiritual essence or reality. The masters explain that we are on the *sthūla* [gross] level, but the guru or teacher conveys the essence which is of the nature of pure light or *jyoti*—or you can call it fire. He conveys it only through a carrier [*mantra*], because otherwise he won't be able to hold it, or seize it; it will immediately burn him. This is also the meaning of the term or word *bhārga* as found in the Gāyatrī-Mantra. The root meaning of the word is that which burns everything. Now the disciple, having received this original fire or pure flame through a covering [*mantra*], has to break open the shell in order to get in touch with the power or flame. The masters explain that the original nature of the *mantra* is Nāda, which you call the flowing sound which had become congealed or concretized in the so-called letters of the alphabet. Now, we generally go on repeating or pronouncing these letters. This is called *japa*; but the main purpose of *japa*—continued repetition or muttering, whatever you may call it—is to kindle or arouse the fire which in the Tantras is called *kuṇḍalinī*. And, as these hard or concretized letters begin to melt, the aspirant or *sādhaka* begins to hear the Nāda. The words melt, leaving only a continuous flow of sound in the consciousness or experience of the aspirant. This is what the masters call the *mantra-caitanya,* or the innate conscious power inhering in the *mantra*. So Nāda is the most convincing sign or proof of the dawning of true consciousness, and as such holds a very important position in *mantra-vijñāna,* or the science of *mantras*. We can also call it the bridge or connecting principle between the material and the spiritual realms, because this continuous unbroken flow of sound, that is Nāda, ultimately takes the aspirant to the Bindu, or the real source of consciousness. In the process of creation, this very Bindu bursts forth; and then again we have Nāda, which ultimately comes down to the material level to become cold inert letters or material things. So, both from the aspect of ascent and descent, dissolution as well as creation, this Nāda plays a very vital role.[30]

In an earlier article Mukhopadhyaya had analyzed the aspect of "heat" in mantra recitation by locating it within specific phonetic sounds and also contrasting it with the "cooling," or "soothing" effect of other letters. This is depicted by recourse to the Vedic names of Agni (the God of fire) and Soma (the God of nectar, which is also prominent in the Gorakhnāth tradition): "The Agni-mātra or the heating or charging factor is encased primarily in the letter 'r'... or *visarga;* and the Soma-mātra is contained in 'ṁ' or *anusvāra* or *candra-bindu*.... These two principles—Agni and Soma—should be recognized in Nāda and Bindu respectively." This means that the initial utterance (especially of r) of the mantra, with its expansion and elongation, result in the heating effect, while the gradual compression and diminishing of the tone produces the soothing effect, which ultimately leads to the merging of consciousness into the Bindu point.

The inner "dialectical" motion of this recitation sets up an inertia, which thus continues onward by itself: "As we cross the level of Vaikharī or outer speech and enter the level of Madhyamā, the middle or intermediate level of subtle sound, we feel that we are no longer doing the *japa* ourselves but it is going on automatically in spite of our remaining inactive or otherwise engaged.... The cold letters of the *mantra* get molten here into a flowing sound (Nāda), which goes on uninterrupted till it reaches its source or point of origin (Bindu)."[31] A sexual metaphor is further suggested. As the heated conjugal act of Śiva and Śakti releases Nāda, the heat generated by the sound of the letters releases Nāda from the mouth: "The two lips are Śiva and Śakti. The movement in utterance is the coition (*maithunā*) of the two."[32]

On a comparative note the Gnostics in classical Greece developed various kinds of vowel and word mysticism. Within their theology and ritual scholars have detected "extended sequences of vowels and cryptic divine names which break abruptly into the petitions and doxologies of the initiatory prayers.... in certain Gnostic writings and in the magical papyri, where sequences of vowels and *nomina sacra*—attributed on one occasion to Hermes Trismegistes himself—are used to invoke gods and concentrate divine powers."[33] A particular selection from the magical papyri is applicable: "Ultimately the initiate says to each of the cosmic elements the whole string of vowels, and ends by invoking the God as the cosmos: *o uu ooo aaa eeeee eeeeee iiiiiii.* The initiate here is called upon to enact with his body and with his voice the entire cosmic scheme."[34]

The mechanical recitation of sacred sounds in Hinduism, known as *japa,* requires the use of the rosary, or *akṣa-mālā* (*akṣa* signifying the entire alphabet of fifty letters beginning with *a,* and ending with *kṣa*). Whereas in the Vedic and early Upaniṣadic period mantra was recited without any external aid, in Śākta-Tantrism, and in Hinduism generally, mantra recitation, or *japa*, is most effective with the use of rosary beads. One of the so-called *Śaiva-Upaniṣads*, the *Akṣamālikā-Upaniṣad* (v. 16), emphasizes the importance of the performance of *japa* with the rosary: "The Upanishad clearly states that any *mantra*, when recited as *japa* with the aid of rosary of *akṣa* beads, becomes efficacious at once."[35]

The practice of counting beads during prayer or petition is well known to Westerners primarily through the Roman Catholic church, which recognizes the bestowal of the rosary from the Blessed Virgin Mary to St. Dominic in twelfth-century Spain. A Jesuit Indologist of this century who researched the subject admitted, however, that "the original invention of the rosary is due to India." The nature of the Hindu rosary beads, and the procedure of counting are outlined by him:

> The rosary should consist of fifty-one beads [either denoting the fifty letters of the Sanskrit alphabet plus a "head bead" or the inclusion of a fifty-first letter, an obscure "Vedic LR"], made of coral, pearl, crystal, conch, silver, gold, sandalwood, *putrajīva*, lotus seeds, and *rudrākṣa* seeds [some obscure Śākta sects have been known to use dead men's teeth]. The rosary of fifty-one beads is to be conceived of as having the import of the fifty-one letters along with their respective *mantras*. . . . The movement of the rosary is always from left to right [the same direction as when circumambulating a temple] when we hold a rosary bead between the thumb and middle finger [of our right hand].[36]

The rosary itself is normally concealed, either under a cloth or contained within a small cloth pouch suspended from the neck or attached directly to the forearm.

A more recent treatment of Tantric practices describes *japa* as "one of the most important elements of Tantric ritual. . . . The only concrete object needed to carry out this ritual repetition of the *mantra* is the rosary, which is very carefully chosen and consecrated. . . . After each round [of chanting], on reaching the *meru* [the center bead], one must not cross over it, but must turn back and retrace the order of the beads. This means that instead of turning the rosary circularwise it is moved forwards and backwards."[37]

According to the sect or division of Hinduism, the rosary beads, as well as the Praṇava, are given certain symbolism. The terminology of Śākta Sound ideology persists, such that the Bījas (letters or beads, seeds) are woven together by the string of Nāda, with a knot (Bindu) ascribed to each one: "A garland of flowers or a rosary of beads is its symbol, where Nāda is the string or thread, the flowers or beads are the *varṇa*-elements or Kalā, and Bindu is the knot that holds them all."[38] *Japa* is indeed performed with a myriad of symbolism attached to nearly every detail, encouraging the aspirant at each step to focus his attention on the salvific vibration.

Regarding the Praṇava, in Vedānta philosophy the fourth *mātra* of A U M was sometimes termed *ardha-mātra*, meaning "half-degree or stage." In the Tantric philosophy the word *ardha* is redefined to encompass the newly discovered or "penetrated" realm of Nāda-Brahman: "The power or Śakti that evolves as such Nāda, Kalā and Bindu from primary Vāk or Logos or Magnum Matrix is Ardha-candra. . . . Ardha-candra is the Mother Divine Herself 'asleep' at our basic center as Kuṇḍalinī. She evolves the cycle of Bindu, Nāda and Kalā for our ascent and when the ultimate *meru* (critical point) is passed, She merges the seeker in the bottomless and shoreless sea of Self-realization. . . . '*Ardha*' from *vṛdh* = to grow, evolve and involve. So it is not 'half.'"[39] The purpose of *japa* is thus to "advance" the consciousness of the votary into newer and higher dimensions of existence by coming in touch with the cosmic sound, or Nāda-Brahman. The linguistic dimensions of *japa*—wherein the syllables, or phonemes, of a mantra have resolute meaning despite slight variations in pronunciation during their extended repetition—have not been sufficiently studied.

The practice of a certain type of *dhikr* in Islam is much like the practice of *japa* in Hinduism, employing as it does the rosary beads for recitation of divine names (99) and being transmitted through a closely guarded system of initiation, awarding a life of bliss in heaven:

> Besides being an excellent means of inducing a sort of ecstatic state, the *dhikr* was also recommended to the faithful as a means of obtaining heavenly reward. . . . The fact that God [Allah] has been described in the Koran as possessing the most beautiful names forms the basis for a whole theology of the divine names. . . . The usual collection of these names of glorification comprises ninety-nine names. The Greatest Name is hidden, but

many a mystic has claimed that he possesses it and that it enables him to perform every kind of miracle. . . . The rosary, with its thirty-three or ninety-nine beads, is used for counting the names. . . . The rules for the use of this or that divine name at a certain moment have been carefully laid down by the Sufi leaders.[40]

In an effort to underscore the importance of *japa* in Hinduism, wherein one particular mantra is repeated almost ad infinitum, Wade Wheelock in a recent article has contrasted the Vedic and Tantric use of mantras. He notes that,

> Instead of repeating many different *mantras* [as in Vedic ritual], the Tantric worshipper reaches the climax of the performance [of *pūjā*, ritual worship] by repeating one *mantra* many times. The Tantric *mantras* take on many forms and perform many ritual functions. . . . However, the end to which they all point is one and the same—realization of identity with the deity. At this point, the *mantra* is no longer a means to an end, it is a manifestation of the goal itself.[41]

After having delineated some of the general patterns of Śākta-Tantra related to sacred sound, we now focus on the specific textual and practical aspects of the two major branches, Śrī-Vidyā and Kālī Śākta-Tantra.

Śrī-Vidyā

The predominant form of Śākta-Tantra in India is the Śrī-Vidyā, or Śrī-Cakra, school. It is also the most sophisticated one regarding sacred sound. Though presently flourishing in south India, it is said to have originated in Kashmir. The tradition of Śrī-Vidyā "rose to eminence in Kashmir during the eleventh century . . . [and] by the twelfth century, had spread to the Tamil country."[42] The cult of Śrī-Vidyā worships the benign goddess Lalitā, Tripurā, or Tripurasundarī. "Tripurasundarī is the foremost benign, beautiful and youthful, yet motherly manifestation of the Supreme Śakti. Her *sampradāya* [tradition] . . . , although presumably not the oldest, seems to have been systematized at a relatively early date [eleventh to twelfth century A.D.]. . . . Its [subsequent] theoreticians seem to have often belonged to the Śaṅkara-Sampradāya."[43]

The Śrī-Vidyā tradition is based on several texts, the foremost being the *Vāmakeśvara-Tantra* (compromising the *Nitya-ṣoḍaśikārṇava* and *Yoginī-hṛdaya-Tantra* composed before the ninth century A.D.), *Tantrarāja-Tantra, Jñānārṇava-Tantra, Śakti-saṅgama-Tantra* (ca. sixteenth century), *Vidyārṇava-Tantra, Saundarya-Laharī,* and *Kāma-kalā-Vilāsa*. The "Vedic" Śrī-Sūkta,[44] three liturgical works by Śivānanda (ca. A.D. 1225–75); the digest known as *Śāradā-Tilaka*; and several of the so-called *Śākta-Upaniṣads* (*Tripurā-tāpinī-Upaniṣad, Tripurā-Upaniṣad, Bhāvana-Upaniṣad,*[45] and *Bahvṛk-Upaniṣad*), are also important works in the canon.[46]

The Tantric axiom "Mantra and Devatā are the same" is indeed exemplified in the Śrī-Vidyā tradition by its assumption about language itself: "In Śrī-Vidyā ideology, there is no disparate existence of signifying sound (*vācaka*) and the signified object (*vācya*); and the expressing consciousness and the expressed energy are fundamentally one. The universe of experience . . . is nothing other than the expressive sounds that constitute the alphabet. . . . The 36 letters (15 vowels taken as one, and the consonants 35) of the alphabet correspond to the 36 principles (*tattvas*) that underlie the constitution and function of the universe."[47] To support this the *Kāmakalā-Vilāsa* (12) emphatically states: "Word (*vāk*) and its meaning (*artha*) are always united. They are Śiva and Śakti."[48]

The Śrī-Vidyā-Mantra, the Pañcadaśī, consists of fifteen syllables—KA E I LA HRĪṀ, HA SA KA HA LA HRĪṀ, SA KA LA HRĪṀ—and is said to symbolically derive from verse 32 of the *Saundarya-Laharī,* a Śākta text traditionally, but perhaps wrongly, ascribed to Śaṅkara. This mantra is also held to have been introduced by the legendary sage Kāmarāja, with another version, beginning with HA, introduced by a princess named Lopamudrā. The translation of verse 32 of the *Saundarya-Laharī* runs as follows: "O Mother! Śiva, Śakti, Kāma and Kṣiti; and then, Ravi, Śītakiraṇa, Smara, Haṁsa and Śakra; and thereafter, Parā, Māra and Hari; these (three sets of) syllables, when conjoined severally at their ends with the three Hṛllekhās [HRĪṀ's], become the components of Thy name."[49]

Lakṣmīdhara, the commentator, explains the formation of the Śrī-Vidyā-Mantra: "The stanza merely mentions fifteen conventional names indicative of syllables, which, when construed in the proper way, would yield the following result; Śiva is 'ka'; Śakti represents 'e'; Kāma, 'i'; Kṣiti, 'la'; this is the first *khaṇḍa*. Ravi is 'ha'; Śītakiraṇa, 'sa'; Smara, 'ka'; Haṁsa, 'ha'; and Śakra, 'la'; this is the second *khaṇḍa*. Parā is 'sa'; Māra, 'ka'; and Hari, 'la'; this is the third *khaṇḍa*. When the Hṛllekhā, i.e., 'hrīṁ,' is added to each of the three *khaṇḍas*, the result is the Pañcadaśākṣarī-Mantra."[50] In concordance with the above theory of language this mantra is believed to be the mother goddess Tripurasundarī herself: "Pañcadaśī (or Ṣoḍaśī [sixteenth], with the addition of another seed-letter ŚRĪṀ) is not merely the *mantra* of the Mother-Goddess; it is itself the Mother-Goddess."[51]

The addition of the sixteenth syllable, ŚRĪṀ, is part of the more esoteric teaching of the Śrī-Vidyā, which is concerned with lunar correspondences and only muttered and transmitted in secret. The letters of the mantra indeed reflect the phases of the moon: "The moon signifying the collective power of 15 vowels tending towards the final unmodified nasal. . . . The moon's parallelism with the 15 vowels taken collectively is derived from the fact that the moon has 15 phases (*tithi*) during each fortnight, the 16th phase being transcendental and unchanging."[52] The mantra has also been made to accord with the words of the Vedic Gāyatrī-Mantra in *Tripurā-tāpanī-Upaniṣad* (1).

As indicated, there are three sections (*kūṭa*) of the Śrī-Vidyā-Mantra, each ending with the syllable *HRĪṀ*. This syllable signifies both Śakti as well as the union of Śiva and Śakti, replaces the Vedic *Om*, and provides a unity to the otherwise manifold nature of syllabic vocalization in the Tantric tradition:

> HRĪṀ is an especially sacred syllable representing the mother-goddess herself. . . . A second explanation is also given; HA stands for Śiva, RA for Śakti, and I for their union resulting in utter tranquility. . . . This seed-syllable, which is extensively employed in Tantric rituals, is described as the Tantric equivalent of the Vedic Om (*tāntrika-praṇava*). It gives the sense of completion; the letters in each unit of the *mantra* are separate by themselves (*vyasti*), but the employment of HRĪṀ at the joints (*kūṭa*) transforms them into a unity (*samasti*).[53]

The power of this mantra is fathomed primarily in its oral form, which is said to be bristling with various energies:

> The terminal sound M̐ (*bindu, anusvāra*) has along with it the crescent moon (*ardha-candra*) and the invisible powers (*rodhinī*,

> *nāda, nādānta, śakti*), which are present only when the seed-syllable is articulated, and not when written. This complex seed-syllable is identified with the supreme mother-goddess (*para-devatā*), whose presence and power are sought to be packed into the *mantra*. The import of each preceding letter is imagined as flowing into the succeeding one, and the imports of the entire series to coalesce in the terminal HRĪṀ.

The immediate sources of power for the consonants themselves are the vowel sounds: "The vowels are said to provide power (Śakti) to the consonants, which are in the nature of mere seeds (*bīja*)... [which]... transform these ordinary letters into the mother-like *mātṛkā* condition."[54]

The soteriological function of the Śrī-Vidyā-Mantra becomes clear as it is identified with the stream of internal sound normally termed Nāda in Śākta-Tantra: "The Pañcadaśī with the above three *kūṭas* are to be regarded as the stream of sound that rises from the basal Mūlādhāra center and goes right up to the thousand-petalled lotus on the crown of the devotee's head. This sound passes through the three 'peaks' (*kūṭas*) symbolized by the sound HRĪṀ, as a thread through three beads of a rosary."[55]

Regarding the *japa* of the Śrī-Vidyā-Mantra, the last chapter of the *Yoginī-hṛdaya-Tantra* contains this curious description, as paraphrased by Padoux:

> The three parts of this *mantra* are visualized as being present in three of the Cakras of the subtle body (placed at different points along the spine of the material body). They are then drawn upwards by the ascending movement of their pronunciation (*uccāra*) which is linked to the cosmic and human movement of "breath" (*prāṇa*). This ascending thrust of the phonic energy of the *mantra* carries upwards the Kuṇḍalinī and culminates in its immobilization at the highest point of both verbal pronunciation and the subtle body. The worshipper is then fused with the Supreme Reality, pure bliss, the "ocean without waves" of the transcendental divinity concealing within itself the totality of cosmic appearances of which it is the source and the foundation.[56]

Schematically, the first section, KA E I LA HRĪṀ, is juxtaposed with the Mūlādhāra, Svādhiṣṭhāna, Maṇipūra, and Anāhata Cakras.

The second section, HA SA KA HA LA HRĪṀ, corresponds to the Viśuddha and Ājñā Cakras. The third and final section, SA KA LA HRĪM, terminates in the Sahasrāra (thousand-petaled lotus). In the upward direction these three sections also reflect the three cosmic processes of creation (*sṛṣṭi*), preservation (*sthiti*), and dissolution (*saṁhāra*), respectively.[57] These correlations are actually not surprising, as the Cakras are also mentioned throughout the *Saundarya-Laharī* (see specifically vv. 36–41), an alleged source of the Śrī-Vidyā-Mantra itself.[58]

Although the term *Nāda* is not within the text of the *Saundarya-Laharī*, it appears throughout the commentaries. In the very first verse, for example, where the unity of Śiva and Śakti is stressed, the commentator Kameśvara-sūrī (ca. sixteenth century) says the following: "Only when brought into union with the Śakti ('A' with ' ़ '), would Śiva (the dyad of 'U' and 'M') acquire the power of assuming the form of Praṇava, the embodied form of Nāda, etc., assuming the stages of Parā, Paśyantī, etc., wherefrom originate the Svaras, Varṇas, Padas and Vākyas galore. If not, the Deva (the dyad of 'U' and 'M') becomes utterly incapable of producing the Praṇava, becoming dumb-founded."[59] Recent studies of the Śrī-Vidyā *japa* practice has revealed a correlation between three types of *japa*, which are all performed using rosary beads, and the three stages of sound (Vaikharī, Madhyamā, and Paśyantī) enunciated by Bhartṛhari:

> In *vācika-japa* [audible repetition] the *mantras* are repeated with the intake of outer air. This is equated with Vaikharī-Vāk, articulated speech, pronounced when the breath strikes different places of articulation. Here there is complete differentiation of the word and its meaning. In the *upāṁśu-japa* [low intonation] the intake of air is considerably reduced. . . . This represents Madhyamā-Vāk, which is less gross than Vaikharī but differentiated. Madhyamā which lies midway between Vaikharī and Paśyantī is apprehended by the mind. In the *mānasa-japa* [silent, mental repetition] the air intake is at its minimum and the *japa* is repeated effortlessly and spontaneously. At this stage the *japa* begins to coalesce with the subtle plane of speech, the Paśyantī-Vāk, which is not subject to the movement of vital breath. Hence, it represents the fusion of word and its meaning and is devoid of every kind of differentiation.[60]

The Śri-Vidyā *japa* practice is meant to accompany meditation on the Śrī-Cakra, the famous *yantra*, or visual diagram composed of nine intersecting triangles within a lotus flower design. "The concomitant recitation (*japa*) of the Śrī-Vidya is meant to accompany a localization of the elements of the Śrī-Cakra in an ascending direction in three centers of the mystic body combined with a mental penetration into ever subtler recesses of the syllable Om."[61] In images reminiscent of the Gorakhnāth tradition the Śrī-Vidyā meditation scenario posits a kind of flooding or bursting of consciousness wherein the elixir of immortality overcomes the aspirant in a state of ecstasy: "The Kuṇḍalinī power is thus starved, and so rises up like a serpent, pierces through the three knots (*granthi*), and entering the thousand-petalled lotus on the crown (Sahasrāra), bites the moon that is lócated in the center of this lotus. The nectar that oozes out of the bitten moon floods the lunar orb that is situated on the top of the Ājñā center (between the eyebrows). Then the entire body is flooded by the flow of nectar."[62]

One of the most esoteric or secretive traditions of Nāda or Nāda-Brahman is the path of the so-called Praṇava-Śaktis, which are said to lie between the sixth and seventh Cakras.[63] After reaching the Ājñā-Cakra "the Yogī then passes to the region of Bindu, the unmanifest sound and from there to the region of causal sound Nāda. In the Yogī's mystic body this causal stage is visualized to exist between Ājñā-Cakra and Sahasrāra. . . . This region between Ājñā-Cakra and Sahasrāra is divided into eight steps representing the gradual fusion of the sonic and phenomenal emanations leading to the final merger of the individual self into the supreme Energy in Sahasrāra."[64] The names of the ten steps (including Ājñā Cakra and Sahasrāra) are the Ājñā-Cakra, or Bindu, Ardha-Candra, Rodhinī, Nāda, Nādānta, Śakti, Vyāpikā, Samanā, Unmanā, and Sahasrāra, or Mahābindu. The text (ca. ninth century A.D.) known as the *Yoginī-hṛdaya-Tantra* (3.179–82), possibly their earliest source, enumerates these steps (Bindu, Ardha-Candra, Rodhinī, Nāda, Nādānta, Śakti, Vyāpikā, Samanā, and Unmanā) in relation to the three "Kūṭas," the three Kuṇḍalīs (three forms of the goddess Kuṇḍalinī), the three cosmic processes (creation, maintenance, and destruction), and the six Cakras, stressing that Nāda is the only unifying factor among these otherwise diverse features.[65] The commentary by Amṛtānandanāth (fourteenth century A.D.) provides additional insight yet remains reticent about the original source of these structures.

By the eighteenth century these steps had been given visual description in the *Varivasyā-Rahasya* (1.21–26) of Bhāskara Rāya:

Nāda emanating from Mūlādhāra functions as the string passing

> through the several letters, forming with them a composite whole, even as the threads in a piece of cloth. The Bindu, circular in form, shines forth like a lamp (with its seat) in the middle of the forehead. Ardha-Candra having its seat just above that, bears a significant name, both in point of brilliance and form (i.e., shines like and assumes the form of the crescent moon). Rodhinī, which is immediately the next, is triangular in shape and has the brightness of moonshine. Nāda, which resembles the ruby has the appearance of a nerve placed between two eggs (i.e., a vertical line between two zeros). Nādānta has the sheen of lightning and resembles a plough with a Bindu attached to the left. Śakti resembles a nerve rising out of the left of two juxtaposed Bindus. Vyāpikā is said to have the form of a Bindu and a triangle with its apex resting thereon. Samanā has the form of two Bindus placed one above the other, with a line connecting them. The same, shorn of the upper Bindu, is Unmanā. Above this lies Mahābindu.[66]

Bhāskara Rāya mentions these same steps in his commentary on the *Lalitā-Sahasranāma* (2.70, no. 299), wherein the name for the goddess Lalitā (Tripurasundarī) is Nāda-rūpā ("in the form of sound"): "There are eight notes (*varṇas*) above the Bindu of the syllable HRĪṀ, etc. such as Ardha-Candra, Rodhinī, Nāda, Nādānta, Śakti, Vyāpikā, Samanā, and Unmanī which are subtle, more subtle, and most subtle; of these the third is Nāda. . . . The Supreme Devī, seated on the lap of that (Nāda), leading upward, should be contemplated."[67] Judging from their initial appearance in the *Yoginī-hṛdaya-Tantra,* these steps cannot be said to be a later accretion but, rather, have formed part of the core of the Śākta-Tantra tradition—at least in its Śrī-Vidyā form—from its earliest theological development.[68]

The *Kāmakalā-Vilāsa,* an important yet undated Śrī-Vidyā text of only fifty-five verses by Puṇyānandanāth (ca. thirteenth century A.D.), describes the stages in the phonic emanation of the universe—in a slightly different way than the *Śāradā-tilaka-Tantra*—by recourse to a primordial triangle recalling the basics of Hindu embryology. This triangle, called the Kāmakalā, consists of three Bindus: "The triad Śiva [Paraśiva as Prakāśa]-Śakti [Vimarśa]-Nāda obtained the name Kāmakalā. . . . The Kāmakalā symbolizes the creative nuclei graphically represented by a white and red dot [semen and menstrual flux] which automatically produce a third point of gravity [Miśra Bindu]."[69]

The names Kāma and Kalā, as well as their role in the origin of language, are explained by the *Kāmakalā-Vilāsa* itself (v. 6 and 7): "The two Bindus, white and red, are Śiva and Śakti, who, in their secret mutual enjoyment, are now expanding and now contracting. They are the cause of the creation of word (*vāk*) and meaning (*artha*), now entering and now separating from one another. Bindu which is Ahaṁkāra . . . is the sun which is the union of these two (white and red Bindus). The sun is Kāma, which is so-called because of its desirableness; and Kalā is the two Bindus which are moon and fire."[70]

Furthermore, the role of Nāda-Brahman is emphasized here (v. 9): "From the Red-Bindu about to create arose sound (*ravaḥ*) which is the Nāda-Brahman sprout. From that (sound) came ether, Air, Fire, water, earth, and the letters of the alphabet." Amid the ensuing discussion of lotus petals, letters, Cakras, Bījas, and elements, the mention of the by now well-known four stages of speech is almost expected (v. 32): "Parā, Paśyantī, and Madhyamā in her form or aspect as (the unuttered) gross letters—by these three is produced Vaikharī who is the fifty-one letters of the alphabet."[71]

Among all of the secondary triangles formed out of the nine intersecting triangles in the Śrī-Cakra-Yantra (diagram), the Kāmakalā is the primordial or primary triangle, and is the "immediate evolute of the central point (Bindu). . . . The three corners of the triangle represent three forms of the power of the Mother-Goddess [Kāmeśvarī, Vajreśvarī, and Bhagamālinī]. . . . The three angles of the triangle also represent three forms of speech: Paśyantī, Madhyamā, and Vaikharī. The triangle is therefore called 'Speech-born' (Vāg-bhava)." The stage of Parā, or Parā-Vāk, is portrayed by the central Bindu, marking the ultimate unity of Śiva and Śakti as well as the word AHAM: "Śiva is the Bindu, symbolized by the initial vowel A in the alphabet; Śakti is the Nāda symbolized by the final consonant HA. Their original union is symbolized by the word AHAM. . . . When the Bindu and the Nāda unite, a compound Bindu emerges, bearing pure affinity to the male Śiva as well as the female Śakti."[72] The Kāma or Miśra-Bindu also represents the *anusvāra*, having one dot, while the other two Kalās represent the "two-dotted" *visarga*.

Nearly every conceivable linguistic permutation has been discussed in the texts of the Śrī-Vidyā, which exemplifies the highest degree of sophisticated speculation on the nature and function of sacred sound as Nāda-Brahman.

Goddess Kālī

The second most fruitful area for the study of sacred sound in Śākta-Tantra is the goddess Kālī tradition, most visible in West Bengal, Assam, Kashmir, and Kerala; all places in which the goddess Kālī, as the Tantric goddess supreme, is the center of Tantric cult and worship. Whereas the tradition of Tripurasundarī is referred to as Śrī-kula, the Kālī tradition is known as Kālī-kula. The transition from the benign Tripurasundarī to the malevolent Kālī is made easier by reference to a key Śākta text: "According to the *Śakti-saṅgama-Tantra*, Kālī, Tārā, Tripurasundarī, and Chinnamastā are one and the same."[73] Indeed, despite some iconographic and even theological differences, the features regarding sacred sound hold true for nearly all of the Śākta traditions.

The Kālī Tantric literary corpus of Bengal abounds in Sanskrit collections and digests, which include material from a vast array of sources. It also includes compendiums that give directions regarding worship activities—namely, *pūjā*, *dhyāna*, and *homa* but including digressions on mantra and *yantra*. As a rule, these texts do not possess the intellectual rigor and literary accomplishment of the Śrī-Vidyā group yet are said to predate the Śrī-Vidyā:

> The beginnings of Kālī-kula literature can be traced back further than those of the Śrī-kula. . . . Perhaps the oldest Tantra on Kālī worship preserved to us is the *Yoni-gahvara* "Recess of the Womb" [ms. dated A.D. 1200]. . . . Among the subjects touched upon is the creation of the Gahvara alluded to in the title; it appears to be the alphabet arranged in a geometrical figure of fifty sections which should be considered the womb of all *mantras*.[74]

The public worship in Bengal of the goddess Kālī postdates, however, the Śrī-Vidyā cult activity: "The public worship of Kālī, which is widespread in Bengal today, does not seem to predate the seventeenth century. . . . The most popular Tantric works of Bengal that celebrate and describe Kālī are also late."[75] The inception of the cult of Kālī in Bengal is probably due to the influence of Kṛṣṇānanda Āgamavāgīśa, said to have been a contemporary of Caitanya (A.D. 1486–1533), the great Vaiṣṇava reformer and inaugurator of Bengali

Vaiṣṇavism: "Kṛṣṇānanda is credited with the conception, for the first time, of the Kālī image current in Bengal. He is also believed to have introduced the worship of this goddess in this province."[76] In addition, Kṛṣṇānanda wrote a large work in Sanskrit, the *Tantra-Sāra* (ca. A.D. 1500), which to this day has formed the basis of Bengali Śākta-Tantra worship and rite: "His *Tantra-Sāra* is looked upon as the most authoritative work on Tantra and as an infallible guide to all Tantric worship."[77]

Kṛṣṇānanda cites many previous Tantric sources in his work, but it seems likely that he is the first to ascribe Kālī with fifty human heads denoting the fifty Sanskrit letters, as he does when describing her form, known as Guhyakālī in *Tantra-Sāra* (1.326).[78] The sixteenth-century Śrī-Vidya text known as *Śakti-saṅgama-Tantra* ("The Tantra of Śakti Communion"), which is quoted extensively by Kṛṣṇānanda, contains descriptions of Guhyakālī as well as the fifteen Nityās (goddesses), all of which resemble in some way the accepted form of Kālī (i.e., dark, terrifying, nude, bloody, disheveled hair, garland of heads, belt of arms, at cremation site, etc.)[79] Yet in none of these descriptions, as far as I can tell, is the garland of heads connected to the Sanskrit alphabet or the number fifty. In verse 6 of *Karpūrādi-Stotram* (ca. tenth century A.D.), however, Kālī is described as being "adorned with a garland of heads." The commentator—date unknown—immediately interprets this as referring to the fifty Sanskrit letters: "She who is Śabda-Brahman consisting of fifty letters. *Niruttara-Tantra* says, 'She is adorned with a garland of heads representing the fifty letters.' The *Kāmadhenu-Tantra* says, 'In my throat is the wonderful Bīja of fifty letters.' Again 'I worship the Mother the source of the universe, Śabda-Brahman itself, blissful.' *Viśvasāra* says, 'Blissful Brahman is adorned with Śabda-Brahman and within the body is represented by all *mantras*.'"[80]

Though the dating of the abovementioned texts (*Niruttara-Tantra* and *Kāmadhenu-Tantra*) is still problematic, further study of these as well as other esoteric Kālī Tantras such as the *Siddhalaharī-Tantra*, *Toḍala-Tantra*, and the *Muṇḍamālā-Tantra* ("Tantra of the Garland of Skulls"), are certain to provide some answers to the vexing question of Kālī's relation to the Sanskrit alphabet.

The Kālī hymn known as the *Karpūrādi-Stotram* is very popular in Bengal, and it is also one of the oldest, according to Agehananda Bharati: "The work is fairly old; though Avalon did not try to establish any date, I would place it between the ninth and eleventh centuries;

its style bears marked similarity to that of the *Saundarya-Laharī* [ca. eighth century]."[81] As the *Saundarya-Laharī* had done for the Śrī-Vidyā tradition, the *Karpūrādi-Stotram* provided a kind of "acrostic foundation" for the main mantra of the practicing Kālī tradition—"KRĪṀ KRĪṀ KRĪṀ HŪṀ HŪṀ HRĪṀ HRĪṀ Dakṣiṇe Kālike KRĪṀ KRĪṀ KRĪṀ HŪṀ HŪṀ HRĪṀ HRĪṀ Svāhā." The title word *Karpūra,* along with the first five verses out of twenty-two, contain esoteric correspondences—that is, they are only understood with reference to the commentaries, between certain words in the text and the above syllables—from which the final twenty-two syllabled mantra is constructed. The mantra is explained further by the commentator Durgārāma with reference to Nāda and Bindu: "in KRĪṀ, K is Kālī, R is Brahmā, I is Mahāmāyā, Nāda is the matrix of the universe, and Bindu is the dispeller of sorrow. In HŪṀ, H is Śiva, Ū is Bhairava, Nāda means the Supreme, and Bindu is the dispeller of sorrow. In HRĪṀ, H is Śiva, R is Prakriti, Ī is Mahāmāyā, Nāda the generatrix of the universe, and Bindu the dispeller of pain. Contemplation of *mantra*s constituted of these letters reveals their *caitanya. Japa* of *mantra* without its *caitanya* is useless."[82] Very often the *japa* of Kālī-Mantras is done without a rosary, using the right thumb to count the recitations by advancing along each of the inside joints of the same hand in a particular fashion known as Kara-Japa, a practice also observed mostly within other Śākta contexts.

Regarding the development of Bengali Śaktism, late seventeenth- and early eighteenth-century Bengal witnessed a revitalization of creative Hindu Śākta-Tantra, which produced a considerable number of mystic hymns in Sanskrit notable for their expression of devotion (Bhakti) toward the Goddess. Often these hymns formed part of a larger text. The famous hymn of the "One Hundred Names of Kālī," known as the "Ādyā-Kālī-Svarūpa," is contained in the *Mahānirvāṇa-Tantra* (7.12–32), an eighteenth-century Kālī text written in Bengal. The text itself proclaims the benefit of its recitation, since the names of Kālī are said to be nondifferent from the goddess herself:

> The hundred names of Kālikā [Kālī], beginning with the letter KA. They are all identical with the image of Kālī. He who in worship recites these names with his mind fixed on Kālikā, for him Mantra-siddhi is quickly obtained, and with him Kālī is pleased. . . . [The repetition of this hymn 108 times] yields all desired fruit. This hymn of praise of a hundred names, which

is the primeval Kālī herself, if read, or caused to be read, if heard, or caused to be heard, frees from all sins and leads to union with Brahman."[83]

In our present age of strife and quarrel, known as the Kali Yuga, this hymn, as well as others, of Kālī is said to be particularly effective for salvation: "In all ages, O Devī! but particularly in the Kali Age, the Mantras of the sacred primeval Kālikā are of great efficacy, and yield complete success."[84]

In the twentieth century several Bengali theorists and practitioners of Śākta-Tantra have made important contributions to the study of Śākta-Tantra and Mantra-Śāstra which deserve mention and which as yet remain unexamined by scholars. Swami Pratyagātmānanda, for example, a nonagenarian, has composed an original Sanskrit-Bengali work in six volumes entitled *Japa-Sūtram,* which is also available in an abridged English edition. Sītārāmdās Oṁkārnāth has published a work entitled *Nāda-Līlāmṛta,* which contains many Sanskrit references to Nāda, as well as a collection of original poems in Bengali on the subject of Nāda-Brahman. The valuable introduction to this work by Gopinath Kaviraj is a Bengali translation of his own essay in Hindī entitled "Nāda-Tattva."

Among the traditions of Hinduism Śākta-Tantra seems to exhibit the highest preoccupation with sonic theology, especially in the articulation of complex strategies and structures of Nāda-Brahman. Yet, the scholarly study of Śākta-Tantra is still in its infancy, as many of the principal Śākta texts remain unexamined and unavailable for cross-comparison with those of the Śaiva and Vaiṣṇava traditions. Though we are somewhat limited to specific Āgamic and Tantric texts, the overwhelming focus of these texts on matters related to mantra and *japa* increase our expectations with regard to the proposed theme of this study. An inspection of the appropriate Śaiva and Vaiṣṇava texts and traditions forms the content of chapters 5 and 6.

Chapter 5

ŚAIVISM

Sacred Sound as the Energy of Śiva

The goddess worshipped by the two major Śākta cults as discussed in the previous chapter is generally understood to be the spouse of Śiva. Though less prevalent in cultic form, the spouse of Viṣṇu also forms an important Śākta dimension of Hinduism. This brings us, in this and the chapter that follows, to an examination of the next two divisions of the Hindu theistic tradition, namely Śaivism and Vaiṣṇavism: "Śaivism and Vaiṣṇavism form the two principal religious currents of classical and modern Hinduism. Śaivism centers on the worship of the god Śiva and Vaiṣṇavism on that of Viṣṇu."[1]

The present chapter will examine the main sectors of the Śaiva tradition, beginning with the Śaiva-Āgama and followed by Śaiva-Siddhānta and Kashmiri Śaivism. The Vaiṣṇava traditions will be examined in chapter 6, beginning with the Pāñcarātra texts and followed by the later Vaiṣṇava sectarian developments and Bhakti movements. We will argue in both chapters that the structure of Ultimate Reality for Hindu theism involves sacred sound as a significant female component and that the techniques for the realization of salvific goals, as in Śākta-Tantra, are significantly centered on exercises involving the transformative power of sacred sound as Nāda-Brahman, that is, sonic theology.

The status of sacred sound (Śabda-Brahman, Nāda-Brahman, or Parā-Vāk) in Śaivism is one of subordination to the supreme deity of Śiva, as noted by Gaurinath Sastri: "In Āgama [early Śaiva texts] the Parā-Vāk occupies a subordinate position, being conceived as the power of the Supreme Reality or Parama-Śiva, and would thus seem to correspond to Śabda-Brahman."[2] Sacred sound is thus conceived as the obedient female counterpart of the male sovereign deity and acts strictly as his energy. This will be seen to apply to Vaiṣṇavism as well. Though the realm of sacred sound is closely identified with the Supreme Reality in these theistic traditions, it contrasts with the supremely autonomous position it holds in the philosophies of Mīmāṁsā and the Grammarians.

The many distinct cults and sects of Hinduism today were supposedly once part of a more unified conglomerate religion: "The three great currents—Vaiṣṇava, Śaiva, and Śākta—have all the chief elements of their cult . . . in common and base these . . . largely on the same theoretical foundations."[3] They shared an outlook that was dualistic: "During (the) early period of Āgamic thought, the philosophy was purely dualistic,"[4] meaning specifically that "all Āgamic schools accept the doctrine of the 'three realities,' viz., the Supreme Being, the individual souls, and the objective universe. That means that they do not take the point of view of Śaṅkara's monism."[5]

On the practical level Thomas J. Hopkins concurs: "There are few sectarian differences between Vaiṣṇavite and Śaivite Tantric practices in the Āgamas. Much more evident is the common Tantric emphasis on internalization of images, identification with the deity and divine powers, use of Tantric *mantras,* and reliance on sectarian or Tantric teachers rather than orthodox Brāhmaṇas for religious instruction."[6] Often it is difficult to differentiate between Tantric and Āgamic practices, regardless of sect. "The specialists in the Tantras and in the Āgamas dealing with temple cults and ceremonials are closely akin and often identical."[7]

Accordingly, the sonic methods of Nāda-Yoga discussed in chapter 3 will be seen to form the foundation of sectarian theology across these divisions of Hindu theism. Many of the Śaiva-Āgama literatures contain metaphysical and cosmological discussions about *nāda, bindu,* the thirty-six *tattvas*, *bīja, mātṛkā,* and the origin of the alphabet. Several of the important Vaiṣṇava Pāñcarātra texts contain similar themes. The Śaiva cults employ a myriad of salvific Yoga practices in their *sādhana,* centering upon sonic meditation, including Nāda-Brahman worship and *japa*. Since most Śaivas and Śāktas practice some form of Yoga, there may appear to be overlaps between some of our chapters. There is almost no Yoga that is free of sectarian connection. The God Śiva is popularly known as Mahā-Yogī, the "Great Yogi," and serves as the Yoga role model par excellence for many Hindu traditions. Even Advaita-Vedānta—and the Yoga practiced therein—which claims to be above sectarian affiliation, is basically Śaivite. The Gorakhnāth Yogīs are generally followers of Śiva, though, according to region, they are sometimes Vaiṣṇavite, as seen in some of the Haṭha-Yoga treatises.

As will be seen, speculation on the nature and function of sacred sound continues throughout the theistic Hindu tradition, from the early Śaiva-Āgamas and Vaiṣṇava-Saṁhitās to the later sectarian ideologies. The actual extent of the later usage of sacred sound and sound formulas by practicing Hindus has, in fact, not been critically studied. When discussed it is too often limited by parochial concerns, temporal borders, and geographic boundaries.

Śaiva-Āgama

The study of sacred sound in medieval Hinduism must be able to incorporate material from diverse sources. Recent scholars have posited the coexistence of two separate corpora, Veda and Āgama, giving each nearly equal authority in terms of guiding the development of Hinduism. The truths outlined in the Vedic corpus (sometimes called "Nigama") are said to be realized practically through the techniques (*sādhana*) inculcated in the Āgamas, a kind of evolved Veda sometimes called the "Fifth Veda" and said to be the prescribed teaching for the present degenerate age of Kali Yuga. A major source for information about India's living religious traditions, yet reflecting many practices over two thousand years old, the Āgamas contain details on all forms and varieties of image worship, pilgrimage, mantra, devotion (Bhakti), festivals, temple construction, and other religious duties. Chronologically, then, the early Āgama and Tantric traditions predate Buddhism and possibly inform it, as noted by a modern scholar: "The Āgamic (Tantric) texts, as we know them today, had for the most part preceded Buddhism."[8]

Though the generic term *āgama* ("tradition" or "sacred traditional doctrine") can be shown to include literatures of virtually all sects, further clarification is needed in order to avoid confusion as we move onward. "Usually the Āgamas of the Śaivas are called Āgama, those of the Śāktas are called Tantra, and those of the Vaiṣṇavas are known as Saṁhitā."[9] The term *Āgama* is now mostly associated with the older Śaiva texts: "In a narrower sense the term Āgama is especially applied to Śaivite works (Śaiva-Āgama)."[10] In south India the word *Āgama* has grown into a common expression for the entire Śaivite canon, including vernacular devotional works (mostly in Tamil) and Śaivite "sayings," all considered on an equal or higher level than the Vedic corpus.

The oral nature of the Āgama texts is understood to mean that they were the original spoken word of Lord Śiva: "The word 'Āgama' is . . . supposed to refer to the śāstra [scripture] that has been related by Śiva to his divine consort Pārvatī [Śakti]."[11] And the same format remains in virtually all the Śaiva literature: "Usually Śiva takes the role of the teacher, Devī of the pupil."[12] Though a large number of Śaiva-Āgamas are said to exist, the basic number of revealed texts containing a common rubric is generally accepted to be twenty-eight. The principal Āgamas are called the "Mūla-Āgamas," or those directly revealed by Śiva, and are generally supposed to expound the four paths of Śaiva philosophy and religion—Jñāna, Yoga, Kriyā including rituals, and Charyā. The Jñāna portion discusses philosophy, while the other three may be taken as dealing with more practical concerns, such as personal *sādhana,* cultic and community affairs. Since only portions of the twenty-eight Āgamas have been recovered, along with fragments supporting a possible larger canon, Āgamic study is still in its beginning stages.

The notion of God as the giver or discloser of an original revelation should not be unfamiliar to Western readers. Just as several of the Hindu gods appear as "speaker" (i.e., Śiva as the speaker of the Śaiva-Āgamas and Viṣṇu as the original revealer of the Pāñcarātra canon), the chief Judaic god, Yahweh, is also celebrated as the primal speaker of the Mosaic law (Torah): "Strict etymology [root HWY = breathe, speak] permits the meaning 'speaker' for the name of Yahweh. The nature of Hebrew religion, especially the tradition regarding Yahwism of the Mosaic period when Yahwism first comes into prominence, supports such an interpretation, for it is preeminently as a 'speaker' that Yahweh is known."[13]

Currently, the most intensive research in the Śaiva-Āgama tradition is being conducted in south India. The French Institute of Indology in Pondicherry, headed by N. R. Bhatt, has been devoted for the past several decades to collecting, editing, and translating many of the important texts and manuscripts.[14] Bhatt emphasized the extreme importance of the Āgamas for our understanding of Hinduism in a recent interview: "The Āgama texts and traditions are as old or older than the Vedas. . . . The sources for the living religion of India are the Āgamas, not the Vedas."[15] In the preface to the institute's recently published *Descriptive Catalogue of Manuscripts* (1986), he explains the antiquity of the Āgamas: "It is better to conclude that the language used in the Āgamas is pre-Pāṇinian [i.e., before the second century B.C.E.] and conformed to the usage of that period." The singular importance of the Āgamas for understanding the practices of Hinduism are underscored, as he continues: "If one goes through this branch of literature [the Vedas], one does not find the type of religion that is now existing in India; these works [Vedas] do not give rules or regulations for personal worship in the form of *pūjā* nor for the temple worship as they are practiced now. It is only the Āgamas which are the basic texts dealing with those regular personal or temple worship [activities,] and with all that pertain to the temple complex."[16]

While not intending to lessen their importance, Jan Gonda is more cautious regarding the date of the Āgamas: "The oldest Āgamas may have been composed in the period between ca. 400 and 800. . . . [But] the earliest manuscript of an Āgama—the Kiraṇa—is dated 924 A.D."[17] On the other hand, there are some who hold an extreme view that the Sanskrit Āgamas were originally written in Tamil and represent a tradition of Śaiva temple worship which vastly predates the entire Vedic culture: "The term *āgama* in Sanskrit may . . . mean that which has come into Sanskrit from Tamil." Gonda is rightly skeptical of this view: "Part of the Śivaites of the South . . . regard their Āgamas as a sanskritization of an originally Dravidian (Tamil) tradition which they believe to have been transmitted orally before disappearing. This cannot however be shown demonstrably."[18]

Still another view posits the origin of the Śaiva-Āgama, not in south India, but in the north: "Despite relatively early references to the existence of Āgamic Śaivism in the South, it seems that the Śaiva-Āgamas originally flourished in northern India, spreading to the South only later."[19] It is difficult to take a stand on this issue, especially since there are thousands of unedited "Āgamic" manuscripts at the institute awaiting further study: "Most of these [Śaiva] Āgamas still lie unpublished, and yet they form the religious kernel of Śaivism as practiced by millions of people in different parts of India."[20] In fact, the future course of indological study is relying on the Āgama research that is presently being carried out in Pondicherry, Tirupati, and Madras.

The Śaiva-Āgama texts are considered the basic canon for nearly all of the Śaiva sectarian divisions of Hinduism. Though the origin and chronology of the Śaiva-Āgamas remain obscure, they are still "considered the basic authoritative texts by Śaiva-Siddhāntins, Kashmir Śaivas, and adherents of Vīraśaivism. . . . It is the common belief of all Śaivas that the Āgamas which, like their Viṣṇuite counterparts, are esoteric and traditionally taught to the worthy initiated, are the spoken word of Śiva. . . . Thus, the inspiration on which the Śaivite schools are believed to be based is eternal and the expression of the

Divine Word."[21] Originally dualistic or pluralistic in outlook, these texts have been supplemented by further revelations to express the nondual position as well, as in Kashmiri Śaivism.

In a second interview N. R. Bhatt enumerated some identifiable characteristics of Śaiva-Āgamic culture which he has compared and contrasted with identifiable Vedic, Yogic, and Tantric features:

> The original Śaiva-Āgama culture was very simple: Liṅga worship, representing the Trimūrti of Brahmā, Śiva, and Viṣṇu in one phallic icon; discussions of the thirty-six Tattvas (truths) including Nāda and Bindu; cosmic bipolarity whereby Śiva is represented by Nāda and Śakti by Bindu; unity of its four parts of Jñāna, Kriyā, Yoga, Charyā, as opposed to the Vedic tradition where there was separation; profusion of Sanskrit texts; the use of Om recitation, as in the Vedas; temple life characterized by music, song, and dance; Yoga practice carried out not necessarily in solitude but in connection with the temple and temple worship. Contrary to the Vedic culture, there were no caste distinctions and no animal offerings allowed.[22]

Bhatt presumably drew upon his extraordinary knowledge of a large range of published and unpublished Āgama texts for this characterization.

For our purposes the recognition of a significant amount of speculation on the nature of Nāda, Bindu, and Praṇava, or Om in the Śaiva-Āgama texts themselves sparks our inquiry. For example: "The *Mṛgendra-Āgama* [1.2] finds the quintessence of Nāda, Bindu or the three gods (Trimūrti), the various elements (the sun, the moon and the fire) in the Praṇava."[23] The *Candrajñāna-Āgama* (Kriyāpāda, Paṭala 3.13) describes the universe as a composite of Śiva, which is Nāda, the Śakti, which is Bindu (*binduḥ śaktiḥ śivo nādaḥ*), while verse 16 portrays the Śiva-Liṅga as both a combination of Nāda and Bindu (*bindu-nādātmakaṁ liṅgam*) as well as the cause of the universe.[24] The *Sūkṣma-Āgama* (Kriyāpāda, Paṭala 1.43–44) mentions similar ideas regarding the Liṅga, which, first, consists of Nāda and Bindu and is the cause of creation, maintenance, and destruction of the universe and, second, is the source of all mantras.[25] The *Candrajñāna-Āgama* and the *Sūkṣma-Āgama* are both included in most lists of the original twenty-eight Āgamas as revealed by Śiva.[26] In reversal of the typology here the later Śaiva-Siddhānta and Kashmiri

Śaiva traditions associated Śiva with Bindu and Śakti with Nāda, as will be shown.

With similarities in both language and symbolism the Āgamic speculation on Om and Nāda-Brahman carried well over into the Purāṇas, a large group of semihistorical and mythological literature growing out of the same theistic background. As in the Śaiva-Āgama texts, the *Liṅga-Purāṇa,* along with the *Skanda-Purāṇa,* amalgamate the Trimūrti (Brahmā, Viṣṇu, Śiva) into both the Liṅga and the Praṇava: "The Liṅga constitutes the Trimūrti and the Nāda in the *Liṅga-Purāṇa.* The Praṇava on the Liṅga synthesizes the Nāda and the *mātṛkā* (syllable). It also symbolizes the quintessence of the three Gods and the Nāda-Brahman—the fourth, by the medium of the three syllables—A + U + M and the eternal sound in the end."[27] Consonant with the *Candrajñāna-Āgama* (and other Āgamas), however, yet contrary to the normal Tantric association of Nāda with Śakti and Bindu with Śiva in later Śaiva theism, the *Śiva-Purāṇa* (16.89–90) explains them as follows: "The unification of the Bindu and the Nāda is called Sakalī-kāraṇa and the universe takes its birth as a result of this Sakalī-kāraṇa. The phallic emblem [Śiva-Liṅga] is the fusion of Bindu and Nāda [*bindu-nādātmakaṁ liṅgam*]. Bindu is the goddess and Śiva is the Nāda and the fusion of the two is the phallic emblem of Śiva [*bindur devī śivo nādaḥ*]."[28]

Deriving many notions from the Śaiva-Āgamas, another source for the study of mantra in Śaivism is the *Śiva-Purāṇa* (ca. before A.D. 700), a text that stresses the intrinsic relation between Lord Śiva and the Praṇava, or Om: "Throughout the text the *Śiva-Purāṇa* expresses in a variety of ways the idea that Śiva IS the Praṇava or that the Praṇava IS Śiva." According to one passage (1.10.16–19), the fivefold Praṇava issued out of Śiva's five mouths: "Om was born from Śiva's mouths. The sound A first came out of his northern mouth, U from his western mouth, M from his southern mouth; the Bindu next came from his eastern mouth, and the Nāda from his central mouth. The result of this fivefold 'gaping' (*vijṛmbhita*) was then made into one in the form of the single syllable OM."[29]

Comparable to this as well as other accounts in the Āgama and Tantra, the Jewish mysticism of the Kabbalah describes the linguistic emanation of the name of God: "God sends a single letter, the *yod,* the first letter of his great name, YHWH, the Tetragrammaton."[30] Further studies in Jewish esoterica reveal descriptions of the Hebrew alphabet vis-à-vis the face and beard of Yahweh as Microprosopus.[31]

Lord Śiva's own abode, or heaven, is said (1.6.23) to be made of Om, or the Praṇava: "Śiva's residence on the summit of Mount Kailāsa is Praṇavākāra, in the form of the Praṇava." The mandatory role of the guru, the divine teacher, in the oral transmission of the Praṇava in Śaivism is explained here also, using the metaphor of human reproduction (1.18.90): "The *mantra* is the semen springing from the guru's tongue (the penis) and deposited in the disciple's ear (the *yoni* [womb])." The idea here is that the guru, the "spiritual father," releases one—by the agency of Praṇava, or mantra—from the material world into which one has been born due to the sexual activities of a natural father. In addition, the word *Praṇava* is subjected to various etymologies in the *Śiva-Purāṇa,* one among which (1.17.5) is as follows: "Praṇava is so called because it is the ideal (*pra*) guide (*ṇa*) to *mokṣa* for you (*va*)."[32]

The "sound system" of the Śaiva-Āgama tradition is referred to as Nāda-Tattva, or Nāda-Bindu-Tattva, and carried well over into Śaiva-Siddhānta metaphysics: "The philosophy of sound in Śiva-Tattva [Śaiva-Āgama and Śaiva-Siddhānta] is known as the Nāda-Bindu-Tattva. . . . Nāda denotes the total sonic action that envelopes the field of sound, and not merely the sound." This coheres with the following statement about their iconic representation: "The Nāda and the Bindu iconically is expressed in the Liṅga and the circular plate or *paṭṭam.*"[33]

As indicated, there is a major emphasis on personal *sādhana,* or spiritual practice, in the Śaiva-Āgama tradition. Personal *sādhana,* which is soteriological for all Āgamic traditions, is said to include three important ingredients; the deity of Śiva, the mantra, and the teacher, or guru: "In the Āgamas, the *sādhana* consists of three essentials—the particular Deity, the *mantra,* and the guru who introduces these." These three in no wise should be considered separate, for they coexist and are interdependent: "The Deity present in the guru, the *mantra* of the Deity, and the *dīkṣā* [initiation] all invest the guru with a transcendental divinity which illumines the novice and helps to lead him on along the chosen path. The Āgamas attach great importance to all these essentials of the Śaiva-Sādhana."[34]

The second of these three essentials is mantra. The most common mantra of the Śaiva-Āgama tradition is the so-called Pañcākṣara, or "five-syllable *mantra*": *namaḥ śivāya*—"I offer obeisance unto Śiva." This is usually prefaced by Om and another *bīja* syllable peculiar to the form of Śiva which has been taught to the disciple: "Without the

Praṇava, the primordial sound Om, no *mantra* for any Deity is valid. The *bīja-mantra* is the most important. *Bīja* is seed. Here it consists of a single sound represented by one voiced letter ending in M. This is different for the different Deities and consists in essence of a sound or syllable which is the principle of the form. It pleases the Deity and makes in come down to the disciple at the time of invocation and *pūjā*."[35]

As the Śaiva-Āgama tradition and literature informed nearly all of the Śaiva sectarian developments in India, the basic tenets remained secure, despite variation in cultic application. And throughout the texts, based on the testimony of Āgama scholars and the limited amount of available texts, the concepts of Nāda, Bindu, and Nāda-Brahman are inseparably woven into the metaphysical and soteriological speculations. In south India and Kashmir the Śaiva-Āgama tradition formed the basis of Śaiva-Siddhānta, which also included the testimonies of the Tamil devotional literature of the Śaiva saints.

Śaiva-Siddhānta

The tradition of Śaiva-Siddhānta, prevalent in the Tamil-speaking areas as well as in Kashmir,[36] represents the most important theological and devotional "living system" of Śaivism. Like the Śaiva-Āgama tradition, Śaiva-Siddhānta accepts the authority of the twenty-eight Śaiva-Āgamas. But it also accepts a large corpus of Tamil writings known as the "Tamil Veda."

As in the Śaiva-Āgama, the primarily dualistic Śaiva-Siddhānta theology posits three eternal realities: God, the living entities, and the material universe. These three realities are labeled as Pati, Paśu, and Pāśa, respectively. "The world being created by God [*pati*] as efficient cause through conscious power (will and creative energy, Śakti) as instrumental cause and Māyā as material cause, is no illusion. The main purpose of its creation is the liberation of the beginningless souls, which are conceived as 'cattle' (*paśu*) bound by the noose (*pāśa*) of impurity (*mala*) or spiritual ignorance, which forces them to produce *karma*."[37]

Śaiva-Siddhānta also accepts the basic Āgama categories of Nāda, Bindu, and so on, yet, differing from Śaiva-Āgama, places Nāda as a feminine dimension of the all-powerful deity of Śiva instead of as Śiva himself. In the Śaiva-Siddhānta cosmogony there is generally a ninefold progression from unmanifest to manifest—in descending order "Śiva, Śakti, Nāda and Bindu as unmanifest, Sadāśiva as manifest-unmanifest, and Maheśvara, Rudra, Viṣṇu and Brahmā as manifest unfoldings of the Absolute."[38] Hence, regarding Nāda, "Śaiva-Siddhānta . . . will look upon Parā or Nāda not as Brahman but as Śakti—Parigraha-Śakti of Brahman and its unfoldment into concrete and overt speech forms as a case of real change of states, modal change (*vṛtti*) not unreal appearances."[39] Thus, Nāda, often equated with Śiva in the Āgamas and Purāṇas, is now used in the sense of an instrument of Brahman, which is Śiva. This was probably due to the influence of the neighboring Śākta ideologies, which unequivocally place Nāda-Brahman as the Śakti, or energy, of Brahman and not Braham itself.

The chief formulators of Śaiva-Siddhānta theology in Sanskrit were Sadyojyoti, Bṛhaspati, Bhoya, Śrīkaṇṭha, Nārāyaṇa Kaṇṭha, Rāmakaṇṭha, Rāmakaṇṭha II, and especially Aghora Śivācārya (twelfth century A.D.).[40] A very small text of twenty-five verses by Rāmakaṇṭha II (eleventh century A.D.) known as the *Nāda-Kārikā*,[41] with Aghora Śivācārya's commentary, survives as the single work on the Śaiva-Siddhānta philosophy of language. Linguistically, Nāda refers to the highest principle of meaning—the source of both *śabda* and *artha*, much like Sphoṭa had done for the Grammarians:

> Nāda . . . and not physical *śabda* possesses the denotative character. . . . The physical *śabda* to which the vocal organ of the speaker gives expression manifests Nāda. Nāda as thus manifested, produces in the hearer the sense of the object meant. Nāda reveals all *śabdas* and *ar. has*. Hence every act of discursive knowledge is impregnated with *śabda*. Nāda is multiple, being unique in each individual, and is a product. Every animal soul, . . . having a nature of its own, experiences its own Nāda which arises from Anāhata-Bindu.[42]

The Ultimate Reality for Śaiva-Siddhānta is, of course, Śiva himself. Yet just below as his Śakti is a reservoir of power which contains a linguistic configuration of the Absolute Word. "Śabda-Tattva . . . is the transcendent reality which reveals itself as many and manifold because of its 'powers.' Without a disruption of its unity, it reveals itself at once as the two poles of language, word and its meaning, and the two poles of experience, viz., subject and object." And the implicit relation between the Śabda-Tattva and its manifestation as spoken language is conceived as Nāda: "There is an isomorphic relation between the transcendent power and the word which is also conceived as an ensemble of power. They may be held together (as in the concept of Parā-Vāk of Kashmir Śaivism) or held apart (as implied in the concept of Nāda of Śaiva-Siddhānta), but their parity of functions is the common presupposition underlying the Śaiva theory of language.[43]

Śaiva-Siddhānta appears to refute the Sphoṭavāda conception of the Grammarians, wherein Śabda-Brahman as Sphoṭa permeates every aspect of creation, from ordinary words to the highest Absolute Truth. "The dualists [pluralistic Āgama traditions] who maintain the doctrine of Nāda repudiate the theory of *sphoṭa* and other allied theories of verbal knowledge and seek to explain the process of the origin of Śabda-Brahman on the basis of this doctrine. Rāmakaṇṭha in his Kārikās [*Nāda-Kārikā*] has tried to show that the doctrine of *sphoṭa* is unable to render an adequate account of the meaning of a word."[44]

A closer look at the textual tradition, however, reveals that the ideas of Nāda and *sphoṭa* are not as dissimilar as Kaviraj makes them out to be. A recent essay by Pierre Filliozat stated that "in the later texts of Śaiva-Siddhānta we can see traces of the acceptance of *sphoṭa.*"[45] Indeed, in the commentary of Umāpati Śivācārya (fourteenth-century Tamil Nadu) on the *Pauṣkara-Āgama* the commentator uses the term *sphoṭa-nāda* ("Nāda which is *sphoṭa*") and "identifies . . . his own Tantric concept of Nāda with *sphoṭa*. . . . This Nāda is a mental entity and as such can be equated with the *sphoṭa* conceived as a mental component."[46] K. Sivaraman also observes the correlation: "The language of *sphoṭa* is . . . used as interchangeable with Nāda in the text of the *Pauṣkara-Āgama* at many places"; and "The lines of clear demarcation if any between Nāda and *sphoṭa* . . . are not clarified by Rāmakaṇṭha or even his commentator."[47]

The overall importance of Nāda in the *Nāda-Kārikā* is revealed in the rather terse statements of this text:

> (This Nāda) makes possible apprehending of all, the word (that reveals meaning) as well as the meaning (that is revealed by the word) [*śabda* and *artha*], wherefore it is the one and only revealer of meaning. By Nāda is it perceived that all things both of the order of being and of non-being alike become thinkable [12]. . . . He that comprehends the word-reality [*vāgbrahmaṇi niṣṇātaḥ*] realizes the reality of consciousness, thus it has been said. (Besides), spiritual accomplishments [*siddhi*], liberation [*mukti*] that is (of the) highest (kind) and spiritual acts (of initiation)

[*parā nāda-jñāna-kriyā*] also accrue as fruits (thus it has been said) [20]. . . . (It thus follows that) [the] Nāda that is generated by the Mahāmāyā is (alone) fit to be the unconditional word (revelatory of meaning) [*paramārtha-vācakaḥ*]. By it comes into operation the manifest forms of sound of the nature of *mantra*, Tantra, etc. (which are therefore revelatory qua manifesters of Nāda) [22].[48]

The role of Nāda as inner speech in the *Nāda-Kārikā* is very close to the concept of *sphoṭa* as the "revealer of meaning," as further elaborated in the rather lengthy commentaries on this text.[49] Filliozat develops the notion of this correlation in another work, wherein he examines the commentary of Aghora Śivācārya regarding Nāda in both the act of speech communication and in the attainment of liberation.[50] The correlation between Nāda and Sphoṭa in Śaiva-Siddhānta does not imply the full acceptance of Bhartṛhari's philosophy, that is, the supremacy of Śabda-Brahman. It only shows the ways in which Bhartṛharian thought has permeated a number of traditions without being accepted in total.

The methods and practices of attaining salvation in Śaiva-Siddhānta follow those categories that appear in the Śaiva-Āgama yet espouse an emphasis on love, thus being part of the Bhakti tradition.

> The three paths of salvation are those of service (Caryā), worship (Kriyā), and meditation (Yoga), all of which should be animated with the love of God. All these ways dispose the soul to receive gratuitously from Śiva divine knowledge (*pati-jñāna*), by which is realized perfect union with Śiva in supreme love. This divine knowledge is imparted to souls either directly through intuition in the case of advanced souls or through a Śiva-Guru to the less advanced.[51]

Appropriately, Nāda plays a vital role in the salvific dimension: "Nāda . . . serves as the platform for the leap into transcendence. . . . It is the medium through which the Śakti intrinsic to Śiva, manifests itself in degrees depending on the intensity of the desire for liberation."[52]

True to the Āgama tradition, followers of Śaiva-Siddhānta practice and advocate the recital of the Pañcākṣara-Mantra (*namaḥ śivāya*) in order to obtain release, or *mokṣa*: "This is also called Mukti-Pañcākṣara in view of the fact that its recital is designed to lead one from the state of *sādhaka* [practitioner] to that of the *mukta* [liberated soul]. . . . It is the direct *sādhana* for Śiva-Darśana [visualization of Śiva]."[53]

The Pañcākṣara-Mantra, of course, includes the recital of Om. In fact, the Śaivite theology lays a particular emphasis on what it terms "Oṁkāra recollection": "The Oṁkāra is Maheśvara [Śiva] himself in so far as he is present as the Om *mantra* in the act of contemplation. . . . Oṁkāra . . . is a linguistically undifferentiated sound that thus can effect Śiva's salvific presence immediately. . . . Such a presence of god, which is no longer conveyed by means of sentence meaning, can only be retained in the heart; that is, in the *ātmā* [inner self] by means of a radical 'recollection of the Oṁkāra.'"[54] The transcending of sentence meaning in the perception of the divine places us closer to the Grammarian position of Sphoṭavāda and farther from the Mīmāṁsā view. Though Tantrism, as noted, is in general more indebted to the Varṇavāda (Mīmāṁsā) theory of language, the notions peculiar to theistic worship and meditation, which can be found in the Bhakti traditions of Śaivism and Vaiṣṇavism, are also curiously reminiscent of Bhartṛhari and the Grammarians.

In sum, within the philosophy of Śaiva-Siddhanta there is a reversal in the status of Nāda and Bindu. While in the Śaiva-Āgamas Nāda denoted Śiva himself, by the eleventh century it has been designated as the power, or Śakti, of Śiva, exercising linguistic and salvific functions. Indeed, this is no mean role, given the importance placed on salvation in this tradition: "In no other system is salvation so much at the center of all reflections as in Śaiva-Siddhānta; all the functions of God are ordered toward salvation. . . . Śiva acts as Guru to the soul; without Śiva's guidance the soul would not be able to reach *mukti* [*mokṣa*]. . . . In every stage the soul is in need of God, in every stage God's presence is acting for the salvation of the soul."[55]

Kashmiri Śaivism

An area of increasing interest for the study of Hinduism is the nondualist school of Kashmiri Śaivism,[56] the most important school of Śaivism in north India, which includes the philosophy of Abhinavagupta, Krama Tantrism, Kashmiri Kuṇḍalinī-Yoga, Spanda theory, and Pratyabhijñā philosophy. The focus here will be the underlying theories of sound which permeate the Kashmiri nondualistic tradition.

As in the Śaiva-Siddhānta, the main emphasis of this school is soteriology: "Kashmiri Śaivism is primarily soteriological. It can be studied as an abstract philosophical system, as an objective body of knowledge to be examined at a discrete academic distance, but the real knowledge that Kashmir Śaivism has to offer arises from the practice of the Yoga of Kashmir Śaivism."[57]

The religious philosophy of Kashmir has been termed "Trika" philosophy—as well as "Triadism"—by Western scholars for various reasons having to do with there being a trinity, or triad, of concepts, categories, scriptures, goddesses, or sages.[58] One of the three categories is nondualism (*adheda*), said to be a special revelation for this age. J. C. Chatterji, referring to the account in Abhinavagupta's *Tantrāloka,* explains the advent of this "new" Śaivism as being due to the growing influence of the degenerate Kali age. As such, Śiva took compassion on men and, appearing on the Kailāsa mountain in the form of Śrīkaṇṭha, commanded the sage Durvāsa to spread in the world the knowledge of the lost Śiva-Āgamas and Śiva-Śāstras again. Durvāsa then created three sons by the power of his mind—Tryambaka, Amardaka, and Śrīnātha. He entrusted them with the mission of teaching human beings over again the ancient and eternal Śaiva faith and doctrine in the three aspects of Abheda, Bheda, and Bhedābheda—Unity, Diversity, and Diversity-in-Unity. Tryambaka was to teach the first, Amardaka the second, while Śrīnātha was to have the charge of the last. It is this nondual Abheda, or Advaya Śaiva, teaching, retaught to the world by Tryambaka, which is spoken of as the Trika.[59]

Jan Gonda further explains these revelations as emanating from Śiva himself through his energy, or Śakti:

> The authoritative texts, having the Parā-Vāk as their source, flow out as spoken words from God's five faces, which represent his fivefold Śakti. The five systems of revelation which owe their existence to this process, are traditionally held to constitute the Śaivite schools or systems. These are divisible into three classes, viz., the Śiva class (ten dualist [Bheda] systems), the Rudra class (eighteen Bhedābheda or duality-unity systems), and the Bhairava class (sixty-four monist [Abheda] systems).[60]

Kashmiri Śaivism introduces the term and concept of *Parā-Vāk.* As explained by Swami Lakshman Jee, a revered guru of this tradition as well as a teacher of both Lilian Silburn and André Padoux, this concept at first appears to coincide with the Grammarian tradition: "The word Parā means 'supreme,' and Parā-Vāk is the supreme speech. It is that soundless sound which resides in your own universal consciousness. It is the supreme sound which has no sound. It is the life of the other three kinds of speech which comprise the kingdom of speech, Paśyantī, Madhyamā, and Vaikharī, and yet it does not come in this kingdom of speech."[61] Accordingly, Parā-Vāk, also referred to as Parā-Nāda, plays a vital role in the salvation scheme, since Parā-Vāk, or "Supreme Speech" is coterminous with the Āgamas themselves and the original spoken Word of Śiva:

> At the basis of these speculations is the conviction that the Highest or All-Transcending Word (Parā-Vāk), which is God's unspoken Thought, germinally contains all the Āgamas in a supersensuous form. It gradually materializes into a physical form as syllables and vocables so as to form the units of speech. Whereas in the first stage of development (Paśyantī) the words and their meanings are not differentiated, in the last stage (Vaikharī) it expresses itself through the audible words."[62]

There is, however, an important and often subtle difference between the Trika philosophy and that of Bhartṛhari regarding the status of Parā-Vāk (Śabda-Brahman). Conforming to the theistic paradigm wherein sacred sound is the female energy of the Supreme Reality, Kashmiri Śaivas place Parā-Vāk as feminine Śakti just below the Parama-Śiva, as noted by Gaurinath Sastri:

> According to the school of Bhartṛhari, Parā-Vāk is the Supreme Reality, while in the opinion of the Trika philosophers, Parā-Vāk is the power of Parama-Śiva which is maintained to be the highest principle. It is of course true that the Trika philosophers entertain the view that Parama-Śiva and his power known as Vimarśa are not different—the two are held to be identical in essence. Still, it cannot be denied that when the two are described as the powerful and the power, they stand in the relation of the substantive and its attribute. Consequently, the latter should be looked upon as subordinate to the former. Thus Vimarśa or Parā-Vāk cannot be viewed as an independent and self-subsistent principle in the same way in which it is conceived in the system of the grammarian.[63]

This same difference has been repeated more recently by K. Sivaraman: "The difference in the conception of Parā-Vāk in the two systems [the Grammarian and Kashmiri Śaivism] is, briefly, that while in the grammarian's system, Parā-Vāk is Brahman, for the [Kashmiri] Śaiva philosopher it is the power of Parama-Śiva. . . . In soteriological terms, it is the difference between achieving of transcendence 'in' language and achieving of transcendence 'of' language itself."[64]

Consequently, the Grammarians can never transcend language because the Ultimate Reality is Śabda-Brahman itself. For different reasons the dualistic, theistic sects of Hinduism likewise almost never advocate a transcendence of language resulting in a silent beatific vision of their respective deity: mantras and corresponding Nāda-Brahman meditation techniques are never given up even after liberation. It is only with the Kashmiri Śaivas, along with Advaita-Vedānta and Buddhism, that language is ultimately replaced by silent contemplation, as characterized by Padoux: "Thus, moving from language to its original levels, one ultimately arrives at its source, at silence: Om merges into the resonance, Nāda, which in turn gradually dissolves in the pure light of consciousness, in the silence of the supreme and transcendent Godhead."[65]

Furthermore, despite the appropriation of technical terms from Bhartṛhari, Kashmiri Śaivism has rejected the linguistic Absolute of the Grammarians. The most poignant criticism of the Grammarian Sphoṭavāda theory by a Kashmiri is found in the *Śiva-Dṛṣṭi* (3.58-61) of Somānanda (tenth century A.D.). Yet, rather than a simple rejection of Bhartṛhari's linguistic scheme, this work builds upon and modifies its structure in a way that suggests that the Grammarian theory presages and influences the Trika system: "Despite Somānanda's acute criticism of *Vākyapadīya* it is perhaps plausible to view the latter as philosophically anticipating the former."[66] For the Grammarian Parā-Vāk is the same as Paśyanti, the Highest Truth, but in Somānanda's view Parā, or Parā-Vāk, is a stage higher than Paśyantī and also represents Vimarśa, or the self-reflective power of Parama-Śiva: "For what reasons the grammarian holds the Paśyantī to be the highest aspect of speech, the Śaiva, thanks to the grammarian, can see it as but the power of knowledge which in his categorical scheme constitutes the Sadāśiva-Tattva. For him, Parā as the highest aspect of speech beyond Paśyanti, is the power of self-awareness or of consciousness being self-aware (Vimarśa)."[67]

The Grammarians hold that Paśyantī is equivalent to Sphoṭa and constitutes the Highest Reality: "Both Paśyantī and Sphoṭa are admitted by the grammarians as eternal (*nitya*) and display one and the same significance expressed by two different terms." Somānanda attempts to show that Paśyantī is not the Supreme Reality since it lacks certain qualities of Śiva: "The doctrine of the grammarians, according to which Paśyantī is the Supreme Cause of the universe, says Somānanda, is acceptable to us if they attribute to it the powers of will [*icchā*], knowledge [*jñāna*], and action [*kriyā*] in subtle forms before it is materialized in the form of the actual creation. In this case it is identical with our Śiva. . . . [But as long as they do not do this,] Śiva and not Paśyantī is the Supreme Being."[68]

Despite the differences between the Grammarian and Kashmiri schools, Sastri and Sivaraman both agree that the school of Bhartṛhari has significantly influenced the Trika philosophy: "Bhartṛhari's work is evidently prior to those of the philosophical classics of the Śaiva and Śākta schools and it is natural that they have been influenced by the former";[69] and "The Grammarian philosophy of language seems to be the precursor for the Śaiva theory."[70] Further issues regarding Parā-Vāk vis-à-vis Grammarian and Trika philosophy are taken up in Abhinavagupta's *Parātriśikā-Vivaraṇa*.[71]

We are told that the Trika accepts the authority of the traditional twenty-eight Āgamas. But, in addition, it accepts the conclusion of its own "Āgama tradition" as well as that of the Spanda and Pratyabhijñā philsophical doctrines, all three of which developed particularly in Kashmir during the ninth through eleventh centuries A.D. The outstanding scholars and philosophers of this period were Vasugupta, Kallaṭa, Somānanda, Utpala, Abhinavagupta, Kṣemarāja, Yogarāja, and Jayaratha. The general thrust of their scholarship had been to reinterpret the Śaiva-Āgama along their peculiar monistic tendency, a kind of "triadic monism": "Triadism soon came into being and spread rapidly; it substituted monism for the dualism of early Āgamic teaching."[72]

In the attempt to reinterpret the pluralistic Āgamas in the light of Śaṅkara's and Bhartṛhari's monism and idealism, Vasugupta (ninth century A.D.) is credited with the promulgation of the first uniquely Kashmiri Śaivite Āgama, the *Śiva-Sūtra*: "Vasugupta is undoubtedly the first historical personage who is deemed to be the founder and originator of Kashmiri Śaivism. . . . The *Śiva-Sūtra* as taught by Vasugupta laid the foundation of Advaita Śaivism of Kashmir."[73] This "nondual Āgama" was said to have been revealed by Śrīkaṇṭha (Śiva) to Vasugupta directly, therefore the classification "Āgama."

The text of the *Śiva-Sūtra* is divided into three sections, each corresponding to the three divisions of Kashmiri Śaiva-Sādhana: Śāmbhava-Upāya, Śākta-Upāya, and Āṇava-Upāya. The first section deals with the Divine Means (Śāmbhava-Upāya) and is the highest of the three. The second section is concerned with the Empowered Means (Śākta-Upāya), and the last with the Individual Means (Āṇava-Upāya), which is the lowest. Regarding the first, "practicing this means the Yogī is carried to the supreme level of consciousness by a powerful and direct awareness of reality awakened in him by Śiva's grace through which he attains identity with Śiva without resorting to any form of meditation."[74] The second and third "Means" deal with internal and external methods, respectively.

The second section, dealing with Śākta-Upāya, begins with a discussion of mantra, focusing on its role of merging with the mind of the aspirant: "By intensive awareness of one's identity with the Highest Reality enshrined in a *mantra* and thus becoming identical with that Reality the mind itself becomes *mantra* [2.1, *cittaṁ mantraḥ*]."[75] Kṣemarāja's commentary, named *Vimarśinī*, explains the rather enigmatic nature of this sūtra: "The mind of the devotee intent on intensive awareness of the deity inherent in the *mantra* acquires identity with that deity and thus becomes that *mantra* itself. It is this mind itself [*cittam*] which is *mantra*, not a mere conglomeration of letters." The translator further explains: "The main technique of Śākta-Upāya is *mantra*, but *mantra* in this context does not mean incantation or muttering of some sacred formula. The word *mantra* is used here in its etymological signification. That which saves one by pondering over the light of Supreme I-consciousness is *mantra*. The divine Supreme I-consciousness is the dynamo of all the *mantras*."[76]

Another important nondualist Āgama text of the Kashmiri tradition is the *Vijñāna-Bhairava*, which purports to describe 112 types of Yoga. After these are given the process of *japa* is highly recommended, as it concentrates on the inner sounding of Nāda and reinforces the concept of mantra described in the *Śiva-Sūtra*: "That creative contemplation which is practiced on the highest Reality over and over again is in this scripture *japa* (recitation in reality). That which goes on sounding spontaneously (inside) [*nāda*] in the form of a *mantra* (mystic formula) is what the *japa* is about [*japaḥ so 'tra svayaṁ nādo*, v. 145]." Indeed, Kṣemarāja, Abhinavagupta's disciple, quotes this verse in his commentary (*Vimarśinī*) on verse 3.27 of *Śiva-Sūtra*, in which the process of *japa* is also recommended by Śiva himself. He continues by stating that "*Japa* consists in the repetition of constant contemplation on the deity that is one's own essential Self."[77]

Parallels to these notions of mantra in Kashmiri Śaivism can be evidenced in the Tibetan school of Tantric Buddhism known as "Vajrayāna": "In Buddhist Tantra *mantras* were used as a means of invoking the deity so that the meditator might become one with him or her. In this sense their full soteriological import becomes apparent."[78] And the practice of mantra repetition in Buddhist Tantra carried similar salvific concerns: "Among the chief features of the ritual of Vajrayāna was the repetition of mystical syllables and phrases (*mantra*), such as the famous *Oṁ maṇi padme hūṁ* ["Ah! The jewel is indeed in the lotus!"]. Yoga postures and meditation were practiced."[79] The *Bardo Thodol* ("Tibetan Book of the Dead"), an eighth-century Tibetan Buddhist text, stresses meditation on the above mantra as containing the cosmic resonance: "When the natural sound of Reality is reverberating (like) a thousand thunders, may they be transmuted into the sounds of the Six Syllables." The notes and commentary of the original translator are helpful: "These [six syllables] are of the essence *mantra* of Chenrazee (Avalokiteśvara), being *Oṁ-ma-ṇi-pad-me-hūṁ*. Chenrazee being the patron-god . . . of Tibet, and this being his *mantra*, its repetition, both in the human world and on the Bardo plane, is credited with bringing to an end the cycle of rebirth and thereby giving entrance to Nirvāṇa; hence its importance in the Bardo prayer."[80]

In consonance with the teachings of Śākta-Tantra reality is described in Trika philosophy according to a system of letters (*varṇamālā*). In fact, as noted by G. Mukhopadhyaya, the entire universe unfolds according to the sequence of the first three vowels, *A*, *I*, and *U*.

> The letter *A*, which is known as the first of all letters, stands for the ultimate reality beyond which there is nothing (*anuttara*). When this *anuttara* duplicates itself and then returns to or is reunited with itself, *A* is born (*A* + *A*), which is *ānanda*. The letter *I* signifies *icchā* or desire for manifestation, and *U* means *unmeṣa*, i.e., subtle manifestation or the sprouting forth of *icchā* in the ideal state of *jñāna*. The long *I* signifies complete mastery over everything desired (*īśāna*) and is thus the fulfillment of *icchā* or return into itself (*I* + *I*). Similarly, the long *U* signifies the ramification of *unmeṣa* into innumerable waves or thought-patterns (*ūrmi*). *A* is thus the ground of all creation and through

the medium of *I* (*icchā*) comes into manifestation (*U*), i.e., *unmeṣa*.[81]

Likewise, the linguistic cosmogony of these three vowels is said to synchronize with the act of speech in the human body:

> A, which is produced from the throat (*kaṇṭha*), comes out without any turn or twist of the tongue or lips, and as such stands for the basic sound which is generated with the least modification of the vocal apparatus. There is, however, a definite projection outward with the raising of the tongue towards the palate (*tālu*) in the production of I. In the utterance of I, the movement is still confined inside the mouth, but in U, it comes outside; . . . what was inside is now spilled out through the lips (*oṣṭha*). Thus the basic ground (A) raising itself or projecting itself through desire (I) comes out into manifestation (U) and thus the entire movement of the creative process is vividly pictured through these three letters, which are more than symbols in the Trika system. They embody the basic vibrations (*spanda*) of the creative process, from the original triangle or field of creative activity. The other vowels are only elongations and combinations of these three basic vowels. . . . Abhinavagupta rightly comments that the primal vibration A (*anuttara*) assumes infinitude of forms through its combination with *icchā*, i.e., I, and *unmeṣa*, i.e., U. This A stretches itself up to Ha and then returns to itself which is signified by the Bindu, encompassing the entire wealth of alphabets within itself. Thus "a-ha-m" denotes or covers the entire gamut of the creative process and is therefore synonymous with the self.[82]

The above is characteristic of what we might call Trika or Kaula "phoneme mysticism" and forms the groundwork of the Kashmiri Śaivite philosophy of sacred sound.

A comparative perspective reveals that meditation on "primal vowels" has also flourished in Japan. In Japanese Buddhism the esoteric tradition known as Shingon, which literally means "true word," "stressed that *mantras* were the living, concentrated essence of the Buddhist teachings. Mikkyo [esoteric teaching] treats *mantras* as embodiments of Truth, affirming that *mantras* themselves are the universal Buddha." Reminiscent of Kashmiri Śaivism and other Tantric groups, Shingon Buddhism, founded in the ninth century A.D.

by Kobo Daishi, stressed the importance of the primal vowel: "The universe is the full development of the meanings condensed in the A-syllable, which, as the essential 'voice' of all things, also embodies the original life-energy penetrating all things. In the *Dainichi-kyo* [the main scripture of Shingon Buddhism] is written, 'The A-syllable is the first life.'"[83]

In its role as the origin of both vowels and consonants Nāda-Brahman is described as *anāhata* (Anāhata-Nāda, "unstruck sound") by the Kashmiri savant Abhinavagupta in the *Tantrāloka* 6.217: "There is one *varṇa* in the form of Nāda (sound vibration) in which lie all the *varṇa*s (letters) latently in an undivided form. As it is ceaseless, it is called Anāhata i.e. unstruck, natural, spontaneous, uncaused. As all the *varṇa*s (letters) originate from this Nāda, therefore, is it called *varṇa* proleptically [*eko nādātmako varṇaḥ*]."[84] Regarding the qualifying adjective *Anāhata* attached to Nāda, Padoux explained that "only a sound that is not caused by a 'shock,' that is to say a material means, can be everlasting."[85]

A simple process of deduction suggests the inherent value of meditation on the original "root" vowels. As noted by a contemporary scholar, "If these sounds are the first rumblings of vibration within the absolute reality as it prepares to manifest, then they are significantly close to the absolute source which the Yogī wishes to approach. Their mutual connections, as they unfold from the absolute, are crucial inasmuch as they grant a knowledge of the salvational combinations of mantric sounds that are structured around these powerful vowels." The inherent value of the fifteen primal vowels (*svara*) is indeed explained by Abhinavagupta himself (*Parātrīśikā-laghuvṛttiḥ* 5–9a) by recourse to etymology: "These fifteen are called vowels (*svara*), because their nature is a sounding whose character results from the self-referral of consciousness, and because they shine by themselves (*svayaṁ rājantaḥ* [*sva* + *ra*]). Thus with respect to the external world they are self-luminous."[86]

Accordingly, Kashmiri Śaivas view the universe as a phonic emanation, a sounding forth from original silence. "The non-dual Kashmir Saivas view the process by which our daily reality is manifested from the infinite reality of Śiva as a 'sounding' forth. . . . This power is the Visarga Śakti [expansive energy]." The process of the sounding forth of reality occurs on four levels, the latter three of which are indebted to Bhartṛhari: "Parā, the supreme level; Paśyantī, the first 'vision' of what is to come; Madhyamā, the intermediate stage; and Vaikharī, the fully embodied stage of everyday speech."[87]

The quintessential nature of the Kashmiri Śaiva Absolute consciousness is described in the *Spanda-Kārikā* as a pulsating, dynamic, ecstatic, throbbing force called "Spanda," or vibration: "Spanda . . . in the case of the Supreme is neither physical motion, nor psychological activity like pain and pleasure, nor pranic activity like hunger or thirst. It is the throb of the ecstasy of the Divine I-consciousness (*vimarśa*). The Divine I-consciousness is spiritual dynamism. It is the Divine creative pulsation. It is the throb of Śiva's *svātantrya* or absolute freedom." In the same *Spanda-Kārikā* (3.10), a Kashmiri text ascribed to either Vasugupta or his disciple Kallaṭa of the tenth century C.E., the principle of Spanda has the attribute of Nāda as "supernormal sound": "From this (*unmeṣa*) appear (supernormal) light, (supernormal) sound, (supernormal) form, (supernormal) taste, in a short time, to the Yogī."[88]

The process of self-manifestation of the Spanda begins with subtle vibrations of the vowels, followed by the remaining phonemes along with the thirty-six Tattvas, and ends with the slowest and grossest vibrations of the inert rock. "The details of this process clarify the intrinsic nature of manifestation as a sounding-forth that begins with the infinitely subtle sounding of the Spanda and becomes progressively more perceptible, dense, gross, and solid."[89]

Abhinavagupta explains the concept of Bindu and Nāda in relation to the cosmos and human physiology in the *Tantrāloka* 3.111b-113a:

> The undivided light which shines in the abodes of the moon, sun, and fire—this is the supreme Bindu. As is said by the Lord in the *Tattva-rakṣā-vidhāna*, the point or dot (*bindu*) which stands within the circle of the lotus of the Heart is to be known by means of a special absorption as characterized by the triad of man, power [Śakti], and Śiva. The point is a stainless liberator. This point is a sound [śabda] whose nature is a vibrating hum (Nāda), and it is to be found in all living beings.[90]

Such affirmative descriptions of reality appear incongruous with the notion of ultimate silence and consciousness dissolution stressed by Padoux and favored by Buddhists and extreme monists. In the face of this ambiguity Paul Muller-Ortega argues that "to wish to define the Ultimate reality as a silence that transcends all characterizations would be to distort and demote the absolute into a powerless and useless ultimate. Such an ultimate would be totally appeased (*śānta*), but would also be incapable of serving as the essence of the finite. The Spanda, the internal movement of the Heart of Śiva, rescues the absolute from a kind of pristine but static inertia." Basing his observation on Abhinavagupta's *Parātriśikā-laghuvṛtti* (5–9a), Muller-Ortega concludes that "absolute consciousness [for the Kashmiri Śaiva] is never inert, it is never inactive; it is continuously throbbing, expanding, and contracting with the movement of the heart."[91] Thus, it is obvious that there are differing streams of thought within this tradition.

But one thing remains certain. Sacred sound or language and the Supreme Reality in Kashmiri Śaivism are not the same at the highest level. Yet, despite this difference, the most effective instrument of release for Kashmiri Śaivism, as in other Hindu traditions, is the linguistic device of a mantra. And, of all mantras, Abhinavagupta recommends the Heart-Mantra, S A U Ḥ, which contains the Visarga (:), and accomplishes the task of liberation by focusing the attention of the aspirant on the expansive aspect of his own heart.[92] Normally, persons are on a particular level of universal expansion or contraction. "In terms of its consciousness, the individual soul (*aṇu*) is caught between the total inertia of a rock and the omniscience of Bhairava [Śiva]." The Heart-Mantra connects the soul with the "flow" of universal processes and thus liberates the individual. "As taught in the *Parātriśikā-laghuvṛtti,* it is clear that the principal purpose of the Heart-*mantra* is the attainment of the freedom of consciousness: the *mantra* is a means toward liberation."[93]

While describing the Yogic process of interior meditation, Abhinavagupta stresses the particular instance wherein the flow of the three mystical channels (Iḍā, Piṅgalā, and Suṣumnā) are united together (*samāpatti*) into one continuous inner resonance, or Nāda (*Tantrāloka* 29.147–49): "Thus the sound vibration, which is perfect Self-awareness, arises in the domain of union during absorption in the consciousness of the triple flow. Such is the power of *mantra*. He alone truly knows the emergence of the *mantra* who, in this very resonance [Nāda], with a wish to obtain such fruits of emergence, remains absorbed in his own *mantra*."[94] In accordance with the teaching of one's guru, the continuous practice of *japa* is then advised in order to sustain the Nāda within the flow of sound (*dhvani*).

Last, we might add that the Kashmiri tradition closely exemplifies the meaning of *theos,* or God, which "shines through" (see intro.), as sacred sound and language participate directly with the qualities of light and consciousness "illumination" such that "the energy of the Word manifests, emits, the universe through a pulsating, radiant light, *sphurattā, prakāśa.*"[95]

Thus, the Kashmiri tradition, while building upon both the Śaiva-Āgama and Grammarian traditions, formulates its own unique triadic monism, wherein sacred sound is fundamental to both the creation of the universe and to the reintegration of the soul, or heart, into the cosmos. The highest reality is the male Parama-Śiva, with the immediately subordinate realm of sacred sound and language characterized as feminine energy (Vimarśa, Parā-Vāk, Paśyantī, etc.). Though sacred sound is not identical with the Absolute, as in Bhartṛhari, it still functions to deliver us from nescience toward a permanent transcendent reality.

The Śaiva traditions, beginning with the Śaiva-Āgamas and culminating in Śaiva-Siddhānta and Kashmiri Trika philosophy, represent an important branch of Hinduism. They include dualistic, theistic sectarian practices as well as an abstract monistic philosophy. Yet, taken together, they reflect a major preoccupation with sacred sound as Nāda-Brahman on both practical and theoretical levels. The next chapter will focus on the texts and practices related to Vaiṣṇavism and the deity of Viṣṇu.

Chapter 6

VAIṢṆAVISM
Sacred Sound as the Energy of Viṣṇu

Vaiṣṇavism is the largest among the Hindu theistic groups, such that the study of contemporary Vaiṣṇavism in India encompasses a broad range of materials all over the South Asian subcontinent. While some historians of religion have traced the origins of Viṣṇu worship to the few selected hymns of the *Ṛg-Veda* which glorify Viṣṇu as the Supreme Lord who "took three strides," the complex religion reflecting a synthesis of the gods Viṣṇu, Nārāyaṇa, Vāsudeva, and Krishna which is achieved by the time of the *Bhagavad-Gītā* (ca. fourth century B.C.E. to the third century A.D.) has continued to puzzle academicians. Without attempting to reconstruct the early Vaiṣṇavism of these periods, we will first examine selected texts of the Pāñcarātra corpus (Vaiṣṇava-Āgama) which detail the rites and practices of medieval Vaiṣṇava communities. Thereafter, we will discuss the development of sectarian Vaiṣṇavism by focusing on the *Bhāgavata-Purāṇa,* followed by evidence gleaned from texts and practices of several of the Sampradāyas, or disciplic lineages, of Vaiṣṇavism—namely, Śrī, Madhva, Nimbārka, Vallabha, and Gauḍīya. Throughout these traditions examples are cited to demonstrate the importance of sacred sound for Vaiṣṇavism, that is, theoretical conceptions of Nāda-Brahman, Praṇava divisions, linguistic levels (Paśyantī, etc.), Varṇavāda/Sphoṭavāda dichotomies, and sonic cosmogonies.

Although many of the Vaiṣṇava traditions exhibit all of these features, the distinguishing factor in Hindu theism, and this is especially visible in Vaiṣṇavism, is the presence of a male Supreme Being (Viṣṇu, Nārāyaṇa, Krishna, Rāma, etc.) who directs and oversees the functioning of these predominantly female features. For Vaiṣṇavism these features are personified most often as the spouse of Viṣṇu known as the goddess Lakṣmī. As in the other Hindu Tantric and theistic traditions, we find that sacred sound and its accompanying techniques of meditation are also believed to endure after liberation of the human soul from the cycle of rebirth, forming a uniquely "personal" sonic theology.

Vaiṣṇava-Āgama: Pāñcarātra

The division of the Āgama which encompasses the worship of Vaiṣṇu, or Nārāyaṇa, has its own terminology. "Whereas the Śākta-Āgamas... are better known as Tantras,... the Vaiṣṇava texts of this category are often called Saṁhitā.[1] Although the term Saṁhitā is still used with reference to a particular text, the category of Vaiṣṇava-Āgama is now more commonly referred to as encompassing two divisions: the Pāñcarātra and Vaikhānasa texts, or traditions. Although the tradition of Vaikhānasa is built largely upon Vedic and Brahmanical standards and, indeed, includes a strong emphasis on sacred sound, the focus here will be primarily on the Pāñcarātra-Āgama, or "Saṁhitā," tradition, since it is closer in spirit to the Āgama traditions, which we have already discussed in Śaivism. Moreover, it is the Pāñcarātra tradition that provides the most authoritative foundation for Vaiṣṇavism in India, as stated by a modern scholar: "All the Vaiṣṇava schools recognize the authority of the Pāñcarātra."[2] Indeed, the unique value of the Pāñcarātra literature,[3] in terms of its breadth and scope for the study of Vaiṣṇavism, has already been established by H. Daniel Smith: "The injunctions found in this Pāñcarātra literature... account for and give textual authority for the bulk of the activities undertaken in temples, in public and in the home by most Viṣṇu-worshippers today."[4]

The concepts of Nāda and Nāda-Brahman appear already in the *Jayākhya-Saṁhitā* and the *Sāttvata-Saṁhitā*, two of the earliest (ca. A.D. 500) and most canonical of the Pāñcarātra texts. The later *Ahirbudhnya-Saṁhitā* is more important for the study of sacred sound in the Pāñcarātra tradition, as it contains in chapters 16 through 19 the best and most characteristic disquisition on Nāda-Brahman. The *Lakṣmī-Tantra* devotes several sections to what the translator calls "linguistic occultism," referring to elaborated Vaiṣṇava discussion on Nāda-Brahman and the origin of mantras and alphabets. The *Śeṣa-Saṁhitā* is an even later text almost totally devoted to mantra. The available portions of these texts will be evaluated with regard to sacred sound, accenting the continuities with both the Śaiva-Āgamas and the Śākta-Tantras.

In harmony with the Śaiva-Āgama tradition the Pāñcarātra texts are ideally divided into the same four principal areas, though one or more of these concerns may be enlarged according to region or school: "The ideal Pāñcarātra-Saṁhitā, like the Śaiva-Āgamas, is said to consist of four 'quarters' (*pāda*) teaching respectively (1) *jñāna*, knowledge; (2) *yoga*, concentration; (3) *kriyā*, making; and (4) *caryā*, doing."[5]

Yet, instead of Śiva, the Pāñcarātras unequivocally worship the personal form of God as Lord Viṣṇu, also known as Nārāyaṇa: "According to the philosophers of the Viṣṇuite Pāñcarātra religion, Viṣṇu, i.e., God, is a Person, eternal, infinite, omniscient, self-existent, pure bliss and self-conscious in Himself. He is the ultimate reality beyond all existence, and at the same time its support. . . . He is the Lord of all and all are in Him. Being spontaneous, He combines in Himself all energies and pervades all things."[6]

Consequently, the primary goal of Pāñcarātra worship is the attainment of the personal abode and association of Lord Viṣṇu, or Lord Nārāyaṇa. And the soteriology of Pāñcarātra duly emphasizes the path of mantra meditation. "The deities, all being aspects of god, save man. And . . . as saviours they are primarily *mantras*. *Mantras* are the pure creation, and at the same time they are the means and the path to salvation. . . . The simultaneous result of such release is to attain Vāsudeva's [Viṣṇu's] highest abode (*paramaṁ padam*), which is the same as his great presence (*dhāman*), the supreme paradise of omniscience and bliss." Moreover, the role of the guru is paramount in their salvific scheme, especially in relation to the mantra which he imparts: "Pāñcarātra *sādhana* is the path of *mantra* (*mantra-mārga*). . . . All the theology, philosophy, and liturgy he learns from his guru, he is to apply to his *mantra* and its relation to his goal, salvation."[7]

The Pāñcarātra attitude toward sacred sound and mantra thus shares common elements with the Śākta-Tantra traditions already discussed, as firmly noted by Sanjukta Gupta: "Pāñcarātra has a great deal in common with other Tantric sects, and this holds also for its attitude to *mantra*. Like the other sects, Pāñcarātra refers to its own scriptures as Mantra-Śāstra and regards them as teaching *mantras*, meditation on those *mantras*, and the ritual accompanying that meditation; the whole constituting the means (*sādhana*) to salvation (*mukti*)."[8]

In conformity with the patterns of the other theistic branches of Hinduism which view Nāda-Brahman as the Sákti of their respective deity (Śaiva-Siddhānta, Kashmiri Śaiva, and forms of Śākta-Tantra traditions), Vaiṣṇavism holds that the Word, Vāk, Nāda-Brahman, or Śabda-Brahman, is the power of Viṣṇu, personified here as his consort Lakṣmī: "As monotheists believing in a personal (*puruṣa*) supreme god, Pāñcarātrins did not accept the theory that the sole ultimate reality was the impersonal Śabda-Brahman [as in the Grammarian tradition]. But they gave it second place in their cosmogony and cosmology, equating it with Śakti in their scheme. . . . Śabda-Brahman or Vāk is in Pāñcarātra identical with god's Śakti, the divine personality hypostatized as the creatrix and indeed personified as Lakṣmī, Vāsudeva's [Viṣṇu's] wife."[9]

The *Jayākhya-Saṁhitā,* one of the earliest known Pāñcarātra texts (ca. A.D. 450), mentions Nāda-Brahman in several places and contains long sections on mantra and mantra-meditation, which are among the first in Vaiṣṇava literature. Benoytosh Bhattacharyya, the general editor of the Gaekwad Oriental Series, gives a translation of some of the more poignant verses regarding mantra from chapter 6 (6.59–61) in his foreword to the edition of this text: "It is necessary that the highest God should be worshipped in the form of *mantras* and images. The *mantras* are parts and parcels of the highest Brahman; his images are parts of his person. The letters of the alphabet originate from him, and their combination makes the *mantras*. And because they come out of him, it is reasonable that his worship should be performed through the agency of *mantras*."[10]

The several references to Nāda-Brahman occur in the last chapter of the *Jayākhya-Saṁhitā.*[11] Within the context of Mantra-Sādhana (33.40) the speaker of this text urges the initiate to meditate gradually on the "shining" sound-syllable, the ultimate end of which is reposed in Nāda (*nādam āśritaḥ*). He then (33.47–50) exhorts the aspirant to concentrate on Lord Nārāyaṇa, whose very essence is mantra and Praṇava. By also meditating on the single-syllable KṢAUḤ or HRĪṀ, one perceives the undivided Bindu in the forehead. This Śakti, appearing as "half-measure," is absorbed in Nāda, which is itself absorbed in the Supreme Lord. Thus, one should certainly contemplate, through the Yoga of meditation, the eternal Parā and Paśyantī consisting of "spiritual sound."[12] The use of the Grammarian terms of *Parā* and *Paśyantī* in this verse is curious, as it is contemporaneous with Bhartṛhari and may even precede him.

In addition, chapter 14 of the *Jayākhya-Saṁhitā,* entitled "Japa-Vidhāna" ("Concerning the Repetition of *Mantras*"), contains many early references to the practice of *japa* with the rosary (*akṣa-mālā*): "There are three aids to doing *japa* repetitions—employing a rosary (*akṣa-mālā*), saying them aloud (*vācika*) or by repeating them in a low voice (*upāṁśu*)—and each of these is of varying value depending on the motives of the aspirant (1-5a). The *akṣa-mālā* rosary is then described and its uses discussed (5b-76a, 90-95a)."[13] This further supports the argument of a pre-Islamic, and thus pre-Christian, provenance of the rosary in Hindu religious meditation.

The *Jayākhya-Saṁhitā* has been normally classified as one of the original "Three Gems," the three most significant Pāñcarātra texts which, according to H. Daniel Smith, "shine out more brightly than others and whose value is treasured beyond count in the canon."[14] The other two "gems" are the *Sāttvata-Saṁhitā* and the *Pauṣkara-Saṁhitā*, both of which emphasize the role of sacred sound as Śabda-Brahman and mantra: "The notion that Śabda [Śabda-Brahman] is the ultimate principle of the universe, comprehending even God, is encountered in both the *Sāttvata* and the *Pauṣkara*."[15] The *Sāttvata-Saṁhitā* is one of the most respected and ancient of the Pāñcarātra works which have survived. While Smith had noted that "the key term for understanding almost 75 percent of the text is *mantra*,"[16] specific references to Nāda-Brahman occur in chapter 12 (v. 68-70), wherein the contemplation of a *varṇacakra* design (letters arranged between the spokes of a wheel image with Brahman at the hub) is detailed. In short, all of the letters of the Sanskrit alphabet from *a* to *h* are said to be born from Nāda, which is Śabda-Brahman, and the Śakti of Viṣṇu, or Nārāyaṇa.[17]

Within the *Pauṣkara-Saṁhitā*, a very esteemed and ancient (ca. A.D. 450) text of nearly six thousand verses, there is a long digression on Mantra-Yoga to be found in chapter 27 (v. 248b-431) and a unique description of the sacred bell (*ghaṇṭā*) sounded during Hindu worship (chap. 34).

The *Ahirbudhnya-Saṁhitā* (before A.D. 800, according to Schrader), one of the more articulately theological Pāñcarātra texts, describes a cosmogony in relation to Nāda-Brahman and the four stages of speech, as paraphrased by Schrader (16.36-77):

> Speech begins with Nāda resembling the sound of a deep bell and perceptible to perfect Yogīs only; the Nāda develops into Bindu (*anusvāra*) which is twofold, as the Śabda-Brahman or "Sound-Brahman" and the Bhūti (related to each other as the

> name and the bearer of the name); and then from the Bindu proceed the two kinds of sounds, to wit the vowels (*svara*) and the consonants (*vyañjana*). . . . In accordance with the theory of the four states of sound (Parā, Paśyantī, Madhyamā, and Vaikharī) it is then shown how . . . [the] fourteen vowels (or rather the *a* as their common root, verse 45) gradually emerge from their latent condition by proceeding, with the Kuṇḍalinī Śakti, from the Mūlādhāra (perineum) to the navel, the heart, and finally the throat where the first uttered sound arising is the aspirate, for which reason the Visarga [:] is interpreted literally as "creation" (*sṛṣṭi*), its counterpart, the *anusvāra* or Bindu being in an analogous way declared to represent the "withdrawal" (*saṁhāra*) of speech. The *anusvāra* is also called "sun" (*sūrya*), and the *visarga* "moon" (Soma), and the sounds *a, i, u, ṛ, ḷ, e, o,* and *ā, ī, ū, ṝ, ḹ, ai, au* are respectively "sun-beams" and "moon-beams" and as such connected with day and night and with the Nāḍīs called Piṅgalā and Iḍā.[18]

This quotation contains nearly all of the ingredients of our concept of Hindu sonic theology: Nāda-Brahman (or Śábda-Brahman), Bindu, Bhartṛharian linguistic levels such as Paśyantī, and sonic creation sequences involving the unfolding of the alphabet. Such patterns and structures subsequently become firmly embedded in Vaiṣṇava vocabulary as found in the *Bhāgavata-Purāṇa* and later sectarian movements.

An interesting comparison from Western religion is suggested by a glance at a linguistic cosmogony in second-century Gnosticism. The commentary by the Gnostic Marcus on the creation account given in the beginning of the Gospel of John (1.1) sounds remarkably similar in spirit to the Hindu scenarios:

> God's creation was linguistic, and the letters of the first potent word that he uttered contained all the forms of creation, each form presided over by the name of a letter of the alphabet, which is in turn composed of letters, each of which has a name, and so on to infinity. . . . Creation, on other words, is eternal and ongoing: "the multitude of letters swells out into the infinitude," and "letters are continually generating other letters." The alphabet speaks a divine language, . . . each letter calling up, but never pinning down, the enigmatic nature of reality, the word of God.[19]

The *Lakṣmī-Tantra* (ca. A.D. 900–1300) is a veritable mine of material for the study of sacred sound in the Pāñcarātra tradition. It contains nearly all of the elements that one might expect in a Śākta-Tantra text (i.e., Śrī-Vidyā) yet persists as a "Pāñcarātra" work due to its conformity to certain Pāñcarātric features, such as the association of Lakṣmī to Viṣṇu as his spouse, or Śakti; discussion of the four Vyūha expansions; and a large number of citations from other Pāñcarātra works, especially the *Jayākhya-Saṁhitā*.[20] A distinctive feature of the *Lakṣmī-Tantra* is that the goddess Lakṣmī, as Śakti, identifies herself as the "mother of all sound": "I (Śabda-Brahman) am essentially consciousness and bliss, the source of all *mantras*; the absolute; the mother of all sound; Śakti not subjected to appearance and disappearance (i.e., she is constantly present)."[21]

The linguistic cosmogony (18.22–27) in the *Lakṣmī-Tantra* also contains the familiar elements of Nāda, Bindu, Paśyantī, Madhyamā, and Vaikharī:

> Śabda is the manifest knowledge (*bodha*), and (*artha*) is the object Śabda (sound) manifests; (whereas) the primary manifestation of sound (arises) from Śakti in the form of Santata, which (aspect of Śakti), known as Nāda does not at that stage carry any implication (*vācyata*). The Śakti attached to Nāda is called Sūkṣma. The second manifestation (*unmeṣa*) after Nāda arising from Śakti is called Bindu which, though carrying implication, is not yet manifestly polarized. This divine and highly efficacious state of mine is referred to as Paśyantī. Besides these manifestations of Śakti, her third manifestation is the state of Madhyamā, in which *saṁgati* (the logical relation of word to meaning) transforms itself into an impression (*saṁskāra*). At this stage, the distinction between the object indicated and the sound denoting it, is (only) discernable in the form of an impression. Śakti's fourth manifestation following that of Madhyamā is the state of Vaikharī, in which syllables and sentences (words) become clearly recognizable.[22]

As in other Hindu traditions, but not in the principal Upaniṣads or Advaita-Vedānta, the syllable *Om* or *AUM*, is divided into four (3 + 1) substantive members, or degrees, in Pāñcarātra and thus in Vaiṣṇavism. In Pāñcarātra fashion the *Lakṣmī-Tantra* (24.6–9) equates the "four" parts of AUṀ, including Nāda and Bindu counted as the fourth, to the four Vyūhas, or emanations, of Viṣṇu.[23] *A* stands for

Aniruddha, the final emanation in the world of the senses. *U* stands for Pradyumna, *M* signifies Saṁkarṣaṇa, and the fourth (*turīya*) represents the original state of Vāsudeva and his consort Lakṣmī:

> Having thus consecrated Om, the adept should first decorate that Brahma-Tāraka [Praṇava] with Bindu, thereupon with Nāda. Then, as accompaniment to this Tāraka he should meditate on the eternal Brahman made up of these three letters in the Vaiṣṇava form (the mind flowing towards it incessantly) like the (continuous) flow of oil. Here (in this Tāraka), A represents Aniruddha, the fifth vowel (U) represents Pradyumna, M (represents) Saṁkarṣaṇa and Bindu (represents) Vāsudeva. O Sureśvara, the indivisibility (i.e., integral nature) of these four (letters) is the Nāda. The highest perfection of Nāda is the I-hood (of God), who is the highest Goddess.[24]

This scenario was presaged by chapter 51 of the earlier *Ahirbudhnya-Saṁhitā,* which had made a total of six subtle distinctions, some of which appear to echo the *Māṇḍūkya-Upaniṣad:*

> The first *mantra* explained is the Tāra or Tāraka Mantra, that is, the sacred syllable Om. . . . In its "subtle sense" it is composed of the letters A U M denoting respectively: (1) the waking state and gross universe with Aniruddha as their protector; (2) the dream consciousness and subtle universe superintended by Pradyumna; (3) the *suṣupti* state and corresponding universe with Saṅkarṣaṇa as their guardian-deity; then (4) the echo of the M (*ardha-mātra*) representing Vāsudeva (the *turīya*); further (5) the last lingering nasal sound, which is the undifferentiated Śakti of the Lord as the "fifth stage"; and, finally, (6) the silence observed after the pronunciation of the syllable, which is Viṣṇu as the Highest Brahman.[25]

Subsequent to this, the *Lakṣmī-Tantra* (52.1–23) incorporated the same states of consciousness into a more typical Śākta-Tantra metaphysics of the fourth degree (*turīya*):

> What is here regarded as (my) Sūrya manifestation corresponds with my waking state. Agni is my dream state and my state of deep sleep is Soma (manifestation) which is otherwise called Māyā. The remaining part called *indu-khaṇḍa* is my *turīya*

> [fourth] state. Nāda is the state beyond that. Śakti, which is the state of inertia (Śānta), is in fact the Nāda's state of existence. Brahman, that exists beyond (even) that, is indeed the (state of union) between Lakṣmī and Nārāyaṇa.[26]

Further explorations of the states of being at the climax of Nāda (*nādānta*) occur in the *Śeṣa-Samhita*, a later Pāñcarātra text that is devoted almost entirely to mantras and sonic themes. In a short section (66) entitled Praṇavārtha ("The Meaning of Om") there is an analysis of the nine components of Om: A U M, Bindu, Nāda, Nādānta, Nādātīta (beyond Nāda), Nādātītānta (the end beyond Nāda), and Nādātītāntāntara (within the end beyond Nāda), with their corresponding Vaiṣṇava meanings, meanings that include a string of names for Viṣṇu or his incarnations such as Nṛsiṁha, Nārāyaṇa, Rāmachandra, Keśava, Vāsudeva, Puruṣottama, and Bhagavān Hari.[27]

Chapter 50 of the *Lakṣmī-Tantra* purports to include a version of the Śrī-Sūkta, an apocryphal "Ṛg-Vedic" hymn of fifteen verses to the goddess Śrī, or Lakṣmī.[28] The original Vedic hymn (v. 3) contains the word *nāda* but only in the sense of "the roar of elephants" at the arrival of Lakṣmī [*hasti-nāda-prabodhinīm*].[29] Vaiṣṇava tradition has extracted fifty-three to fifty-four names of the goddess from the hymn which have been enlarged upon and included in the *Lakṣmī-Tantra*. Therein the goddess Lakṣmī, in the first person, expounds her own glories in fifty-three names. The first few lines of the redacted hymn (*Lakṣmī-Tantra* 50.37–42) contain the metaphysical elements of Nāda and Paśyantī:

> I am immanent in all beings and I hum like the female bumble bee. From my abode in Sūrya and Candra I gush forth in an unbroken flow of absolute sound (Nāda) like the flow of oil during the interval between the closing and opening of (God's) eyes. As I travel (in turn through) all the centers of the body, from Mūlādhāra to the Dvādaśānta [the end of the twelve lotuses in the body] with the brilliance of thousands of risen suns, fires and moons, I unfold (myself) from the Cakraka, the air-repository, as (manifested sound) Śānta [Parā], Paśya [Paśyantī], Madhyamā and Vaikharī.

Accordingly, goddess Lakṣmī explains her presence in the Praṇava syllable in subsequent verses (*Lakṣmī-Tantra* 50.136–42): "My sound-body is the subtle flame of Praṇava and resembles the continuing resonance of a ringing bell like a flow of oil. He who has realized Brahman will soon recognize my presence there (in Praṇava) and I, consisting of sound, come together with all sounds produced from the Âditya-sound (i.e., Praṇava)."[30] Obviously, the Yogic, Āgamic, and Bhartṛharian influences have overtaken what must originally have been purely a laudatory poem attached to the *Ṛg-Veda*.

The presence of the sacred in Pāñcarātra is contained first and foremost in sound form, which, as we have seen, is the power or energy of God. Accordingly, the diverse parts of God's nature are represented by mantras, which, in turn, are able to sanctify and transform nonsound forms of land and material into sacred temples, diagrams, and icons: "The power (*bala*) of the deity inheres in the first instance in the *mantra* form and attaches itself to the other two forms (personification, *devatā*, and visual diagram or icon, *yantra*) by derivation."[31]

The Pāñcarātric process whereby an icon or image of God is installed for worship (*pratiṣṭhā*) in a temple or holy shrine involves a complicated procedure of "Nāda-Brahman infusion." After the sound form of the particular deity is created within the body of the priest or preceptor through the correct mantra intonation, the sound-power (Nāda) of that deity is then infused into the icon or image according to the four stages of Nāda, or Śabda-Brahman. The *Lakṣmī-Tantra* (49.135–41) contains a description of the ritual Yoga involved in this process of *pratiṣṭhā*:

> Whereupon, identifying his (own) body as identified with the conscious sound [Śabda-Brahman] in all (its states of) distinction, (namely) the absolute (transcendent), the subtle etc., (the preceptor) should envisage the image as incorporating (that sound-body). Then following the Yoga of sonic dissolution (Śabda-Saṁhāra) he should visualize the two bodies, his own and that of the image, as merged in the unflickering conscious sound. After which, following the previously mentioned order, he should envisage the unaffected Śabda-Brahman inhering the sound (-pervaded) image, through the successive (states of) Paśyantī etc. Having thus introduced the presence of Śabda (in the image) and having finished the Mantra-introduction, the wise (preceptor) should start the ritual Yoga in the following way. (Envisaging) the integral absolute (sound) as reaching the Paśyantī state at the navel, (he should then visualize it as) approaching his lotus heart through the middle channel [Suṣumnā],

> which resembles the fibre of a lotus stalk. After allowing it to tarry there awhile, he should then envisage it as entering the heart of the image through the Vaikharī (manifestation). Whereupon he should visualize the Lord of the world in *mantra* form manifested as the glorious Nāda, pervading all *mantras* and present in the heart of the image.[32]

In agreement with this description P. P. Apte, a Pāñcarātra scholar, added that "Nāda-Brahman gives life to the deity, . . . [and] *mantra* makes the deity powerful."[33]

In order to obtain the "secrets" of sound, or mantra, power in Pāñcarātra, it is essential, as in other Hindu traditions, to receive initiation (*dīkṣā*) and instruction (śikṣā) from a guru. A specific ritual whereby the guru imparts to the disciple the method of *mantroddhāra*, or "culling the power of the mantra," is described in the *Lakṣmī-Tantra*. After the guru has inscribed the *Om* in the center of a lotus *maṇḍala* he or she "worships this diagram and demonstrates how to envisage it as the manifest Śabda-Brahman in its seminal state of Nāda. The *sādhaka* learns to imagine Nāda as a luminous entity existing inside his heart, which he imagines to be inside two lotuses. . . . This brilliant Nāda is visualized as constantly pouring out the vibrating *mātṛkā*, the potential Vāk. Om represents this Nāda form of Śabda-Brahman before it is disseminated over the cosmos."[34]

The guru knows the secret powers of each of the letters and infuses them into the total mantra, which, in turn, begins to act on the consciousness of the disciple. "By extracting his *mantra* letter by letter from the body of the *mātṛkā* (Vāk, visualized as Lakṣmī, whose body is entirely made of the Sanskrit alphabet, *Lakṣmī-Tantra* 23.13–29), the *sādhaka* enacts a birth of the *mantra* from its source. This strengthens his conviction that his *mantra* is a part of the totality of the sonic emanation of Śakti, namely Nāda."[35]

In consonance with Mīmāṁsā and the Varṇavāda position the Pāñcarātra tradition perceives the essential power of language in the letters themselves. Unlike the Mīmāṁsā, however, in which the letters are autonomously empowered by their very presence in the Veda, the letters of mantras in Hindu theism are purposely empowered by the deity and the deity's own power. In the case of Vaiṣṇavism the letters are both named and empowered by the goddess Lakṣmī (*Lakṣmī-Tantra* 25.30–33):

> Letters are the source of all *mantras*. They are made strong by the Lakṣmī-Śakti. They are reverentially praised, worshipped

and meditated upon (by the adept) by means of (their) names. They bestow great prosperity (on the adept) and produce (promote) the highest knowledge (in his mind); when used in *mantras* they become parts of each other. There is nothing in this world of movables and immovables that is not produced by them. Although the forms of the *mantras* are divine and eternal, yet *mantras* are thus conceived to be produced by letters.[36]

Furthermore, the *Ahirbudhnya-Saṁhitā* (chap. 17) contains information regarding certain "occult" (that is, ecumenical, in the sense of hidden correspondences between otherwise rival groups) meanings of the individual letters:

> Each letter of the alphabet has (1) three "Vaiṣṇava" forms, namely a "gross," "subtle," and "highest" one, expressed by certain names of Viṣṇu; (2) one "Raudra" form called after one of the Rudras (that is, by one of the names of Śiva); and (3) one "Śākta" form being the name of one of the limbs, organs, or ornaments of the Śakti of Viṣṇu. . . . For *mantras* connected with Viṣṇu, Śiva, or Śakti the respective alphabets should always be employed. These alphabets seem to serve a double purpose: enabling the initiate to quote the *mantras* without endangering their secrecy, and providing him with a handle for their mystic interpretation. These lists, then, are an indispensable key to the *mantras*.[37]

In summary, the Pāñcarātra tradition displays the features of a fully developed sonic theology, perhaps even more than its Śaiva-Āgamic counterpart. The soteriological dimension of this tradition being centered on the use of sacred sound as mantra, meditation and repetition of the letters of the mantras consisting of Nāda-Brahman as the Śakti of the Supreme Deity enable the adept to reach the highest possible level of Ultimate Reality for the Vaiṣṇava—the abode of Lord Viṣṇu.

Bhāgavata-Purāṇa and the Sectarian Movements

The study of later Vaiṣṇavism (post-Pāñcarātra) must begin with an examination of the *Bhāgavata-Purāṇa* (ca. A.D. 900), a large Purāna that reflects the devotional milieu of south India plus the syncretism of Vedic, Āgamic, Yogic, and philosophical sources. Regarding content, it centers on the by then standard mythology concerning Viṣṇu and his incarnations known as the Avatāras (22)—especially notable is the presence here of a narrative framework for Krishna's childhood—and presents a relatively coherent Vaiṣṇava philosophy through the mouths of both divine incarnations and human sages. Regarding the *Bhāgavata-Purāṇa* and its role in propagating the Krishna tradition, Daniel P. Sheridan remarked that "it is the main channel through which the stories and legends about Krishna have entered the length and breadth of Hindu civilization. . . . The *Bhāgavata* is a literary masterpiece, . . . but more than that it is a religious document which is the dynamic force behind a long and glorious chapter in the religious history of the Indian people."[38] Appropriately, this text, including several canonical Vaiṣṇava commentaries, provides a solid point of departure for understanding certain normative Vaiṣṇava positions after A.D. 1000.

The *Bhāgavata-Purāṇa* has been significantly influential on the major Vaiṣṇava Sampradāyas (disciplic lineages—e.g., Rāmānuja, Madhva, Nimbārka, Vallabha, Caitanya) as well as innumerable other subsects and cults. In fact, "later Vaiṣṇava devotional movements almost all had the *Bhāgavata* as a base, and almost all were characterized in their initial stages by intense devotional fervor."[39]

The unique synthesis achieved by the "Bhāgavat" provided additional theological foundation, along with the Pañcarātra, for the further development of the sectarian movements. "The *Bhāgavata-Purāṇa* has blended the Upaniṣadic path of knowledge with Yoga technique of Patañjali and the Tantric method of worship and opening of the mystic plexuses (*kamala*) located in the body, along with the nine-fold path of devotion. The result is the unique doctrine of Love of Bhāgavata-Dharma."[40] Indeed, the text (11.27.7,8) betrays its own syncretistic nature, wherein Lord Viṣṇu, himself the original "speaker," agrees to receive both Vedic and Tantric modes of worship: "My worship is of three kinds—according to the Veda, according to the Tantra and according to a mode that combines both. A man may worship me according to whichever of these modes appeals to him."[41]

The important role of sacred sound in the *Bhāgavata-Purāṇa* comes clearly into view near the end of the text (12.6.37–44), wherein a detailed description of its own sonic origin, including the theologies of Śabda-Brahman and Nāda-Brahman, is presented and discussed in the terms with which we are by now familiar. When questioned regarding the origin of the *Bhāgavata-Purāṇa* itself, Sūta Goswami, the narrator, replies with an explanation of the origin of Om, the Vedas, and the Sanskrit alphabet:

> The Sūta Answered: From the space in the heart of Brahmā, the Chief of all Creators, rose Nāda (unarticulated sound) when his mind was stilled in contemplation, that Nāda which any one may perceive by stopping his ear. It is by devout meditation thereon that the Yogīs free themselves from all taint of what are known as substance, action, and agent, and win release from saṁsāra. From that issued the triform "Om" whose origin is unapparent; it is self-luminous, and it signifies the exalted Lord, the Brahmā, Supreme Spirit, Who hears this indistinct Oṁkāra even when he is unreceptive, since He perceives without the aid of the senses. It was this Oṁkāra which, being made manifest [*sphoṭam*] in the space of the heart by the Ātman Itself, revealed the whole corpus of speech. It directly signifies the Supreme Soul, the Brahmā, its own Origin. It is the subtle form of the Vedic *mantras*, and the source, eternal and immutable, of the Veda. It has three letters, *ākāra* and the rest [A U M], O exalter of the Bhṛgus, which produce the triad of existents—the guṇas, the names (Ṛg, Yajus and Sāman) and the states (waking and the rest).[42]

The importance of Oṁkāra here is self-evident, being the first linguistic manifestation of Nāda-Brahman and the source of the Vedas, language, and consciousness. Also, the creator-god Brahmā holds a distinctive place in the lineage of several Vaiṣṇava Sampradāyas, since he is said to have also inaugurated the initiatory tradition (*dīkṣā*) whereby sacred sound as mantra (e.g., Om, Gopāla-Mantra, Viṣṇu-Gāyatrī, Mahā-Mantra, etc.) is first received by him from Lord Krishna (Viṣṇu) and then passed down to succeeding generations.

The theoretical continuity of the *Bhāgavata-Purāna* with the Upaniṣadic tradition of sacred sound is evident. We had previously seen in the *Śvetāśvatara-Upaniṣad* (1.14) that God, or Brahman, is "kindled" by the rubbing together of two friction-sticks (Om and the human body). Similarly, Lord Krishna reveals his personal appearance as sacred sound in the *Bhāgavata-Purāṇa* (11.12.18) using the same metaphor: "When kindling wood is rubbed together, heat is produced by contact with air, and by vigorously rubbing the sticks, a spark of fire appears. Once the fire is kindled, ghee is added and the fire blazes. Similarly, I become manifest in the sound vibration of the Vedas [*vāṇī*]."[43]

In addition, the reliance on the Bhartṛharian divisions of language and the vocabulary of Tantric Yoga is continued. The *Bhāgavata-Purāṇa* (11.12.17) depicts Lord Krishna as manifesting Nāda-Brahman within the human body in terms of the Cakra itinerary:

> This is that perceptible Supreme Lord who infuses life in all and who manifests himself within the nerve-centers or plexuses (Cakras) known as Mūlādhāra and others (existing in the internal parts of the human body). With the Prāṇa impregnated with Nāda (called Parā speech), he enters the "cave" (known as Ādhāra-Cakra, located near the anus). He proceeds (ahead) assuming the subtle mental form (known as Paśyantī, and Madhyamā forms of speech) in the spiritual plexuses called Maṇipūra and Viśuddhi located at the navel and at the throat respectively. He reveals himself in the mouth in the form of short and long notes, accents (such as *udatta, anudatta* and *svarita*) and articulate sounds (like the velars, palatals, dentals, etc.). This is the grossest speech form (called Vaikharī) of the Vedas and its branches.[44]

An important Gauḍīya-Vaiṣṇava commentator known as Viśvanāth Cakravartī (born ca. A.D. 1654) has given a further explanation of this verse, stressing the presence of God in the form of sound in the energy centers:

> Lord Krishna became manifest from the mouth of Lord Brahmā [demiurge] in the form of the Vedas. The word *vivara-prasūti* in this verse also indicates that the Lord is manifest within the *ādhārādi-cakras* [the Mūlādhāra-Cakra, etc.] situated within the body of Lord Brahmā. The word *ghoṣeṇa* means "subtle sound," and *guhaṁ praviṣṭaḥ* also indicates that Lord Krishna enters within the *ādhāra-cakra* [Mūlādhāra-Cakra]. The Lord can further be perceived within other Cakras such as the Maṇipūra-Cakra, located around the navel, and the Viśuddha-Cakra [at the throat].[45]

The subtle form of Krishna is to be perceived within the worshipper's body at the very culmination of Nāda itself, according to the *Bhāgavata-Purāna* (11.27.23-24): "In his own body, purified by the Vāyu and the Agni within, the worshipper should contemplate on My highest form, atomic in size, located in the heart lotus, which the perfected meditate upon as being beyond the 'Nāda' [*nādānte,* literally "at the end of Nāda"].[45] Having thus perceived the Lord at the apex of Nāda, the adept is now able to transfer the sacred power into an otherwise material object for the purpose of worship and *darśana* (visual adoration), through the Pāñcarātra method of Nāda-infusion: "When his body is irradiated by That Presence with which he identifies himself in thought, he should worship It with all honors mentally offered, and then, filled with Its afflatus, invoke It in the image or other vehicle of worship, and establish it there."[46]

Śrīdhara Swami, a fourteenth- to fifteenth-century Advaita commentator much favored by Vaiṣṇavas, remarks here that the syllable *Om* has four to five parts, as in the Śaiva and Śākta ideologies: "Praṇava, or Oṁkāra, has five parts; A, U, M, the nasal Bindu and the reverberation (Nāda). Liberated souls meditate upon the Lord at the end of that vibration."[47] The *Bhāgavata-Purāṇa* (11.15.16) has even blended Lord Nārāyaṇa (Viṣṇu) into the concept of *turīya,* or the fourth degree, of Praṇava: "The Yogī who focuses his mind on me as Nārāyaṇa, the Fourth Principle [*nārāyaṇe turīyākhye*], one specifically designated by the term Bhagavan, attains the same characteristics as mine."[48]

The various Vaiṣṇava sectarian movements that followed the *Bhāgavata-Purāṇa* continued to emphasize the role of sacred sound as the Śakti of a male deity, a deity known formally as Viṣṇu but more popularly worshipped in his more accessible form of Rāma, or Krishna. The personal role of the Supreme Lord becomes more important, as the power of mantra is based solely on the initiative that he takes toward the redemption of the devoted followers. This initiative, while taking many forms, is known as grace, or *anugraha,* and is especially present in mantra: "All *mantras* are manifestations of god in his pristine glory as saviour. God decides to make himself available to his devotee in a form he can understand and approach. . . . *Mantras* are god's forms assumed out of grace, embodiments of that grace (*anugraha-mūrti*). The *sādhaka* identifies himself with his *mantra* in love and trust, as he knows it to be a form of god's presence."[49] For instance, the personal dimension of the goddess Lakṣmī, the spouse of Viṣṇu, was already evident in the *Lakṣmī-Tantra* (24.3) by her willingness to "incarnate" into language itself for the salvation of souls: "In order to help all living beings, I voluntarily manifest myself in the forms of Mātṛkā-Mantras, containing Śabda-Brahman."[50]

This notion of grace has its counterpart in the branch of Śaivism known as Śaiva-Siddhānta (or Pāśupata):

> There can be no doubt that these *mantras* can be traced back to nothing but the decree of Śiva himself.... In using these *mantras* in meditation, Śiva communicates himself for the salvation of men. This is because... he alone enables these *mantras* to mediate himself as the means of salvation in an actual encounter. It is only in this encounter that the mediating subject opens himself up in actual worship to the god who is mediated through the *mantra*. Thus, he can become the recipient of salvation.[51]

Such initiative taken by the Supreme Being to "impregnate" ordinary human language with sacred potencies is often accompanied by directives on the manner and frequency of mantra recitation and repetition (*japa*). We may note here that, contrary to Mīmāṁsā—in which the sacred Vedic texts exist a priori without a Supreme Being overseeing their dissemination—certain types of language (i.e., mantras) for the Hindu theistic traditions are deliberately impregnated with divine energies by a personal Lord. This squares well with the general notion of *avatāra,* in which Viṣṇu descends to save the faithful.

The appropriate response by the faithful involves a devotional attitude known as "Bhakti," which normally manifests in devotional activities such as chanting God's name and glories. In fact, "taking the name" (*nāma-japa*) is an essential step in professing one's Bhakti, since most sects hold that God and his name are somehow identical. Because God has revealed and empowered his names (or a specific set of syllables or phrases) with his energies, they are extremely effective in bringing about purity and liberation. As noted by Klaus K. Klostermaier, "In order to be effective, the *nāma-japa* must be undertaken with a name that God himself has revealed in the Scriptures. God is identical with such a self-revealed name, God's *śabda,* and that lends power to the sound of the name itself. Repetition of the name is the most powerful remedy against all sins and faults."[52]

While followers of Śiva and the Goddess venerate the name of Śiva and Śakti with devotion, numerically the Vaiṣṇavas with their many subsects and lineages are the most important group among the

Bhakti practitioners of *nāma-japa.* They attach a particular importance to the continuous recitation of God's name, as explained by an Indian scholar: "Vaiṣṇavism holds that the name of God contains within it all the values of holiness. The process of recital brings these values down to the level of daily life, sanctifying all thoughts, acts and desires.... Devotion to the name... is the same thing as reverential worship of Hari.... If the name of God is same as God, a continuous process of recital signifies a continuous presence of God in the mind of the devotee."[53]

What now follows is a brief "sonic survey" of the major theological lineages, or Sampradāyas, of Vaiṣṇavism. Though they all accept the supremacy of Viṣṇu, or Krishna, as inculcated in the *Bhāgavata-Purāṇa,* they differ in their interpretation of the relationship between the individual souls and God. The names and basic doctrines of these schools are: (1) Viśiṣṭādvaita ("qualified monism"), associated with the name of Rāmānuja (eleventh century) and continued by the Śrī-Vaiṣṇava sect, yet prominent in south India; (2) Dvaita ("dualism"), the main exponent of which was Madhva (thirteenth century), who taught that souls have eternal separateness from God, the only independent reality; (3) Dvaitādvaita ("dualistic monism"), taught by Nimbārka (twelfth century), according to which the world of souls and matter is simultaneously different and nondifferent from God; (4) Śuddhādvaita ("pure monism") of Vallabha, which explains the universe and God as One without recourse to the doctrine of Māyā (illusion); (5) Acintya-bhedābheda ("inconceivable duality and nonduality"), the doctrine of Caitanya (Bengal, early sixteenth century), in which the relation between the world of souls and matter on the one hand and God on the other is beyond conception but is both different and nondifferent.

Inspired by the work of the renowned saint-scholar Rāmānuja (A.D. 1050–1137), the Śrī-Vaiṣṇava sect represents the earliest as well as the most enduring formalization of Vaiṣṇava theistic worship. Though originally founded by Nāthamuni on the basis of both the devotional hymns of the Āḷvārs and the Pāñcarātra texts, the establishment of Śri-Vaiṣṇavism as a major sectarian system was largely the work of Rāmānuja, the fifth in the line of Ācharyas after Nāthamuni and the leader of the sect in the eleventh and early twelfth centuries. Rāmānuja's entire argument in his interpretations of Vedānta was for the purpose of defending theistic devotion as philosophically and scripturally valid and effective for salvation. "The Śrī-Vaiṣṇavas have continued down to modern times as a model of sectarian theism, establishing a pattern followed by many other sectarian groups."[54]

In an attempt to establish theistic devotion on philosophical grounds Rāmānuja indeed took up the task of writing a commentary on Bādarāyaṇa's *Vedānta-Sūtra,* which had earlier been interpreted in purely monistic terms by Śaṅkara (ca. A.D. 800). And characteristic of most Vedāntins—Rāmānuja's version of Vedānta being Viśiṣṭa-Advaita—was the preoccupation with the questions of the eternity of the Veda and the creation of the universe through linguistic emanation. Rāmānuja's apposite statements in his own commentary on the *Vedānta-Sūtra,* known as *Śrī-Bhāṣya* (1.3.27–29), are interesting for his reliance on the Mīmāṁsā viewpoint shared by Śaṅkara and for his understanding of a Creator-Lord: "The creator at first bethinks himself of the characteristic make [form] of a thing, in connection with the word denoting it, and thereupon creates an individual thing characterized by that make [form]. . . . The superhuman origin and the eternity of the Veda really mean that intelligent agents having received in their minds an impression due to previous recitations of the Veda in a fixed order of words, chapters, and so on, remember and again recite it in that very same order of succession."[55]

Though Rāmānuja and Śaṅkara disagreed on many major points, they both categorically rejected Sphoṭavāda, as noted by Surendranath Dasgupta: "Neither Śaṅkara nor the Śrī-Vaisnavas admit the Sphoṭa theory."[56] Rāmānuja's acceptance of Mīmāṁsā doctrines (Varṇavāda) is more understandable than Śaṅkara's,[57] since the theistic schools of Vedānta (Uttara-Mīmāṁsā) adopt the Pūrva-Mīmāṁsā as a necessary prerequisite for knowledge of Brahman, while Śaṅkara has rejected Pūrva-Mīmāṁsā outright.

Rāmānuja, however, was not in total agreement with Mīmāṁsā philosophy either, especially the noncognitivist branch advocated by Prabhākara. Instead of viewing Vedic language in the performative context whereby only natural objects are denoted, Rāmānuja argued that "Vedic words terminate referentially in Brahman, the very ground of being." He diverged from Śaṅkara regarding the nature of Brahman. For Rāmānuja there was no division between Nirguṇa ("without qualities") and Saguṇa ("with qualities") Brahman as in Advaita-Vedānta. The unified Absolute is Lord Nārāyaṇa, who is also known as Brahman, consisting of ultimate pure consciousness, knowledge, and bliss. And words do not merely point toward a "nameless" and "formless" Brahman, as in Śaṅkara, but can ultimately signify and partake of the divine form and qualities of God. Thus, for Rāmānuja "a purified use of language can designate the supreme being."[58]

Parāśara, a great teacher or Āchārya succeeding Rāmānuja to the pontifical chair at Śrīraṅgam, wrote a small work of eight verses entitled *Aṣṭaślokī*. Therein the importance and significance of the syllable *Om* is briefly explained, followed by an explanation of the main Śrī-Vaiṣṇava mantra *Oṁ namo nārāyaṇāya*. In the opening verse he analyzes Om: Om contains *A, U,* and *M. A* stands for Viṣṇu, who is responsible for the creation, maintenance, and dissolution of the universe. *M* stands for the *jīva,* the individual soul, who is always dependent on the Lord for his very existence, for his control and success. The intervening *U* belongs to the *paramātman,* or Supersoul, which connects the two. In later language Jīva is called a Śeṣa, "existing for the sake of somebody else," having no independence at any time.[59]

A south Indian scholar of Śrī-Vaiṣṇavism, M. Narasimhachary, has explained in a recent interview the soteriological significance of Om in relation to the mantra used by Śrī-Vaiṣṇavas:

> The Śrī-Vaiṣṇavas attach very great importance to the syllable Om. In fact, it forms part of a *mantra* which is very sacred to them and is called the Aṣṭākṣarī Mantra, or "eight-syllabled *mantra*." The *mantra* goes like this; *Oṁ namo nārāyaṇāya.* So Om is a part of it—it is called *aṣṭākṣarī*. And there are some specifications as to how to use this *mantra*. Supposing you want liberation of *mokṣa,* then you have to use Om along with it; *Oṁ namo nārāyaṇāya.* Then one is assured of getting *mokṣa.* If, however, you want material prosperity in this universe, and freedom from other problems of life, the aim being different, you can use this *mantra* without Om: *nārāyaṇāya,* you can say. *Namaḥ* means "salutations." So *nārāyaṇāya* alone will be enough if you want some specific gain other than liberation.[60]

Rāmānuja had given his own explanation of the Praṇava within the context of an exergesis of a section of the *Śvetāśvatara-Upaniṣad*. This has been cited by Julius Lipner in his work on Rāmānuja's Vedantic theology:

> The Praṇava has been said to be the root of the whole collection of the Vedas, and the A [the first letter of the Praṇava] is the root of the Praṇava. That is, the Vedas, but a transformation

of the Praṇava, are resolved in it, their root, the Praṇava itself being a transformation of the A and resolved in the A which is its root. Now, since only that one who is the highest being expressed by the A, which is the Praṇava's root, is the great Lord, it is Nārāyaṇa who is the great Lord, since it is He alone who is expressed by the A, the root of the whole collection of words, and is the [ontological] root of the whole collection of beings.[61]

Liberation, or *mokṣa,* for the Śrī-Vaiṣṇavas follows the Pāñcarātra conception of a transcendent deity with an eternal abode and a female consort. For Rāmānuja, and for subsequent theistic Vaiṣṇavas, God as Viṣṇu, or Nārāyaṇa, has an eternal bodily form, consort, and abode to which the liberated soul repairs after death. "The Supreme Person who is the Supreme Brahman is none other than Nārāyaṇa, who is always in his unique transcendent form in his transcendent abode, accompanied by or united with His Divine Consort Śrī and waited upon by celestial ministers and attendants, as well as by the hosts of liberated souls [who] . . . exist in the Lord's supreme abode." As emphasized by John B. Carman, this abode is not superseded by a formless Absolute so favored by the Advaita-Vedāntins: "Just as there is no qualityless Being at a higher level of reality than the Lord possessing all auspicious qualities, so there is no formless Absolute that transcends the Deity with bodily form."[62] It follows from this that the continuous utterance of mantra by the residents is part of that eternal abode said to be full of all "qualities."

Madhva (A.D. 1199–1294 or 1238–1317), the formulator of Dvaita-Vedānta and the founder of the Madhva-Sampradāya, was the champion of unqualified dualism (Dvaita), directing most of his polemic against Śaṅkara and the Advaita-Vedānta school. In consonance with Śaṅkara, however, Madhva appears to have aligned himself with the Varṇavāda theory of the Mīmāṁsā philosophers and declared that *varṇas,* or letters, are eternal substances: "The doctrine of *varṇa* as professed in the Madhva system has much in common with the interpretation of the Mīmāṁsakas and the later grammarians [i.e., Nāgeśa and others who later modified the sonic absolutism of Bhartṛhari]. . . . *Varṇa* is a substance, because of being all-pervasive like *ākāśa.* Because 'pervasiveness' is an attribute that is concomitant only with 'substance,' it is illogical to propound the doctrine that *varṇa* is only an attribute of *ākāśa.*"[63]

Furthermore, Dvaita scholarship reveals that Madhva, in consonance with Rāmānuja and the Pāñcarātra texts, had refuted the Grammarian position of Sphoṭavāda:

> The phonemes (*varṇas*) are eternal and all-pervasive substances according to Madhva. Though eternal they manifest themselves through primary sounds (*dhvanis*) which are non-eternal. As soon as they reach the sense of hearing they remind the hearer of the corresponding *varṇas*. . . . The only type of order that the followers of Madhva recognize in the *varnas* is the order imposed by the speaker and hearer. . . . No other order is possible among letters because they exist always and in all places. . . . According to Madhva there is no separate sentence-meaning apart from the word meanings put together. . . . The Madhvas criticize the Vākya-Sphoṭa on the ground that there is no separate sentence-sense apart from word-sense and words denote their own sense as well as their syntactical relation. . . . Madhva is of the opinion that words denote only particulars [as against a class or a universal].[64]

Thus, for the Madhvaites and other theists language as mantra is an eternal substance due to its being made up of separate *varṇas*.

Madhva provides a personalistic analysis of the importance of meditation on Oṁkāra in his *Anuvyākhyāna,* a summary of his conclusions regarding the *Vedānta-Sūtra.* According to Dasgupta, "He [Madhva] says in the first chapter that the Oṁkāra which designates the Brahman and which is also the purport of Gāyatrī is also the purport of all the Vedas and one should seek to know it. Those who seek to know the Brahman please God by such an endeavor, and by His grace are emancipated."[65] Madhva also provides an elaborate discussion on the importance of Om in his commentary on some selected verses of the *Ṛg-Veda* known as *Ṛg-Bhāṣya.*

The importance of mantra in the worship of Viṣṇu is stressed in Madhva's work *Tantra-sāra-Saṅgraha,* in which there are four chapters devoted to the ritualistic details of Viṣṇu worship. Another ritual text of his, the *Sadācāra-smṛti* in forty verses, accents the importance of mantra. Furthermore, the primary role of meditation on Viṣṇu's, or Krishna's, form, and especially his name, is underscored in the small work of Madhva known as *Kṛṣṇāmṛta-Mahārṇava.*

Compared to the other Vaiṣṇava Sampradāyas, very little is known about either the founder, Nimbārka (ca. A.D. 1120–1200), or the sect itself, which maintains headquarters in the Mathurā District of Uttar Pradesh. He is said to have been born in Andhra Pradesh yet spent the majority of his life around Mathura. Nimbārka propounded a version of Vedānta known as "Dvaitādvaita," in which God and the souls are the same yet different. Instead of the worship of Viṣṇu and his consort Lakṣmī, as in Rāmānuja, Nimbārka advocated a personal devotion to their alternate forms of Krishna, or Gopāla, and his consort, Rādhā.

The most comprehensive account of the use of mantras in the Nimbārka-Sampradāya is contained in the *Krama-Dīpikā,* a work by Keśava Kashmiri Bhaṭṭa (ca. fourteenth century). A learned study of the Nimbārka tradition by Roma Bose, who translated Nimbārka's commentary on *Vedānta-Sūtra* known as the *Vedānta-Pārijāta-Saurabha,* reveals the use of the Gopāla-Mantra by the sect. Drawing from the *Krama-Dīpikā* (2d Patala, pp. 32–55), Bose explains that a member of the Nimbārka-Sampradāya "must be initiated to the Viṣṇu-Mantra. . . . Now, there are various kinds of Viṣṇu Mantras, of which the Gopāla-Mantra of eighteen syllables is the best [*klīṁ kṛṣṇāya govindāya gopījana-vallabhāya svāhā*]."[66] This is the same mantra that gains enormous currency in Gauḍīya-Vaiṣṇavism.

The followers of Nimbārka, as well as most Krishnaite sects, perform *japa* of their particular Krishna mantra on a rosary made of beads from the Tulasī plant. While observing the temple activities of the sect's headquarters at the Śrījī Mandira in Vṛndāvana, the present author noticed that, in addition to daily *japa,* members continuously chant and sing the names of Rādhā and Śyāma (Krishna) in the following form: *rādhe krishna rādhe krishna krishna krishna rādhe rādhe rādhe śyāma rādhe śyāma śyāma śyāma rādhe rādhe.* A daily routine would consist of the singing of this mantra, along with Braj Bhāṣā poems composed by eminent saints of the sect, such as Śrī Bhaṭṭa (immediate disciple of Keśava Kashmiri Bhaṭṭa) and his disciple Harivyāsadevāchārya (ca. sixteenth century).

Vallabha or Vallabhācārya (A.D. 1479–1533), the founder of the Vallabha-Sampradāya said to be based on the teachings of Viṣṇuswamin (ca. thirteenth century), was a Vaiṣṇava scholar-saint who, though originally hailing from southern Andhra Pradesh, focused his preaching efforts mostly in northern Uttar Pradesh, with subsequent sectarian fruition mainly in the states of Rajasthan and Gujarat. He propagated Śuddhādvaita-Vedānta, a theistic version of Vedānta aimed at establishing "purified" Brahman as Krishna. "Śrī Krishna, according to him [Vallabha], is not only an incarnation of God like other incarnations; He is Brahman himself, the ultimate reality."[67]

Vallabhite tradition records that Vallabha received the principal initiatory mantra of the sect, the so-called Brahmasambandha-Mantra (the mantra that binds one, *sambandha,* to Brahman, which is Krishna), directly from Śrī Krishna himself in Gokula near Mathurā one night in the year A.D. 1494. "On the morning of the next day, Vallabhācārya initiated Dāmodaradāsa [the first disciple in the Sampradāya] with the Brahmasambandha-Mantra that had been given the night before by Śrī Krishna, thus making Dāmodaradāsa the first member of the new Sampradāya." Thereupon, the continuing tradition of initiation into the Vallabha-Sampradāya includes the benefaction of this mantra, which is unique to their tradition: *śrī-kṛṣṇaḥ śaraṇaṁ mama*—"Lord Krishna is my refuge." "When one receives the eight-syllabled *mantra—śrī-kṛṣṇaḥ śaraṇaṁ mama,* he is said to have received the divine name and is admitted into the Vallabha-Sampradāya. This is the Brahmasambandha initiation by which one's sins are destroyed."[68] Illustrating the steps taken by the initiate toward full realization of Lord Krishna, there is an esoteric interpretation of the mantra given by the sect, not unlike many of the Śākta-Tantra schemes:

> *śrī*—this syllable brings wealth and good fortune; *kṛ*—this syllable withers and destroys sin; *ṣṇaḥ*—this syllable drives away *adhibhautika* (relating to matter), *adhyātmika* (relating to the individual self), and *adhidaivika* (relating to the divine) sorrows and misfortunes; *śa*—this syllable dispels the sorrows of birth and death; *ra*—this syllable gives one knowledge related to Śrī Krishna; *ṇam*—this syllable causes one's devotion (Bhakti) to Śrī Krishna to be firm; *ma*—this syllable brings the affection of one's guru who teaches one the methods of divine *seva* [service]; *ma*—this syllable unites one with Śrī Krishna so that one need never again be born on the *laukika* [worldly] plane.[69]

In consequence of Vallabha's direct association with the sacred sound emanating from Krishna's mouth, Vallabha has been given the epithet Mukhāvatāra: "The mouth of Bhagavān Śrī Krishna is the source of speech, of the eternal cosmic sound. . . . Vallabhācārya is called in the Sampradāya the Mukhāvatāra of Bhagavān (the incarnation of the mouth of Bhagavān Śrī Krishna). As such, Vallabhācārya has . . . the divine speech for instructing his followers."[70] During his lifetime the only person authorized to initiate disciples (that is, to impart the holy sound of the mantra given by Śrī Krishna) was Vallabha himself. After his demise this privilege was handed to his two sons by divine decree and then on to his seven grandsons.

The full doctrine of Vallabha is known as Puṣṭi-Mārga ("the Way of God's Grace," taken himself from the words *poṣaṇaṁ tad-anugrahaḥ* in the *Bhāgavata-Purāṇa* 2.10.4) and is a lifetime agenda for complete surrender to the will of Krishna. Superior to the individuals who follow the other Vaiṣṇava paths to *mokṣa* in gradual stages (i.e., the paths of Rāmānuja, Nimbārka, or Madhva), those souls who adopt the path of Puṣṭi-Mārga, "get immediate *mokṣa* after coming out of the body;. . . they immediately merge into Brahman. After this merger, God takes them out of His body [Brahman] and bestows upon them the divine bodies and allows them to participate in His eternal *rāsa-līlā* (love-dance). Thus the highest *mokṣa*, according to Vallabha, is to participate in the *rāsa-līlā* with God and enjoy the bliss of devotion."[71] And this eternal *mokṣa* is facilitated and sustained by constant repetition of the Brahmasambandha-Mantra, along with continued remembrance of Krishna's pastimes.

Gauḍīya-Vaiṣṇavism, though attaching itself to the lineage of Madhva, actually began with the immediate followers of Caitanya (A.D. 1485–1533), a Bengali ecstatic who preached widely and established a fervently devotional religion over a large part of India. Caitanya, originally a logician, renounced all scholastic duties and dedicated himself to chanting, dancing, and spreading his unique form of Bhakti devotion. His group of followers, including the so-called Six Goswamis and Krishnadās Kavirāj, author of Caitanya's biography known as *Caitanya-Caritāmṛta,* were settled in the newly rediscovered region of Brajabhūmī in India's Uttar Pradesh. "Gauḍīya-Vaiṣṇava theology was really the formulation of Sanātana Goswami, Rūpa Goswami, their nephew Jīva Goswami, and Krishnadās Kavirāj." Krishnadās Kavirāj's *Caitanya-Caritāmṛta,* as well as the philosophical work of Jīva Goswami, were attempts to provide a solid intellectual foundation to a devotional movement with the help of a scholastic philosophy borrowed from Śrīdhara Swami (ca. A.D. 1350–1450), a renowned scholar who wrote a famous commentary on the *Bhāgavata-Purāṇa* known as the *Bhāvārtha-Dīpikā.* "Śrīdhara Swami's commentary on the *Bhāgavata-Purāṇa* provided for the theologians of the Caitanya order a contemporary theological apparatus.

This commentary was improved upon by Jīva Goswami in his *Krama-Sandarbha*."[72]

Like Śaṅkara, Rāmānuja, and Madhva before him, Śrīdhara Swami rejected the Grammarian theory of Sphoṭavāda in his works, especially the *Nyāya-Kandalī*: "The following arguments, among others, are sought by Śrīdhara to refute the existence of Sphoṭa: Sphoṭa is never directly perceived, but falsely assumed by the grammarians; the denotation lies within the word and not with an imperceptible entity as Sphoṭa. To assume Sphoṭa, as distinct from letters, is as fallacious as to conceive a 'flower in the sky.'"[73]

Jīva Goswami (A.D. 1513–98), the most prolific and most celebrated theologian of the Gauḍīya-Sampradāya, also rejected the Sphoṭavāda doctrine and adhered to the views of Madhva and Śrīdhara indicated above, in consonance with the Mīmāṁsā position of Varṇavāda. This was noted by Stuart Elkman in his recent translation of Jīva's *Tattva-Sandarbha*:

> Jīva Goswami . . . offers arguments in favor of the eternal nature of the Vedas, the origin of the universe from the Vedas, and the authoritative nature of both imperative and declarative statements of the Vedas. . . . Having established the Vedas to be the source of all knowledge, Jīva discusses different theories of language and meaning. He refutes the doctrine of Sphoṭavāda, which posits an indefinable power, or *sphoṭa,* above and beyond the linguistic elements of words, in order to explain the emergence of their meanings, and embraces the doctrine of Varṇavāda, which reduces the meanings of words to their elements which, being both universal and eternal, render the Vedas also universal and eternal. Jīva supports his arguments by quoting Śaṅkara's *Bhāṣya* on *Brahma-Sūtra* 1.3.28, which he relies on heavily for his exposition of this topic.[74]

It is interesting to note here that, while Jīva accepts the eternity of the Veda which is not accepted by Śaṅkara, he relies on Śaṅkara for his refutation of Sphoṭavāda when, in fact, he would be more consistent had he quoted one of the Mīmāṁsā philosophers.

Gopāla Bhaṭṭa Goswami, a Caitanya disciple and former Śrī-Vaiṣṇava from Śrīraṅgam, compiled the authoritative Gauḍīya-Vaiṣṇava work known as the *Hari-Bhakti-Vilāsa* (before A.D. 1541), in which Śākta-Tantra texts are strongly represented: "In this work Gopāla cites a large number of Tantras and Āgamas as authorities [including the *Śāradā-tilaka-Tantra*, from which several sections, including material on *dīkṣā*, have been reproduced]. According to Gopāla, the Vaiṣṇava guru must have a knowledge of the Tantras and their *mantras* or ritual formulas."[75] Indeed, several important mantras are described within the twenty chapters, or "Vilāsas," among which are the Śrī-Krishna-Mantra of eighteen syllables (Vilāsa 1), the Kāma-Gāyatrī (Vilāsa 3), and the Gopāla-Gāyatrī (Vilāsa 3). These are all prefaced by "Klīṁ," the Tantric Bīja-syllable for both Kāmadeva and Krishna known as the "Kāma-Bīja."

As in other forms of Hinduism, especially Śākta-Tantra, the Gauḍīya-Vaiṣṇava tradition has incorporated various seed-syllables, or Bījas, of tremendous power. The Bīja, known as Kāma-Bīja, of Krishna is Klīṁ, and that of Hlādinī-Śakti, or Rādhā, is Hrīṁ (cf. the use of Hrīṁ in the Śrī-Vidyā-Mantra). The *Hari-bhakti-Vilāsa*, from *Gopāla-tāpanī-Upaniṣad* (3.25), describes the creation of the universe from this syllable. This description, along with some additional remarks, is paraphrased by Dimock: "The Bīja has five 'letters'—KA, LA, I, M, and the sign of nasalization (Bindu). These five are the five elements: KA is the earth, LA the water, I the fire, M [Nāda] the wind, and Bindu is the sky. . . . And in realized form, KA is Krishna, LA is Radha, I is bliss [Hlādinī], M [Nāda] is Rūpa, and Bindu is Vṛndāvan.' Through the Bīja the worshipper appropriates the universe. Through the Bīja he covers all of space and exists through all of time."[76]

A textual source for several standard Gauḍīya-Vaiṣṇava mantras, the *Gopāla-tāpanī-Upaniṣad* (before A.D. 1500),[77] also contains the well-known Krishna-Mantra: *klim kṛṣṇāya govindāya gopījana-vallabhāya svāhā* (1.11–13): "I offer oblations unto Lord Krishna, who is Govinda, the beloved of the Gopīs (cowherd women)."[78] A late Pāñcarātra text,[79] the *Nārada-Pāñcarātra*, contains an elaborate discussion of this same Krishna-Mantra: "Then the highest eighteen-lettered *mantra* is spoken *klīṁ kṛṣṇāya govindāya gopījana-vallabhāya svāhā*. This is the secret of the secret *mantras*. It is the desired *cintāmaṇi* (the philosopher's stone)" (3.3.21). In a later chapter of this work (5.1.66–67) the same mantra has accumulated several of the characteristic Bīja letters of Śākta-Tantra: "Now about the 'Siddha-Gopāla-Mantra' praised by Garuḍa, of Śrī Gopāla . . . the *mantra* runs as follows—*Oṁ Śrīṁ Hrīṁ Klīṁ Śrī Kṛṣṇāya Śrī Govindāya Śrī*

Gopījana-vallabhāya Śrīṁ Śrīṁ."[80] This is perhaps the same mantra that appears under the name Siddha-Gopāla-Mantra in another late Pāñcarātra work (ca. A.D. 1600) known as *Śāṇḍilya-Saṁhitā* (1.13.1–5), wherein it is remarked that "the 18-syllable 'Siddha-Gopāla-Mantra' is said to be the essence of all the Vedas, and it belongs only to the initiated."[81]

The importance of this Krishna-Mantra for Gauḍīya-Vaiṣṇavism is made clearer by Baladeva Vidyābhūṣaṇa (A.D. 1720–90) in his commentary on *Vedānta-Sūtra* (3.3.32), wherein he, while referring to this Upaniṣad, delineates the five parts of the mantra in relation to five parts of the human body:

> Meditating with concentrated heart on Krishna, a man is freed from the cycle of births and deaths. Reciting his *mantra* and doing *pūjā* to him, is like the conjunction of the moon with the earth. . . . His *mantra* consists of five words, namely, (1) *klīṁ kṛṣṇāya,* (2) *govindāya,* (3) *gopījana,* (4) *vallabhāya,* and *svāhā.* Reciting this fivefold *mantra,* on the five parts of one's body, namely, (1) heart, (2) head, (3) *śikhā* or tuft lock, (4) breast, and (5) hands with five elements heaven, earth, the sun, moon and fire, one assuming these forms, attains Brahman, verily he attains Brahman.[82]

The *Kali-santaraṇa-Upaniṣad* (ca. before A.D. 1500) is a very short work, which contains possibly the earliest reference to the famous Gauḍīya-Vaiṣṇava "Mahā-Mantra," the string of names most commonly recited in Vaiṣṇava *nāma-japa*: "*Hare Rāma, Hare Rāma, Rāma Rāma, Hare Hare, Hare Krishna, Hare Krishna, Krishna Krishna, Hare Hare* [O Hari, O Rāma, O Krishna, etc.]—This collection of sixteen names is destructive of the baneful influences of Kali [Kali Yuga, the age of Kali]. . . . Beyond this there is not other better means to be found in all the Vedas."[83] Though the standard biographies of Caitanya mention only a ten-syllabled mantra, the above Mahā-Mantra is believed by popular tradition to be the same mantra that Caitanya received at his initiation (*dīkṣā*) in Gayā and which he propounded as the surest means of salvation in the present age of Kali Yuga. According to sectarian etymology, the expression *Hare* is the vocative form of *Harā,* a name for Rādhā, or the Śakti of Krishna, and betrays the presence of the Śakti, the energy of God, in the mantra itself: "Now the name 'Hare' means 'O Harā,' 'O Stealer.' Harā is she who steals the mind of Krishna; she is Rādhā. The eight

'Hare's' in the Mahā-Mantra call out to Rādhā in the eight phases of her love for Krishna."[84]

In Japanese Buddhism a similar process of name repetition is found in the prayer of the Nembutsu ("name of Buddha"), recited by the Pure Land sect founded in the twelfth century A.D. by Honen. Just as the Hindu practitioners of Bhakti make themselves an empty channel through which the divine word can reverberate, the members of this Japanese sect recite the name of the Buddha with complete sincerity. The name of Buddha which is pronounced "namu Amida," or "namu Amida Butsu," is derived from the Sanskrit name of Buddha known as Amitābha and is repeated with the intended meaning: "I put my faith in Amida Buddha." In its earlier phases "the Nembutsu meant meditation on Amida, but the element of meditation was soon replaced by fervent devotion and endless repetition." In contrast to the more difficult paths of salvation in earlier Buddhist sects, "Honen proposed the easy means of salvation available to all: rebirth in Amida's Pure Land [heaven] by means of invoking Amida's name."[85]

Initiation into Gauḍiya-Vaiṣṇavism frequently includes a series of stages, the first of which is the benefaction of the Mahā-Mantra followed by more esoteric mantras meant for the development of perfected spiritual bodies (*siddha-rūpa*) needed to participate in eternal Krishna pastimes in the afterlife. "The first stage of the initiation is a very general one. It involves the whispering of the well-known and public Mahā-Mantra of the Gauḍīya-Vaiṣṇava-Sampradāya into the ear of the initiate. The initiate is to meditate with this *mantra* until he is ready for the second stage of the initiation, the imparting of the secret and private *dīkṣā-mantra*." The system of Mañjarī-Sādhana in the Gauḍīya-Sampradāya enjoins that the practitioner develop his or her own spiritual body as a *mañjarī*, assistant to Krishna's maid-servants, the *gopī*s. Among a number of possible choices, the special mantra given by the guru gives the aspirant a new birth and a new identity. "With the *mantra*, the practitioner comes to know more and more about the ultimate world and his place in it. Moreover, it is the *mantra* that nourishes the growth of this new body with its particular identity and relationship with Krishna. . . . The early Vṛndāvana Goswamins [sixteenth century A.D.] thought that knowledge of the *siddha-rūpa*, with its inherent relationship to Krishna, was solely acquired through the *mantra*."[86] During the ensuing centuries a third stage of initiation (*siddha-praṇālī-dīkṣā*) was introduced, which involved knowledge of one's particular spiritual lineage.

Gauḍīya-Vaiṣṇavism lays great emphasis on Nāma-Saṅkīrtana, the loud chanting or singing of the name of God propounded by Caitanya. Whereas other Vaiṣṇava and Śaiva sects had advised that the silent or low-volume muttering of mantra, or *japa,* was as efficacious as loud chanting, Caitanya and his followers proclaimed that the loud singing of God's name(s) was more effective in the requisition of salvation, since the loud exclamation (*saṅkīrtana*) of God's name is more expressive and thus conducive of the kind of Bhakti sentiments required for the highest spiritual experience, namely, love of God.

Such "high-volume sound" is indeed considered transcendental by Gauḍīya-Vaiṣṇavas, especially the Gauḍīya Maṭh, the main institutional artery of Gauḍīya-Vaiṣṇavism founded in 1920.[87] Śrīla Bhaktisiddhānta Sarasvatī (1874–1937), the founding Āchārya of the Gauḍīya Maṭh, revealed the movement's rather fervent and ascetic position regarding sacred or "transcendental sound" in an interview with the American Indologist Stella Kramrisch on 12 July 1931:

> We should always be hearing the Absolute through the transcendental Sound. The sound of our atmosphere describes nature's products. It informs us about America or any corner of the globe. The aptitude should be dismissed in the case of transcendental Sound which is not from this region of three dimensions. Sound from the Absolute Realm (Vaikuṇṭha) has a peculiar reference. It requires no corroboration by the other senses. In the case of mundane sound nasal activity is required to test its correctness, the tongue and other senses must also help in the process. There are always the four corroborative senses that are engaged in testing the validity of the mundane sound. But they are quite unserviceable in the case of the transcendental Sound. The transcendental Sound has got a popular distinctive reference of its own. It refers to non-divisible Absolute Knowledge (Advaya-jñāna). No challenge is to be offered to that Sound.
>
> The transcendental Sound comes here to designate Godhead. The transcendental Sound is the Name of Godhead. The mundane sound designates something else than itself. The transcendental Sound should be heard and no challenging question should be placed to contradict it. . . . The transcendental Sound should come through the uncontaminated pipe of the true devotee. One who thinks that he should have anything to do with this world cannot be the bearer of the message of the Absolute.[88]

The idea here is that such transcendental sound, itself a divine category overpowering by nature, cannot be experienced within ordinary human consciousness at low volume. It can only be experienced by the loud exclamation of God's name with a full throat and surrendered mind. This activity is believed to remove sinful propensities in the heart and foster "true" Bhakti sentiments. In fact, both Śrīla Bhaktivinode Ṭhākur and his son Śrīla Bhaktisiddhānta Sarasvatī preached publicly that "the Mahā-Mantra is for both *japa* and *kīrtana* [loud chanting or singing], and that *kīrtana* is ultimately superior to *japa*." They had based this understanding on the authority of Rūpa Goswami, who had written in his short work of eight verses, *Prathama-Caitanyāṣṭaka* (5), that Caitanya himself had chanted "the Māha-Mantra in a loud voice" (*hare kṛṣṇety uccaiḥ*).[89]

The loud recital of the name of God is thus of paramount importance for the Gauḍīya-Vaiṣṇavas. Their method of *japa* also employs the *akṣa-mālā*, or rosary, of which the beads are normally counted as 108 and made of Tulasī wood sacred to Nārāyaṇa, or Krishna. Members of the group known as ISKCON, for example, the worldwide "offspring" of the Gauḍīya Maṭh founded by A. C. Bhaktivedanta Swami (1896–1977) and first brought to the West in 1965, practice "loud" *japa* daily as the most important part of their spiritual *sādhana*: "It is the duty of each initiated ISKCON devotee to chant sixteen rounds each day on the 108-bead rosary that he or she is given in initiation. There is, in ISKCON, no religious practice that supersedes the chanting of the Krishna Mantra, or prayer formula."[90]

A comparative perspective on the intense utterance of religious names or words suggests a possible corollary in evangelical Christianity. Research on glossolalia, or "speaking in tongues," in modern American Pentecostalism revealed that "individuals abandon themselves totally to the work of the Spirit, and lose all individuality in the process of participation in a greater, transcendent reality. . . . In the repudiation of rational discourse for the ecstatic utterance of a rapid flow of syllables with no discursive content, the forms of structured, everyday modes of communication are left behind in favor of pure, unmediated flow."[91] Indeed, current fieldwork has suggested that persons experiencing glossolalia are overcome by a variety of purely physical symptoms, such as flowing of tears, closed eyes, rapid breathing, flushed face, salivation, perspiration, trembling, kinetic behavior, spasms, and crying.[92] These kinds of symptoms are also witnessed in Hindu practices. In fact, they were especially believed to have been displayed by Caitanya himself during his ecstatic moments. But, unlike the act of mantra recitation and *nāma-japa,* in which the average Hindu practitioner must remain conscious of the object of affection at all times, the speakers in tongues, while in the throes of vocalic effusion, are totally unconcerned with the meaning of what they are repeating. The Hindu practice of *japa,* unlike glossolalia, requires the user's full awareness of the efficacy of selected words or names, which are initially received from and monitored by an authoritative teacher though also repeated in pure, unmediated flow. Cross-cultural studies of ecstatic symptoms and utterances might yield more insight into these issues.

Insofar as the key traditions can be examined within limited space, it can be said that sacred sound in Vaiṣṇavism conforms to the basic patterns of Hindu theism. From the speculation on Nāda-Brahman as the female energy of Viṣṇu to the soteriological efficacy of mantra in the form of the divine name (e.g., Viṣṇu, Nārāyaṇa, Krishna) or as *japa* recitation of specific phrases (e.g., *Oṁ namo Nārāyaṇāya, Hare Krishna, Rādhe Śyāma*), sacred sound constitutes a central feature of Vaiṣṇava theology and practice.

Conclusion

Sonic Theology, the Study of Religion, and Hermeneutics

The quotation from the *Parama-Saṁhitā* cited at the beginning of this book pointed to aspects of Indian tradition which were thought to be best kept "undescribed." This book has sought to explore these "unseen" mysteries using a barrage of text and testimony from diverse parameters of the Hindu world. Now, with this material in place, it is possible to review, and reassemble, several common assumptions regarding both Hinduism and the study of religion—and, too, the salient points of hermeneutics vis-à-vis sonic phenomena.

What is immediately clear from the rather lengthy explication of Indian texts and traditions undertaken in this work is that the sonic, or oral, dimension of Hinduism is of utmost significance. Indeed, speculation on the sonic dimension of reality has been found to occupy the minds of the most sapient thinkers of India. It is also clear that, while language was almost never conceived as separate from the oral word, the power of transformation inherent in sacred sound continued to operate in ways that were true to accepted canons of execution yet remained mysterious in its inability to be described, classified, or defined by common consensus.

In the foregoing chapters an attempt has been made to present sonic themes from a broad range of significant sectors of Hinduism. Though the emphasis has been primarily on the Sanskrit texts, the discussion has also drawn from scholars and personal informants. The mélange of data which has arisen in this line of exploration has made it apparent that the study of sacred sound in India is also very complex. Yet the apparent complexity did not obscure the significance and underlying centrality of sacred sound for the Hindu tradition.

To facilitate an overall design this study has concentrated on a number of target areas within Hinduism and Indian thought such as Vedic sound, Indian philosophies of language, Nāda-Yoga, Śākta-Tantra, Śaivism, and Vaiṣṇavism. These areas were then investigated in light of the following: the confrontation between the Varṇavāda and Sphoṭavāda schools; speculation on the primal syllable *Om*, or *AUM*, and its parsing into at least four or five degrees after the time of the principal Upaniṣads; sonic creation scenarios involving Vāk and Śabda-Brahman (Nāda-Brahman); the sequential levels of language within human consciousness known as Paśyantī, Madhyamā, and Vaikharī; the physiological, "mystic" centers, or Cakras, in the human body and their connections to letters of the Sanskrit alphabet as well as musical notes; the soteriological importance given to mantra utterance and the verbal repetition (*japa*) of Sanskrit syllables, names, and phrases.

As we have seen, the role of sacred sound in the Vedic period was bound up with the Vedic sacrifice. The notions of *vāk* and Vāk, the goddess of speech, were among many implements to be coordinated in the rather complex ritual detail outlined in the Vedic texts. Yet it is the emerging notion of "speech as power" inherent in the pronunciation and metrical structure of the mantras, or "ritually applied Vāk," which is striking. The mantras became more powerful than the gods themselves, who were dependent on the sacrificial offerings, and invited access to the unseen world of supernatural forces and energies. Gradually, as the natural metaphors and powers associated with Vāk became compacted into the metaphysical, seed-syllable *Om* of the Upaniṣads, the notion of Śabda-Brahman emerged.

Thus, the prevailing terms denoting sacred sound in the Vedic canon are *Vāk*, *Śabda-Brahman*, *Om* (in three divisions of *A + U + M*), *Praṇava*, and *Udgītha*. They have slightly different shades of meaning yet are often used interchangeably in the texts. The Upaniṣadic Śabda-Brahman signifies the merging of Brahman with Om, such that Om in triplicate as AUM is the Sound Brahman. And the Upaniṣadic Om as friction-stick served to alert us to its increasingly important role in theistic meditation: to invoke or "verbally ignite" the interior manifestation of God, or Brahman, in the human heart prior to the external, visual perception of the deity. The speculation on the Praṇava, Om, in the principal Upaniṣads (as well as in the Vedas, Brāhmaṇas, and Āraṇyakas), though somewhat extensive, was indeed limited to divisions and correspondences in triplicate: A U M. This triune division was best exemplified in the *Māṇḍūkya-Upaniṣad*, wherein a fourth stage is mentioned but which is defined as "no stage" (*amātra*). An inquiry into the subsequent developments of Om has shown that the Vedic and Upaniṣadic Om differed from the Yogic,

Tantric, or theistic Om, which consisted of a number of additional degrees. Yet the triune division of Om in the principal Upaniṣads formed the foundation for the addition of a "substantive" fourth degree (*turīya*) by the Yoga tradition, comprised of Nāda and Bindu as sonic building blocks. Though the term *Nāda-Brahman* was curiously omitted in both the Vedas and the main Upaniṣads, the rudimentary discussion of *nāda* in the early phonetic texts and Mīmāṁsā verses—as being the voiced sound produced by the combination of internal fire and air in the human body—provided the basic raw material from which the extensive physiological and linguistic elaborations found in Yoga and Tantrism were constructed.

The present exposition of the polemic between the Varṇavāda and Sphoṭavāda theories has indicated the serious implication of the following issue for the practicing Hindu: though both schools agreed on the absolute ultimacy of "the Word," does it inhere only in an external Absolute such as the Veda, or is it already present within human consciousness as Sphoṭa? The confrontation between these rival schools, while reflecting a major dialectic among linguistic philosophers in India, has also formed a valuable methodological apparatus for the investigation of the Yogic and sectarian theories and practices of sacred sound.

Here it is useful to stress the seminal nature of Bhartṛhari's work, still largely unrecognized in Indology, which revolved around his articulation of the theory of Sphoṭavāda and the three levels of linguistic apprehension in human consciousness, namely Paśyantī, Madhyamā, and Vaikharī. Bhartṛhari's concept of Sphoṭa as being identical with Brahman and Praṇava assures us of his ties to Vedic orthodoxy, yet the question of Bhartṛhari's indebtedness to Āgamic or Tantric sources for other aspects is still unanswered. Nevertheless, the study of Bhartṛhari provides us with a kind of missing link (namely, his articulation of Sphoṭavāda and the levels of language apprehension), without which an inquiry into the Hindu sectarian traditions of sacred sound is labyrinthine.

The levels of interior language apprehension, together with the Sphoṭavāda doctrine, formed a distinct "theological package" for Bhartṛhari and the succeeding Grammarians. Yet the theory of Sphoṭavāda has been refuted by all the major schools of Vedānta, beginning with Śaṅkara. The question of "what is at stake" in this refutation has indeed prodded us onward toward the next discovery, the fact that his linguistic levels of sacred sound formed part of the theological nomenclature of nearly every Hindu sectarian tradition, indicating a rather large outreach for this aspect of his thought. Since the nature of Sphoṭa is explained and understood by the Grammarians in reference to the Paśyantī, Madhyamā, and Vaikharī levels of consciousness, the acceptance of the latter without the former by so many traditions is perplexing. Most of the Hindu sectarian traditions overtly align themselves with the Mīmāṁsā standpoint of Varṇavāda yet coopt the Bhartṛharian speech levels in the explication of their particular salvific theories of mantra and Om recitation. The concept of Varṇavāda and the notion of the three internal speech levels are philosophically irreconcilable, at least without some outstanding feats of logic and sophistry by sectarian proponents, of which there are none. There are only nodding assents as to the feasibility of the Varṇavāda position without any attempt to justify it theologically.

The dilemma in a nutshell was this: the highest level of Paśyantī is an internal state of pure cognition and apprehension of Śabda-Brahman in which there is no necessity of sequence in language. In Varṇavāda there is no intuitive revelation of truth since the Veda is an external body of revelation dependent upon its unique sequence of syllables. A proper hermeneutic for the study of mantra recitation (the flow of meaningful syllables) in any tradition, especially those that accept both Varṇavāda and Paśyantī, has to face this difference. The splitting of Bhartṛhari's "package" and the lack of philosophical justification thereof by the sectarian traditions adopting this particular portion of Bhartṛhari's thought (Paśyantī, etc.) represents a newly recognized problematic in Hindu thought.

The Grammarians never transcend language because Ultimate Reality is Śabda-Brahman itself. Though, for different reasons, the dualistic, theistic sects of Hinduism also never advocate a transcendence of language resulting in a silent beatific vision of their respective deity: mantras and corresponding Nāda-Brahman meditation are never given up or discarded even after liberation. It is only with some of the Kashmiri Śaivas, along with Advaita-Vedānta and Buddhism, that language is ultimately replaced by silent contemplation.

In Mīmāṁsā the divine potencies of language are compacted into the text of the Veda, that is, the syllables themselves. Theistic Hinduism accepted that sacred potencies are indeed contained in the syllables of mantras, Vedic or otherwise, but that particular energies in particular syllables are mandated by a Supreme Being for the purpose of bringing about salvation for human beings. Thus, sonic theology, though composed of important, structural components said to be grounded in the Vedic tradition—such as Mīmāṁsā doctrines, Om divisions, and Bhartṛharian levels of linguistic function—reaches full consummation in the Hindu theistic traditions.

As we have seen, Nāda-Yoga forms the basis for a large variety of sonic meditational techniques that are shared by many other traditions. Patañjali and the *Yoga-Sūtra* commentarial tradition, including the work of Vyāsa, Vācaspati, and Vijñāna Bhikṣu, endorses the practice of Om meditation and provides a solid ground for the development of Yoga techniques of Nāda-Brahman meditation. The concept of Nāda-Brahman, having undergone a kind of "hypostatization," made its grand debut there in the commentary of Vācaspati by becoming a synonym for *Param Brahman*. As the classical Yoga school propounded the merit of Om meditation and seemed to accept the doctrine of Sphoṭavāda, the tentative equation of Praṇava = Sphoṭa = Nāda = Brahman = Turīya = Paśyantī to designate the highest reality seemed virtually unavoidable at this point in the tradition.

Several of the *Yoga-Upaniṣads*, texts that share similar terminology with the earlier members of this class of literature, developed the principles outlined in the classical Yoga tradition and embrace speculation on and application of Nāda and Nāda-Brahman. The texts and doctrines of the Gorakhnāth tradition as the largest and most important Yoga lineage disclosed a previously unrecognized fidelity to the principle of Nāda-Brahman, adopted the levels of Paśyanti, and enlarged upon the physiological and sidereal dimensions of sacred sound. The three major Haṭha-Yoga texts, *Śiva-Saṁhitā, Gheraṇḍa-Saṁhitā,* and *Haṭha-Yoga-Pradīpikā,* also exhibited an overwhelming concern for meditation on Nāda by practitioners of Yoga and, in fact, continue to inform Nāda-Yoga today. The subtlety of the Yogic discussions therein regarding *bīja* and *bindu,* terms that also have great provenance, suggested a compromise in the apparent dispute between Varṇavāda and Sphoṭavāda by including both concepts within a single letter of the alphabet. The feminine concept of *mātṛkā* provided the theoretical basis for this fusion, which, as we have seen, was exemplified on a larger scale in the female Nāda-Brahman. The gender polarization within each letter or syllable was seen to reflect the Āgamic, or Tantric, notion that viewed Om as the perfect embodiment of Śiva and Śakti.

The extra-Vedic Nāda-Brahman—AUM with its fourth (*turīya*) stage of Nāda-Bindu as Sound Brahman—thus gradually overshadowed Śabda-Brahman and became the dominant cosmological and psychological characterization of sacred sound in the Hindu tradition, in which it is connected to either Śiva, Viṣṇu, or the Goddess in a number of ways. The initiative taken by the Supreme Lord in the Bhakti movements to impregnate human language with sacred potencies is often accompanied by directives on the manner and frequency of mantra recitation and repetition (*japa*). We may recall here that, contrary to Mīmāṁsā, in which the sacred Vedic texts exist a priori without a Supreme Being overseeing their dissemination, words and syllables for the theistic Hindu have been deliberately impregnated with divine energies by a personal Lord.

A major objective in this work has been to evaluate the variety of Hindu sectarian developments in terms of their adoption of similar configurations of sacred sound: Śaiva-Āgamas, Śaiva-Siddhānta, Kashmiri Śaivism, Śākta-Tantra, the Pāñcarātra texts, and the major Vaiṣṇava Sampradāyas. The initial discussion of the Śaiva-Āgama tradition made it clear that there are serious alternatives to the common assumption that "everything comes from the Vedas." In fact, the south Indian Śaiva-Āgamas, insofar as texts are available, offer some unique root sources for theories of Om, as well as speculations on Nāda and Bindu and their relationship to the god Śiva and his spouse, or Śakti. Since the enlarged concepts of Nāda and Bindu are nowhere to be found in the Vedic canon, the value of the Śaiva-Āgama texts—most of which are unpublished or otherwise unavailable for study—for the understanding of the Śaivite practices of mantra and Om meditation is overwhelming. A number of Śaivite traditions claim allegiance to the Śaiva-Āgama texts, among which are Śaiva-Siddhanta and those groups reflected in the *Śiva-Purāṇa*. Kashmiri Śaivism, tending toward nondualism, offers some interesting developments of vowel, or phoneme, mysticism as well as the novel theories of Parā-Vāk (Parā-Nāda) via Bhartṛhari and Spanda, or cosmic vibration. The utilization of the Bhartṛharian levels of language apprehension (Paśyantī), as well as the equation of Śiva with either Nāda, Bindu, or Praṇava, is indisputable within nearly all of Śaivism.

Though most Hindu traditions have elements of the feminine in their teachings, the worship of the Goddess as Supreme constitutes the essence of Śākta-Tantra. The *Śāradā-tilaka-Tantra,* a crucial text for the study of Nāda-Brahman in the Śākta tradition, is observed to have been referenced and accepted as authoritative by the Śākta tradition as well as by Vaiṣṇava and Śaiva authors. This text embraced the Grammarian levels of Paśyantī. Several of the Śākta texts indeed accent the importance of mantra, *bīja,* and Nāda in the actualization of the highest goals of Śākta worship, such that the goddess Tripurasundarī has been formally identified as being either Praṇava, Nāda, or the essence of mantra (*mātṛkā*). The goddess Kālī is also identified with Śabda-Brahman and Nāda. The internalization of the alphabet (*mātṛkā*) vis-à-vis the Cakra centers form the substance of the practice of Kuṇḍalinī-Yoga, which, though also present in Śaiva and Vaiṣṇava practices, is the hallmark of Śākta-Tantra.

The Vaiṣṇava tradition showed similar features. The key Pāñcarātra texts displayed significant attention to sacred sound (for example, to Nāda-Brahman, Bindu, Praṇava, Paśyantī), especially in relation to the attainment of Vaiṣṇava aspirations. The *Jayākhya-Saṁhitā, Sāttvata-Saṁhitā, Pauṣkara-Saṁhitā, Ahirbudhnya-Saṁhitā, Lakṣmī-Tantra,* and *Śeṣa-Saṁhitā* were found to contain pertinent digressions on Om, Nāda-Brahman, and the Grammarian levels, the main points of which informed the theology and practice of a number of later Vaiṣṇava sects. In the later Bhakti movements, influenced largely by the *Bhāgavata-Purāṇa,* the role of sacred sound as Nāda-Brahman, Praṇava, mantra, or the names of Viṣṇu becomes even more acute in the salvific practices of a number of sects. While primary sources are still scarce regarding the early history and theology of the major Vaiṣṇava Sampradāyas (Śrī, Madhva, Nimbārka, Vallabha, Gauḍīya), the evidence based on secondary sources as well as interviews with scholarly practitioners wields a strong case: throughout the texts and traditions of Vaiṣṇavism, both by direct statement and by implication, the identification of Nāda-Brahman as the energy of Viṣṇu, or Krishna, is incontrovertible. Judging from an overview of the various theistic traditions examined, it is possible to postulate the theoretical—if not practical—equivalence, the "interchangeability," of Nāda-Brahman with the Śakti of either Śiva or Viṣṇu: the common denominator disclosed as the mysterious substance and nature of sacred sound.

At this point it is possible to offer some concluding remarks regarding the radical ascension of Nāda-Brahman in these Hindu traditions. Though not unaware of them, sectarian Hinduism speaks very little of Sphoṭa and Varṇa; in fact, as we have seen, Sphoṭavāda is rejected outright by many of the traditions, while Varṇavāda remains in somewhat ambiguous favor. Sphoṭavāda as a total package is unacceptable to theistic Hindus, for, if it were true, then anyone without proper initiation could achieve spiritual elevation simply by meditating on the sentence meanings of ordinary language, since there is ultimately no difference between ordinary and revealed language for this school. In fact, there is no special revealed language at all for the Grammarians. Moreover, the ultimacy of Śabda-Brahman for the Grammarians, and the Vedas for the Mīmāṁsās (Varṇavāda), would factor out the supremacy of a personal deity for the theists.

Varṇavāda, though often tacitly accepted by theists, cannot be squared with Hindu theism in the strict sense either. Theists mostly acknowledge Varṇavāda on the basis of its emphasis on the power of individual letters or syllables. Yet, since theists generally ascribe divine authorship to their scriptures, the power of syllables must ultimately rest in their being specifically created or empowered by a personal deity or energy and not on any kind of supremely autonomous quality. Varṇavāda not only claims that the Veda is "authorless" but also proscribes any arbitrary "illumination" as bestowed by divine benefaction and represented by the interior notion of Paśyantī, or Pratibhā.

As we have seen, however, one of the foundations of Hindu theism is its indulgence in meditative forms of Yoga employing interior sonic techniques and mantra recitation in which sacred sound appears within the human body and mind. Hindu theism thus needed a concept of sacred sound that was subordinate to a principal deity yet could manifest itself at random in the real world, that is, within human consciousness. Nāda-Brahman proved to be the most likely choice, since it incorporated the dimensions of both Varṇavāda and Sphoṭavāda, exterior and interior, and was seldom billed as the Supreme Reality in itself. As surmised from an overview of the available sources, Nāda-Brahman seems to act as a kind of synthesis, fusing the basic ingredients of Varṇa (external Śabda-Brahman) and Sphoṭa (internal Śabda-Brahman) into one essential concept that forms a conspicuous bridge between the sectarian movements, including the tradition of classicial music.

Whether the choice of Nāda-Brahman was a conscious one, selected by a particular sage on a fixed date in history, or an unconscious one, borne out by an evolving inertia of anonymous ritual practice and recitation, cannot be evidenced from the available materials. We do know, however, that at some point between the completion of the principal Upaniṣads and the first appearance of Nāda-Brahman in

Vācaspati's *Yoga-Sūtra* commentary—or in the *Nādabindu-Upaniṣad*, whichever came first—the concept of Nāda-Brahman had become anchored in the classical Hindu tradition as the vehicle through which to express notions of both sonic cosmogony and interior sonic meditation.

The notion of Nāda-Brahman may have even broader implications for the study of ancient civilization. Related to the word *Nāda* in Sanskrit is *nadī*, which means "river," or "stream," or the "sound of rushing water." According to linguistic studies, the root of both words *Nāda* and *nadī*, *nad*, "is hidden in the names of rivers all over the world, from the German Nidda and the Polish Nida to the Norwegian Nid and the British Nidd, from the Italian Niete to the Nidwan in Afghanistan, from the Italian Nera to the Russian Ner, Nara, Narova, and Narym, and from the German Nahe to the African Nahil and the Spanish Narcea."[1] And, since rivers are generally considered "female" in India, as in Gaṅgā, Yamunā, or Sarasvatī Rivers, there is further cause to speculate on the connection between sacred sound and the feminine.

At any rate, throughout the vast canvas of Indian history and soil the basic sacrality of sound has persisted, despite sectarian "coloring." At this stage in our research, it is unclear exactly why this is so. We can only say that the arcane or enigmatic nature of sacred sound somehow prevents us from knowing its full mystery. Perhaps we need a "supersonic" theology. Yet, despite this conundrum, the conclusion here, based as it is on an attempt at sonic theology, is deep-seated and resonant. Though it has undergone several metamorphoses over the centuries, it is clear that sacred sound in Hinduism, regardless of its particular name or context, continues to operate in a mysterious way that is both central and soteriological. And the Hindu tradition—both consciously and "unconsciously"—seeks this original centrum again and again to renew the very power that originally impelled it.

The act of "intoning" sacred sound—the oral "sonic act"—has been seen to both inaugurate and sustain the soteriological quest toward whichever Hindu god, goddess, or heaven is targeted, according to sectarian definition. Indeed, similar trajectories of Nāda-Yoga have been observed to be practiced by Hindus who had entirely different or mutually irreconcilable theological aims and goals. The religious life of a person aspiring for *mokṣa*, reflecting any particular Hindu sect, is observed to be inaugurated by the founding of a personal interior sonic world, created initially by receiving the sound seed (*bīja*, or *mantra*) from the guru. This "sonic world" is then sustained and developed by quotidian practices of mantra recitation and *japa*, being literally carried around within the body with its own self-preserving inertia like a kind of battery. At the time of death the accumulated sonic "charge" secures for an individual both release from the material suffering of rebirth and an eternal life of bliss in the kingdom of one's chosen deity, wherein the interaction with sacred sound continues. Relying on a visual metaphor, we can surmise that the sound seed is first "watered" by constant reciting, or chanting, until it "sprouts"; then it continues to grow upward and, ultimately, is transplanted into the eternal "spiritual garden" above. Such being the case, the soteriological modus operandi for the Hindu aspiring for liberation or association with a chosen deity involves a sonic act informed by a sonic theology.

Patterns that we have observed in Indian thinking about sacred sound may further illuminate our understanding of other religious traditions, particularly those that also claim to have an orally revealed canon. Indeed, within the domain of those Western religions (Judaism, Christianity, Islam) that have been known as "peoples of the book," the importance of the oral dimension of scripture can now be recalled. "Even within the traditions of the book, sound played and continues to play an important role in the transmission and assimilation of holy words in the actual life of persons. Religious scholars in many different areas are taking, with increasing seriousness, the oral-aural qualities of scripture." It is unfortunate that the word *scripture* (from *scribere*, "to write") has been used to signify what in many cases is an oral transmission: "the inter-relatedness of the oral-aural and the written aspect of holy words has become sufficiently apparent . . . that the limitation of 'scripture' to written forms only is sometimes quite misleading."[2]

The general importance of orality for human beings as a species has, of course, been proclaimed by scientific opinion: "From the standpoint of human evolution a perspective on the 'orality' . . . of the human animal requires us to recognize that oral language is fundamental to our species, whereas reading and writing wear the appearance of a recent accident."[3] But the implications arising out of comparative studies of oral chant among differing religions have not been consummated fully. A comparative study of sacred chant, for instance, suggested that "Shintoist, Buddhist, Brahman, Moslem and Hebrew sacred chant reveal a striking similarity to one another."

Indeed, in many of the world's traditions of sacred chant, as in the familiar Western forms of Gregorian chant, "the natural flow of the speaker's voice, with its constant change of pitch, is channelled into a magico-hypnotic one-note recitation."[4] Such "monotone" recitation and its connection to experiences of the numinous in religion is a unique characteristic warranting further study.

The growing field of hermeneutics offers a potential aegis for further exploration into sonic phenomena. Indeed, the much broader scope of what has been called the "new hermeneutic" of twentieth-century theology involves the deeper understanding of the oral word-event, as characterized in the following statement: "The etymological origin of *hermeneuein*... points in the direction of roots with the meaning 'speak,' [or] 'say' (connected with the Latin *verbum* or *sermo*)."[5] An important proponent for the current theological response to the new hermeneutic contends that "the content and object of hermeneutics is the word-event as such.... Hermeneutics as the theory of understanding must therefore be the theory of words." The hermeneutical process itself is also linguistic:

> For hermeneutics is of course not a departure from the linguistic realm in order to understand by means of language.... The primary phenomenon in the realm of understanding is not understanding of language, but understanding through language.... The word is what opens up and mediates understanding, i.e., brings something to understanding. The word itself has a hermeneutic function.[6]

As noted by modern theology, "There is no contradiction between God and word any more than between man and word; rather it is the word which binds God and man together."[7]

The main presupposition of any hermeneutical undertaking is the lack of understanding or "clarity" in a text or religious act. Consequently, the task of hermeneutics is the removal of obstacles (whether seen as things, thoughts, misunderstandings, etc.) which prevent the *kairos*, or "fullness," of participation in the word. Again, in the words of Gerhard Ebeling: "Hermeneutics is requisite only in the case where the word-event is hindered for some reason or other....The hermeneutic aid can only consist in removing hindrances in order to let the word perform its own hermeneutic function."[8] This view of the word, or language, is extended further in Martin Heidegger's notion that it is language itself that speaks, such that "it is indeed not man at all who is expressing himself in language..., basic is what wills fundamentally to show [or sound] itself and have its say prior to or apart from any subjective intent."[9]

Though the term in general has come to mean almost any activity that is involved in bringing whatever is unclear to clarity, in its archaic sense hermeneutics as a tool was primarily applied to "the messages of the gods, in that they are by their very nature mysterious, obscure, and in need of clarification." This orientation resurfaces in Heidegger's hermeneutic as he restores pre-Hellenic heroes such as Prometheus, Tantalus, and Sisyphus to their "original position of honor as hermeneuts of the gods.... [Thus] the role of the new hermeneutic as a new orientation for theology [i.e., to interpret the numinous messages of the gods] is prefigured by his work."[10]

If hermeneutics is based originally on the principle that the word is what opens up and mediates understanding, then the oral word itself has a hermeneutical function. Often this "understanding" is the result of a creative dynamic whereby something previously undescribed, "unthought," is disclosed. "Hermeneutical theology, or more appropriately a theological thinking that is hermeneutically grounded, strives irrepressibly for the recovery of what is unthought. Its concern is not merely the hidden sense of the *verba divina* that appear in the guise of antique documents, but the creative 'word' that manifests itself through the archives, leavings, and sundry objectivities of history and culture." And, consequently, what is unthought is often perceived as a central mystery in need of interpretation: "Hermeneutics... tends to disclose the absent object, the mysterium lurking behind the iconic material that requires interpretation.... hermeneutics intends to pierce the veil of secrecy."[11] Carl Raschke proposes that hermeneutics be a radical form of dialogue which he calls "Hermeneutical dialogy," not a "tug-of-war" rhetoric but, rather, "a mutual penetration of cognitive armor which leads to a bipolar manifestation of the ultimate mysterium."[12]

As indicated in the introduction, sonic theology as a theological hermeneutic amounts to both a brush-clearing activity within the sonic or verbal realm and a powerful sonic act of penetration which renders or engages the omnipresent, Eternal Truth (Śabda-Brahman or otherwise). Sacred sound as a hermeneutic would thus act to uncover, or "un-sound," the Ultimate Reality, or God. Such Ultimate Truth is not lying naked before our eyes (or ears), ready to be apprehended by our senses or intellect, but is, instead, unveiled within the context of a radical experience: "Truth is no longer to be found in the agreement of the intellect with the subject matter, but is to be understood in terms of the Greek notion of *a-letheia,* an unveiling or unconcealing, an occurrence. Such truth must be experienced." Harking back to the pre-Socratic philosophers, this notion of "unveiling" is receiving increasing audience in current scholarship. "This is a vision of reality that begins with Heraclitus, for whom Logos not only meant *a-letheia,* as Heidegger reminds us, but for whom it also meant utterance—as though the whole of things were essentially the speech of Being."[13]

This notion of uncovering has another early counterpart in Buddhist thought. Regarding *Nirvāṇa,* a term that has been said to be the Buddhist equivalent of the Hindu *mokṣa,* the following etymology is instructive: "Many Buddhist authors have derived the word 'Nirvāṇa' from the [Sanskrit] root *vri,* 'to cover,' interpreting it as that which is quite 'unobstructed,' or 'free.' Nirvāṇa is therefore here envisaged as the final stage of the removal of all obstructions, of the uncovering process."[14]

Our exploration has noticed the importance of word repetition (*japa*) for the Hindu in engaging, unveiling, Ultimate Reality. Yet an objection may be raised as to the feasibility of this act. According to a modern scholar of linguistics, "Nothing in the real world is, strictly speaking, repeatable; only when one is dealing with an ideality of some kind does the possibility of its being repeatable make sense." Moreover, from an empirical view "no intended repetitions of the same sound even by one individual speaker can be shown to be precisely and in every respect the same on different occasions." The point is made, however, that "what is essential is not what is physically pronounced, but what these sounds are taken as representing in terms of the phonological structure of our language."[15] Accordingly, "where the actual 'teachings' are mainly phonetic rather than semantic, as in Vedic education, the living context is of the highest importance, for it makes clear the 'sense' of the sacred sounds or *mantras* and gives meaning to what otherwise could appear as mindless repetition and recitation."[16]

The same holds true for the religious votaries of the ancient Greco-Roman world: "It is clear that for the ancient writer the inspired language of the alphabet did carry meaning and could be interpreted."[17] Thus, as in the Hindu worldview, the most legitimate and consistent posture within the general study of religion will be that sacred words and syllables are never meaningless or nonsense but, rather, retain meaning both in themselves and as part of a vast universe of discourse.

Various occult traditions in the West have labored to uncover the essential word or mystical language by which to pierce an alleged veil of secrecy. Their general point of outlook has been noted by George Steiner: "The image of the world as a concatenation of secret syllables, the notion of an absolute idiom or cosmic letter—alpha and aleph—which underlies the rent fabric of human tongues, the supposition that the entirety of knowledge is prefigured in a final tome containing all conceivable permutations of the alphabet."[18]

Consequently, viewing the collapse of Babel (Genesis 11.1-9) as the "second Fall," an overriding concern of many Western occult traditions has been to recover the singular "Adamic language," which was dispersed. Jacob Boehme (1575-1624) was an original thinker along these lines who greatly influenced philosophers such as Leibniz, Schopenhauer, and Hegel and writers such as Goethe, Novalis, and C. G. Jung. For Boehme the Word of God is "identical with the heart of God as the essence of all things: it is the great mystery [*mysterium magnum*] enshrined in all things. . . . Adam's fall results in the loss of the essential word." This is termed by him "*Natursprache*": "As far as its origin is concerned, the *Natursprache* is the language of Adam, the first of mankind, and consists of the names by which, according to scripture, he called everything."[19] Boehme claimed a qualified understanding of this language, which is both partially recoverable in the "sensual" aspects of human speech and also understood by birds and animals.

The original language of Adam is also believed by some occult groups to be recoverable from the East through esoteric initiation. The tradition of Freemasonry, for example, continually seeks to recover the "lost word" in many of its rituals. Curiously, perhaps in partial fulfillment of their search, the Hindu syllable *AUM* has been incorporated into one of the "higher degrees" by Scottish rite masons during this century. Earlier attempts at uncovering the primordial linguistic revelation in Hinduism took place within the Theosophical Society, founded in 1875 by Madame Blavatsky. In her book *The Voice of the Silence* (1889) *Nāda* had been eulogized as the "soundless sound," the "voice of the spiritual sound."[20] Specific passages on

Nāda and Om from this work then made their way into William James's *The Varieties of Religious Experience* (1902),[21] giving them a kind of legitimacy in Western psychological and religious discourse.

According to Steiner,

> The occult holds that a single primal language, an *Ur-Sprache*, lies behind our present discord, behind the abrupt tumult of warring tongues which followed on the collapse of Nimrod's ziggurat. This Adamic vernacular not only enabled all men to understand one another, to communicate with perfect ease. It bodied forth, to a greater or lesser degree, the original Logos, the act of immediate calling into being whereby God had literally "spoken the world."

As in the Hindu sonic cosmogonies, wherein the naming of a thing brought it into being, "the vulgate of Eden contained . . . a divine syntax—powers of statement and designation analogous to God's own diction, in which the mere naming of a thing was the necessary and sufficient cause of its leap into reality."[22]

In terms of the onset of postmodernism the French philosopher Michel Foucault envisions a kind of unitive linguistic mysticism: "total reabsorption of all forms of discourse into a single word, of all books into a single page, of the whole world into one book."[23] Likewise, sonic theology in terms of the "death-of-God" question holds promise: "what is signified by this death is not the impossibility of the theological quest . . . but its relocation. The angle of theological vision is now toward the forgotten and archaic, toward the 'word' as aboriginal schema, as pre-utterance."[24] Thus, the future of hermeneutics requires the task of being thoroughly in touch, or "in tune," with the complexities of the sonic realm.

Upon final reflection the presence of sacred sound looms large on the Hindu horizon, a horizon enriched by centuries of religious dedication. Ostensibly, South Asia is a vast landscape of temple architecture and artifact, a veritable paradise for the visually acute. Yet, as we have endeavored to demonstrate, "Hindu" India, as legitimized by the Veda and Āgama, is also a "soundscape," an immense "auditorium" of sonic manifestations backed by centuries of theoretical formulation. Inversely, there are very few "soundproof" corners in the Hindu topography. The numerous Hindu temples that dot the landscape are not silent monoliths but, rather, house living deities who require "soundful" worship on a regular schedule. From morning to evening throughout the year one hears recitations and discussions of sacred lore, the resonance of mantra and *japa* repetitions, the singing of sacred hymns, or the peal of temple bells, conches, and musical instruments. Sacred sound thus forms a kind of nucleic substance—binding all Hindu activities and acting as the vital yet inexplicable nexus between temporal life and eternal beatitude.

We close with an observation by a Western musicologist, Hans Kayser, who, having spent a lifetime researching cosmic sound and world harmonics, reached an absorbing and similar conclusion:

> There are powers above and shapes written in the sky which sound in your own soul, which concern you most vitally, and which belong to the Godhead as much as do you in your innermost self.[25]

NOTES

INTRODUCTION

1. Johannes Fabian, *Time and the Other: How Anthropology Makes its Object* (1983), 106.
2. Ibid., 107.
3. Jacques Ellul, *The Humiliation of the Word* (1985), 155.
4. Ibid., 27.
5. Ernst Cassirer, *Language and Myth* (1946), 61.
6. Walter J. Ong, S. J., *The Presence of the Word: Some Prolegomena for Cultural and Religious History* (1967), 112, 162.
7. William A. Graham, *Beyond the Written Word: Oral Aspects of Scripture in the History of Religion* (1987), 65.
8. Harold Coward, *Sacred Word and Sacred Text: Scripture in World Religions* (1988), x.
9. Walter J. Ong, 15.
10. H. Daniel Smith, *Vaiṣṇava Iconography* (1969), xix (intro. M. Narasimhachary).
11. Diana L. Eck, *Darśan: Seeing the Divine Image in India* (1981), 1.
12. George Michell, *The Hindu Temple: An Introduction to Its Meaning and Forms* (1977), 14.
13. Rudolf Otto, *The Idea of the Holy* (1923, 1958), 6, 13.
14. Kees W. Bolle, *Secrecy in Religions* (1987), 5, 10, 14.
15. Walter J. Ong, 324.
16. Rudolf Otto, 190.
17. J. G. Arapura, *Hermeneutical Essays on Vedantic Topics* (1986), 164.
18. Harold Coward, 111.
19. Ernst Cassirer, *An Essay on Man: An Introduction to a Philosophy of Human Culture* (1944), 126.
20. Thomas B. Coburn, "Scripture in India: Towards a Typology of the Word in Hindu Life" (1984), 437, 447.
21. Harold Coward, 116.
22. William A. Graham, 69.
23. Monier Monier-Williams, *A Sanskrit-English Dictionary* (1988 repr.), 1052.
24. K. Kunjunni Raja, *Indian Theories of Meaning* (1963), 11.
25. F. J. Smith, "Prelude to a Phenomenology of Sound" (1973), 14–15.
26. Frits Staal, *Exploring Mysticism: A Methodological Essay* (1975), 175.
27. Kees W. Bolle, 17.

28. Brian K. Smith, "Exorcising the Transcendent: Strategies for Defining Hinduism and Religion" (1987), 40.
29. S. N. Dasgupta, *Hindu Mysticism* (1927), 16.
30. Wilfred Cantwell Smith, "Theology and the World's Religious History," *Toward a Universal Theology of Religion* (1987), 52.
31. Carl A. Raschke, "Religious Pluralism and Truth: From Theology to a Hermeneutical Dialogy" (1982), 41.
32. John B. Carman, *The Theology of Rāmānuja: An Essay in Interreligious Understanding* (1974), 201.
33. J. A. B. Van Buitenen, trans., *Rāmānuja's Vedārthasaṅgraha* (1956), 48.
34. Robert Jackson and Dermot Killingley, *Approaches to Hinduism* (1988), 168.
35. Pramod Kumar, *Mokṣa: The Ultimate Goal of Indian Philosophy* (1984), 6.
36. Klaus K. Klostermaier, *Indian Theology in Dialogue* (1986), 196.
37. Gerhard Ebeling, *Word and Faith* (1963), 323.
38. Paul Tillich, "The Word of God," *Language: An Inquiry into its Meaning and Function* (1957), 125.
39. Thomas Matus, *Yoga and the Jesus Prayer Tradition* (1984), 45.
40. J. G. Arapura, "Language and Knowledge in the Theology of Karl Barth and Vedanta," *Hermeneutical Essays on Vedāntic Topics* (1986), 183-84.
41. Paul Tillich, *Systematic Theology* (1951), 1:124.

CHAPTER 1

1. Richard Lannoy, *The Speaking Tree: A Study of Indian Culture and Society* (1971), 275.
2. Harold Coward, *Sacred Word and Sacred Text: Scripture in World Religions* (1988), 10, 11.
3. Labib al-Said, *The Recited Koran* (1975), 56.
4. Frederick M. Denny, "Islam: Qur'an and Hadith," in *The Holy Book in Comparative Perspective*, ed. Frederick M. Denny and Rodney L. Taylor (1985), 84.
5. Subhash C. Kak, "On the Chronology of Ancient India" (1987). Also, evidence linking the Aryan languages (Brahmī script) to the Indus script of Harappan civilization (ca. 2500 B.C.E.) has been assembled and studied through computer analysis by Kak in his "Frequency Analysis of the Indus Script" (1988).
6. Jim G. Shaffer, "The Indo-Aryan Invasions: Cultural Myth and Archaeological Reality," *The People of South Asia* (1984), 86.
7. P. Chakravarti, *The Linguistic Speculations of the Hindus* (1933), 23.
8. Monier-Williams, *A Sanskrit-English Dictionary*, 936.

9. J. G. Arapura, "Some Perspectives on Indian Philosophy of Language," *Revelation in Indian Thought* (1977), 21.
10. G. K. Bhat, "Vāk in Śatapatha Brāhmaṇa" (1977–78), 34.
11. W. Norman Brown, "The Creative Role of the Goddess Vāc in the Rig Veda," *Pratidānam* (1968), 394.
12. Ibid.
13. M. P. Lakhera, "Indra and Vāk" (1980), 21.
14. Quoted in ibid., 19–20.
15. Ibid., 18.
16. Robert E. Hume, trans., *The Thirteen Principal Upanishads* (1921), 200, 330 (cf. vowels as considered the "soul of language" in phonetics).
17. Wendy Doniger O'Flaherty, trans., *The Rig Veda: An Anthology* (1981), 63.
18. See W. D. Whitney, trans., *Atharva-Veda-Saṁhitā* (1962), 1:200–201.
19. Sudhendu Kumar Das, *Śakti or Divine Power* (1934), 25.
20. Quoted in K. Madhava Krishna Sarma, "Vāk before Bhartṛhari" (1943), 22.
21. Sudhendu Kumar Das, 30, 34.
22. M. Bloomfield, *The Atharva Veda and the Gopatha Brāhmaṇa* (1978 repr.), 108–9.
23. Frits Staal, "Ritual Syntax," *Sanskrit and Indian Studies: Essays in Honor of D. H. H. Ingalls* (1980), 122.
24. Thomas J. Hopkins, *The Hindu Religious Tradition* (1971), 19.
25. J. A. B. Van Buitenen, "Akṣara" (1959), 178.
26. Jan Gonda, *Vedic Literature* (1975), 83.
27. G. K. Bhat, 37.
28. Thomas J. Hopkins, 20.
29. George Steiner, *After Babel: Aspects of Language and Translation* (1975), 32.
30. S. J. Tambiah, "The Magical Power of Words" (1968), 179.
31. Frits Staal, "Ritual, Mantras and the Origin of Language," *R. N. Dandekar Felicitation Volume* (1984), 413.
32. Frits Staal, "Oriental Ideas on the Origin of Language" (1979), 10.
33. Frits Staal, "The Origin and Development of Linguistics in India," *Studies in the History of Linguistics* (1974), 66.
34. Frits Staal, "The Meaninglessness of Ritual" (1979), 9.
35. Frits Staal, "Ṛgveda 10.71 on the Origin of Language," *Revelation in Indian Thought* (1977), 11.
36. Jan Gonda, *Vedic Literature*, 84.
37. Wade T. Wheelock, "A Taxonomy of the Mantras in the New- and Full-Moon Sacrifice" (1980), 352.
38. C. Kunhan Raja, *Vedas* (1957), 41, 70.
39. John Taber, "Are Mantras Speech Acts? The Mīmāṁsā Point of View," *Mantra* (1989), 158.

40. Gerardus Van der Leeuw, *Religion in Essence and Manifestation* (1938), 405–6.
41. Ernst Cassirer, *Language and Myth* (1946), 48.
42. Richard Cavendish, *The Black Arts* (1967), 141–42.
43. Jan Gonda, "The Indian Mantra," *Selected Studies* (1975), 4:249.
44. Wendy Doniger O'Flaherty, trans., 61–62.
45. Frits Staal, "Ṛgveda 10.71 on the Origin of Language" (1977), 9.
46. P. Chakravarti, *The Linguistic Speculations of the Hindus* (1933), 82–83.
47. Ibid., 79–80, 87.
48. Ibid., 86.
49. Robert E. Hume, trans., 180.
50. P. Chakravarti, 91.
51. Robert E. Hume, trans., 214.
52. Madhav M. Deshpande, "On the Ṛk-Prātiśākhya 13.5–6" (1976), 176–77, 174.
53. W. D. Whitney, trans., "Taittirīya-Prātiśākhya and Tribhāshyaratna" (1871), 49–54.
54. Richard Cavendish (1967), 150.
55. The work by Sudhendu Kumar Das entitled *Śakti or Divine Power* (1934) is one of the first to examine the idea of the Śakti, or power of Vāk present, in Vedic meters. The more recent article by G. U. Thite, "The Doctrine of Meters in the Veda" (1987), provides a more thorough elaboration of a relatively unexplored field.
56. Sudhendu Kumar Das, *Śakti or Divine Power* (1934), 22.
57. G. U. Thite, 446–47.
58. Sudhendu Kumar Das, 24, 23.
59. G. U. Thite, 448.
60. The range of meters begins with the Gāyatrī of 24 syllables (8 syllables × 3 lines or 6 × 4) as the shortest and extends beyond the Atikṛti of 100 syllables. Some of the important ones after Gāyatrī are the following: Uṣṇik 28 (7 × 4), Anuṣṭubh 32 (8 × 4), Bṛhatī 36 (9 × 4), Paṅkti 40 (10 × 4), Triṣṭup 44 (11 × 4), Jagatī 48 (12 × 4), Atijagatī 52 (13 × 4), Śakvarī 56 (14 × 4), Atiśakvarī 60 (15 × 4), Kṛti 80 (20 × 4).
61. G. U. Thite, 435–36.
62. Ibid., 450.
63. Sudhendu Kumar Das, 25.
64. Robert E. Hume, trans., 177.
65. Ibid., 201, 279.
66. Ibid., 348–49.
67. Ibid., 372.
68. Ibid., 387–88.
69. Ibid., 426.
70. S. Radhakrishnan, trans., *The Principal Upanishads* (1953), 672.
71. Robert E. Hume, trans., 391–93.

72. Ibid., 437-38.
73. Ibid., 438.
74. Ibid., 441, 457, 437.
75. Ibid., 396.
76. Thomas J. Hopkins, 72.
77. Ibid.

CHAPTER 2

1. Edmund Husserl, *Formal and Transcendental Logic* (1929), 19.
2. A. J. Ayer, *Philosophy in the Twentieth Century,* 218.
3. W. Sidney Allen, *Phonetics in Ancient India,* 3.
4. Quoted in ibid., 3.
5. George Steiner, *After Babel,* 61.
6. W. Sidney Allen, 7.
7. See Harold Coward, *Derrida and Indian Philosophy* (1990), for a stimulating comparison between literary deconstruction (Derrida) and the thought of Bhartṛhari, Śaṅkara, and Nāgārjuna.
8. T. R. V. Murti, "The Philosophy of Language in the Indian Context," *Studies in Indian Thought* (1983), 361.
9. K. A. Subramania Iyer, "The Doctrine of Sphoṭa" (1948), 123.
10. See Sastri (1959), Kunjunni Raja (1963), and Coward (1980).
11. Franklin Edgerton, "Some Linguistic Notes on the Mīmāṁsā System," 171.
12. Benson Mates, *Stoic Logic,* 12.
13. George Steiner, *After Babel,* 60.
14. Sir Monier Monier-Williams, *A Sanskrit-English Dictionary,* 818.
15. Surendranath Dasgupta, *History of Indian Philosophy,* 1:370.
16. Ganganath Jha, *Pūrva-Mīmāṁsā in its Sources* (1942), 111.
17. Pt. Mohan Lal Sandal, trans., *Mīmāṁsā-Sūtras of Jaimini* (1923–25), 3–5.
18. Ganganath Jha, trans., *Śābara-Bhāṣya* (1933), 1:32–37.
19. Pt. Mohan Lal Sandal, trans., 5.
20. Ganganath Jha, trans., *Śābara Bhāṣya,* 37.
21. Franklin Edgerton, 171.
22. Mysore Hiriyanna, *Outlines of Indian Philosophy* (1932), 309.
23. Surendranath Dasgupta, *History of Indian Philosophy,* 1:395–96.
24. Susan Handelman, *The Slayers of Moses: The Emergence of Rabbinic Interpretation in Modern Literary Theory* (1982), 32.
25. Frank Paul Bowman, "Occultism and the Language of Poetry," *The Occult in Language and Literature* (1980), 54.
26. Ganganath Jha, trans., *Śābara-Bhāṣya,* 145.
27. Mysore Hiriyanna, 311–12.
28. John Taber, "Are Mantras Speech Acts? The Mīmāṁsā Point of View," in *Understanding Mantras,* ed. Harvey P. Alper (1989), 151.

29. Othmar Gachter, *Hermeneutics and Language in Pūrva Mīmāṁsā: A Study in Śabara-Bhāṣya* (1983), 36–37.
30. Ibid., 22.
31. Paul Tillich, "The Word of God," *Language: An Inquiry into Its Meaning and Function* (1957), 126.
32. Jacques Ellul, *The Humiliation of the Word*, 28, 32.
33. Surendranath Dasgupta, *History of Indian Philosophy*, 1:395.
34. Monier-Williams, 924.
35. K. Kunjunni Raja, *Indian Theories of Meaning* (1963), 204.
36. Upavarṣa is important, as he is Śaṅkarācārya's principle source for his own acceptance of the Varṇavāda doctrine in the *Brahma-Sūtra-Bhāṣya* (1.3.28).
37. K. A. Subramania Iyer, "The Doctrine of Sphoṭa," 125.
38. Gaurinath Sastri, *The Philosophy of Word and Meaning* (1959), 112. Sastri has reminded us further that the words *mantra* and *mīmāṁsā* are linguistically related: "Both the expressions *mantra* and *mīmāṁsā* are derived from the same root *man*" (Gaurinath Sastri, "Some Reflections on Veda" [1978], 941).
39. K. A. Subramania Iyer, "The Doctrine of Sphoṭa," 129.
40. Ibid., 133.
41. There has been a resurgence of interest in the Indian Grammarians among modern scholars. Pandit Gaurinath Sastri initiated this in India by solidly presenting the entire subject from the traditional Indian viewpoint in his well-known *The Philosophy of Word and Meaning* (1959), followed competently by K. Kunjunni Raja and his *Indian Theories of Meaning* (1963). The latter work differs from the first in that it appropriates some of the work of European linguistics (Firth and Brough) in its evaluation of the Indian materials. K. A. Subramania Iyer's translation (1965) and interpretation (1969) of Bhartṛhari's major work, the *Vākyapadīya*, has become the standard for any future work on Bhartṛhari. Among Western scholars preliminary work had been done early in this century by the British linguist John Brough, followed by the Canadian Harold G. Coward, whose excellent study *Bhartṛhari* (1976) has revealed important connections between Bhartṛhari and the Yoga tradition as well as the various contributions of this Grammarian. Coward's *Sphoṭa Theory of Language* (1980) provides a thorough elucidation of the arguments in the debate over the value of the Sphoṭa doctrine. The current standard reference source in English, *The Philosophy of the Grammarians* (1990), co-authored by Harold Coward and K. Kunjunṇi Raja, contains an exhaustive bibliography on the entire subject.
42. P. Chakravarti, *The Philosophy of Sanskrit Grammar* (1930), 34, 3.
43. Bishnupada Bhattacharya, "Philosophical Data in Patañjali's Mahābhāṣya," 52.
44. K. Raghavan Pillai, trans., *The Vākyapadīya* (1971), 5.

45. K. A. Subramania Iyer, trans., *The Vākyapadīya of Bhartṛhari with the Vṛtti,* (1965), chap. 1, pp. 205, 211.
46. K. V. Abhyankar and J. M. Shukla, eds. and trans., *Patañjali's Vyākaraṇa-Mahābhāṣya,* Āhnikas 1–3 (1975), 6–7.
47. Kshitish Chandra Chatterji, ed. and trans., *Patañjali's Mahābhāṣya,* Paspaśāhnika (1972), 16, 22.
48. Hartmut Scharfe, *Grammatical Literature* (1977), 172.
49. This question needs to be addressed, especially in the context of Harold Coward's noteworthy attempt to reconstruct the nature of Bhartṛhari's "Yoga" in chapter 4 of his book on Bhartṛhari (1976).
50. A. L. Herman, "Sphoṭa" (1963), 20.
51. Gaurinath Sastri, *The Philosophy of Word and Meaning,* 1, 24.
52. K. Raghavan Pillai, trans., 1.
53. Gopinath Kaviraj, *Aspects of Indian Thought* (1966), 21.
54. K. Raghavan Pillai, trans., xxiii.
55. Harold Coward, *The Sphoṭa Theory of Language* (1980), 72.
56. P. Chakravarti, *The Philosophy of Sanskrit Grammar* (1930), 89.
57. Monier-Williams, 1270.
58. Betty Heimann, "Sphoṭa and Artha," *A Volume of Studies in Indology Presented to Prof. P. V. Kane* (1941), 225.
59. Ibid., 225.
60. K. A. Subramania Iyer, *Bhartṛhari* (1969), 158–59.
61. John Brough, "Theories of General Linguistics in the Sanskrit Grammarians," in *A Reader on the Sanskrit Grammarians,* ed. Frits Staal (1972), 408.
62. P. Chakravarti, *The Philosophy of Sanskrit Grammar,* 99.
63. John Brough, 409.
64. Ibid., 413, 416.
65. Ibid., 417, 420.
66. Gopinath Kaviraj, "The Doctrine of Pratibhā in Indian Philosophy," *Aspects of Indian Thought,* 1, 29.
67. Gaurinath Sastri, *The Philosophy of Word and Meaning,* 87, 89.
68. P. Chakravarti, *The Philosophy of Sanskrit Grammar,* 88.
69. Kunjunni Raja, *Indian Theories of Meaning* (1963), 121.
70. Quoted by Kunjunni Raja, 121.
71. "Patañjali . . . is not acquainted with the divisions of Vāk into paśyantī etc. or *parā* etc. or *bindu* and *nāda.*" (K. Madhava Krishna Sarma, "Vāk Before Bhartṛhari" [1943], 33).
72. K. A. Subramania Iyer, trans., *The Vākyapadīya of Bhartṛhari with the Vṛtti,* 1, p. 55.
73. K. Raghavan Pillai, trans., 23.
74. K. A. Subramania Iyer, trans., 100.
75. Ibid., 84–85.

76. Harold Coward, "The Meaning and Power of Mantras in Bhartṛhari's Vākyapadīya," in *Understanding Mantras*, ed. Harvey P. Alper (1989), 172–73.
77. Harold Coward, *The Sphoṭa Theory of Language*, 134–35.
78. Harold Coward, "The Yoga of the Word (Śabdapūrva Yoga)," 12.
79. Harold Coward, "The Meaning and Power of Mantras in Bhartṛhari's Vākyapadīya," 173.
80. K. A. Subramania Iyer, trans., 21.
81. Harold Coward, "The Meaning and Power of Mantras," 168.
82. K. A. Subramania Iyer, trans., 125.
83. Jan Gonda, "The Indian Mantra," *Selected Studies* (1975), 4:277n.
84. Klaus Klostermaier, "The Creative Function of the Word," *Language in Indian Philosophy and Religion* (1978), 8.
85. K. Raghavan Pillai, trans., 3–4.
86. Interview with Pt. Guarinath Sastri in Calcutta on 12 June 1988. The passage was transcribed from a tape recording in English.
87. K. A. Subramania Iyer, *Bhartṛhari*, 142–43.
88. K. A. Subramania Iyer, "Bhartṛhari on Vyākaraṇa as a Means of Attaining Mokṣa" (1964), 128.
89. Harold Coward, "The Yoga of the Word (Śabdapūrva Yoga)" (1985), 6.
90. There are implications here in terms of religious fundamentalism and the so-called religions of the book,—for example, how dependent is the doctrine of scriptural inerrancy on the precise word order in the New Testament or the Koran?
91. Gaurinath Sastri, *A Study in the Dialectics of Sphoṭa* (1980), 83.
92. Ibid., 84.
93. Harold Coward, *Bhartṛhari*, 106.
94. Gaurinath Sastri, *A Study in the Dialectics of Sphoṭa*, 79–80.
95. P. Chakravarti, *The Philosophy of Sanskrit Grammar*, 112–13.
96. Shiv Kumar, *Sāṁkhya-Yoga Epistemology* (1984), 169.
97. A. L. Herman, "Sphoṭa," 9.
98. George Thibaut, trans., *Śaṅkara's Commentary on the Brahma-Sūtras* (1962), 210.
99. Karl H. Potter, ed., *Advaita Vedānta up to Śaṁkara and His Pupils* (1981), 60.
100. Susan Handelman, 5, 7, 8.
101. Karl H. Potter, ed., 54.
102. P. K. Sundaram, *Advaita Epistemology* (1968), 158.
103. Ibid., 137.
104. Harold Coward, *Bhartṛhari*, 109.
105. Ibid., 107.
106. Ibid., 109.

Chapter 3

1. Monier-Williams, *Sanskrit-English Dictionary*, 534, 731, 41.
2. T. R. Srinivasa Ayyangar, trans., *The Yoga Upanishads* (1938), 151.
3. Mircea Eliade, *Yoga: Immortality and Freedom* (1958), 75.
4. Surendranath Dasgupta, *A History of Indian Philosphy* (1952–55), 1:229.
5. Although these issues remain outside the scope of this work, research contained in articles by Varma (1960–61) and Werner (1975) engage our speculation about the earliest practices of meditation and Yoga technique.
6. *Yoga: Immortality and Freedom* (1958) is his major work on Yoga. He calls brief attention to sacred sound in Yoga in the small sections on "Mystical Sounds" (390–91) and "Mantras and Dhāraṇīs" (407–8).
7. Surendranath Dasgupta, *The Study of Patañjali* (1920), 207.
8. The Theosophical Society, founded in 1875 in New York City, stimulated a revival of interest in Hinduism and Yoga. At the turn of this century Rama Prasada supplied early information on Yoga and Hindu Tantra to Western magical and occultist groups, such as the Order of the Golden Dawn: "The Tantric elements in the Golden Dawn system were derived from an early publication of the Theosophical Society entitled *Nature's Finer Forces*, a Bengali Tantric text translated into English by a certain Rama Prasad" (Francis King, *Tantra for Westerners: A Practical Guide to the Way of Action* [1986], 77).
9. Mircea Eliade, 370–71.
10. Georg Feuerstein, "Patañjali," *Encyclopedia of Religion* (1987), 11:206.
11. Surendranath Dasgupta, 238n.
12. Mircea Eliade, 371.
13. Rama Prasada, trans., *Patañjali's Yoga Sūtras* (1912), 208.
14. Georg Feuerstein, *The Philosophy of Classical Yoga* (1980), 119.
15. "Vācaspati in his gloss under the aphorism *viśoka vā jyotiṣmatī* [1.36] has attempted to show the internal aspect of Sphoṭa" (P. Chakravarti, *The Philosophy of Sanskrit Grammar* [1930], 88).
16. Rama Prasada, trans., 212, 215.
17. Rammurti S. Mishra, M. D. *The Textbook of Yoga Psychology* (1963), 243–45.
18. Rama Prasada, trans., 49–50.
19. Ibid., 49.
20. James H. Woods, *The Yoga System of Patañjali* (1914), 60.
21. Georg Feuerstein, *The Philosophy of Classical Yoga*, 12.
22. Rama Prasada, trans., 51.
23. Ibid., 50.
24. Ibid.
25. Ibid., 51.
26. Ibid., 236.

27. Ibid., 240–41.
28. Alf Hiltebeitel, "Mahābhārata," *Encyclopedia of Religion* (1987), 9:118.
29. Georg Feuerstein, *Textbook of Yoga*, 85.
30. Ibid., 63.
31. Since the word *mātra* is directly related to the word for "measure," the translation of the word *mātra* as "degree" is more accurate than "element," which is used in most editions.
32. Swami Nikhilānanda, trans., *The Māṇḍūkyopanishad with Gauḍapāda's Kārikā and Śaṅkara's Commentary* (1955), 77, 82, 84.
33. Ibid., 80, 79.
34. Mircea Eliade, 70–71.
35. In his recent study *The Triadic Heart of Śiva* (1989), 73–74.
36. Georg Feuerstein, *Textbook of Yoga* (1975), 77.
37. The *Yoga-Upaniṣads* consist of the *Advayatāraka*, *Amṛtabindu*, *Amṛtanāda*, *Brahmabindu*, *Brahmavidyā*, *Darśana*, *Dhyāna-bindu*, *Haṁsa*, *Kṣurika*, *Mahāvākya*, *Maṇḍalabrāhmaṇa*, *Nādabindu*, *Pāśupatabrahma*, *Śāṇḍilya*, *Tejobindu*, *Triśikhibrāhmaṇa*, *Varāha*, *Yogacūḍāmaṇi*, *Yogakuṇḍali*, *Yogaśikha*, and *Yogatattva*. In our study we will consult the Adyar Sanskrit edition (1920) of Pandit A. Mahadeva Sastri, which includes the commentary of Śrī Upaniṣad Brahmayogin. The English translation of T. R. Srinivasa Ayyangar (Adyar, 1938) will be used with some modifications.
38. Jean Varenne, *Yoga and the Hindu Tradition* (1976), 182.
39. Mircea Eliade (1958), 127.
40. T. R. Srinivasa Ayyangar, trans., *The Yoga Upanishads* (1938), 365.
41. Georg Feuerstein, *Textbook of Yoga*, 88.
42. Mircea Eliade, 132, 133.
43. T. R. Srinivasa Ayyangar, trans., pp. 177–78, 179–80.
44. Ibid., 500.
45. Mircea Eliade, 241, 333.
46. T. R. Srinivasa Ayyangar, trans., 359–60.
47. Ibid., 361–63.
48. Ibid., 141.
49. Ibid., 299, 244.
50. Ibid., 367–68.
51. Ibid., 417, 435.
52. Varenne, *Yoga and the Hindu Tradition*, 8.
53. The Gorakhnāth tradition of Yoga has been studied by G. W. Briggs (1938), S. B. Dasgupta (1946), and A. K. Banerjea (1962).
54. Mircea Eliade, 308.
55. G. W. Briggs, *Gorakhnāth and the Kānphaṭa Yogīs* (1938), 228.
56. Ibid., 250.
57. Mircea Eliade, 306.
58. Shashibhusan Dasgupta, *Obscure Religious Cults* (1946), 218.

59. G. W. Briggs, 2.
60. Michael Magee, trans., *Kaulajñāna-nirṇaya* (1986), 18.
61. Ibid., 75–76.
62. G. W. Briggs, 256–57, 300, 301.
63. Ibid., 304.
64. The Devanāgarī text of this work is included as appendix 1 in A. Banerjea, *Philosophy of Gorakhnāth* (1962), 333–44.
65. A. K. Banerjea, *Philosophy of Gorakhnāth*, 191.
66. Ibid., 150.
67. Harvey P. Alper, ed., *Understanding Mantras*, 372.
68. A. K. Banerjea, 150–51.
69. Ibid., 151.
70. Mircea Eliade, 301.
71. Rai Bahadur S. C. Vasu, trans., *The Gheraṇḍa-Saṁhitā* (1914), 49.
72. Rai Bahadur S. C. Vasu, trans., *The Śiva-Saṁhitā* (1914), 57–58.
73. Pancham Sinh, trans., *The Haṭha-Yoga-Pradīpikā*, (1915), 56.
74. Ibid., 57–58.
75. Besides stating directly that "Bhartṛhari became a Gorakhnāthī" (244), there are references throughout Briggs's book about the legends surrounding Bhartṛhari's Nāth affiliation.
76. Smt. Vimala Musalagaonkar, "Music and Sound in Yoga," *Psychology of Music: Selected Papers* (1980), 44.
77. G. W. Briggs, 318.
78. Shashibhusan Dasgupta, *Aspects of Indian Religious Thought* (1957), 161.
79. G. W. Briggs, 318.
80. Ibid., 244.
81. Shashibhusan Dasgupta, *Obscure Religious Cults*, 242.
82. Daniel M. Neuman, *The Life of Music in North India* (1980), 60.
83. V. Raghavan, "Sāmaveda and Music" (1962), 127.
84. S. S. Janaki, "The Role of Sanskrit in the Development of Indian Music" (1985), 67.
85. The *Sāma-Veda* hymns are generally arranged in two primary sections, Arcika and Gāna. The Arcika is divided as Pūrvārcika and Uttarārcika. The Gāna portion is divided into Grāmageya and Āraṇyageya. The Pūrvārcika verses were arranged in the order of the deities propitiated, while the Uttarārcika verses were arranged according to ritual order. The Grāmageya-Gānas were those melodies to be sung in public, and the Āraṇyageya-Gānas were those melodies only to be sung in solitude in the forest. The Pūrvārcika collection consists of about 585 single stanza hymns, which were sung to melodies contained in the Grāmageya songbooks. The rules of adaptation of verses to melodies are contained in a very old musicological text in Sanskrit, the *Puṣpasūtra*.
86. V. Raghavan, 129.

87. S. S. Janaki, 68–70.
88. Robert E. Hume, trans., *The Thirteen Principal Upanishads* (1977), 177.
89. Donna M. Wulff, "On Practicing Religiously: Music as Sacred in India," *Sacred Sound: Music in Religious Thought and Practice* (1983), 154.
90. Smt. Vimala Musalagaonkar, "Music and Sound in Yoga," 56.
91. Ibid., 56. The translations of the verses are my own. For a scholarly discussion of this text, see Prem Lata Sharma, "Brihaddeśī of Mataṅga," (1970, 1971).
92. Gaurinath Sastri and Govinda Gopal Mukhopadhyaya, eds., *Sangīta Dāmodaraḥ of Śubhaṅkara* (1960), 16.
93. Śrīpād Nandalāl Vidyāsāgara, ed., *Śrī-Śrī-Bhakti-Ratnākara* of Śrīla Narahari Cakravartī (1960), 232.
94. Prem Lata Sharma, "Brihaddeśī of Mataṅga" (1971), 59.
95. "The largest work that has for a long time been the most important source of information on the ancient period, is the famous *Sangīta-Ratnākara*" (Emmie Te Nijenhuis, *Musicological Literature* [1977], 12).
96. R. K. Shringy and Prem Lata Sharma, eds., and trans., *Sangīta-Ratnākara* of Śārṅgadeva (1977), 108–9.
97. Ibid., 21–22, 115–16.
98. Ibid., 113.
99. Richard Lannoy, *The Speaking Tree: A Study of Indian Culture and Society* (1971), 276.
100. Interview on 10 June 1988 at the Calcutta home of M. R. Gautam.
101. Interview on 12 June 1988 with Sri Sailen Banerjee at the Tansen Music College in Calcutta.
102. Interview conducted with Prof. N. Ramanathan at the University of Madras on 24 June 1988.
103. Pandit Usharbudh Arya (1933–), *Nāda Yoga Meditation*, phonotape (n.d.).
104. Ibid.
105. Ibid.
106. Swami Śivānanda, *Japa Yoga* (1986), 3, 17.
107. Swami Śivānanda, *Philosophy and Meditation on Om* (1941), ix.
108. Swami Śivānanda, *Tantra Yoga, Nāda Yoga, and Kriyā Yoga* (1955), 103–4.
109. See ibid., 142–50; Swami Nādabrahmānanda, "The Science of Thaan."
110. C. W. Sanders, *The Inner Voice* (1948), 24–25.
111. Vishal Mangalwadi, *The World of Gurus* (1977), 206.
112. Harold Coward, *Sacred Word and Sacred Text*, 133.
113. Lawrence A. Babb, *Redemptive Encounters: Three Modern Styles in the Hindu Tradition* (1986), 53.
114. Vishal Mangalwadi, 196–97.
115. Bhagwan Shree Rajneesh, *Meditation: The Art of Ecstasy* (1976), 245–46.

116. Ibid., 246.
117. Lama Anagarika Govinda, *Creative Meditation and Multi-Dimensional Consciousness* (1976), 72–73.
118. Personal interview with Dr. C. R. Sankaran at his home in Poona on 13 July 1988. For more information, see C. R. Sankaran, "Theory and Experiment Concerning the Ultimate Unit of Speech," *Journal of the Acoustical Society of India* (1981); and C. R. Sankaran, *Process of Speech* (1963).
119. Shri R. J. Sahu, "The Rationale of Praṇava Japa" (1982), 89.
120. Shri R. J. Sahu and B. V. Bhole, "Effect of Two Types of Praṇava (Om) Recitations on Psycho-Motor Performance" (1983–84), 28.
121. Shri R. J. Sahu and B. V. Bhole, "Prāṇadhāraṇa and Nādānusandhāna as Contributing Factors in Inner Experience of Yogic Nature" (1983–84), 33.

Chapter 4

1. Teun Goudriaan and Sanjukta Gupta, *Hindu Tantric and Śākta Literature* (1981), 2.
2. André Padoux, "A Survey of Hindu Tantrism for the Historian of Religions" (1981), 347.
3. Swami Pratyagātmānanda Sarasvatī, "Tantra as a Way of Realization," *The Cultural Heritage of India* (1957–62), 4:227.
4. S. K. Das's *Śakti or Divine Power* (1934) describes the history of the feminine concept in Tantrism. P. C. Bagchi's *Studies in the Tantras* (1939), Chakravarti's *The Tantras: Studies on their Religion and Literature* (1963), and N. Bhattacharya's *History of the Tantric Religion* (1982), though useful for the historical study of Tantrism, are less informative regarding the role of sacred sound. Although based mainly on Buddhist-inspired texts, Agehananda Bharati's *The Tantric Tradition* (1965) provides an excellent chapter (5) on the esoteric and linguistic aspects of *mantras* and phonemes, or syllables. Recent studies include *Hindu Tantrism* (1979) by Sanjukta Gupta, Dirk Hoens, and Teun Goudriaan and *Hindu Tantric and Śākta Literature* (1981) by Gupta and Goudriaan.
5. Surendranath Dasgupta, "General Introduction to Tantra Philosophy," *Philosophical Essays* (1941), 160, 274.
6. Ibid., 282.
7. André Padoux, "Hindu Tantrism," *The Encyclopedia of Religion* (1987), 14:274.
8. Agehananda Bharati, "Tantrism," *Abingdon Dictionary of Living Religions* (1981), 735–36.
9. André Padoux, "Survey of Hindu Tantrism," 357.
10. André Padoux, "Hindu Tantrism," 277.

11. Sanjukta Gupta, "Mantra," *The Encyclopedia of Religion* (1987), 9:177.
12. André Padoux, "Hindu Tantrism," 278.
13. Ibid., 277.
14. Surendranath Dasgupta, "General Introduction to Tantra Philosophy," *Philosophical Essays* (1941), 171, 172.
15. Ibid., 172, 173.
16. See P. G. Lalye, "The *Devī-Bhāgavata* and *Śāradā-Tilaka*," *Studies in Devī-Bhāgavata* (1973), 97–101.
17. From this point forward *nāda* will appear as "Nāda," since it is nearly always synonymous with Nāda-Brahman.
18. Translation from Arthur H. Ewing, "The Śāradā-Tilaka Tantra" (1902), 70.
19. Gopinath Kaviraj, *Aspects of Indian Thought* (1966), 193–94.
20. Umesha Mishra, "Physical Theory of Sound and Its Origin in Indian Thought" (1926), 241–47.
21. Surendranath Dasgupta, 169.
22. Philip Rawson, *The Art of Tantra* (1973), 59.
23. Agehananda Bharati, *The Tantric Tradition* (1965), 111.
24. "It is the fifty (or as some count them fifty-one) letters of the Sanskrit alphabet which are denoted by the garland of severed heads which the naked Mother Kālī, dark like a threatening rain-cloud, wears as she stands amidst the bones and carrion, beasts and birds, in the burning ground, on the white corpse-like (Śava-rūpa) body of Śiva" (Sir John Woodroffe [Arthur Avalon], *The Garland of Letters* [1922], p. 225).
25. "The Mūlādhāra [Cakra] is a lotus of four petals. The petals are red, and have the letters VA, ŚA (palatal), ṢA (cerebral), SA, in colors of gold. . . . The Svādhiṣṭhāna-Cakra is of the color of vermilion, and has six petals. On its six petals are the six letters BA, BHA, MA, YA, RA and LA, with the Bindu placed thereon. . . . The Nābhi-Padma (Navel Lotus) [Maṇipūra-Cakra] is of the color of the rain-cloud and has ten petals; on each of its petals are each of the ten letters, ḌA, ḌHA, ṆA, TA, THA, DA, DHA, NA, PA, PHA, and of a lustrous blue color, with the Bindu above each of them. . . . The Heart Lotus [Anāhata-Cakra] is of the color of the Bandhūka flower, and on its twelve petals are the letters KA to THA [KA, KHA, GA, GHA, NA, CA, CHA, JA, JHA, NA, ṬA, ṬHA], with the Bindu above them, of the color of vermilion. . . . At the base of the throat is the Viśuddha-Cakra, with sixteen petals of smoky purple hue. Its filaments are ruddy, and the sixteen vowels [A, Ā, I, Ī, U, Ū, Ṛ, Ṝ, Ḷ, Ḹ, E, AI, O, AU, Anusvāra, Visarga] which are red and have the Bindu above them, are on the petals. . . . The Ājñā-Cakra has two petals and is white. The letters HA and KṢA, which are white, are on the two petals." (Arthur Avalon [Sir John Woodroffe], *The Serpent Power* [1919], 355, 365, 370, 382, 391, 413).

26. Dirk Jan Hoens, "Tantric Transmission," *Hindu Tantrism*, 86–87.
27. Lilian Silburn, *Kuṇḍalinī: The Energy of the Depths* (1988), 93-94.
28. Madhu Khanna, *Yantra: The Tantric Symbol of Cosmic Unity* (1979), 36.
29. Philip Rawson, 202.
30. Personal interview with Govinda Gopal Mukhopadhyaya, retired head of the Sanskrit Department at the University of Burdwan, conducted on 15 June 1988 in Calcutta.
31. Govinda Gopal Mukhopadhyaya, "The Secret of Japa" (1971), 277, 280-81.
32. Arthur Avalon (Sir John Woodroffe), *Shakti and Shakta* (1918), 514.
33. Garth Fowden, *The Egyptian Hermes: A Historical Approach to the Late Pagan Mind* (1986), 118.
34. Patricia Cox Miller, "In Praise of Nonsense," *Classical Mediterranean Spirituality* (1986), p. 499.
35. Tulsi Ram Sharma, *Studies in the Sectarian Upanishads* (1972), 120.
36. Jose Pereira Diogo (Andrade), *Historical Studies of the Rosary in Hinduism, Buddhism, Mohamedanism, and Christianity* (1937), 3, 115.
37. Sanjukta Gupta, Dirk Hoens, and Teun Goudriaan, *Hindu Tantrism* (1979), 155.
38. Govinda Gopal Mukhopadhyaya, "The Secret of Japa," 289.
39. Ibid.
40. Annemarie Schimmel, *Mystical Dimensions of Islam* (1975), 176–77.
41. Wade T. Wheelock, "The Mantra in Vedic and Tantric Ritual," *Understanding Mantras* (1989), 119.
42. Alexis Sanderson, "Śaivism in Kashmir," *The Encyclopedia of Religion* (1987), 13:17.
43. Teun Goudriaan and Sanjukta Gupta, *Hindu Tantric and Śākta Literature* (1981), 58–59.
44. See the recent text and translation by S. K. Ramachandra Rao, *Śrī-Sūkta* (1985).
45. See the recent translation and study by S. K. Ramachandra Rao, *The Tantra of Śrī-Cakra (Bhāvanopanishat)* (1983).
46. For a survey of the primary texts, the reader is directed to Teun Goudriaan and Sanjukta Gupta, *Hindu Tantric and Śākta Literature* (1981), 58–74. For a critical review of the secondary scholarship as well as a more in-depth study of the cult and liturgy, however, there are two recent Ph.D. dissertations on the Śrī-Vidyā or Śri-Cakra cult: Madhu Khanna, "The Concept and Liturgy of the Śrī-Cakra Based on Śivānanda's Trilogy" (Oxford University, 1986); and Douglas R. Brooks, "The Śrī-Vidyā School of Śākta Tantrism: A Study of the Texts and Contexts of the Living Traditions in South India" (Harvard University, 1987).
47. S. K. Ramachandra Rao, *Śrī-Cakra: Its Yantra, Mantra and Tantra* (1982), 38.

48. Sir John Woodroffe, trans., *Tantrarāja-Tantra and Kāmakalā-Vilāsa* (1921), 167.
49. Pandit S. Subrahmanya Sastri and T. R. Srinivasa Ayyangar, trans., *Saundarya-Laharī* (1965), 123–24.
50. Ibid., 124–25.
51. S. K. Ramachandra Rao (1982), 41.
52. Ibid., 39.
53. Ibid., 50.
54. Ibid., 50–51, 77.
55. Ibid., 54.
56. André Padoux, "Survey of Hindu Tantrism," 360.
57. See the chart in Madhu Kahnna's *Yantra*, 42, which is based on Bhāskara Rāya's eighteenth-century *Varivasyā-Rahasya*.
58. Douglas R. Brooks has documented evidence of a fifth century A.D. inscription bearing the Pañcadaśī-Mantra in Tamil Nadu, thus opening the question of the Kashmiri origin of the Śrī-Vidyā cult as well as the earliest source for the Śrī-Vidyā-Mantra. See the abovementioned dissertation.
59. Subrahmanya Sastri and T. R. Srinivasa Ayyangar, trans., *Saundarya-Laharī*, 15.
60. Madhu Khanna, "The Concept and Liturgy of the Śri-Cakra Based on Śivānanda's Trilogy" (1986), 276–77.
61. Teun Goudriaan and Sanjukta Gupta, *Hindu Tantric and Śākta Literature*, 64.
62. S. K. Ramachandra Rao (1982), 79.
63. See chapter 19 of Woodroffe's *The Garland of Letters* (196–204) for an early though unsystematic discussion of them.
64. Sanjukta Gupta, *Hindu Tantrism*, 177.
65. See Upendra Kumar Das, ed., *Yoginī-Hṛdayam* (1987), 296.
66. Pandit S. Subrahmanya Sastri, trans., *Varivasyā-Rahasya of Śrī Bhāskara-Rāya Makhin* (1948), 20.
67. R. Ananthakrishna Sastry, trans., *Lalitā-Sahasranāman with Bhāskararāya's Commentary* (1951), 162–63.
68. The enumeration of these subtle distinctions of Praṇava or Nāda has also been done, in whole or in part, in other Śākta texts such as the *Svacchanda-Tantra, Sammohana-Tantra, Śāradā-tilaka-Tantra* and the commentary on the *Ṣaṭcakra-Nirūpaṇa*. There are, no doubt, many more references, such that it remains another hermeneutical task for scholars to unravel the various ramifications of this rather recondite legacy.
69. Dirk Jan Hoens, "Mantra and Other Constituents of Tantra Practice," *Hindu Tantrism*, 95.
70. Sir John Woodroffe, *Tantrarāja-Tantra and Kāmakalā-Vilāsa* (1921), 155.
71. Ibid., 162, 205.
72. S. K. Ramachandra Rao (1982), 31–32, 72–73.

73. N. N. Bhattacharya, *History of the Tantric Religion* (1982), 350.
74. Teun Goudriaan and Sanjukta Gupta, *Hindu Tantric and Śākta Literature*, 75–76.
75. David R. Kinsley, *The Sword and the Flute* (1975), 99–100.
76. S. C. Banerji, *Tantra in Bengal* (1978), 79.
77. Govinda Gopal Mukhopadhyaya, "Tantras in Bengal" (1975), 85.
78. David R. Kinsley, 81.
79. Benoytosh Bhattacharyya, ed., *Śakti-Saṅgama-Tantra*, vol. 2 (1941). The description of Guhyakālī is in vol. 4 (1978), 9–10.
80. Sir John Woodroffe, *Hymns to the Goddess* (1973), 299.
81. Agehananda Bharati, *The Tantric Tradition*, 72.
82. Sir John Woodroffe, *Hymns to the Goddess*, 297, 300.
83. Arthur Avalon (Sir John Woodroffe), trans., *Tantra of the Great Liberation (Mahānirvāṇa Tantra)* (1972), 146–48.
84. Ibid., 153.

CHAPTER 5

1. David N. Lorenzen, "Śaivism," *The Encyclopedia of Religion* (1987), 13:7.
2. Gaurinath Sastri, *The Philosophy of Word and Meaning* (1959), 77.
3. Jan Gonda, *Medieval Religious Literature in Sanskrit* (1975), 4.
4. N. R. Bhatt, Preface, xiii in *Descriptive Catalogue of Manuscripts*, ed. V. Varadachari (1986).
5. Jan Gonda, 4.
6. Thomas J. Hopkins, *The Hindu Religious Tradition* (1971), 115.
7. Kees W. Bolle, *The Persistence of Religion*, 68.
8. M. Arunachalam, *The Śaivāgamas* (1983), 3.
9. Andre Padoux, "Hindu Tantric Literature," *Encyclopedia of Religion* (1987), 6:365. Variation in terminology is exemplified by the fact that Vaiṣṇava Pāñcarātra texts are sometimes referred to as Pāñcarātra-Āgama, and the *Lakṣmī-Tantra*, though having strong Śākta tendencies, is considered a Vaiṣṇava text.
10. Jan Gonda, 2.
11. Chintaharan Chakravarti, *The Tantras: Studies on Their Religion and Literature* (1963), 25.
12. Kees W. Bolle, *The Persistence of Religion*, 46.
13. Raymond A. Bowman, "Yahweh the Speaker" (1944), 8.
14. "In recent decades, the most sustained and significant work on the [Śaiva] Āgamic tradition has been done at the Institut Français d'Indologie in Pondicherry, particularly by the head pandit, N. R. Bhatt, and Helene Brunner" (in *Understanding Mantras*, ed. Harvey P. Alper, 418).
15. Personal interview with Pandit N. R. Bhatt in Pondicherry on 5 July 1988, conducted in English and transcribed from written notes.

16. N. R. Bhatt, preface, xiii, xv.
17. Jan Gonda, 164–65.
18. M. Arunachalam, *The Śaivāgamas*, 12, 5.
19. Mark S. G. Dyczkowski, *The Canon of the Śaivāgama and the Kubjikā Tantras of the Western Kaula Tradition* (1988), 6.
20. Surendranath Dasgupta, *A History of Indian Philosophy*, 5:20.
21. Jan Gonda, 163.
22. Personal interview with N. R. Bhatt in Pondicherry on 6 July 1988, conducted in English and transcribed from written notes.
23. B. Patni, *Śiva Purāṇa: A Poetic Analysis* (1980), 58. The same, we assume, is found in the *Vātulaśuddhākhya-Āgama*, according to Patni. According to S. N. Dasgupta, the *Mṛgendra-Āgama* "is said to be a subsidiary part of *Kāmika-Āgama*, supposed to be one of the oldest of the Āgamas [one of the original 28], and has been referred to in the *Sūta-Saṁhitā* which is regarded as a work of the sixth century" (*History of Indian Philosophy*, 5:21). Though sometimes considered an apocryphal Upāgama (of which there are said to be 107), with limited clientele, the *Mṛgendra-Āgama* has indeed been profusely quoted as a great authority (i.e., in the fourteenth-century *Sarva-darśana-Saṁgraha* of Mādhavācarya).
24. See *Candrajñāna-Āgama*, ed. Pt. Kashinath Shastri (1940).
25. See *Sūkṣma-Āgama*, ed. Pt. Kashinath Shastri (1942).
26. See M. Arunachalam, 100–103.
27. B. Patni, 51.
28. Ganesh V. Tagare, trans., *Śiva-Purāṇa* (1970), 1:103.
29. Ludo Rocher, "Mantras in the *Śiva-Purāṇa*," in *Understanding Mantras*, ed. Harvey P. Alper, 182, 183.
30. Susan Handelman, *The Slayers of Moses*, 40.
31. See S. L. MacGregor Mathers, trans., *The Kabbalah Unveiled* (1968).
32. Ludo Rocher, 184, 183, 179.
33. B. Bhattacharya, *Śaivism and the Phallic World* (1975), 2:605, 615.
34. M. Arunachalam, 39, 40.
35. Ibid., 40.
36. "In the tenth and eleventh centuries, . . . it was the Śaiva-Siddhānta that was the dominant Śaiva doctrine (*jñāna*) in Kashmir" (Alexis Sanderson, "Śaivism in Kashmir," *The Encyclopedia of Religion* [1987], 13:16).
37. Jan Gonda, *Medieval Religious Literature*, 159.
38. J. W. V. Curtis, "Space Concepts and Worship Environment in Śaiva-Siddhānta," *Experiencing Śiva: Encounters with a Hindu Deity* (1983), 92.
39. K. Sivaraman, *Śaivism in Philosophical Perspective* (1973), 229.
40. They are discussed in a recent book by Rohan A. Dunuwila, *Śaiva Siddhānta Theology* (1985), as well as in Sivaraman's and Pandey's earlier works. Another valuable presentation on Śaiva-Siddhānta is Mariasusai

Dhavamony's *Love of God according to Śaiva Siddhānta: A Study in the Mysticism and Theology of Śaivism* (1971).

41. This work is translated and discussed by a contemporary scholar prominent in this tradition, K. Sivaraman, as part of an article entitled, "The Word as a Category of Revelation." Sivaraman's *Śaivism in Philosophical Perspective* (1973) focuses mainly on the philosophical doctrines of Śaiva-Siddhānta yet mentions the *Nāda-Kārikā,* and discusses the Śaivite Pañcākṣara-Mantra, *namaḥ śivāya* (401–4).
42. Gopinath Kaviraj, *Aspects of Indian Thought* (1966), 211.
43. K. Sivaraman, "Word as a Category of Revelation," *Revelation in Indian Thought* (1977), 50, 51.
44. Gopinath Kaviraj, 210.
45. Pierre Filliozat, "On the Semantic Use of the Word Sphoṭa," *Amṛtadhara: Prof. R. N. Dandekar Felicitation Volume* (1984), 138.
46. Ibid.
47. K. Sivaraman, "Word as a Category of Revelation," 63.
48. Ibid., 57–59.
49. The Government Oriental Manuscripts Library at the University of Madras contains the following hand-copied transcriptions of the Sanskrit commentaries on the *Nāda-Kārikā: Nāda-Kārikā-Vṛtti* (#R16819) and *Nāda-Kārikā-Vyākhyā* (#R14719 and #R147200). The latter is 472 pages in length.
50. Pierre-Sylvain Filliozat, "Les *Nāda-Kārikā* de Rāmakaṇṭha," *Bulletin de l'École Français d'Extrême Orient,* 73 (1984): 223–55. He presents a French translation of the *Nāda-Kārikā,* with many useful comments regarding the similarity or difference between the concepts of *nāda* and *sphoṭa,* especially on pages 236–40. In addition, he accents the role of *nāda* and Nāda-Brahman in both human communication and in ultimate realization: "In the transmission of a message from one person to another by speaking, the role of *nāda* is primary" (224); "The attainment of wonderful things in this world as well as the highest kind of liberation are the workings of the realization of Nāda-Brahman" (252). The translations are my own.
51. Mariasusai Dhavamony, "Śaiva Siddhānta," *The Encyclopedia of Religion* (1987), 13:12.
52. Jayandra Soni, *Philosophical Anthropology in Śaiva Siddhānta* (1989), 140.
53. K. Sivaraman, *Śaivism in Philosophical Perspective,* 402.
54. Gerhard Oberhammer, "The Use of Mantra in Yogic Meditation: The Testimony of the Pāśupata," in *Understanding Mantras,* ed. Harvey P. Alper, 216–17.
55. Klaus K. Klostermaier, *Mythologies and Philosophies of Salvation in the Theistic Traditions of India* (1984), 177.
56. Kashmiri Śaivism is recently receiving scholarly attention from the SUNY

Series in the Shaiva Traditions of Kashmir, which has been publishing (or republishing) many works of important scholarship: Jaidev Singh, Lilian Silburn, André Padoux, Harvey P. Alper, Mark S. G. Dyczkowski, and Paul E. Muller-Ortega. Singh's translations of several of the important shorter texts provide us with primary source references in English. Padoux's work on Vāc (1990) remains among the best secondary sources for the study of mantra and sound in this tradition. For a good update on Kashmiri Śaiva scholarship, the reader is referred to pages 18–24 of Muller-Ortega's *The Triadic Heart of Śiva* (1989).

57. William Barnard, Preface, J. C. Chatterji, *Kashmir Shaivism* (1986 repr. of 1949 ed.), viii.
58. "Principally because of its triadic structure, the literature often refers to Kashmir Śaivism by the term Trika, which may be translated as Triadism" (Paul E. Murphy, *Triadic Mysticism: The Mystical Theology of the Śaivism of Kashmir* [1986], vii).
59. J. C. Chatterji, *Kashmir Shaivism* (1986 repr. of 1914 ed.), 133.
60. Jan Gonda, *Medieval Religious Literature,* 162.
61. Swami Lakshman Jee, *Kashmir Shaivism: The Supreme Secret* (1988), 41.
62. Ibid.
63. Gaurinath Sastri, *Philosophy of Word and Meaning,* 77.
64. K. Sivaraman, "The Śaiva and the Grammarian Perspectives of Language," *Language in Indian Philosophy and Religion* (1978), 27.
65. André Padoux, *Vāc: The Concept of the Word in Selected Hindu Tantras* (1990), 428.
66. Ibid., 25.
67. Ibid.
68. R. K. Kaw, *The Doctrine of Recognition* (1967), 83–84, 87.
69. Gaurinath Sastri, 82.
70. K. Sivaraman, 20.
71. Jaideva Singh, trans., *Abhinavagupta: A Trident of Wisdom* (1989).
72. Paul E. Murphy, 3.
73. Pranabananda Jash, *History of Śaivism* (1974), 123–24.
74. Mark S. G. Dyczkowski, *The Doctrine of Vibration: An Analysis of the Doctrines and Practices of Kashmir Śaivism* (1987), 172–73.
75. Jaideva Singh, trans., *Śiva Sūtras: The Yoga of Supreme Identity* (1979), 82.
76. Ibid., 83, 85–86.
77. Jaideva Singh, trans., *Vijñāna Bhairava or Divine Consciousness* (1981), 133, 134.
78. Richard H. Robinson and Willard L. Johnson, *The Buddhist Religion: A Historical Introduction* (1977), 118.
79. Wm. Theodore de Bary, ed., *The Buddhist Tradition in India, China and Japan* (1972), 113–14.

80. W. Y. Evans-Wentz, ed., *The Tibetan Book of the Dead* (1960), 149–50.
81. G. Mukhopadhyaya, "Reality as Viewed in the Trika System of Philosophy" (1968), 238–39.
82. Ibid., 239.
83. Taiko Yamasaki, *Shingon: Japanese Esoteric Buddhism* (1988), 77, 80.
84. Quoted in Jaidev Singh, trans., *Vijñāna Bhairava or Divine Consciousness*, xvi.
85. André Padoux, *Vāc: The Concept of the Word in Selected Hindu Tantras*, 100.
86. Paul E. Muller-Ortega, *The Triadic Heart of Śiva: Kaula Tantricism of Abhinavagupta in the Non-dual Shaivism of Kashmir* (1989), 153, 210.
87. Ibid., 172.
88. Jaidev Singh, trans., *Spanda-Kārikās: The Divine Creative Pulsation* (1980), xvii, 146.
89. Ibid., 147.
90. Ibid., 156.
91. Paul E. Muller-Ortega, 120, 139.
92. The linguistic details of this mantra are contained in Abhinavagupta's commentary on verse 9 and on verses 22–24 of his *Parātrīśikā-laghuvṛtti*, trans. Muller-Ortega, in the above cited volume. Muller-Ortega's remarks cited here are from his study of Abhinavagupta's original Sanskrit text.
93. Ibid., 172, 170.
94. Lilian Silburn, *Kuṇḍalinī: Energy of the Depths* (1988), 197.
95. André Padoux, *Vāc*, 110.

CHAPTER 6

1. Jan Gonda, *Medieval Religious Literature* (1975), 2.
2. Chandradhar Sharma, *A Critical Survey of Indian Philosophy* (1960), 336.
3. Until the twentieth century the Pāñcarātra tradition was a largely neglected area for academic study. The first serious work was done by F. Otto Schrader, who published his *Introduction to the Pāñcarātra and the Ahirbudhnya-Saṁhitā* in 1916. For decades this was the only volume known to non-Sanskritists and was slightly misleading as to the nature of the entire Pāñcarātra corpus. The work of H. Daniel Smith redressed that imbalance with his *Descriptive Bibliography of the Printed Texts of the Pāñcarātrāgama* (1975), which provides a content outline of the published texts as well as noteworthy evaluations on their place in the canon. A glance over the highly condensed descriptions of the thirty or so texts that Smith examines furnishes us with accessible information regarding the use of mantra and sacred sound in Vaiṣṇavism. Further guidance is provided by Smith in a companion volume (1980), which is

a topical index to subjects treated in the printed Pāñcarāta texts. See especially entries under "Mantra," 78-84. For descriptions of contents of unpublished Pāñcarātra manuscripts, see Smith, *The Smith Āgama Collection* (1978).

4. H. Daniel Smith, "The Three Gems of the Pāñcarātrāgama Canon—An Appraisal" (1972), 45.
5. F. O. Schrader, *Introduction to the Pāñcarātra and the Ahirbudhnya-Saṁhitā* (1916), 22.
6. Jan Gonda, "The Concept of a Personal God in Ancient Indian Religious Thought," *Selected Studies* (1975), 4:14.
7. Sanjukta Gupta, "The Pāñcarātra Attitude to Mantra," in *Understanding Mantras*, ed. Harvey P. Alper (1989), 227-28, 236.
8. Ibid., 224.
9. Ibid., 228-29.
10. Benoytosh Bhattacharyya, Foreword, *Jayākhya-Saṁhitā* (1931), 23-24.
11. Acknowledgment is given here to the assistance provided by S. D. Joshi of Deccan College, Pune, India. The current project there known as the "Scriptorium" is nothing less than a comprehensive word index of all Sanskrit texts and literatures, enabling researchers to locate words that are not sufficiently referenced in other published indices. The present author visited the institution during July of 1988.
12. See Embar Krishnamacharya, ed., *Jayākhya-Saṁhitā* (1931), 362. The translations are my own.
13. H. Daniel Smith, *A Descriptive Bibliography*, 121.
14. H. Daniel Smith, "Pāñcarātra Literature in Perspective," 50.
15. H. Daniel Smith, "The 'Three Gems' of the Pāñcarātrāgama Canon," 51.
16. H. Daniel Smith, *A Descriptive Bibliography*, 514.
17. Details regarding the *Pauṣkara-Saṁhitā* and the *Sāttvata-Saṁhitā* are taken from Smith, *A Descriptive Bibliography*, 277, 514-16, while references to Nāda in the *Sāttvata-Saṁhitā* are found in the original text edited by P. B. Anantha Chariar (Conjeevaram: Sudarsana Press, 1902), 28.
18. F. O. Schrader, 118-19.
19. Quoted in Patricia Cox Miller, "In Praise of Nonsense," *Classical Mediterranean Spirituality* (1986), 500.
20. "In form, the *Lakṣmī-Tantra* follows the tradition of both the *Sāttvata-Saṁhitā* and the *Jayākhya-Saṁhitā*. It deals extensively with the *vyūha* theory [theory of emanation]. . . . In regard to the ritualistic aspect of worship, the *Lakṣmī-Tantra* follows the tradition of the *Jayākhya-Saṁhitā*, which accords a central position to the worship of Viṣṇu and His consort Lakṣmī. . . . Indeed, the *Lakṣmī-Tantra* depends so largely on the *Jayākhya-Saṁhitā* that it frequently quotes lengthy passages of it" (Sanjukta Gupta, trans., *Lakṣmī-Tantra* [1972], xviii).

21. Ibid., 99.
22. Ibid., 100.
23. The Śaivites generally consider these five parts of Om (A, U, M, Nāda, Bindu) "as an equivalent to the five syllables of their mantra *namaḥ śivāya* [*na-maḥ-śi-vā-ya*]" (Jan Gonda, *Viṣṇuism and Śivaism: A Comparison* [1976 repr. of 1970 London ed.], 67).
24. Sanjukta Gupta, trans., *Lakṣmī-Tantra*, 127.
25. F. O. Schrader, 141.
26. Sanjukta Gupta, trans., *Lakṣmī Tantra*, 359.
27. This previously rare text has been reprinted in South India without chapter numbers and edited by G. R. Josyer (1981). The descriptions of Nāda are found on 118–19.
28. The original hymn "is probably pre-Buddhist in date" (David R. Kinsley, *Hindu Goddesses*, 20).
29. S. K. Ramachandra Rao, trans., *Śrī Sūkta: Text and Translation* (1985), 34.
30. Sanjukta Gupta, trans., *Lakṣmī-Tantra*, 338, 347.
31. Sanjukta Gupta, "The Pāñcarātra Attitude to Mantra," 230.
32. Sanjukta Gupta, trans., *Lakṣmī-Tantra*, 333.
33. Interview conducted in English with P. P. Apte at Deccan College on 12 July 1988.
34. Sanjukta Gupta, "The Pāñcarātra Attitude to Mantra," 237.
35. Ibid.
36. Sanjukta Gupta, trans., *Lakṣmī-Tantra*, 136–37.
37. F. O. Schrader, 120–21.
38. Daniel P. Sheridan, *The Advaitic Theism of the Bhāgavata Purāṇa* (1986), 2, 16.
39. Thomas J. Hopkins, *The Hindu Religious Tradition* (1971), 124–25.
40. Ganesh V. Tagare, trans., *The Bhāgavata Purāṇa* (1978), 1:lxv.
41. N. Raghunathan, trans., *Śrīmad-Bhāgavatam* (1976), 2:628.
42. Ibid., 668.
43. Ibid., 566.
44. Ganesh V. Tagare, trans., pt. 5, 1978. Cf. N. Raghunathan, trans., 2:566.
45. Quoted in Bhaktivedanta Swami, trans., *Śrīmad-Bhāgavatam*, canto 11, pt. 3 (1982), 145.
46. N. Raghunathan, trans., 2:629–30.
47. Quoted in Bhaktivedanta Swami, trans., canto 11, pt. 5 (1984), 577.
48. Ganesh V. Tagare, trans., pt. 5, 1999.
49. Sanjukta Gupta, "The Pāñcarātra Attitude to Mantra," 243.
50. Sanjukta Gupta, trans., *Lakṣmī-Tantra*, 127.
51. Gerhard Oberhammer, "The Use of Mantra in Yogic Meditation: The Testimony of the Pāśupata," in *Understanding Mantras*, ed. Harvey P. Alper (1989), 220.
52. Klaus K. Klostermaier, *A Survey of Hinduism* (1989), 216.

53. N. N. Sen Gupta, "A Historical and Comparative Study of the Practice of Religious Recital (or Japa)" (1939), 40–41.
54. Thomas J. Hopkins (1971), 122–23.
55. George Thibaut, trans., *Vedānta-Sūtras with the Commentary of Rāmānuja* (1904), 32–34.
56. Surendranath Dasgupta, *A History of Indian Philosophy*, 3:108.
57. See chapter 2 for a discussion of Śaṅkara's position vis-à-vis Sphoṭavāda and Mīmāṁsā.
58. Julius J. Lipner, *The Face of Truth: A Study of Meaning and Metaphysics in the Vedāntic Theology of Rāmānuja* (1986), 21, 28.
59. See T. Bheemacharya and S. N. Shastri, eds. and trans., *Aṣṭaślokī* of Śrī Parāśara (1971), 1–9.
60. Personal interview with M. Narasimhachary, professor and head of the Department of Vaiṣṇava Studies at the University of Madras, on 27 June 1988 in Madras.
61. Julius Lipner, 21.
62. John Braisted Carman, *The Theology of Rāmānuja* (1974), 174.
63. K. Narain, *An Outline of Madhva Philosophy* (1962), 84.
64. P. Nagaraja Rao, *The Epistemology of Dvaita Vedānta* (1976), 99–100, 103.
65. Surendranath Dasgupta, *A History of Indian Philosophy*, 4:63.
66. Smt. Roma Bose, trans., *Vedānta-Pārijāta-Saurabha of Nimbārka and Vedānta-Kaustubha of Śrīnivāsa* (1943), 3:256.
67. Pramod Kumar (1984), 124.
68. Richard Barz, *The Bhakti Sect of Vallabhācārya* (1976), 18. The entire "message" of Śrī Krishna revealed to Vallabha that particular night—a theophany considered by members of the Sampradāya to be the single most important event in its history—is recorded by Vallabha in his Sanskrit work *Siddhānta-Rahasya*, the relevant passage of which is translated into English by Barz in his book (17–18). Barz's source for the text of Vallabha's *Siddhānta-Rahasya* is a Hindi work by Sitaram Caturvedi, entitled *Mahāprabhu Śrīmad-Vallabhācārya aur Puṣṭi-Mārga* (1967), 292–93.
69. Ibid., 20. Barz's source here is a work by Harishankarajī Cimmanalāla, entitled *Puṣṭimārgopadeshikā*, trans. Shrimadhava Sharma (Sanskrit into Hindī) (1941), 28–30.
70. Ibid., 22.
71. Pramod Kumar (1984), 128.
72. Ramakanta Chakravarti, *Vaiṣṇavism in Bengal* (1985), 91, 95.
73. P. Chakravarti, *The Philosophy of Sanskrit Grammar* (1930), 121.
74. Stuart M. Elkman, *Jīva Goswami's Tattva-Sandarbha* (1986), 75.
75. Edward C. Dimock, Jr., *The Place of the Hidden Moon* (1966), 82.
76. Ibid., 233–34.
77. This text belongs to the group of Vaiṣṇava-Upaniṣads which are held

by serious scholars to be both "apocryphal" and late (after the tenth century) in composition. Though these works often include nomenclature similar to the so-called Principal Upaniṣads, they, in fact, clearly exhibit tendencies accumulated in medieval times. This, however, does not necessarily deter us from recognizing the "canonical" status of some of them, especially the *Gopāla-tāpanī-Upaniṣad,* for Vaiṣṇavism.

78. This translation is my own.
79. "As a document representing the cult of Rādhā-Krsna, it must be dated among the latest of the Saṁhitā-type works" (H. Daniel Smith, *A Descriptive Bibliography,* 131).
80. Swami Vijñānānanda, trans., *Śri Nārada Pañcharatnam* (1921), 127, 217.
81. H. Daniel Smith, *A Descriptive Bibliography,* 423.
82. Rai Bahadur Srisa Chandra Vasu, trans., *The Vedānta-Sūtras of Bādarāyaṇa with the Commentary of Baladeva* (repr. 1974), 554. This commentary on the *Vedānta-Sūtra* by Baladeva Vidyābhūṣaṇa is known as the *Govinda-Bhāṣya* and is the standard definition of Vedānta philosophy for Gauḍīya-Vaiṣṇavism. In commenting on the earlier sutra 1.1.5 (*Īkṣater nāśabdam*) Baladeva explains, in reference to Brahman—which for Vaiṣṇavas is Viṣṇu or Krishna—that "Brahman is not *aśabdam.* On the contrary He [Krishna or Govinda] is *śabdam* or expressed by words" (23). This is at loggerheads with the Advaita-Vedānta interpretation that Brahman is *aśabdam,* or inexpressible in words or sound.
83. T. R. Srinivasa Ayyangar, trans., *Vaiṣṇava Upanishads* (1953), 19.
84. Basanti Choudhury, "Love Sentiment and Its Spiritual Implications in Gauḍīya Vaiṣṇavism" (*Bengal Vaiṣṇavism, Orientalism, Society and the Arts* [1985], 4).
85. H. Byron Earhart, *Japanese Religion: Unity and Diversity* (1969), 46, 47.
86. David L. Haberman, *Acting as a Way of Salvation* (1988), 117, 118.
87. For a historical and critical assessment of the Gauḍīya Maṭh, see Joseph T. O'Connell, "The Social Implications of the Gauḍīya Vaiṣṇava Movement" (1970).
88. Bhaktisiddhānta Sarasvatī Goswami Mahārāj, *Shri Chaitanya's Teachings* (1967), 419–20. In a letter dated 24 July 1989 Paul H. Sherbow, Sanskritist and Gauḍīya-Vaiṣṇava historian, mentioned a lecture in Bengali on "Sphoṭa" delivered by Śrīla Bhaktisiddhānta Sarasvatī in 1929. The lecture, transcribed in the Calcutta periodical *Gauḍīya-Darśana,* revealed that, for Śrīla Bhaktisiddhānta Sarasvatī and Gauḍīya-Vaiṣṇavas, the ultimate referent and nature of Sphoṭa is God, or "Krishna."
89. Rūpa Vilāsa Dāsa (Robert D. MacNaughton), *A Ray of Vishnu* (1988), 22.
90. Larry D. Shinn, *The Dark Lord: Cult Images and the Hare Krishnas in America* (1987), 101.

91. Peter W. Williams, *Popular Religion in America* (1980), 144.
92. Felicitas D. Goodman, *Glossolalia: Speaking in Tongues* (1972), 58–59.

Conclusion

1. Joachim-Ernst Berendt, *Nāda Brahma: The World Is Sound* (1987), 16.
2. C. Mackenzie Brown, "Purāṇa as Scripture: From Sound to Image of the Holy Word in the Hindu Tradition" (1986), 69.
3. Eric Havelock, *Origins of Western Literacy* (1976), 6.
4. Edith Gerson-Kiwi, "Religious Chant: A Pan-Asiatic Conception of Music" (1961), 65, 64.
5. James M. Robinson, ed., *The New Hermeneutic* (1964), 3.
6. Gerhard Ebeling, *Word and Faith* (1963), 318–19.
7. S. Paul Schilling, *Contemporary Continental Theologians* (1966), 124.
8. Ibid.
9. James M. Robinson, *New Hermeneutic*, 46.
10. Ibid., 1, 49.
11. Carl A. Raschke, *Theological Thinking: An In-quiry* (1988), 92–93, 96.
12. Carl A. Raschke, "Religious Pluralism and Truth: From Theology to a Hermeneutical Dialogy" (1982), 44.
13. Stanley Romaine Hopper and David L. Miller, eds., *Interpretation: The Poetry of Meaning* (1967), xiv, xx.
14. Edward Conze, trans., *Buddhist Wisdom Books Containing the Diamond Sūtra and the Heart Sūtra* (1972), 97.
15. James M. Edie, *Speaking and Meaning: The Phenomenology of Language* (1976), 23, 24, 26.
16. C. Mackenzie Brown, 74.
17. Patricia Cox Miller, "In Praise of Nonsense" (1986), 485.
18. George Steiner, *After Babel* (1975), 67.
19. Klaus K. Klostermaier, "Man Carries the Power of All Things in His Mouth: Jacob Boehme's Ideas on Word and Language" (1977), 93–94, 89.
20. H. P. Blavatsky, *The Voice of the Silence* (repr., 1976), 1, 73.
21. William James, *The Varieties of Religious Experience* (1982), 421.
22. George Steiner, 58.
23. Michel Foucault, *The Order of Things* (1970), 305–6.
24. Carl Raschke, *Theological Thinking*, 98.
25. Hans Kayser, *Akroasis: The Theory of World Harmonics* (1970), 60.

GLOSSARY

Āgama: a textual tradition; refers often to a body of Sanskrit texts associated with Śaivism, as in Śaiva-Āgama.

Agni: fire; Vedic god of fire.

Akṣamālā: a rosary for chanting mantras or names of divinities.

Akṣara: "imperishable"; refers to the power of a single syllable, such as *Om*.

Amātra: "without measure"; refers to a state of being which is immeasurable or beyond measure.

Anāhata: "unstruck"; often associated with Nāda (Anāhata-Nāda) as the unstruck sound before creation said to be heard by Yogīs and musicians.

Anusvāra: "after-sound"; refers to the dot (Bindu) above the *M* in final position of a word or phoneme; a cerebral sound.

Apūrva: technical term in Mīmāṁsā philosophy for the unseen and not-yet-realized effect of a sacrifice.

Ardha-Candra: "half-moon" symbol for the reverberation of sacred sound known as Nāda-Brahman.

Ardha-mātra: "half-measure"; the semi-degree (sometimes half-moon) following the three degrees, or measures, of AUM and signifying Nāda-Brahman.

Artha: the meaning of a word or sentence.

Aśabda: "soundless"; refers to a state beyond sound mentioned in the Upaniṣads.

AUM (Om): the primal syllable or Bīja said to contain the entire Sanskrit alphabet in seed form; Praṇava.

Bhajan: devotional song in praise of a deity.

Bhakti: devotion, love.

Bīja: seed; one-syllable phoneme ending in *M*.

Bindu: dot above the half-moon in the symbol for Nāda-Brahman; primal seed or semen; represents Śiva or Viṣṇu at the end of Nāda (Nādānta).

Brahman: the Absolute described in the Upaniṣads.

Cakra: wheel; refers to the energy centers along the spine in Tantrism and Kuṇḍalinī-Yoga.

Candra-Bindu: symbol for Nāda-Brahman as the combination of the half-moon (Candra) with dot above (Bindu) placed over the *M̐* in final position of a phoneme; the source of the power of sacred sound that accumulates within persons who recite the Bījas.

Chandas: the Vedic science of prosody.

Darśana: the act of seeing the divine, such as the form of a deity in the temple; system of Indian philosophy.

Dharma: righteousness, religion, law, sacred duty, support.

Dhvani: any audible sound produced in the world.

Dīkṣā: initiation by a guru into a sect or teaching of Hinduism.

Guru: teacher or spiritual master.

Haṭha-Yoga: Yoga of physical exercises.

Indra: major god of the Vedic religion, sometimes known as the first Grammarian.

Īśvara: lord or master, referring to any principal deity.

Japa: the act of repeating mantras or divine names, counted normally on rosary beads or the joints of the fingers.

Jñāna: knowledge, divine wisdom.

Kālī: terrifying goddess, spouse of Śiva.

Kali Yuga: present age of quarrel and corruption.

Kāma-Bīja: KLĪṀ, the Bīja of the deity Kāmadeva which is also used to symbolize the god Krishna in Vaiṣṇavism.

Kīrtana: praise of a deity.

Krishna: Hindu god who plays the flute; speaker of the *Bhagavad-Gītā*.

Kuṇḍalinī: the female serpent coiled at the base of the spine in Tantrism.

Kuṇḍalinī-Yoga: practice of Yoga in which the serpent within the body is raised to the top of the skull.

Lakṣmī: goddess of fortune, spouse of Viṣṇu.

Liṅga: phallic form or symbol of Śiva.

Madhyamā: the second linguistic level of the Grammarians in which word and meaning (signifier and signified) are united in the mind.

Mantra: sacred word or phrase used in worship or prayer.

Mātra: measure, degree.

Mātṛkā: "little mothers"; refers to the Bījas as sources of female power in Tantrism.

Māyā: the illusory status of reality.

Mokṣa: liberation or release from rebirth (Saṁsāra).

Mukti: the state of being liberated from Saṁsāra.

Mūrti: form or image of a deity.

Nāda: sound.

Nāda-Brahman: sacred sound, including both the concept of Śabda-Brahman (linguistic Word) and non-linguistic, or non-verbal, sound as in music; female "sonic" power of a god in Hinduism.

Nāda-Yoga: Yoga theory and practice involving sound.

Nādānta: "at the end of Nāda"; refers to the Absolute which is accessible through sacred sound.

Nāḍīs: natural Yogic channels of energy within the human body.

Nārāyaṇa: a name of Viṣṇu.

Nāth Yoga: sect of Yoga founded by Gorakhnāth.

Nirvāṇa: the extinction of suffering, the release from rebirth in Buddhism.

Nyāya: system of Indian logic.

Pāñcarātra: important branch of early Vaiṣṇavism.

Parā: beyond, supreme.

Parā-Vāk: sacred sound in Kashmir Śaivism, similar to Nāda-Brahman.

Paśupati: lord of the animals; name of Śiva.

Paśyantī: the first linguistic level of the Grammarians, equivalent to Śabda-Brahman.

Prajāpati: lord of creatures; major god in Brāhmaṇa literature.

Prakṛti: nature or matter, depicted as female.

Prāṇa: life force; breath.

Praṇava: name for the syllable *Om* (AUM).

Pratibhā: intuitive flash within the mind; revelation.

Pūjā: Hindu worship.

Purāṇa: early Hindu literatures containing mythologies and detailing sectarian rites and practices.

Puruṣa: male, person, supreme spirit.

Ṛṣis: seers who revealed the Veda to humankind.

Śabda: any word or verbal sound with meaning.

Śabda-Brahman: primal or absolute Word in the Upaniṣads.

Śabdapūrva-Yoga: Yoga of the Word outlined by the Grammarians.

Sādhana: religious practice aimed at *mokṣa*.

Śaiva: follower of the god Śiva; related to Śiva.

Śākta: follower of the goddess; related to the goddess.

Śakti: female power; spouse of male god (Śiva).

Samādhi: deep absorption and concentration in Yoga.

Sāman: Vedic verses set to music.

Sāṁkhya: analytical system of Indian philosophy.

Saṁkīrtana: loud congregational chanting in praise of a deity.

Sampradāya: religious sect with a lineage of teachers.

Saṁsāra: the wheel of rebirth; the material world.

Saṁskāra: trace; sacrament.

Śikṣā: instruction; group of early phonetic texts.

Śiva: one of the great gods of Hinduism.

Soma: moon god; intoxicating drink used in Vedic rituals.

Spanda: primal vibration in Kashmir Śaivism.

Sphoṭa: the "flashbulb effect" of comprehending sentence-meaning in the Grammarian tradition.

Sphoṭavāda: refers to the Grammarian tradition of sentence-meaning comprehension by means of Sphoṭa.

Śrī-Vidyā: a particular Śākta tradition of goddess worship.

Śruti: "that which is heard"; the Vedas and Upaniṣads.

Stotra: hymn in praise of a deity.

Suṣumnā: main Nāḍī channel along the spine.

Sūtra: concise textbook expounding a teaching.

Svarga: heaven.

Tantra: loom; texts and traditions of esoteric goddess worship.

Tantrism: dimension of Hinduism involving female worship and extensive rituals.

Tattva: truth, principle.

Turīya: the fourth *mātra* or degree in the sequence of AUM; designates Brahman, highest reality in Vedānta.

Udgītha: loud chanting of the Veda; Ultimate Reality in the Upaniṣads.

Upaniṣads: fourth division of the Vedic literatures; wisdom texts.

Upāsana: worship.

Vāg-Yoga: early Yoga of the Word in the Grammarian tradition; similar to Śabdapūrva-Yoga.

Vaikharī: third linguistic level of the Grammarians, designating actual speech sounds and their separate meanings.

Vaikuṇṭha: Viṣṇu's heaven.

Vaiṣṇava: follower of the god Viṣṇu; related to Viṣṇu.

Vāk: early Vedic term for the Absolute Word and for the goddess of speech.

Varṇa: the individual letter in the Sanskrit language.

Varṇamālā: a garland of letters around the neck of the goddess.

Varṇavāda: the Mīmāṁsā tradition of sentence-meaning comprehension by means of the individual letters rather than the sentence as a whole.

Veda: knowledge; earliest revealed texts of the Hindus.

Vedānta: "end of the Veda"; system of Indian philosophy.

Vidhi: ritual; Vedic injunction.

Viṣṇu: one of the great gods of Hinduism.

Vyākaraṇa: science of grammar.

Vyūha: manifestation of Viṣṇu.

Yajña: Vedic fire sacrifice.

Yantra: diagram used in meditation; Tantric device.

Yoga: yoke; system of Indian philosophy and practice in which the mind is brought under control and "yoked" with Brahman.

Yogī: person who practices Yoga.

Yuga: cosmic time cycle.

BIBLIOGRAPHY

Abhyankar, K. V., and J. M. Shukla, eds. and trans., *Patañjali's Vyākaraṇa-Mahābhāṣya, Āhnikas 1–3*. Poona: Bhandarkar Oriental Research Institute, 1975.

Agnihotri, B. S. "The Implication of Om in Philsophy." *Journal of the Oriental Institute* 14 (1964–65): 70–74.

Allen, William Sidney. *Phonetics in Ancient India*. London: Oxford University Press, 1953.

Alper, Harvey P. "The Cosmos as Śiva's Language-Game: Mantra according to Kṣemarāja's Śivasūtravimarśinī." In *Understanding Mantras*, edited by Harvey P. Alper, 249–94. Albany: SUNY Press, 1989.

———, ed. *Understanding Mantras*. Albany: SUNY Press, 1989.

Anantha Chariar, P. B., ed. *Sāttvata-Saṁhitā*. Conjeevaram: Sudarsana Press, 1902.

Ananthakrishna Sastry, R. *Lalitā-Sahasranāman with Bhāskararāya's Commentary*. Adyar: Theosophical Publishing House, 1951.

Anantharangachar, N. S. *The Philosophy of Sādhana in Viśiṣṭādvaita*. Mysore: University of Mysore, 1967.

Andrare, Diogo Jose Pereira. *Historical Studies of the Rosary: In Hinduism, Buddhism, Mohammedanism, and Christianity*. Bastoia-Portuguese, India: Tipografia Rangel, 1937.

Arapura, J. G. *Hermeneutical Essays on Vedāntic Topics*. Delhi: Motilal Banarsidass, 1986.

———. "Some Perspectives on Indian Philosophy of Language." In *Revelation in Indian Thought*, edited by Harold Coward and K. Sivaraman, 15–43. Emeryville, Calif.: Dharma Publications, 1977.

Arunachalam, M. "The Prasāda Yoga in Śaiva Siddhānta." *Śaiva Siddhānta* 9 (Dec. 1974): 120–26.

———. *The Śaivāgamas*. Trichi: Gandhi Vidyalayam, 1983.

Arya, Pandit Usharbudh. *Nāda Yoga Meditation*. Phonotape. Minneapolis: Center for Higher Consciousness, n.d.

Avalon, Arthur (Sir John Woodroffe). *The Garland of Letters*. Madras: Ganesh, 1955.

———. *Hymns to the Goddess*. Madras: Ganesh, 1973.

———. *The Serpent Power*. 1919. Reprint. New York: Dover, 1974.

———. *Shakti and Shakta*. 1918. Reprint. New York: Dover, 1978.

———. *Tantra of the Great Liberation (Mahānirvāṇa-Tantra)*. 1913. Reprint. New York: Dover, 1972.

———. *Tantrarāja-Tantra and Kāmakalā-Vilāsa*. Madras: Ganesh, 1921.

Ayer, A. J. *Philosophy in the Twentieth Century*. New York: Vintage Books, 1982.

Babb, Lawrence A. *Redemptive Encounters: Three Modern Styles in the Hindu Tradition*. Berkeley and Los Angeles: University of California Press, 1986.

Bagchi, P. C. *Studies in the Tantras*, pt. 1. 1939. Reprint. Calcutta: University of Calcutta, 1975.

Banerjea, Akshaya Kumar. *Philosophy of Gorakhnāth with Goraksha-Vacana-Saṅgraha*. Gorakhpur: Gorakhnath Temple, 1962.

Banerji, Suresh Chandra. *A Brief History of Tantra Literature*. Calcutta: Naya Prakash, 1988.

———. *Tantra in Bengal: A Study in its Origin, Development and Influence*. Calcutta: Naya Prakash, 1978.

Bary, Wm. Theodore de., ed. *The Buddhist Tradition in India, China, and Japan*. New York: Vintage Books, 1972.

Barz, Richard. *The Bhakti Sect of Vallabhācārya*. Faridabad: Thomson Press, 1976.

Berendt, Joachim-Ernst. *Nāda Brahma: The World is Sound*. Rochester, Vt.: Destiny Books, 1987.

Bhaktisiddhānta Sarasvatī Goswami Mahārāj. *Shri Chaitanya's Teachings*. Madras: Sree Gaudiya Math, 1967.

Bhaktivedanta Swami, A. C., trans. *Śrīmad-Bhāgavatam*. New York and Los Angeles: Bhaktivedanta Book Trust, 1972–89.

Bhandarkar, R. G. *Vaiṣṇavism, Śaivism, and Minor Religious Systems*. Strasbourg: K. J. Trubner, 1913.

Bharadwaj, K. D. *The Philosophy of Rāmānuja*. New Delhi: Sri Shankar Lall Charitable Trust Society, 1958.

Bharati, Agehananda. *The Tantric Tradition*. New York: Doubleday/Anchor, 1970.

———. "Tantrism." In *Abingdon Dictionary of Living Religions*, edited by Keith Crim, 734–38. Nashville: Abingdon Press, 1981.

Bhat, G. K. "Vāk in Śatapatha Brāhmaṇa." *Journal of the Asiatic Society* (Bombay) 52, no. 3 (1977–78): 32–38.

Bhatt, N. R. Preface. V. Varadachari. *Descriptive Catalogue of Manuscripts*, v–xxi. Pondicherry: Institute Français D'Indologie, 1986.

Bhattacharya, B. *Śaivism and the Phallic World*. 2 vols. New Delhi: Oxford, 1975.

———. *The World of Tantra*. New Delhi: Munshiram Manoharlal, 1988.

Bhattacharya, Bishnupada. "Constitution of Words: Sphoṭa Theory and Its Opponents." *Our Heritage* 4, no. 2 (July–Dec. 1956): 217–26.

———. "Philosophical Data in Patañjali's Mahābhāṣya." *Our Heritage* 4, no. 1 (Jan.–June 1956): 51–65.

Bhattacharya, N. N. *History of the Śākta Religion*. New Delhi: Munshiram Manoharlal, 1974.

———. *History of the Tantric Religion*. New Delhi: Munshiram Manoharlal, 1982.

Bhattacharyya, Benoytosh, ed. *Śakti-saṅgama-Tantra*. 4 vols. (GOS 61,91, 104,166). Baroda: Oriental Institute, 1932, 1941, 1947, 1978.

Bheemacharya, T., and S. N. Shastri, eds. and trans. *Aṣṭaślokī of Śrī Parāśara*. Indore: Bharati Publications, 1971.

Biardeau, Madeleine. *Theorie de la Connaissance et Philosophie de la Parole dans le Brahmanisme—Classique*. Paris: Mouton, 1964.

Blavatsky, H. P. *The Voice of the Silence*. 1889. Reprint. Pasadena, Calif.: Theosophical University Press, 1976.

Bloom, Harold. *Kabbalah and Criticism*. New York: Seabury, 1975.

Board of Scholars, trans. *Liṅga-Purāṇa*. Delhi: Motilal Banarsidass, 1973.

———, trans. *Mahīdhara's Mantra-Mahodadhi*. Delhi: Satguru Publications, 1984.

Bolle, Kees W. *The Persistence of Religion*. Leiden: E. J. Brill, 1965.

———. *Secrecy in Religions*. Leiden: E. J. Brill, 1987.

Bose, Roma, trans. *Vedānta-Pārijāta-Saurabha of Nimbārka and Vedānta-Kaustubha of Śrīnivāsa*. 3 vols. Calcutta: Asiatic Society, 1940, 1941, 1943.

Bowman, Frank Paul. "Occultism and the Language of Poetry." In *The Occult in Language and Literature*, edited by Hermine Riffaterre, 51–63. New York: New York Literary Forum, 1980.

Bowman, Raymond A. "Yahweh the Speaker." *Journal of Near Eastern Studies*, 3, no. 1 (Jan. 1944): 1–8.

Briggs, George Weston. *Gorakhnāth and the Kānphaṭa Yogīs*. Calcutta: YMCA Publishing House, 1938.

Brooks, Douglas R., *The Secret of the Three Cities: An Introduction to Hindu Śākta Tantrism*. Chicago: University of Chicago Press, 1990.

———. "The Śrī-Vidyā School of Śākta Tantrism: A Study of the Texts and Contexts of the Living Traditions in South India." Ph.D. diss., Harvard University, 1987.

Brough, John. "Auḍumbarāyaṇa's Theory of Language." *Bulletin of the School of Oriental and African Studies* 14 (1952): 73–77.

———. "Some Indian Theories of Meaning" (1953). In *A Reader on the Sanskrit Grammarians*, edited by Frits Staal, 414–23. Cambridge: MIT Press, 1972.

———. "Theories of General Linguistics in the Sanskrit Grammarians" (1951). In Staal, *Reader on the Sanskrit Grammarians*, 402–14.

Brown, C. Mackenzie. "Purāṇa as Scripture: From Sound to Image of the Holy Word in the Hindu Tradition." *History of Religions* 26, no. 1 (Aug. 1986): 68–86.

Brown, W. Norman. "The Creative Role of the Goddess Vāc in the Rig Veda." In *Pratidānam: Indian, Iranian, and Indo-European Studies Presented to F. B. J. Kuiper*, edited by J. C. Heesterman, G. H. Schokker, and V. I. Subramoniam, 393–97. The Hague and Paris: Mouton, 1968.

———. "Theories of Creation in the Rig Veda." *Journal of the American Oriental Society* 85 (1965): 23–24.

Brunner, Hélène. "Un Tantra du Nord: Le Netra Tantra." *Bulletin de l'école français d'Extrême-Orient* 61 (1974): 125–97.

Carman, John B. *The Theology of Rāmānuja*. New Haven, Conn.: Yale University Press, 1974.

Cassirer, Ernst. *An Essay on Man: An Introduction to a Philosophy of Human Culture*. New Haven, Conn.: Yale University Press, 1944.

———. *Language and Myth*. New York: Harper, 1946.

Caturvedi, Sitaram. *Mahāprabhu Śrīmad-Vallabhācārya aur Puṣṭi-Mārga*. Varanasi: Hindi Sahitya Kutira, 1967.

Cavendish, Richard. *The Black Arts*. London: Routledge and Kegan Paul, 1967.

Chakravarti, Chintaharan. *Tantras: Studies On Their Religion and Literature*. Calcutta: Punthi Pustak, 1963.

Chakravarti, Hemendranath. *Tantra-Sāra of Abhinavagupta*. Varanasi: Varanaseya Sanskrit Samsthan, 1986.

Chakravarti, Prabhatchandra. *The Linguistic Speculations of the Hindus*. Calcutta: Calcutta University, 1933.

———. *The Philosophy of Sanskrit Grammar*. Calcutta: Calcutta University, 1930.

Chakravarti, Ramakanta. *Vaiṣṇavism in Bengal*. Calcutta: Sanskrit Pustak Bhandar, 1985.

Chakravarti, Tarapada. *Indian Aesthetics and Science of Language*. Calcutta: Sanskrit Pustak Bhandar, 1971.

Chatterjee, Ksitish Chandra, ed. and trans. *Patañjali's Mahābhāṣya, Paspaśāhnika*. Calcutta: A. Mukherjee, 1972.

Chatterji, J. C. *Kashmir Shaivism*. 1914. Reprint. Albany: SUNY Press, 1986. Preface by William Barnard, vii–xv.

Choudhury, Basanti. "Love Sentiment and Its Spiritual Implications in Gauḍīya Vaiṣṇavism." In *Bengal Vaiṣṇavism, Orientalism, Society and the Arts*, edited by Joseph T. O'Connell. East Lansing, Mich.: Asian Studies Center, Michigan State University, 1985.

Cimmanalāla, Harishankarajī. *Puṣṭimārgopadeshikā*, trans. from Sanskrit into Hindī by Shrimadhava Sharma. Varanasi: Shrimadhava Sharma, 1941.

Coburn, Thomas B. "Scripture in India: Towards a Typology of the Word in Hindu Life." *Journal of the American Academy of Religion* 52, no. 3 (Sept. 1984): 435–59.

Conze, Edward, trans. *Buddhist Wisdom Books containing the Diamond Sūtra and the Heart Sūtra*. New York: Harper Torchbooks, 1972.

Coward, Harold. *Bhartṛhari*. Boston: G. K. Hall, 1976.

———. "Bhartṛhari vs. Śaṅkara on the Overcoming of Error." In *Buddhist Thought and Asian Civilization*, edited by L. S. Kawamura. Emeryville, Calif.: Dharma Publishing, 1977.

———. *Derrida and Indian Philosophy*. Albany, New York: SUNY Press, 1990.

———. "The Meaning and Power of Mantras in Bhartṛhari's Vākyapadīya." *Studies in Religion* 11, no. 4 (1982): 365–75.

———. *Sacred Word and Sacred Text: Scripture in World Religions*. Maryknoll, New York: Orbis Books, 1988.

———. *The Sphoṭa Theory of Language*. Delhi: Motilal Banarsidass, 1986.

———. "The Yoga of the Word (Śabdapūrvayoga)." *Brahmavidyā* 49 (1985): 1–13.

———, ed. *Language in Indian Philosophy and Religion*. Waterloo: Wilfrid Laurier University Press, 1978.

———, ed. *Studies in Indian Thought*. Delhi: Motilal Banarsidass, 1983.

Coward, Harold, and David Goa. *Mantra: Hearing the Divine in India*. Chambersburg, Pa.: Anima Books, 1991.

Coward, Harold, and K. Kunjunni Raja. *The Philosophy of the Grammarians*. Encyclopedia of Indian Philosophies, vol. 5. Princeton, N.J.: Princeton University Press, 1990.

Coward, Harold, and K. Sivaraman, eds. *Revelation in Indian Thought*. Emeryville, Calif.: Dharma Publications, 1977.

Curtis, J. W. V. "Space Concepts and Worship Environment in Śaiva Siddhānta." In *Experiencing Śiva: Encounters with a Hindu Diety*, edited by Fred W. Clothey and J. Bruce Long. Columbia, Mo.: South Asia Books, 1983.

Das, Sudhendu Kumar. *Śakti or Divine Power*. Calcutta: University of Calcutta Press, 1934.

Das, Upendra Kumar, ed. *Yoginī-Hṛdayam*. Calcutta: Navabharat Publishers, 1987.

Dasgupta, Shashibhusan. *Aspects of Indian Religious Thought*. Calcutta: Firma KLM, 1957.

———. *Obscure Religious Cults*. Calcutta: Firma KLM, 1946.

———. "The Role of Mantra in Indian Religion." *Aspects of Indian Religious Thought*, 22–41. Calcutta: Firma KLM, 1957.

Dasgupta, Surendranath. "General Introduction to Tantra Philosophy." *Philosophical Essays*, 151–78. Calcutta: University of Calcutta, 1941.

———. *Hindu Mysticism*. Delhi: Motilal Banarsidass, 1927.

———. *A History of Indian Philosophy*. Cambridge: Cambridge University Press, 5 vols. 1952–55.

———. *The Study of Patañjali*. Calcutta: University of Calcutta, 1920.

———. *Yoga as Philosophy and Religion*. London: Kegan Paul, 1924.

———. *Yoga Philosophy in Relation to Other Systems of Indian Thought*. Calcutta: University of Calcutta, 1930.

———. "Yoga Psychology." *Philosophical Essays,* 179–97. Calcutta: University of Calcutta, 1941.

Davis, Lawrence Ward. "Studies in Bhartṛhari's Vākyapadīya." Ph.D. diss., University of Massachusetts, 1978.

Davis, Richard. "Ritual in an Oscillating Universe." Ph.D. diss., University of Chicago, 1986.

De, Sushil Kumar. *Early History of the Vaiṣṇava Faith and Movement in Bengal.* Calcutta: General Printers and Publishers, 1942.

Denny, Frederick M. "Islam: Qur'an and Hadith." In *The Holy Book in Comparative Perspective,* edited by Frederick M. Denny and Rodney L. Taylor, 84–108. Columbia, S.C.: University of South Carolina Press, 1985.

Deshpande, Madhav M. "On the Ṛk-Pratiśākhya 13.5–6." *Indian Linguistics* 37, no. 3 (1976): 171–81.

Deussen, Paul. *The Philosophy of the Upanishads.* 1906. Reprint. New York: Dover, 1966.

Dhavamony, Mariasusai. *Love of God according to Śaiva Siddhānta.* Oxford: Clarendon Press, 1971.

———. "Śaiva Siddhānta." In *The Encyclopedia of Religion* (Mircea Eliade, editor-in-chief), 13:11–12. New York: Macmillan, 1987.

Dimock, Edward C. *The Place of the Hidden Moon: Erotic Mysticism in the Vaiṣṇava-Sahajīyā Cult of Bengal.* Chicago:.University of Chicago Press, 1966.

Dunuwila, Rohan A. *Śaiva Siddhānta Theology.* Delhi: Motilal Banarsidass, 1985.

Dyczkowski, Mark S. G. *The Canon of the Śaivāgama and the Kubjikā Tantras of the Western Kaula Tradition.* Albany: SUNY Press, 1988.

———. *The Doctrine of Vibration: An Analysis of the Doctrine and Practices of Kashmir Shaivism.* Albany: SUNY Press, 1987.

Earhart, H. Byron. *Japanese Religion: Unity and Diversity.* Belmont, Calif.: Dickenson, 1969.

Ebeling, Gerhard. *Word and Faith.* Philadelphia: Fortress Press, 1963.

Eck, Diana L. *Darśan: Seeing the Divine Image in India.* Chambersburg, Pa.: Anima Books, 1981.

Edgerton, Franklin. "Some Linguistic Notes on the Mīmā;admsā System." *Language* 4 (1928): 171–77.

Edie, James M. *Speaking and Meaning: The Phenomenology of Language.* Bloomington: Indiana University, 1976.

Eggeling, Julius. *The Śatapatha-Brāhmaṇa according to the Text of the Madhyandina School.* 5 vols. Delhi: Motilal Banarsidass, 1963.

Eliade, Mircea. *Occultism, Witchcraft, and Cultural Fashions.* Chicago: University of Chicago, 1976.

———. *Patañjali and Yoga.* New York: Schocken Books, 1975.

———. *Yoga: Immortality and Freedom.* New York: Bollingen Foundation, 1958.

Elkman, Stuart M. *Jīva Gosvamin's Tattva Sandarbha: A Study on the Philosophical and Sectarian Development of the Gauḍīya Vaiṣṇava Movement.* Delhi: Motilal Banarsidass, 1986.

Ellul, Jacques. *The Humiliation of the Word.* Grand Rapids, Mich.: William B. Eerdmans, 1985.

Entralgo, Pedro Lain. *The Therapy of the Word in Classical Antiquity.* New Haven, Conn.: Yale University Press, 1970.

Evans-Wentz, W. Y., ed. *The Tibetan Book of the Dead.* London: Oxford University Press, 1960.

Ewing, Arthur H. "The Śāradā-tilaka Tantra." *Journal of the American Oriental Society* 23 (1902): 65–76.

Fabian, Johannes. *Time and the Other: How Anthropology Makes Its Object.* New York: Columbia University Press, 1983.

Feuerstein, Georg. "The Concept of God (Īśvara) in Classical Yoga." *Journal of Indian Philosophy* 15 (1987): 385–97.

———. "Patañjali." In *The Encyclopedia of Religion* (Mircea Eliade, editor-in-chief), 11: 206–7. New York: Macmillan, 1987.

———. *The Philosophy of Classical Yoga.* New York: St. Martin's Press, 1980.

———. "Some Notes on the Final Stages of Yoga according to Patañjali." *Bharatiya Vidya* 28 (1968): 1–12.

———. *Textbook of Yoga.* London: Ryder, 1975.

Filliozat, Pierre-Sylvain. "Les Nāda-Kārikā de Rāmakaṇṭha." *Bulletin de l'école français d'Extrême-Orient* 73 (1984): 223–55.

———. "On the Semantic Use of the Word *Sphoṭa*." *Amṛtadhara: Prof. R. N. Dandekar Felicitation Volume,* 1331–40. Poona: Ajanta, 1984.

Foucault, Michel. *The Order of Things: An Archaeology of the Human Sciences.* 1970. Reprint. New York: Vintage Books, 1973.

Fowden, Garth. *The Egyptian Hermes: A Historical Approach to the Late Pagan Mind.* Cambridge: Cambridge University Press, 1986.

Gachter, Othmar. *Hermeneutics and Language in Pūrva Mīmāṃsā.* Delhi: Motilal Banarsidass, 1983.

Gajendragadkar, A. B. "Speculation on Sound in Sanskrit Literature." *Aryan Path* 44, no. 10 (Dec. 1973): 425–30.

Gerson-Kiwi, Edith. "Melodic Patterns in Asiatic Rituals: The Quest for Sound Alienation." *Israel Studies in Musicology,* vol. 2. Jerusalem: Israel Music Society, 1978.

———. "Religious Chant: A Pan-Asiatic Conception of Music." *Journal of the International Folk Music Council* 8 (Jan. 1961): 64–67.

Ghosh, Atul Behari. "The Spirit and Culture of the Tantras." In *The Cultural Heritage of India,* edited by H. Bhattacharya, 4:241–51. Calcutta: Ramakrishna Institute of Culture, 1957–62.

Gilson, Etienne. *Linguistics and Philosophy.* 1969. Reprint. Notre Dame, Ind.: Notre Dame University, 1988.

Gnoli, Raniero. "The Śivadṛṣṭi of Somānanda," canto 1. *East and West* 8 (1957): 16–22.
Gonda, Jan. *Aspects of Early Viṣṇuism*. Utrecht: NV. A. Oosthoek, 1954.
———. "The Concept of a Personal God in Ancient Indian Religious Thought." *Selected Studies*, 4:1-26. Leiden: E. J. Brill, 1975.
———. "The Indian Mantra." *Selected Studies*, 4:248–301. Leiden: E. J. Brill, 1975.
———. *Medieval Religious Literature*. Weisbaden: Otto Harrassowitz, 1975.
———. *Notes on the Name and the Names of God in Ancient India*. Amsterdam: N. Holland, 1970.
———. *Vedic Literature*. Wiesbaden: Otto Harrassowitz, 1975.
———. *Vision of the Vedic Poets*. The Hague: Mouton, 1963.
———. *Viṣṇuism and Śivaism: A Comparison*. University of London: Athlone Press, 1970.
Goodman, Felicitas D. *Glossolalia: Speaking in Tongues*. Chicago: University of Chicago, 1972.
Goudriaan, Teun, and Sanjukta Gupta. *Hindu Tantric and Śākta Literature*. Weisbaden: Otto Harrassowitz, 1981.
Govinda, Lama Anagarika. *Creative Meditation and Multi-Dimensional Consciousness*. Wheaton, Ill.: Quest Books, 1976.
Graham, William A. *Beyond the Written Word: Oral Aspects of Scripture in the History of Religion*. Cambridge: Cambridge University Press, 1987.
Gupta, Sanjukta. "Mantra." In *The Encyclopedia of Religion*, edited by Mircea Eliade, 9:177. New York: Macmillan, 1987.
———. "The Pāñcarātra Attitude to Mantra." In *Understanding Mantras*, edited by Harvey P. Alper, 224–48. Albany: SUNY Press, 1989.
———, trans. *Lakṣmī Tantra*. Leiden: E. J. Brill, 1972.
Gupta, Sanjukta, Dirk Hoens, and Teun Goudriaan. *Hindu Tantrism*. Leiden: E. J. Brill, 1979.
Haberman, David L. *Acting as a Way of Salvation: A Study of Rāgānuga Bhakti Sādhana*. New York: Oxford University Press, 1988.
Handelman, Susan A. *The Slayers of Moses: The Emergence of Rabbinic Interpretation in Modern Literary Theory*. Albany: SUNY Press, 1982.
Harland, Richard. *Superstructuralism*. London: Methuen, 1987.
Havelock, Eric. *Origins of Western Literacy*. Toronto: Ontario Institute for Studies in Education, 1976.
Heimann, Betty. *Facets of Indian Thought*. London: Allen and Unwin, 1964.
———. "Sphoṭa and Artha." In *A Volume of Studies in Indology Presented to Prof. P. V. Kane*, edited by S. M. Katre and P. K. Gode, 221–27. Poona: Oriental Book Agency, 1941.
Herman, A. L. "Sphoṭa." *Journal of the Ganganath Jha Research Institute* 19, nos. 1–4 (Nov. 1962–Aug. 1963): 1–21.
Hicks, Harry H., and Robert N. Anderson. "Analysis of an Indo-European

Vedic Aryan Head—4th Millennium B.C." *Journal of Indo-European Studies* 18 (1990): 425–46.

Hiltebeitel, Alf. "Mahābhārata." In *The Encyclopedia of Religion* (Mircea Eliade, editor-in-chief), 9:118–19. New York: Macmillan, 1987.

Hiriyanna, Mysore. *Outlines of Indian Philosophy.* London: Allen and Unwin, 1932.

Hopkins, E. Washburn. "Yoga-technique in the Great Epic." *Journal of the American Oriental Society* 22, no. 2 (1901): 333–79.

Hopkins, Thomas J. *The Hindu Religious Tradition.* Encino, Calif.: Dickinson, 1971.

Hopper, Stanley Romaine, and David L. Miller, eds. *Interpretation: The Poetry of Meaning.* New York: Harcourt Brace and World, 1967.

Hume, Robert E. *The Thirteen Principal Upanishads.* London: Oxford University Press, 1958.

Husserl, Edmund. *Formal and Transcendental Logic.* 1929. Reprint. The Hague: Mouton, 1969.

Jackson, Robert, and Dermot Killingley. *Approaches to Hinduism.* London: John Murray, 1988.

Jaiswal, Suvira. *The Origin and Development of Vaiṣṇavism.* New Delhi: Munshiram Manoharlal, 1967.

James, William. *The Varieties of Religious Experience.* New York: Penguin, 1982.

Janaki, S. S. "The Role of Sanskrit in the Development of Indian Music." *Journal of the Music Academy of Madras* 56 (1985): 66–98.

Jash, Pranabananda. *History of Śaivism.* Calcutta: Roy and Chaudhury, 1974.

Jha, Ganganath. *Pūrva-Mīmāṁsā in Its Sources.* Varanasi: Benares Hindu University, 1942.

———, trans. *The Pūrva-Mīmāṁsā Sutras of Jaimini.* 1916. Reprint. New York: AMS Press, 1974.

———, trans. *Śābara Bhāṣya.* Baroda: Oriental Institute (Gaekwad Oriental Series), 1933, 1934, 1936.

Joshi, K. S. "On the Meaning of Yoga." *Philosophy East and West* 15, no. 1 (Jan. 1965): 53–64.

Joshi, S. D. "Bhartṛhari's Concept of Pratibhā: A Theory on the Nature of Language Acquisition." In *Some Aspects of Indo-Iranian Literary and Cultural Traditions,* edited by T. G. Mainkar, 71–76. Delhi: Ajanta, 1977.

Joshi, S. D. and J. A. F. Roodbergen, eds. *Patañjali's Vyākaraṇa-Mahābhāṣya.* Poona: Samarthahnika, 1968.

Josyer, G. R., ed. *Shesha-Saṁhitā.* Mysore: Coronation Press, 1981.

Kak, Subhash C. "A Frequency Analysis of the Indus Script." *Cryptologia* 12 (1988): 129–43.

———. "On the Chronology of Ancient India." *Indian Journal of History of Science* 22, no. 3 (1987): 232–33.

Kaviraj, Gopinath. *Aspects of Indian Thought*. Burdwan: University of Burdwan, 1984.

———. "Nāda, Bindu and Kalā." *Journal of the Ganganath Jha Research Institute* 3 (1945–46): 47–62.

———. "Nāda Tattva." In *Tantrik Vāṅmayamen Śākta-dṛṣṭi* (Hindī), 292–310. Patna: Bihar-Rāṣṭrabhāṣā Parishad, 1963.

Kaw, R. K. *The Doctrine of Recognition*. Hoshiarpur: Vishveshvaranand Institute, 1967.

Kayser, Hans. *Akroasis: The Theory of World Harmonics*. Boston: Plowshare Press, 1970.

Keith, A. B. *The Veda of the Black Yajus School Entitled Taittirīya Saṁhitā*. 2 vols. 1914. Reprint. Delhi: Motilal Banarsidass, 1967.

Khanna, Madhu. "The Concept and Liturgy of the Śrī-Cakra Based on Śivānanda's Trilogy." Ph.D. diss., Oxford University. 1986.

———. *Yantra: The Tantric Symbol of Cosmis Unity*. London: Thames and Hudson, 1979.

Killingley, Dermot. "Om: The Sacred Syllable in the Veda." In *A Net Cast Wide: Investigations into Indian Thought in Memory of David Friedman*, edited by Julius J. Lipner, Newcastle-upon-Tyne: Grevatt and Grevatt, 1986.

King, Francis, *Tantra for Westerners: A Practical Guide to the Way of Action*. New York: Destiny Books, 1986.

Kinsley, David R. *Hindu Goddesses: Visions of the Divine Feminine in The Hindu Religious Tradition*. Berkeley: University of California Press, 1986.

———. *The Sword and the Flute*. Berkeley: University of California Press, 1975.

Klostermaier, Klaus. "The Creative Function of the Word." In *Language in Indian Philosophy and Religion*, edited by Harold Coward, 5–18. Waterloo: Wilfrid Laurier University Press, 1978.

———. "Man Carries the Power of All Things in His Mouth: Jacob Boehme's Ideas on Word and Language." In *Revelation in Indian Thought*, edited by Harold Coward and K. Sivaraman, 87–98. Emeryville, Calif.: Dharma Publications, 1977.

———. *Mythologies and Philosophies of Salvation in the Theistic Traditions of India*. Ontario: Canadian Corporation for Studies in Religion, 1984.

———. *A Survey of Hinduism*. Albany: SUNY Press, 1989.

Krishnamacharya, Embar, ed. *Jayākhya-Saṁhitā* (GOS 54). Baroda: Oriental Institute, 1931. Foreword by Benoytosh Bhattacharyya.

Krishnaswami Aiyangar, S., ed. and trans., *Parama-Saṁhitā* (GOS 86). Baroda: Oriental Institute, 1940.

Kristeva, Julia. *Desire in Language*. Oxford: Basil Blackwell, 1980.

Kumar, Pramod. *Mokṣa: The Ultimate Goal of Indian Philosophy*. Ghaziabad: Indo-Vision, 1984.

Kumar, Pushpendra. *Śakti Cult in Ancient India*. Varanasi: Bhartiya, 1974.

Kumar, Shiv. *Sāṁkhya-Yoga Epistemology.* Delhi: Eastern Book Publishers, 1984.

Kumarappa, Bharatan. *The Hindu Conception of the Deity as Culminating in Rāmānuja.* London: Luzac, 1934.

Kunhan Raja, C. *The Vedas: A Cultural Study.* Waltair: Andhra University, 1957.

Kunjunni Raja, K. *Indian Theories of Meaning.* Madras: Adyar, 1963.

Labib al-Said. *The Recited Koran.* Princeton, N.J.: Darwin Press, 1975.

Lakhera, M. P. "Indra and Vāk." *Journal of the Ganganath Jha Kendriya Sanskrta Vidyapeeth* 36 (1980): 13–23.

Lalye, P. G. "The *Devī-Bhāgavata* and *Śāradā-Tilaka.*" *Studies in Devī-Bhāgavata.* Bombay: Popular Prakashan, 1973.

Lancaster, Lewis. "Buddhist Literature: Its Canons, Scribes, and Editors." In *The Critical Study of Sacred Texts,* edited by Wendy Doniger O'Flaherty, 215–29. Berkeley: Berkeley Religious Studies Series, 1979.

Lannoy, Richard. *The Speaking Tree: A Study of Indian Culture and Society.* London: Oxford University Press, 1971.

Lester, Robert C. *Rāmānuja on the Yoga.* Madras: Adyar, 1976.

Lipner, Julius. *The Face of Truth: A Study of Meaning and Metaphysics in the Vedāntic Theology of Rāmānuja.* Albany: SUNY Press, 1986.

Lorenzen, David N. "Śaivism." In *The Encyclopedia of Religion* (Mircea Eliade, editor-in-chief), 13:6–11. New York: Macmillan, 1987.

McDermott, A. S. C. "Towards a Pragmatics of Mantra Recitation." *Journal of Indian Philosophy* 3 (1975): 283–98.

MacDonell, A. A. *The Vedic Mythology.* Varanasi: Indological Book House, 1963.

Magee, Michael, trans. *Kaulajñāna-Nirṇaya.* Varanasi: Prachya Prakashan, 1986.

Mangalwadi, Vishal. *The World of Gurus.* New Delhi: Vikas, 1977.

Mates, Benson. *Stoic Logic.* Berkeley: University of California Press, 1961.

Matus, Thomas. *Yoga and the Jesus Prayer Tradition.* Ramsey, N.J.: Paulist Press, 1984.

Mehta, N. D. "Evolution of the Concept of Praṇava or Om in Sanskrit Literature, and Its Theological and Philosophical Implications." *Sanskrit Research* 1, nos. 3–4 (1916): 213–40.

Michell, George. *The Hindu Temple: An Introduction to Its Meaning and Forms.* Chicago: University of Chicago Press, 1977.

Miller, Patricia Cox. "In Praise of Nonsense." In *Classical Mediterranean Spirituality,* edited by A. H. Armstrong, 481–505. New York: Crossroad, 1986.

Mishra, Rammurti S., M. D. *The Textbook of Yoga Psychology.* New York: Julian Press, 1987.

Mishra, Umesha. "Physical Theory of Sound and Its Origin in Indian Thought." *Allahabad University Studies* 2 (1926): 239–90.

Mishra, Vidhata. *A Critical Study of Sanskrit Phonetics*. Varanasi: Chowkhamba Sanskrit Series Office, 1972.

Mitra, Rajendra Lal, ed. *Gopath Brāhmaṇa*. Delhi: Indological Book House, 1972.

Mookerjee, Ajit. *Kālī: The Feminine Force*. New York: Destiny Books, 1988.

———. *Kuṇḍalinī: The Arousal of the Inner Energy*. London: Thames and Hudson, 1982.

Mookerjee, Ajit, and Madhu Khanna. *The Tantric Way: Art, Science, Ritual*. London: Thames and Hudson, 1977.

Mukharji, Justice P. B. "The Metaphysics of Sound." In *Japa Sūtram: The Science of Creative Sound*, edtied by Swami P. Sarasvati, 1-19. Madras: Ganesh, 1971.

Mukhopadhyaya, G. "Reality as Viewed in the Trika System of Philosophy." *Annals of the Bhandarkar Oriental Research Institute* 48–49 (1968): 231–40.

Mukhopadhyaya, Govind Gopal. "The Secret of Japa." In *Japa Sūtram: The Science of Creative Sound*, edited by Swami P. Sarasvati, 273–89. Madras: Ganesh, 1971.

———. "Tantras in Bengal." In *Proceedings of the 1st International Sanskrit Conference*, edited by V. Raghavan, 1 (pt. 1): 80–89. New Delhi: Ministry of Education and Social Welfare, 1975.

Muller-Ortega, Paul E. *The Triadic Heart of Śiva: Kaula Tantricism of Abhinavagupta in the Non-dual Shaivism of Kashmir*. Albany: SUNY Press, 1989.

Murphy, Paul E. *Triadic Mysticism: The Mystical Theology of the Saivism of Kashmir*. Delhi: Motilal Banarsidass, 1986.

Murti, T. R. V. "The Philosophy of Language in the Indian Context." In *Studies in Indian Thought*, edited by Harold Coward, 357–76. Delhi: Motilal Banarsidass, 1983.

———. "Some Comments on the Philosophy of Language in the Indian Context." *Journal of Indian Philosophy* 2 (1974): 321–31.

Musalagaonkar, Vimala. "Music and Sound in Yoga." In *Psychology of Music: Selected Paters*, edited by R. C. Mehta, 44–65. Bombay and Baroda: Indian Musicological Society, 1980.

Nādabrahmānanda, Swami. "The Science of Thaan." In *Tantra Yoga, Nāda Yoga and Kriyā Yoga*, edited by Swami Śivānanda, 142–50. Rsikesh: Yoga Vedanta Forest University, 1955.

Nagaraja Rao, P. *The Epistemology of Dvaita Vedānta*. Madras: Adyar, 1976.

Naidu, S. Shankar Raju. "Supreme Sound: The Ultimate Reality." *Indian Philosophical Annual* 10 (1974–75): 59–72.

Narain, K. *An Outline of Madhva Philosophy*. Allahabad: Udayana Publications, 1962.

Narayana Murti, M. S. "Philosophy of Sanskrit Grammar." *Sri Venkatesvara University Oriental Journal* 16 (1973): 37–54.

Neuman, Daniel M. *The Life of Music in North India.* Detroit: Wayne State University Press, 1980.

Nijenhuis, Emmie Te. *Musicological Literature.* Wiesbaden: Otto Harrassowitz, 1977.

Nikhilānanda, Swami, trans. *The Māṇḍūkypaniṣad with Gauḍapāda's Kārikā and Śaṅkara's Commentary.* Mysore: Śrī Rāmakrishna Ashrama, 1955.

Oberhammer, Gerhard. "The Use of Mantra in Yogic Meditation: The Testimony of the Pāśupata." In *Understanding Mantras,* edited by Harvey P. Alper, 204–23. Albany: SUNY Press, 1989.

O'Connell, Joseph T. "Social Implications of the Gauḍīya Vaiṣṇava Movement." Ph.D. diss., Harvard University 1970.

Oṁkārnāth, Śrī Sītārāmdās. *Śrī Śrī Nāda-Līlāmṛta* (Bengali). Dumurdaha, Hugali: Sri Vrajanath Niketan, 1956.

Ong, Walter J. *The Presence of the Word: Some Prolegomena for Cultural and Religious History.* New Haven, Conn.: Yale University Press, 1967.

Otto, Rudolf. *The Idea of the Holy.* 1923. Reprint. New York: Oxford University Press, 1958.

Padoux, André. "Contributions à l'étude du Mantra Śāstra." *Bulletin de l'école français d'Extrême-Orient* 65 (1978): 65–85.

———. "Mantras—What Are They?" In *Understanding Mantras,* edited by Harvey P. Alper, 295–318. Albany: SUNY Press, 1989.

———. *Recherches sur la symbolique et l'énergie de la parole dans certains textes tantriques.* Paris: E. de Boccard, 1963.

———. "A Survey of Tantric Hinduism for the Historian of Religions." Review. *History of Religions* 20, no. 4 (May 1981): 345–60.

———. "Tantrism (An Overview, Hindu Tantrism)." *The Encyclopedia of Religion* (Mircea Eliade, editor-in-chief), 14:272–80. New York: Macmillan, 1987.

———. *Vāc: The Concept of the Word in Selected Hindu Tantras.* Albany: SUNY Press, 1990.

Pandey, K. C. *Abhinavagupta: An Historical and Philosophical Study.* Varanasi: Chowkhamba Sanskrit Series Office, 1963.

———. *Indian Aesthetics.* 2 vols. Varanasi: Chowkhamba Sanskrit Series Office, 1959.

———. *An Outline of History of Śaiva Philosophy.* 1954. Reprint. Delhi: Motilal Banarsidass, 1986.

Pandeya, Kalika Charan. "The Theory of Śabda Brahma and Sphoṭa." *Journal of the Ganganath Jha Research Institute* 17, nos. 3–4 (May–Aug. 1961): 235–55.

Pandeya, R. C. *The Problem of Meaning in Indian Philosophy.* Delhi: Motilal Banarsidass, 1963.

Parthasarathi, T. S. "Worship of Nāda Brahman." *Tattvāloka* 10, no. 3 (Aug.–Sept. 1987): 11–14.

Patni, B. *Śiva Purāṇa: A Poetic Analysis.* Delhi: Ajanta Publications, 1980.

Pepin, Jean. "Logos." In *The Encyclopedia of Religion* (Mircea Eliade, editor-in-chief), 9:9-15. New York: Macmillan, 1987.

Potter, Karl, ed. *Advaita Vedānta up to Śaṁkara and His Pupils*. Princeton, N.J.: Princeton University Press, 1981.

Prasada, Rama, trans. *Patañjali's Yoga Sūtras*. Allahabad: Panini Office, 1912.

Radhakrishnan, S., trans. *The Principal Upanishads*. London: Allen and Unwin, 1953.

Radhakrishnan, Sarvepalli, and Charles A. Moore, eds. *A Sourcebook in Indian Philosophy*. Princeton, N.J.: Princeton University Press, 1967.

Raghavan, V. "Sāmaveda and Music." *Journal of the Music Academy of Madras* 33 (1962): 127-33.

Raghavan Pillai, K., trans. *The Vākyapadīya*, cantos 1 and 2. Delhi: Motilal Banarsidass, 1971.

Raghunathan, N., trans. *Śrīmad-Bhāgavatam*. 2 vols. Madras: Vighnesvara, 1976.

Rai, Ram Kumar, trans. *Śiva-Svarodaya*. Varanasi: Prachya Prakashan, 1987.

Rai, Ram Kumar, ed. and trans. *Dictionaries of Tantra Śāstra*. Varanasi: Prachya Prakashan, 1984.

Rajneesh, Bhagwan Shree. *Meditation: The Art of Ecstasy*. New York: Harper Colophon Books, 1976.

Ramachandra Rao, S. K. *Śrī-Cakra: Its Yantra, Mantra and Tantra*. Bangalore: Kalpatharu Research Academy, 1982.

———. *The Tantra of Śrī-Cakra (Bhāvanopanishat)*. Bangalore: Sharada Prakashana, 1983.

———, trans. *Śrī-Sūkta: Text and Translation*. Bangalore: Kalpatharu Research Academy, 1985.

Raschke, Carl A. "Religious Pluralism and Truth: From Theology to a Hermeneutical Dialogy." *Journal of the American Academy of Religion* 50 (1982): 35-48.

———. *Theological Thinking: An In-quiry*. Atlanta: Scholars Press, 1988.

Rastogi, Navjivan. "Abhinavagupta's Notion of Tantra in the Tantrāloka." *Indian Theosophist* 82, nos. 10-11 (Oct.-Nov. 1985): 110-20.

———. *Introduction to the Tantrāloka: A Study in Structure*. Delhi: Motilal Banarsidass, 1987.

———. *The Krama Tantricism of Kashmir: History and General Sources*. Delhi: Motilal Banarsidass, 1979.

Rawson, Philip. *The Art of Tantra*. London: Thames and Hudson, 1973.

Renou, Louis. *Religions of Ancient India*. London: Athlone Press, 1953.

Robinson, James M., ed. *The New Hermeneutic*. New York: Harper and Row, 1964.

Robinson, Richard H., and Willard L. Johnson. *The Buddhist Religion: A Historical Introduction*. Encino, Calif.: Dickenson, 1977.

Rocher, Ludo. "Mantras in the Śivapurāṇa." In *Understanding Mantras*, edited by Harvey P. Alper, 177–203. Albany: SUNY Press, 1989.

Rukmani, T. S., trans. *Yogavārttika of Vijñānabhikṣu*. 4 vols. Delhi: Motilal Banarsidass, 1981.

Rūpa Vilāsa Dāsa (Robert D. MacNaughton). *A Ray of Vishnu*. Washington, Miss.: New Jaipur Press, 1988.

Sahu, Shri R. J. "The Rationale of Praṇava Japa." *Yoga-Mīmāṁsā* 21 (1982): 81–90.

Sahu, Shri R. J., and Dr. B. V. Bhole. "Effect of Two Types of Praṇava (Om Recitations) on Psycho-Motor Performance." *Yoga-Mīmāṁsā* 22 (1983–84): 23–29.

———, "Prāṇadhāraṇa and Nādānusandhāna as Contributing Factors to Inner Experience of Yogic Nature." *Yoga-Mīmāṁsā* 22 (1983–84): 30–35.

Sandal, Pt. Mohan Lal. *Introduction to the Mīmāṁsā Sūtras of Jaimini*. 1925. Reprint. New York: AMS, 1974.

———, trans. *Mīmāṁsā-Sūtras of Jaimini*. Allahabad: Panini Office, 1923–25.

Sanders, C. W. *The Inner Voice*. Amritsar: Rādhā Soami Satsaṅg Beas, 1948.

Sanderson, Alexis. "Shaivism in Kashmir." In *The Encyclopedia of Religion* (Mircea Eliade, editor-in-chief), 13:16–17. New York: Macmillan, 1987.

Sankaran, C. R. "Theory and Experiment concerning the Ultimate Unit of Speech." *Journal of the Acoustical Society of India* 9, no. 3 (1981): 79–81.

Sarasvatī, Swami Pratyagātmānanda, ed. *Japa Sūtram* (Sanskrit and Bengali). 6 vols. Madras: Ganesh, 1961. English summary published as *Japa Sūtram: The Science of Creative Sound*, one volume (1971).

———. "Tantra as a Way of Realization." In *The Cultural Heritage of India*, edited by H. Bhattacharya, 4:227–40. Calcutta: Rāmakrishna Institute of Culture, 1957–62.

Sarma, K. M. "Gleanings from the Commentaries on the Vākyapadīya." *Annals of the Bhandarkar Oriental Research Institute* 23 (1942): 405–12.

———. "Vāk before Bhartṛhari." *Poona Orientalist* 8, nos. 1–2 (1943): 21–36.

Sastri, Gaurinath. "The Doctrine of Śabdabrahman: A Criticism by Jayanta Bhaṭṭa." *Indian Historical Quarterly* 15 (1939): 441–53.

———. *The Philosophy of Word and Meaning*. Calcutta: Sanskrit College, 1959.

———. "Some Reflections on Veda." *Annals of the Bhandarkar Oriental Research Institute* 59 (1978): 939–53.

———. *A Study in the Dialectics of Sphoṭa*. Delhi: Motilal Banarsidass, 1980.

Sastri, Gaurinath, and Govinda Gopal Mukhopadhyaya, eds. *Saṅgīta Dāmodaraḥ of Śubhaṅkara*. Calcutta: Sanskrit College, 1960.

Sastri, Pancanana, ed. and trans. (Bengali) *Śāradā-Tilaka-Tantram* (Sanskrit). Calcutta: Nava Bharat, 1983.

Sastri, Pasupatinath. *Introduction to the Pūrva Mīmāṁsa*. Varanasi: Chaukhambha Orientalia, 1980.

Sastri, Sitaram. *Kaula and Other Upanishads*. Tāntrik Texts XI, Calcutta, 1992.

Sathyanarayana, R. "Śruti, Dhvani and Sphoṭa." *Indian Theosophist* 82, nos. 10–11 (Oct.–Nov. 1985): 30–47.

Scharfe, Hartmut. *Grammatical Literature*. Wiesbaden: Otto Harrassowitz, 1977.

Schilling, S. Paul. *Contemporary Continental Theologians*. New York: Abingdon Press, 1966.

Schimmel, Annemarie. *Mystical Dimensions of Islam*. Chapel Hill: University of North Carolina Press, 1975.

Scholem, Gershom. *Kabbalah*. Jerusalem: Keter, 1974.

Schrader, F. O. *Introduction to the Pāñcarātra and the Ahirbudhnya Saṁhitā*. Adyar: Adyar, 1916.

Sen Gupta, N. N. "A Historical and Comparative Study of the Practice of Religious Recital (or Japa)." *Journal of the U.P. Historical Society* 12, no. 2 (1939): 22–48.

Seshasayee, T. *The Concept of Praṇava: Its Meaning and Significance in Hindu Religion*. Ph.D. diss., University of Madras, 1988.

Shaffer, Jim G. "The Indo-Aryan Invasions: Cultural Myth and Archaeological Reality." In *The People of South Asia*, edited by John R. Lukacs, 77–90. New York: Plenum, 1984.

Sharma, Chandradhar. *A Critical Survey of Indian Philosophy*. Delhi: Motilal Banarsidass, 1960.

Sharma, Prem Lata. "Brihaddeśī of Mataṅga." *Indian Music Journal* 6 (1970): 54–58; 7 (1971) 56–66.

Sharma, Tulsi Ram. *Studies in the Sectarian Upanishads*. Delhi: Munshiram Manoharlal, 1972.

Shastri, Pandit Kashinath, ed. *Candrajñāna-Āgama*. Mysore, 1940.

———, ed. *Sūkṣma-Āgama*. Mysore, 1942.

Sheridan, Daniel P. *The Advaitic Theism of the Bhāgavata Purāṇa*. Delhi: Motilal Banarsidass, 1986.

Shinn, Larry D. *The Dark Lord: Cult Images and the Hare Krishnas in America*. Philadelphia: Westminster Press, 1987.

Shringy, R. K., and Prem Lata Sharma, eds. *Saṅgīta-Ratnākara of Śārṅgadeva*, vol. 1. Delhi: Motilal Banarsidass, 1978.

Silburn, Lilian. *Kuṇḍalinī: The Energy of the Depths*. Albany: SUNY Press, 1988.

Singh, Himat. *The Philosophical Conception of Śabda*. Patiala: University Campus, 1985.

Singh, J. D. "Pāṇini's Theory of Language." *Kuruksetra University Research Journal* 5 (1971): 73–86.

Singh, Jaideva. "Nāda in Indian Tradition." *Psychology of Music: Selected Papers*, 37–43. Bombay and Baroda: Indian Musicological Society, 1980.

———, trans. *Abhinavagupta: A Trident of Wisdom: Translation of Parātriśikā-Vivaraṇa*. Albany: SUNY Press, 1989.

———, trans. *Pratyabhijñāhṛdayam: The Secret of Self-Recognition*. 1963. Reprint. Delhi: Motilal Banarsidass, 1987.

———, trans. *Śiva Sūtras: The Yoga of Supreme Identity*. 1979. Reprint. Delhi: Motilal Banarsidass, 1982.

———, trans. *Spanda-Kārikās: The Divine Creative Pulsation*. Delhi: Motilal Banarsidass, 1980.

———, trans. *Vijñāna Bhairava or Divine Consciousness*. 1979. Reprint. Delhi: Motilal Banarsidass, 1981.

Sinh, Pancham, trans. *The Haṭha-Yoga-Pradīpikā*. Allahabad: Panini Office, 1915.

Śivānanda, Swami. *Japa Yoga: A Comprehensive Treatise on Mantra Śāstra*. Shivanandanagar: Divine Life Society, 1986.

———. *Philosophy and Meditation on Om*. Rsikesh: Śivānanda Publication League, 1941.

———. *Tantra Yoga, Nāda Yoga and Kriya Yoga*. Rsikesh: Yoga Vedanta Forest University, 1955.

Sivaraman, K. "The Śaiva and the Grammarian Perspectives of Language." In *Language in Indian Philosophy and Religion*, edited by Harold Coward, 19-31. Waterloo: Wilfrid Laurier University Press, 1978.

———. *Śaivism in Philosophical Perspective*. Delhi: Motilal Banarsidass, 1973.

———. "The Word as a Category of Revelation." In *Revelation in Indian Thought*, edited by Harold Coward and K. Sivaraman, 45-64. Emeryville, Calif.: Dharma Publications, 1977.

Smith, Brian K. "Exorcising the Transcendent: Strategies for Defining Hinduism and Religion." *History of Religions* 27, no. 1 (Aug. 1987): 32-55.

Smith, F. C. "Prelude to a Phenomenology of Sound." *Main Currents in Modern Thought* 30, no. 1 (Sept.-Oct. 1973): 12-17.

Smith, H. Daniel. *A Descriptive Bibliography of the Printed Texts of the Pāñcarātrāgama*. 2 vols. (GOS 158, 168). Baroda: Oriental Institute, 1975, 1980.

———. "Pāñcarātra Literature in Perspective." *Journal of Ancient Indian History* 12 (1978-79): 45-58.

———. *The Smith Āgama Collection: Sanskrit Books and Manuscripts relating to Pāñcarātra Studies: A Descriptive Catalog*. Syracuse: Maxwell School of Citizenship and Public Affairs, 1978.

———. "The 'Three Gems' of the Pāñcarātrāgama Canon—An Appraisal." *Vimarśa* 1, no. 1 (1972): 45-51.

———. *Vaiṣṇava Iconography*. Madras: Pāñcarātra Pariśodhana Pariṣad, 1969.

Smith, Wilfred Cantwell. "Theology and the World's Religious History." In

Toward a Universal Theology of Religion, edited by Leonard Swidler, Maryknoll, N.Y.: Orbis Books, 1987.

Soni, Jayandra. *Philosophical Anthropology in Śaiva Siddhānta*. Delhi: Motilal Banarsidass, 1989.

Sreekrishna Sarma, E. R. "Bhartṛhari and Maṇḍana." *Brahmavidyā* 49 (1985): 66–78.

Srinivasa Ayyangar, T. R., trans. *The Vaiṣṇava Upanishads*. Madras: Adyar, 1953.

———, trans. *The Yoga Upanishads*. Madras: Adyar, 1938.

Staal, Frits. *Exploring Mysticism: A Methodological Essay*. London: Penguin, 1975.

———. "The Meaninglessness of Ritual." *Numen* 26 (1979): 2–22.

———. "Ṛgveda 10.71 on the Origin of Language." In *Revelation in Indian Thought*, edited by Harold Coward and K. Sivaraman, 3–14. Emeryville, Calif.: Dharma Publications, 1977.

———. "Ritual, Mantras and the Origin of Language." In *Amṛtadhara*. Prof. R. N. Dandekar Felicitation Volume, 403–25. Poona: Ajanta, 1984.

———. "Sanskrit Philosophy of Language." In *History of Linguistic Thought and Contemporary Linguistics*, edited by Herman Parret, 102–36. Berlin: de Gruyter, 1976.

———. "Vedic Mantras." In *Understanding Mantras*, edited by Harvey P. Alper, 48–95. Albany: SUNY Press, 1989.

———, ed. *A Reader on the Sanskrit Grammarians*. Cambridge: MIT Press, 1972.

Steiner, George. *After Babel: Aspects of Language and Translation*. London: Oxford University Press, 1975.

———. "The Language Animal." *Encounter* 33, no. 2 (Aug. 1969): 7–24.

Stutley, Margaret and James. *Harper's Dictionary of Hinduism*. London: Harper and Row, 1977.

Subrahmanya Sastri, Pandit S., trans. *Varivasyā-Rahasya of Bhāskara-Rāya Makhin*. Adyar: Adyar, 1948.

Subrahmanya Sastri, Pandit S., and T. R. Srinivasa Ayyangar. *Saundarya-Laharī*. Adyar: Theosophical Publishing House, 1965.

Subramania Iyer, K. A. *Bhartṛhari: A Study of the Vākyapadīya in the Light of Ancient Commentaries*. Poona: Deccan College Series, 1969.

———. "Bhartṛhari on Vyākaraṇa as a Means of Attaining Mokṣa." *Brahmavidyā* 28 (1964): 112–31.

———. "The Doctrine of Sphoṭa." *Journal of the Ganganath Jha Research Institute* 5, no. 2 (Feb. 1948): 121–47.

———. "Sanskrit and the Philosophy of Language." *Proceedings of the First International Sanskrit Conference*, edited by V. Raghavan, 2, pt. 2 (26–31 March 1972): 70–81.

———, trans. *Sphoṭasiddhi of Maṇḍana Miśra*. Poona: Deccan College Institute, 1966.

———, trans. *The Vākyapadīya of Bhartṛhari with the Vṛtti*, chap. 1. Poona: Deccan College, 1965.

Sundaram, P. K. *Advaita Epistemology with Special Reference to Iṣṭa-siddhi*. Madras: University of Madras, 1968.

Suryanarayana, V. "Nāda—the Legendary Reality." *Tattvāloka* 10, no. 3 (Aug.-Sept. 1987): 15–19.

Svaminathan, Sri V. "On Auṁkāra-Maṇḍana Miśra and Śaṅkarācārya." *K.S.R.I. Silver Jubilee Volume* (Madras 1981): 105–16.

Swami Laksman Jee. *Kashmir Shaivism: The Secret Supreme*. Albany: Universal Shaiva Trust, 1988.

Taber, John. "Are Mantras Speech Acts? The Mīmāṁsā Point of View," In *Understanding Mantras*, edited by Harvey P. Alper, 144–64. Albany: SUNY Press, 1989.

Tagare, Ganesh V., trans. *The Bhāgavata-Purāṇa*. Delhi: Motilal Banarsidass, 1978.

———, trans. *Śiva-Purāṇa*. Delhi: Motilal Banarsidass, 1970.

Tambiah, Stanley J. "The Magical Power of Words." *Man* 3, no. 2 (1968): 175–208.

Thibaut, George, trans. *Śaṅkara's Commentary on the Brahma-Sūtras*. New York: Dover, 1962.

———, trans. *Vedānta-Sūtras with the Commentary of Rāmānuja*. Delhi: Motilal Banarsidass, 1904.

Thite, G. U. "The Doctrine of Metres in the Veda." *Annals of the Bhandarkar Oriental Research Institute* 68 (1987): 425–55.

Tillich, Paul. *Systematic Theology*, vol. 1. Chicago: University of Chicago Press, 1951.

———. "The Word of God." In *Language: An Inquiry into Its Meaning and Function*, edited by Ruth Nanda Anshen, 122–33. New York: Harper and Row, 1957.

Theodore de Bary, William, ed. *The Buddhist Tradition in India, China and Japan*. New York: Vintage Books, 1972.

Tola, Fernando, and Carmen Dragonetti. "Yogic Trance in the Oldest Upanishads." *Annals of the Bhandarkar Oriental Research Institute* 68 (1987): 377–92.

Van Buitenen, J. A. B. "Akṣara." *Journal of the American Oriental Society* 79 (1959): 176–87.

———, trans. *Rāmānuja's Vedārthasaṅgraha*. Poona: Deccan College Postgraduate and Research Institute, 1956.

Van der Leeuw, Gerardus. *Religion in Essence and Manifestation*. 2 vols. Gloucester, Mass.: Peter Smith, 1967.

Varadachari, V. *Āgamas and South Indian Vaiṣṇavism*. Triplicane, Madras: Prof. Rangacharya Memorial Trust, 1982.

———, ed. *Descriptive Catalogue of Manuscripts*, vols. 1 and 2. Pondicherry: French Institute of Indology, 1986–87. Preface by N. R. Bhatt.

Varenne, Jean. *Yoga and the Hindu Tradition*. Translated by Derrek Coltman. Chicago: University of Chicago Press, 1976.

Varma, Satyakama. *Studies in Indology*. Delhi: Bharatiya Prakashan, 1976.

Varma, Siddheshwar. *Critical Studies in the Phonetic Observations of Indian Grammarians*. 1929. Reprint. Delhi: Munshiram Manoharlal, 1961.

———, trans. *The Śvetāśvatara-Upaniṣad*. Allahabad: Panini Office, 1916.

Varma, Vishwanath Prasad. "The Origins of Yoga." *Journal of the Ganganath Jha Research Institute* 17, nos. 1-2 (Nov. 1960–Feb. 1961): 42-58.

Vasu, Rai Bahadur Srisa Chandra, trans. *The Gheraṇḍa-Saṁhitā*. Allahabad: Panini Office, 1914.

———, trans. *The Śiva-Saṁhitā*. Allahabad: Panini Office, 1914.

———, trans. *The Vedānta-Sūtras of Bādarāyaṇa with the Commentary of Baladeva* (Sacred Books of the Hindus, vol. 5). 1912. Reprint. New York: AMS, 1974.

Vidyāsāgara, Śrīpād Nandalāl, ed. *Śrī-Śrī-Bhakti-Ratnākara* of Śrīla Narahari Cakravartī. Calcutta: Gaudiya Mission, 1960.

Vijñānānanda, Swami, trans. *Śrī Nārada Pañcharatnam*. Allahabad: Panini Office, 1921.

Werner, Karel. "Religious Practice and Yoga in the Time of the Vedas, Upanishads and Early Buddhism." *Annals of the Bhandarkar Oriental Research Institute* 56 (1975): 179-94.

Wheelock, Wade T. "The Mantra in Vedic and Tantric Ritual." In *Understanding Mantras*, edited by Harvey P. Alper, 96-122. Albany: SUNY Press, 1989.

———. "The Problem of Ritual Language: From Information to Situation." *Journal of the American Academy of Religion* 50, no. 1 (March 1982): 49-71.

———. "Sacred Language." In *The Encyclopedia of Religion* (Mircea Eliade, editor-in-chief), 8:439-46. New York: Macmillan, 1987.

———. "A Taxonomy of the Mantras in the New- and Full-Moon Sacrifice." *History of Religions* 19 (1980): 349-69.

Whitney, W. D., ed. and trans. "Atharva-Prātiśākhya." *Journal of the American Oriental Society* 7, no. 2 (1862): 333-615.

———, trans. *Atharva-Veda-Saṁhitā*. 2 vols. Delhi: Motilal Banarsidass, 1962.

———, trans. "Taittirīya-Prātiśākhya." *Journal of the American Oriental Society* 9, nos. 1-2 (1871): 1-240, 241-469.

Williams, Peter W. *Popular Religion in America*. Englewood Cliffs, N.J.: Prentice-Hall, 1980.

Wood, Ernest. "The Use of Sounds in Yoga Practice." *Yoga*, 186-215. London: Penguin, 1959.

Woods, J. H., trans. *The Yoga System of Patañjali*. Harvard Oriental Series XVII, Cambridge 1924.

Wulff, Donna Marie. "On Practicing Religiously: Music as Sacred in India."

In *Sacred Sound: Music in Religious Thought and Practice*, edited by Joyce Irwin, 149–72. Chico, Calif.: Scholars Press, 1983.

Yamasaki, Taiko. *Shingon: Japanese Esoteric Buddhism*. Boston and London: Shambhala, 1988.

Young, Katherine. "Dying for *Bhukti* and *Mukti*: The Śrī-Vaiṣṇava Theology of Liberation as a Triumph over Death." *Studies in Religion* 12, no. 4 (1983): 389–96.

Zaehner, R. C. *Hinduism*. London: Oxford University Press, 1962.

Index

Abhinavagupta, 160, 161, 164, 165, 170; on *nāda*, 130, 169; on Nāda-Brahman, 168
Advaita Śaivism. *See* Kashmiri-Śaivism
Advaita-Vedānta school, 65, 91, 113; and Brahman, 45; language replaced by silent contemplation in, 163, 207; meditation on sacred sound in, 90–91; and Nāda-Brahman, 92; and Om, 90, 178; and the relationship between word and meaning, 54; Śabda-Brahman in, 66; and Śaivism, 149; Sphotavāda rejected by, 17, 77–78; and the Upaniṣads, 45, 92; and Vaiṣṇavism, 192; and the Vedas, 79
Agama Anusandhana Samiti, 122
Āgamas, 65, 147, 206 (*see also* Śaiva-Āgamas); antiquity and origins of, 151, 152; dualism in, 149, 153, 158, 164, 171; Indian classical music in, 107; and Kashmiri-Śaivism, 19, 152, 164–66, 171; living religious traditions of India reflected in, 150 151–52; monism in, 153, 164, 171; *nāda* in, 19, 153–54, 157, 160, 209; Om in, 48, 153–54, 208, 209; sacred sound in, 107, 108, 118, 148, 171, 218; and Śiva, 19, 150–51, 152–54, 155, 157, 159, 164–65, 209; and Tantra, 149, 150; and Vaiṣṇavism, 181, 183, 198; and the Vedas, 150, 153
Āgamavāgīśa, Krsnānanda, 144–45
Agni, 27, 39; and *nāda*, 40, 110, 133, 206; in Śākta-Tantra, 133; in Vaiṣṇavism, 179, 187
Ahirbudhnya-Saṁhitā, 173, 176, 179, 183, 210
Allen, W. Sidney, 50, 51
Anuvyākhyāna (Madhva), 193
Apte, P. P., 182
Āraṇyakas, 23, 47, 92, 205
Artha, 9, 99; and the Grammarians, 52, 63, 84; as internal, 71; and the Mīmāṁsās, 52; and *nāda*, 157, 158; and *śabda*, 8, 31–32, 49, 52, 63, 84; in Śaivism, 157, 158; in Śrī-Vidyā, 143; in Vaiṣṇavism, 178; in the Vedas, 31, 35, 49
Arya, Usharbudh, 111–12
Aryans, 24–25
Atharva-Veda, 23, 28, 33, 82
Ātman, 43, 45, 94, 95
AUM. *See* Om
Avalon, Arthur. *See* Woodroffe, Sir John

Babb, Lawrence A., 114
Bagchi, P. C., 122
Banerjea, A. K., 100, 101
Banerjee, Sri Sailen, 111
Barth, Karl, 15–16
Bhāgavad-Gītā, 41, 172
Bhāgavata-Purāṇa, 19, 172, 183–87; influence of, on Vaiṣṇava sects, 177, 184, 196; Visnu in, 183–84, 187, 189
Bhakti, 148, 200, 209; and *nāma-japa*, 188–89; in Savism, 159, 160; in Vaiṣṇavism, 160, 188–89, 196, 201, 202, 210

Bharati, Swami Agehananda, 12, 123, 124, 128, 145
Bhaktivedanta Swami, A. C., 202
Bhartṛhari: and cognition, 71–72, 79; and grammar, 63, 65, 72, 74–75; and the Grammarians, 17, 52, 53, 160, 164; influence of, 76, 79, 159, 163, 164, 168–69, 175, 177, 181, 192, 206–7; and Kashmiri Śaivism, 19, 76, 160, 162, 163, 164, 168–69, 209; language divisions of, 72–73, 177, 186, 206–7, 208, 209 (*see also* Madhyamā; Paśyanti; Vaikharī); and *nāda*, 57, 70, 102; and Patañjali, 65; and the relationship between word and meaning, 53, 63–64, 68; on Śabda-Brahman, 17, 53, 65, 66, 75–76, 80, 159; and *śabdapurva-yoga*, 74–76; and sacred sound, 162, 171, 209; and Saussure, 51; Sphoṭavāda supported by, 67–68, 69, 70, 80, 96, 206; and Vaiṣṇavism, 175, 176; and the Vedas, 65, 206; and Yoga, 83
Bhāskara Rāya, 141–42
Bhāṣya (Śabara), 58, 61
Bhatt, N. R., 151, 153
Bhaṭṭa, Keśava Kashmiri, 194
Bhaṭṭa, Kumārila, 55, 80
Bhaṭṭa, Śrī, 194
Bhattacharyya, Benoytosh, 175
Bhāvārtha-Dīpikā (Śrīdhara Swami), 196–97
Bhikṣu, Vijñāna, 82, 83, 85, 91, 208
Biardeau, Madeleine, 5
Bīja, 18, 208, 212–13; in Śaivism, 149, 155–56; in Śākta-Tantra, 127, 198, 210; in Vaiṣṇavism, 198
Bindu, 11, 81; in Kālī-kula, 146; and *nāda*, 81–82, 128, 154; in Nāda-Yoga, 17, 115; in the Pāncarātra texts, 210; in Śaivism, 19, 149, 153–54, 155, 156, 160, 169, 209; in Śākta-Tantra, 127, 130, 132, 135, 141–43, 146, 154; and Soma, 133; in Śrī-Vidyā, 141–43; in Vaiṣṇavism, 176, 177, 178, 179, 180, 187; in Yoga, 93, 99, 104, 105, 206, 208
Blavatsky, Madame, 217–18
Bloomfield, Maurice, 29
Boehme, Jacob, 217
Bolle, Kees W., 4–5, 10
Bose, Roma, 194
Brahmā, 28, 41, 44, 94; and Indra, 27; and Krishna, 185, 186; and mantras, 185; and Nāda-Brahman, 109; and Om, 27, 29, 42; in Śaivism, 153–54, 157; and Śiva and Viṣṇu, 153 (*see also* Trimūrti); in Vaiṣṇavism, 185, 186
Brahman, 8, 18, 173; in Advaita-Vedāntas, 45, 190; and the Grammarians, 65, 66, 73–74; and Krishna, 194; and mantras, 175, 213; and the Mīmāṁsās, 190–91; and *nāda*, 8, 157, 208; and Nāda-Brahman, 7, 8, 157; and Om, 39, 41, 42, 43, 45–46, 47, 48, 118, 205, 208 (*see also* Śabda-Brahman); and Oṁkāra, 193; and Parā-Vāk, 163; and Śabda-Brahman, 45, 66, 118, 205; and Śaṅkara, 78–79, 80, 190–96; and Śiva, 9, 157; and Sound and non-Sound, 45–46, 48, 66; in Tantra, 18, 123–24, 131, 145; in the Upaniṣads, 42, 43–48, 89–90, 185; in Vaiṣṇavism, 175, 176, 180–81, 185, 190–91, 192, 194–95, 196, 199; and Vāk, 7, 18, 29, 41; and the Vedānta, 18, 190, 194; in the Vedas, 44, 66; and Viṣṇu, 9, 45, 48, 96; in Yoga, 89–90, 91, 94, 95, 96
Brāhmaṇas, 16, 92, 149; Indra as the first Grammarian in, 26–27;

Brāhmaṇas, *continued*
language as sacred speech or sound in, 23; meter in, 40; Om in, 29, 48, 205; Vāk in, 28–29, 41
Brahma-Sūtra, 78, 197
Bṛhaddesī (Mataṅga), 108–9
Briggs, G. W., 98
Brough, John, 68
Buddhism, 9, 51, 150, 216; mantras in, 166, 167–68, 200, 213; relationship between word and meaning in, 53; silent contemplation in, 6, 14, 163, 169, 207; sound in, 38, 116; Vedas as revelatory rejected by, 52–53
Buitenen, J. A. B., 30

Caitanya, 144, 184, 189, 196, 203; soteriology of, 199, 201, 202
Cakras, 11; in Haṭha-Yoga, 104; and Indian music, 205; in Kuṇḍalinī-Yoga, 106, 110, 210; in Nāda-Yoga, 112, 114; in Śaivism, 210; in Śākta-Tantra, 104, 128, 129–30, 139–41, 143, 210; and Sanskrit, 7, 205; in Śrī-Vidyā, 139–41, 143; in Tantra, 97; in the Upaniṣads, 94–96; in Vaiṣṇavism, 177, 186, 210; in Yoga, 94, 98–99
Cakravartī, Narahari, 109
Cakravartī, Viśvanāth, 186
Candrajñāna-Āgama, 153, 154
Carman, John B., 13, 192
Cassirer, Ernst, 34
Chakravarti, Chintaharan, 122
Chakravarti, P., 37–38, 66, 69
Chāndogya-Upaniṣad, 39–40, 42, 108
Chatterji, J. C., 161
Christianity, 12, 134; glossolalia in, 202–3; language in, 14–16, 60; orality in, 2, 213, 214
Cidananda, Swami, 112
Coward, Harold, 5, 72, 76
Cratylus (Plato), 53, 78
Creation: and sound, 16, 35; in Tantra, 123–24; in Vaiṣṇavism, 177; and Vāk, 73; in Western occult traditions, 58

Dasgupta, Surendranath, 57, 190, 193; and Patañjali, 83, 84; on the rejections of Sphoṭavāda, 190; on sacred sound, 83, 123
Deśika, Lakṣmaṇa, 126
Dharma, 99; Grammarian position on, 74, 75, 76; Mīmāṁsā position on, 55, 57
Dhvani, 8, 67, 70, 170

Ebeling, Gerhard, 14, 214
Eliade, Mircea, 3, 88, 98; on Indra, 94; on Vyāsa, 88; and Yoga, 83, 84, 91, 105, 112; on the *Yoga-Upaniṣads*, 92, 93
Elkman, Stuart, 197
Ellul, Jacques, 1–2, 4, 60

Feuerstein, Georg, 84, 86, 87
Filliozat, Pierre, 158, 159
Firth, J. R., 50
Foucault, Michel, 218
Frazer, James, 32

Gauḍīya-Vaiṣṇavism, 54, 186, 194, 196–202, 210
Gautam, M. R., 111
Gāyatrī, 40–41, 193
Gheraṇḍa-Saṁhitā, 18, 102–3, 208
Ghosh, Atul Behari, 122
Glossolalia, 202–3
Gonda, Jan, 3, 73, 152, 161
Gopāla Bhaṭṭa Goswami, 197–98, 200
Gorakhnāth, 99, 97–102, 105; Agni and Soma in, 133; and Bhartṛhari, 83; and Nāda-Brahman, 98, 99, 208; and Paśyanti, 208;

and Śaivism, 149; and Śākta-Tantra, 101, 106; tradition of, 17-18, 81, 83, 92, 118, 141; and Vaiṣṇavism, 149; and Vāk, 100
Gorakṣa-Śataka, 99, 105
Goudriaan, Teun, 121
Govinda, Lama, 116-17
Grammarians, 49, 50, 62 (*see also* Sphoṭavāda); and Bhartṛhari, 17, 52, 53, 160, 164; and consciousness, 72-73, 207; contributions of, 52; divinity in, 82; and the ego sense, 75; and Indra, 26, 27, 68; influence of, 163; and Kashmiri Śaivism, 162-64, 171; language in, 14, 23, 52, 71-72, 73, 75-76, 97, 164, 206, 207, 211; *nāda* for, 65, 70, 89; Parā-Vāk in, 161-63; Paśyanti in, 163-64, 175, 207, 210; and *pratibhā*, 69; and Śabda-Brahman, 8, 14, 17, 18, 53, 54, 62-76, 158, 159, 162-63, 175, 207, 211; and Śaivism, 158; soteriology of, 14, 52, 73; sound in, 52, 53, 61, 63-64, 68-69, 148 (*see also* Sphoṭa; Sphoṭavāda); and *sphoṭa*, 17, 76, 78, 79, 80, 84-85, 94, 157, 158, 163-64, 193, 197, 207 (*see also* Sphoṭavāda); and Vaiṣṇavism, 192, 210; and the Vedas, 63, 64, 65, 69, 75; and Yoga, 83-85, 105
Greeks, ancient, 12; alphabet in, 216; language for, 54, 78; word mysticism in, 6, 14, 133
Gupta, Sanjukta, 174

Hari-Bhakti-Vilāsa (Gopāla Bhatta Goswami), 197-98
Haṭha-Yoga, 98, 100, 115; treatises of, 18, 81, 92, 102, 118 (*see also* *Gheraṇḍa-Saṁhitā; Haṭha-Yoga-Pradīpikā; Śiva-Saṁhitā*)
Haṭha-Yoga-Pradīpikā, 102, 110, 208; Nāda-Brahman in, 18, 99-100, 104-5
Harā. *See* Rādha
Hebrew, 51, 54, 57-58, 151, 213
Heidegger, Martin, 34, 214-15, 216
Heimann, Betty, 66-67
Herder, J. G., 67
Herman, A. L., 65
Hermeneutics, 20, 204, 215; and linguistics, 50, 214-15; and sonic theology, 14-15, 19, 214, 215-16, 218; and the unthought, 215-16
Hinduism: definition of, 10; God conceived in, 12; revelation in, 12, 13; sects of, 13, 14, 18, 19-20, 23, 80, 149 (*see also* Śaivism; Vaiṣṇavism); visual dimension of, 3-4
Hindu theism: Brahman in, 18, 45; formative stages of, 47; mantras in, 62; male Supreme Being overseeing female features in, 172; *nāda* in, 40; Śabda-Brahman in, 45; and Śakti, 28; sound in, 45; and Sphoṭavāda, 211; and Varṇavāda, 211
Hiriyanna, Mysore, 57, 58
Hopkins, Thomas J., 32, 47, 149
Husserl, Edmund, 50

Indra, 26-27, 40, 68, 94
Islam, 24, 135-36, 213
Īśvara, 87, 95, 97; and Om, 82, 86, 102
Iyer, Kuppuswami. *See* Śivānanda, Swami

Jacobi, H., 84, 87
Jaimini, 55-56
Jainism, 6, 38, 52-53
James, William, 218
Janus, 54, 70
Japa, 7, 92, 113, 209, 219; compared to Christian glossolalia, 202-3;

Japa, continued
correlated to Bhartṛhari's stages of sound, 140; feasibility of, 216; in Kālī-kula, 146, 147; in Śaivism, 149, 165–66, 170, 201; soteriological import of, 113, 205, 213; in Śrī-Vidyā, 139–41; taking the name in, 188–89; in Tantra, 123, 131–32, 133–36, 139–41, 146, 147; in Vaiṣṇavism, 176, 194, 199, 201, 202, 203; in the *Yoga-Upaniṣads*, 93
Jayākhya-Saṁhitā, 173, 175–76, 178, 210
Jee, Swami Lakshman, 161
Jha, Ganganath, 55
Ji, Guru Maharaj, 114–15
Jīva Goswami, 80, 196–97, 200
Jones, Sir William, 50
Judaism, 24, 54, 151, 154, 213

Kabbalah, 54, 154
Kālī, 18, 129, 144–47, 210
Kālī-kula, 144–47
Kālī Śākta-Tantra, 18, 121, 136, 144–47
Kallaṭa, 164, 169
Kāmakalā, 142–43
Kāmakalā-Vilāsa, 137, 142–43
Kameśvara-sūrī, 140
Karpūrādi-Stotram, 145–46
Kashmiri Śaivism, 91, 126, 158, 160–71; Bhartṛhari's influence on, 19, 76, 160, 162, 163, 164, 168–69, 209; *Bindu* in, 153–54, 169; compared to Grammarians, 162–64, 171; consciousness in, 169–70; dualism in, 171; language replaced by silent contemplation in, 14, 19, 207; language theory in, 54, 163, 170, 209; monism of, 19, 153, 171; *nāda* in, 153–54, 163, 165, 168, 169, 170; and Nāda-Brahman, 14, 168, 171, 175; nondualism of, 160, 161, 168, 209; Parā-Vāk in, 148, 158, 161–62, 171, 209; reality described according to letter system in, 166–69; and the Śaiva-Āgamas, 19, 152, 164–66, 171; Śakti in, 153–54, 161, 162, 169; Śiva in, 153–54, 161, 162, 164–66, 169, 170, 171; soteriology of, 160–61, 163; sound theories of, 14, 158, 160, 167, 168, 170–71; Spanda in, 124, 169, 170, 209; and Sphoṭavāda, 53, 80, 163; triadic monism of, 171; Trika philosophy in, 161, 162, 163, 164, 166–67, 171
Kātyāyana, 61, 63
Kaviraj, Gopinath, 66, 69, 122, 147, 158
Kavirāj, Krishnadās, 196
Kayser, Hans, 219
Keith, A. B., 84
Khanna, Madhu, 131
Khecarī-Mudrā, 106
Klostermaier, Klaus K., 188
Koran, 2, 24, 135
Kramrish, Stella, 201
Krishna (*see also* Nārāyaṇa; Viṣṇu); and Brahmā, 185, 186; and Brahman, 194–95; and *nāda*, 186–87; and Nāda-Brahman, 96, 186, 210; in Śaivism, 19; and Śakti, 199; in Vaiṣṇavism, 13, 19, 172, 184, 185–87, 189, 193, 194–96, 198–99, 200, 202, 203, 210
Ksemarāja, 164, 165
Kumārila, 60, 61, 78
Kuṇḍali, 129, 141
Kuṇḍalinī, 114, 130, 135, 139, 141
Kuṇḍalinī-Yoga, 118; Cakras in, 106, 110, 129–30, 210

Lakṣmī: and Brahman, 180–81; and language, 187–88; and Om, 179; personal role of, 187–88, 209,

211; and Śabda-Brahman, 188; as Śakti, 178, 179; and Sanskrit, 182–83; and Viṣṇu, 172, 175, 178
Lakṣmi-Tantra, 173, 178–83, 187–88, 210
Lalita. *See* Tripurasundarī
Language, 204; Christian and Hindu compared, 15–16; and consciousness, 5–6, 7, 23, 50, 73; derived from mantras, 32–33; and the divine, 15, 23, 110; eternity of, 37–39, 55–56, 58; and hermeneutics, 214; in India, 25, 32, 63; Indian philosophies of, 16, 17, 49, 50, 51–52, 204 (*see also* Sphoṭavāda; Varṇavāda); meaning in, 51–52, 53–54; oral dimension of, 1, 2–3, 6, 23, 213; origin and development of, 25, 36–37, 217, 218; power of, 23, 34–35, 40, 51, 75; in ritual, 31 (*see also* Mantras); sacred, 110; and sound, 14, 15, 16, 20, 51, 53–54; and speech formation, 38–40; and thought, 50; and the West, 50–51, 62–63, 217–18
Liebich, B., 84
Linguistics: dual nature of sign in, 69–70; and the feasibility of *japa,* 216; and hermeneutics, 50, 214–15; Indian study of, 50; and phonetics, 35–36; and Sanskrit, 51; and *sphoṭa,* 69; and traditional Western magic, 34–35
Lipner, Julius, 191–92
Logos, 6, 216

Madhva, 172, 184, 189, 192–93, 210; *mokṣa* followed in gradual stages by, 196; Sphoṭavāda rejected by, 80, 193, 197
Madhva-Sampradāya, 192–93, 210 (*see also* Madhva)
Madhyamā, 7, 11, 205; and the Grammarians, 96, 207; in Kashmiri Śaivism, 162, 169; in Śrī-Vidyā, 143; in Vaiṣṇavism, 177, 178, 180, 186
Magical theory, 34–35
Mahābhārata, 41, 88, 92
Mahābhāsya (Patañjali), 63, 64, 74, 83
Mahānirvāna-Tantra, 122, 146
Maitri-Upaniṣad: Brahman in, 45, 46, 66, 89, 90; and Nāda-Yoga, 92; Om in, 44, 46
Mantras, 7, 20, 182, 219 (*see also Japa*); in Buddhism, 166, 167–68, 200, 213; and cognition, 71–72; defined, 30–31, 35; in dualistic, theistic Hindu sects, 163; and the Grammarians, 71–72, 76; impregnated with divine energy by a personal Lord, 1, 187–88, 209, 211; in injunctions, 34; in Kālī-kula, 145, 146; in Kashmiri-Śaivism, 165–66, 170; language derived from, 33; and meaning, 57, 59, 71–72, 216; meter in, 28, 40–41; and the Mīmāṁsā, 71, 72; modification required in performance of, 64; and *nāda,* 97; and Nāda-Yoga, 112, 113; and the Nāth tradition, 101–2; and Om, 17, 29; in the Pāncarātra texts, 19, 182, 198–99; and Paśyanti, 207; power of, 72, 129, 205; pronunciation of, 35–36, 51, 205; rosary beads used in, 134–35, 140; in Śaiva-Siddhanta, 159; in Śaivism, 154, 155–56, 159, 165–66, 170, 183, 188, 201, 209; and Śakti, 183; and the Sāṁkhya, 77; soteriological import of, 14, 62, 166, 203, 205, 207–8, 212–13; and Sphoṭavāda, 71, 72; in Śrī-Vidyā, 18, 137–41; and Tantra, 67, 101, 122, 123, 124,

Mantras, *continued*
125-26, 128-29, 130, 131-41, 145, 146, 147, 149, 195, 210; as Tripurasundarī, 210; in the Upaniṣads, 95, 134, 179, 199-200; in Vaiṣṇavism, 19, 173, 174-76, 178-79, 180, 181, 182-83, 187, 188, 191, 192, 193, 194, 195, 198-99, 200-201, 210; and Vāk, 8, 23, 29, 51, 182, 205; and Varṇavāda, 207; in the Vedas, 23, 29, 30-41, 47, 134, 136, 185; Western similarities to, 15, 202-3, 213-14; the whole resulting from the sum of its parts in, 76; in Yoga, 83, 86, 87, 92, 93, 97, 211
Mantra-Śāstra, 129, 147, 174
Mantaṅga, 108-9
Merleau-Ponty, Maurice, 50
Meter, 23, 28, 82; in the Vedas, 40-41, 47, 51
Mīmāṁsās, 52, 55, 57; divinity in, 82; language in, 38, 58-59, 60, 62, 65, 71, 125-26, 148, 207; and mantras, 71, 72; and *nāda,* 89, 102, 206; and Nāda-Brahman, 92; and the Pāncarātra tradition, 182; and *pratibhā,* 69; realist position of, 60-61; and the relationship between word and meaning, 53, 55, 59, 60-61, 62, 64, 68; *śabda* in, 31-32, 38, 49, 52, 54, 56, 59, 61, 126, 148; Śabda-Brahman in, 52, 63; Sanskrit in, 182; soteriology of, 14, 52; sound and language viewed in, 38, 148; Sphoṭavāda rejected by, 76, 77; and Tantra, 125-26, 160; and Vaiṣṇavism, 190-91, 192; Vāk in, 52; and Varṇavāda (*see* Varṇavāda); and the Vedas, 32, 55, 57, 58-59, 61, 62, 63, 64, 65, 68, 182, 188, 207, 208, 209, 211
Mīmāṁsā-Sūtras (Jaimini), 55-56, 65, 68, 70
Mishra, Umesha, 122, 127
Miśra, Maṇḍana, 53, 63, 72, 80
Misra, Rammurti, 85
Mokṣa, 14, 216; and the Grammarians, 72, 74, 75; and the Nāth Yogis, 98; in Śaivism, 155; and Śaṅkara, 79; and sacred sound, 9, 212; in Vaiṣṇavism, 196; and Yoga, 99
Mookerjee, Ajit, 122
Mukhopadhyaya, Govinda Gopal, 122, 131-33, 166-67
Müller, Max, 24, 51
Muller-Ortega, Paul, 91, 169-70
Muṇḍaka-Upaniṣad, 43, 44-45
Muni, Bhārata, 108
Murti, T. R. V., 52
Musalagaonkar, Vimala, 105
Music, Indian classical, 7, 118; and the Āgamas, 107; chanting in, 107; and the creation of musical sound, 39; instruments in, 108, 110; and Nāda-Brahman, 18, 35, 40, 48, 80, 81, 107, 108-10, 111; and Nāda-Yoga, 107-11; and sound detached from linguistic meaning, 35; and Tantra, 96, 109; and the Upaniṣads, 107, 108, 110; in the Vedas, 107-8, and Yoga, 96, 109, 110

Nāda, 11, 17; and *agni,* 40, 110, 133, 206; and *artha,* 157, 158; and *bindu,* 81-82, 128, 154; and Brahman, 8, 157, 208; defined, 40, 81; as external, 71; as feminine, 156; and the Grammarians, 65, 70, 89; in Haṭha-Yoga, 104, 105, 208; in Kālī-kula, 146, 147; in Kashmiri-Śaiva, 153-54, 163, 165, 168, 169, 170; and linguistic studies, 212; in Mīmāṁsā, 39, 89, 102, 206; as Nāda-Brahman, 8, 107; in Nāda-Yoga, 82, 110; and

Om, 82, 154, 206, 208; and *śabda*, 157, 158; and Śabda-Brahman, 56–57, 176, 181; and Śabda-Tattva, 157–58; in the Śaiva-Āgamas, 19, 153–54, 157, 160, 209; in Śaiva-Siddhanta, 19, 153–54, 156–59, 160; in Śaivism, 149, 154, 155, 156–59, 160, 163, 165, 168, 169, 170, 209; in Śākta-Tantra, 18, 127–28, 131, 132, 135, 139, 140, 141–42, 143, 146, 147, 210; and Śakti, 127, 133, 154, 157; and Śiva, 133, 153, 154, 156–57, 160, 209; in soteriology, 159; and *sphoṭa*, 158–59, 208; in Śrī-Vidyā, 140, 141–42, 143; in Tantra, 82, 123, 154, 158; as Tripurasundarī, 210; in the Upaniṣads, 94, 96; in Vaiṣṇavism, 173, 175, 176, 178–79, 180, 181, 182, 185, 186; in Western studies, 91, 217–18; in Yoga, 8, 71, 83, 89, 91, 92, 93, 97, 99, 100, 102, 105, 206, 208

Nāda-Bindu, 48, 125

Nādabindu-Upaniṣad, 93, 105, 110

Nāda-Brahman, 7, 11, 14–15, 20, 207; in Āgamas, 107, 108, 154, 171; and ancient civilization, 212; and Brahmā, 109; and Brahman, 8, 17, 157; as bridge between sectarian movements, 211; created by *prana* and *agni*, 39; current trends in, 18; in dualistic, theistic Hindu sects, 163; as female energy, 8, 17, 18, 19, 48, 66, 203, 208, 209; four forms of, 96, 176–77; and Gorakhnāth, 98, 99, 208; and Haṭha-Yoga, 104, 105; in Hindu theism, 40, 48; and Indian classical music, 18, 35, 40, 48, 80, 81, 107, 108–10, 111; in Kashmiri Śaivism, 168, 171; and Krishna, 186, 210; and *nāda*, 8, 107; in Nāda-Yoga, 113, 118; and nonlinguistic sound, 46; and Om, 44, 97; omitted in Vedas and Upaniṣads, 8, 206; Oṁkāra as first linguistic manifestation of, 185; and the origin of vowels and consonants, 168; in the Pāñcarātra texts, 19, 48, 210; and Śabda-Brahman, 35, 45, 46, 66, 81, 97, 205, 211; in Śaiva-Siddhanta, 171, 175; in Śaivism, 8, 19, 149, 154, 156, 163, 171; in Śākta-Tantra, 8, 18, 35, 40, 44, 46, 48, 97, 121, 126–29, 135, 141–42, 143, 147, 148, 175, 209–10, and Śakti, 18, 109, 128, 157, 183, 210; and the Sanskrit alphabet, 129–31; and Śiva, 18, 48, 98, 99, 109, 209, 210; and sonic cosmogony, 211–12; and Sphoṭavāda, 211; in Śrī-Vidyā, 18, 121, 141–42, 143–44; in Tantra, 9, 48, 124–25; and Vaiṣṇavism, 8, 19, 109, 172, 173, 174, 176, 181, 182, 183, 184, 185, 186, 210; and Vāk, 46, 97; and Varṇavāda, 211; and Viṣṇu, 48, 109, 203, 209, 210; in Western studies, 91; in Yoga, 8, 17–18, 35, 40, 44, 46, 80, 81, 89–90, 91, 92, 102, 103, 107, 108, 208

Nādabrahmānanda, Swami, 111, 113

Nāda-Kārikā (Rāmakaṇṭha II), 19, 157, 158

Nāda-rupa. *See* Tripurasundarī

Nāda-Yoga: Cakras in, 112, 114; current trends in, 81, 111–18; and Gorakhnāth, 102; and Haṭha-Yoga, 102–6, 112, 115, 208; and Indian classical music, 107–11; mantras in, 112, 113; Om in, 111, 112, 113, 116–17, 118; practiced for differing goals, 212; and sacred sound, 16, 17–18, 84, 86, 108, 113, 118; sonic meditation in, 17, 149; and the Upaniṣads, 91–92, 97, 112; and the West, 111

Nāgeśa, 53, 80, 192
Nakamura, Hajime, 88
Nāma-japa, 188–89
Nanak, Guru, 114
Nārada-Pāncarātra, 198
Narasimhachary, M., 191
Nārāyaṇa, 19, 172, 202, 203 (*see also* Krishna; Viṣṇu) and Brahman, 180, 190; and *praṇava,* 175, 187, 192
Nārāyaṇa Kaṇṭha, 157
Nathamuni, 189
Nāth Yoga, 97-102, 106 (*see also* Gorakhnāth)
Nikhilānanda, Swami, 90
Nimbārka, 172, 184, 193–94, 196, 210
Nyāya, 38, 52–53, 54, 76, 77

Om, 7, 11, 20, 205, 207 (*see also* Praṇava); in Advanta-Vedānta, 90, 178; in the Āgamas, 48, 153–54, 160, 208, 209; in the Aranyakas, 205; and *bindu,* 206; and Brahmā, 27, 29, 42; and Brahman, 39, 41, 42, 43, 45–46, 47, 48, 118, 205, 208 (*see also* Śabda-Brahman); in the Brāhmaṇas, 29, 48, 205; in Buddhism, 166; and the Grammarians, 64, 76; as hermeneutic and as vehicle, 45; and meter, 82; and *nāda,* 82, 154, 206, 208; and Nāda-Brahman, 94, 97; and Nāda-Yoga, 111, 112, 113, 116–17, 118; origin of, 42, 185; parts of, 43–45, 48, 135, 187, 205, 208–9; and Patañjali, 85; as *śabda,* 8; and Śabda-Brahman, 16, 43, 48, 118, 205; in Śaiva-Siddhanta, 160; in Śaivism, 153–54, 155–56, 160, 187; in Śākta-Tantra, 128, 131, 141, 187, 204–5, 208; and Śakti, 208; and Śaṅkara, 78, 90; and Śiva, 9, 154, 155, 208; in Śrī-Vidyā, 18; in the Upaniṣads, 16, 42–48, 82, 89–90, 92, 95, 110, 118, 178, 179, 185, 205–6; in Vaiṣṇavism, 48, 178–79, 180, 182, 185, 187, 191, 193, 210; and Vāk, 205; in the Vedānta, 135; and the Vedas, 29, 64, 66, 69, 128, 138, 153, 205; and Viṣṇu, 9, 46, 175, 179, 187, 191; in Western word mysticism, 217–18; in Yoga, 9, 82, 83, 86, 89–90, 91, 92, 93, 94, 97, 99, 100, 102, 205, 206
Oṁkāra, 185, 187, 193
Oṁkārnath, Sītārāmdās, 147
Ong, Walter J., 2, 4, 5
Otto, Rudolf, 4, 5

Padmapāda, 80
Padoux, André, 5, 161; on Kashmiri Śaivism, 163, 168, 169; on mantras in Tantra, 125, 139
Pancakṣara-Mantra, 159–60
Pāncarātra texts, 172, 173–83; mantras in, 19, 182, 198–99; and Mīmāṁsā, 182; *nāda* in, 187; *pratiṣṭhā* in, 181–82; and the relationship between word and meaning, 54; sacred sound in, 19, 173, 174, 178, 181, 209; and the Śaiva-Āgamas, 173–74, 183, 184; and Śākta-Tantras, 173, 174, 179; and Sanskrit, 182; soteriology of, 174; Sphoṭavāda rejected in, 193; and the Vaiṣṇava sects, 19, 148, 184, 189, 192, 198, 210; and Varṇavāda, 182; and Viṣṇu, 151
Pāṇini, 70, 63, 83, 151
Parā, 96, 143, 168; in Vaiṣṇavism, 175, 177, 180, 186
Parama-Saṁhitā, 1, 204
Parama-Śiva, 162–63
Parāśara, 191
Parātrīśikā-laghuvṛttiḥ (Abhinavagupta), 168, 170
Parātrīśikā-Vivarana, 164

Parā-Vāk; in the Āgamas, 148, 162; Bhartṛhari on, 162, 209; and Brahman, 163; and the Grammarians, 161–63; in Kashmiri Śaivism, 158, 161–62, 171, 209; and Paśyanti, 163–64; and Śabda-Brahman, 148, 162; in Śaivism, 148, 158, 161–62, 171; and Śakti, 162; and Śiva, 162
Paśyantī, 7, 19, 205; and the Gorakhnāth tradition, 35, 76, 208; for the Grammarians, 163–64, 175, 207, 210; in Kashmiri-Śaivism, 162, 168, 171; and the Mīmāṁsās, 211; in Śaivism, 168, 171, 209; in Śrī-Vidyā, 143; and Vaiṣṇavism, 172, 175, 177, 178, 180, 181, 186, 210; in the *Yoga-Upaniṣads,* 96
Patañjali, 17, 74, 81, 118; on *dhvani,* 70; and grammar, 63, 64–65, 75; identity of, 83–84; on language, 64; and Om, 85, 208; and *śabda* and *sphoṭa,* 53, 67, 70, 76, 80, 84–85; and Vaiṣṇavism, 184; and Yoga, 82, 97
Pauṣkara-Saṁhitā, 176, 210
Phenomenology, 10, 50
Phonetics, 16, 23, 35–36, 39–40, 50
Pillai, 66
Plato, 53, 78
Prabhākara, 55, 60, 80 190
Prajāpati. *See* Brahmā
Prāna, 38, 39, 40, 110, 123
Praṇava, 205, 208 (*see also* Om); divisions of, 187, 205; and the Grammarians, 64, 66; in the Pāncarātra texts, 210; in Śaivism, 154, 209; in Śākta-Tantra, 135, 140, 210; and *sphoṭa,* 163–64, 206, 208; as Tripurasundarī, 210; in the Upaniṣads, 205, 206; in Vaiṣṇavism, 172, 175, 180–81, 187, 191–92; in the Vedas, 46, 64, 66, 205; and Viṣṇu, 187; in Yoga, 93, 95
Prasada, Rama, 83
Pratibhā, 69, 74–75, 211
Pratyabhijñā philosophy, 160, 164
Pratyagātmānanda, Swami, 147
Puñyānandanāth, 142–43
Purāṇas, 41, 88, 154, 157
Pythagoras, 110–11

Rādhā, 194, 198, 199–200
Rādhā Soami sect, 111, 113–14, 115
Rāghavabhaṭṭa, 126
Raghavan, V., 107
Raja, C. Kunhan, 33
Rajneesh, Bhagwan Shree, 111, 115–16, 117
Rāma, 13, 19
Rāmakaṇṭha, 157
Rāmakaṇṭha II, 157, 158
Ramanathan, N., 111
Rāmānuja, 184, 189–92, 194, 196; Sphoṭavāda rejected by, 80, 180, 193, 197
Raschke, Carl, 215
Religious studies, 204, comparative, 12, 51; in India, 5; language studied in, 50, 62–63; and oral word, 2–3, 213–14; and sound in, 3, 5, 9–10, 19, 213; visual dimension of, 3; visualist bias in, 3, 10
Ṛg-Veda, 16, 33, 41, 44, 193 (*see also* Vedas); and Indian classical music, 107, 108; language in, 23, 31, 36, 77; Vāk in, 25–29; and Vaiṣṇavism, 172, 181
Rosary beads, 134–35, 140, 146; in Vaiṣṇavism, 176, 194, 202
Rudra, 27, 28, 44, 47 (*see also* Śiva)
Rukmani, T. S., 83
Rūpa Goswami, 196, 200, 202

Śabara, 38, 55, 56, 68; on speech, 38, 58, 59, 61
Śabara-Bhasya (Śabara), 55, 56

Śabda: and *artha,* 8, 31–32, 49, 52, 63, 84; Bhartṛhari on, 66, 67–68; defined, 8; for the Grammarians, 52, 63, 66, 67; in Kashmiri Śaiva, 169; for the Mīmāṁsās, 31–32, 38, 49, 52, 54, 56, 59, 61, 126; in Nāda-Yoga, 84, 108; Patañjali on, 64, 67–68; Śabara on, 56, 61; in Śaiva-Siddhanta, 157, 158; in Śaivism, 157, 158, 169; in the Sāṁkhya doctrine, 77, 79; and *sphoṭa,* 67–68; in Tantra, 123, 126; in Vaiṣṇavism, 181
Śabda-Brahman, 7, 11, 15, 20, 215; and *artha,* 9; and Bhartṛhari, 17, 53, 65, 66, 75–76, 80, 159; and Brahman, 45, 66, 118, 205; and cognition, 71–72; as external, 54, 55–62, 211; and the Grammarians, 8, 14, 17, 18, 53, 54, 62–76, 158, 159, 162–63, 175, 207, 211; in Indian classical music, 35, 107; as internal, 54, 62–76, 211; and Kālī, 210; in Kālī-kula, 145; and Lakṣmi, 188; as the merging of Om and Brahman, 16, 41, 43, 48, 118, 205; and the Mīmāṁsās, 54, 55–62, 211; and *nāda,* 56–57, 176, 181; and Nāda-Brahman, 35, 45, 46, 66, 81, 97, 205, 211; and Parā-Vāk, 148, 162; in Tantra, 35, 145, 210; in the Upaniṣads, 8, 9, 16, 17, 18, 23, 31, 35, 41, 42–48, 49, 66, 205; in Vaiṣṇavism, 175, 176–77, 178, 181, 182, 184; and Vāk, 16–17, 42, 46, 52, 205; and Varṇavāda, 211; in the Vedas, 54, 81; in Yoga, 35, 52–53
Śabda-Tattva, 53, 157
Sadyojyoti, 157
Śaiva-Āgamas, 150–56 (*see also* Āgamas); *bindu* in, 19, 149, 153–54, 155, 156, 160, 169, 209; compared to the Vedas, 153; and Kashmiri Śaivism, 19, 152, 164–66, 171; *nāda* in, 19, 153–54, 157, 160, 209; Om in (*see* Om, in the Āgamas); and the Pāncarātra texts, 173–74, 183, 184; and Śaiva-Siddhanta, 152, 156, 159, 209; Śakti in, 153–54, 160
Śaiva-Siddhanta: Bhakti in, 159; *Bindu* in, 19, 153–54, 156, 160; dualism of, 156, 171; formulators of, 157; language theory in, 54, 157–58; monism in, 171; *nāda* in, 19, 153–54, 156–59, 160; Nāda-Brahman in, 171, 175; and the Śaiva-Āgamas, 152, 156, 159, 209; Śakti in, 19, 153–54, 156–57, 159, 160; Śiva in, 19, 153–54, 156, 157, 158, 159; soteriology in, 159–60, 188; Sphoṭavāda rejected by, 80, 158
Śaivism, 147, 173 (*see also* Kashmiri Śaivism; Śaiva-Siddhanta); dualism in, 19, 149, 171; literature of, 150 (*see also* Āgamas; Śaiva-Āgamas); monism in, 171; *nāda* in (*see Nāda,* in Śaivism); Nāda-Brahman in, 8, 19, 149, 154, 156, 163, 171; Om in, 153–54, 155–56, 160, 187; and sacred sound in, 8, 16, 19, 52, 121, 148, 149, 154, 156, 163, 171; Śakti in (*see* Śakti, in Śaivism); and Śiva (*see* Śiva, in Śaivism); soteriology of, 188, 201; and Sphoṭavāda, 158, 163
Śākta-Āgamas. *See* Tantra
Śāktas. *See* Śākta-Tantra
Śākta-Tantra, 164, 166, 179 (*see also* Tantra); in Bengal, 18, 144–47; *bindu* in, 127, 130, 132, 135, 141–43, 146, 154; branches of (*see* Kālī Śākta-Tantra; Śrī-Vidyā); Cakras in, 104, 128, 129–30, 139–41, 143, 210; gender polarization in, 102, 106, 124, 149; and Gorakhnāth,

101, 106; and Kundalini-Yoga, 106; language in, 28, 54, 65, 123, 125–26, 129; mantras in, 123, 125–26, 128–29, 195; meter in, 41; *nāda* in (*see* Nāda, in Śākta-Tantra); Nāda-Brahman in (*see* Nāda-Brahman, in Śākta-Tantra); Om in, 128, 131, 141, 187, 204–5, 208; and the Pāncarātra texts, 173, 174, 179; rosary beads in, 135; Śakti in, 13, 18, 121, 123–24, 127, 128, 129, 133, 209; and Sanskrit, 104, 145; Śiva in (*see* Śiva, in Tantra); sound in, 16, 35, 39, 123, 125, 126, 148; soteriology in, 148; and Vaiṣṇavism, 178, 195, 198
Śakti, 28, 35, 188; and *bindu*, 153; in Kashmiri Śaivism, 153–54, 161, 162, 169; and Krishna, 199; in mantras, 183; and *nāda*, 102, 127, 133, 154, 157; and Nāda-Brahman, 18, 109, 128, 157, 183, 210; and Om, 208; in Śaiva-Siddhanta, 19, 153–54, 156–57, 159, 160; in Śaivism, 153–54, 156–57, 159, 160, 161, 162, 169, 209; in Śākta-Tantra, 13, 18, 121, 123–24, 127, 128, 129, 133, 209; and Śiva, 106, 121, 124–25, 126, 150, 159, 160, 161 (*see also* Śiva-Śakti); in Śrī-Vidyā (*see* Tripurasundarī); in Tantra, 28, 121, 123–24, 128, 129, 133, 136, 137, 138, 139, 142, 143, 154; and Vaiṣṇavism, 174, 175, 178, 179, 180, 182, 183, 187; and Vāk, 175; in Yoga, 94, 95, 99, 104, 105
Śakti-saṅgama-Tantra, 137, 144, 145
Śaktism. *See* Śākta-Tantra
Sāma-Veda, 23, 42, 44, 48, 107–8
Sāṁkhya school, 52, 54, 87, 91; and *śabda*, 52, 77, 79; Sphoṭavāda rejected by, 17, 76, 77, 80, 84–85
Sampradāyas. *See* Vaiṣṇavism, sects of
Sanātana Goswami, 196, 200
Sandal, Pt. Mohan Lal, 56
Śāṇḍilya-Saṁhitā, 199–200
Saṅgīta. *See* Music, Indian classical
Śaṅkara, 79, 90, 205, 210, 216; and Bhartṛhari, 65, 79–80; and Brahman, 78–79, 80, 190–91; and Mīmāṁsā, 190, 192; monism of, 42, 149, 190; and Om, 78, 90; Sphoṭavāda rejected by, 77–78, 80, 190, 197, 206; and Vaiṣṇavism, 192, 210
Sankaran, C. R., 117
Sanskrit, 20, 31, 63, 65; and the Cakras, 7, 205; and Kālī, 145; and the Mīmāṁsās, 182; and Nāda-Brahman, 129–31; origin of, 122, 185; and rosary beads, 134; sacred sound in, 5, 6, 7–9, 129–31; in Śākta-Tantra, 104, 145; in Vaiṣṇavism, 175, 176, 177, 182–83, 185, 192–93; Western discovery of, 50, 51
Śāradā-tilaka-Tantra, 122, 130–31, 137, 142, 198; Nāda-Brahman in, 18, 126–27, 209–10
Sarasvatī, 96
Sarasvatī, Śrīla Bhaktisiddhānta, 201–2
Sarasvatī, Swami Pratyagātmānanda, 122
Śārṅgadeva, 109
Śastri, Gaurinath, 61, 164; on Parā-Vāk, 148, 162; on Paśyanti, 76; on grammar, 69, 74
Śatapatha-Brāhmaṇa, 26–27, 40–41
Ṣaṭcakra-Nirūpaṇa (Pūrnānanda, Swami), 129–30
Sāttvata-Saṁhitā, 173, 176, 210
Saundarya-Laharī, 137, 146
Saussure, Ferdinand de, 51, 69
Schrader, F. O., 176

Śeṣa-Saṁhitā, 173, 180, 210
Sheridan, Daniel P., 184
Silburn, Lilian, 5, 130, 161
Singh, Maharaj Charan, 113–14
Śiva, 47, 95, 183, 188; in the Āgamas, 9, 150–51, 152–54, 155, 157, 159, 164–65, 209; and *bindu,* 81, 154, 209; and Brahman, 9, 157; in Haṭha-Yoga, 104, 105; in Kālīkula, 146; in Kashmiri-Śaiva, 153–54, 161, 162, 165–66, 169, 170, 171; mantras decreed by, 188; and *nāda,* 133, 153, 154, 156–57, 160, 209; and Nāda-Brahman, 18, 48, 98, 99, 109, 209, 210; and the Nāth Yogis, 98, 99, 102; and Om, 9, 154, 155, 208; and Parā-Vāk, 162; and Paśyanti, 164; in Śaiva-Siddhanta, 19, 153–54, 156, 157, 158, 159; in Śaivism, 13, 148, 150, 152–54, 155, 156, 157, 158, 159, 161, 162, 164–66, 169, 170, 171, 188, 209; and Śakti, 106, 121, 124–25, 126, 150, 159, 160, 161 (*see also* Śiva-Śakti); in Śrī-Vidyā, 137, 142, 143; in Tantra, 18, 121, 123, 124–25, 126, 127, 133, 137, 142, 143, 146, 154; in Vaiṣṇavism, 19; in Yoga, 149
Śivācārya, Aghora, 157, 159
Śivācārya, Umāpati, 158
Śivānanda, 137
Śivānanda, Swami, 111, 112–13
Śiva-Purāna, 154, 155, 209
Sivaraman, K., 158, 162–63, 164
Śiva-Śakti (*see also* Nāda-Brahman, in Tantra): and *nāda,* 81, 100, 102; in Nāth-Yoga, 101; in Śākta-Tantra, 124–25, 126; in Śrī-Vidyā, 138, 140, 143
Śiva-Saṁhitā, 18, 102, 103–4, 208
Śiva-Sūtra (Vasugupta), 164–65
Smith, Brian K., 10
Smith, F. J., 10
Smith, H. Daniel, 173, 176
Smith, Wilfred Cantwell, 12
Soma, 26, 105, 133; in Vaiṣṇavism, 177, 179; in the Vedas, 27, 37
Somānanda, 163, 164
Sonic: defined, 3, 15
Sonic theology, 13, 14, 15; and the death of God, 218; and hermeneutics, 215–16, 218; and religious studies, 19
Soteriology: and Caitanya, 199, 201, 202; for the Grammarians, 14, 52, 73; in Hinduism, 13–14; in Kashmiri Śaivism, 160–61, 163; for the Mīmāṁsās, 14, 52; and *nāda,* 159; in the Pāncarātras, 174; in the Śaiva-Āgamas, 159–60, 188; in Śaivism, 188, 201; in Śākta-Tantra, 148; and sound, 7, 9, 211; in Vaiṣṇavism, 187–88, 201; in Yoga, 97
Sound, sacred, 4, 5, 6–7, 51, 204; in Advaita-Vedānta, 90–91, 92; in the Āgamas, 107, 108, 118, 148, 171, 218; in Bhartṛhari, 79, 162, 171, 209; and the Brāhmaṇas, 23; in Buddhism, 38, 116; as common thread in Hinduism, 3, 7, 11, 13, 19–20; and consciousness, 211; and creation, 16, 35; and the divine, 3, 7, 15, 17, 47; eternity of, 37–39, 53, 56; as feminine energy, 7, 8, 15, 17, 18, 19, 121, 129, 148, 162, 171, 212; for the Grammarians, 52, 53, 61, 63–64, 68–69, 148, 161–63; in Hinduism, 204, 212, 218–19 (*see also* individual traditions); in Kashmiri Śaivism, 14, 148, 158, 160, 161–62, 167, 168, 170–71, 209; linguistic, 3, 7; and meaning, 35, 216–17; and the Mīmāṁsās, 38, 92, 148; and *mokṣa,* 9, 212; and music, 110–11; and mythology, 16,

35; in Nāda-Yoga, 16, 17–18, 84, 86, 108, 113, 118, 149; nonlinguistic, 3, 7, 9, 46, 81; origin of, 39; in the Pāncarātras, 19, 173, 174, 178, 181, 209; power of transformation in, 204; in Śaivism, 8, 16, 19, 52, 121, 148, 149, 154, 156, 163, 171; in Śākta-Tantra, 16, 35, 39, 123, 125, 126, 148 (*see also* Nāda-Brahman, in Śākta-Tantra); and soteriology, 7, 9, 211; in Tantra, 9, 48, 122, 123, 124–25, 126, 172; in Vaiṣṇavism, 16, 19, 52, 121, 148, 172–73, 176, 187, 201, 202 (*see also* Nāda-Brahman, in Vaiṣṇavism); in the Vedas, 16, 23–24, 35, 37–38, 46, 51, 53, 59, 81, 204, 205, 218; in Yoga, 16, 17–18, 20, 35, 46, 48, 52, 81, 83, 85–88, 91, 92 (*see also* Nāda-Brahman, in Yoga)

Spanda, 209; and Kashmiri Śaivism, 19, 124, 160, 164, 169, 170, 209

Speech. *See* Language

Sphoṭa, 60, 210 (*see also* Grammarians; Sphoṭavāda); and Brahman and *praṇava*, 206, 208; and cognition, 71–72; defined, 8, 66–67; as external and internal, 54, 69–70, 71; and the Grammarians, 17, 35, 53, 63, 76, 78, 79, 80, 84–85, 94, 157, 158, 163–64, 193, 197, 207; levels of, 96; and *nāda*, 158–59, 208; and Nāda-Brahman, 92; and Paśyanti, 163–64, 206, 208; and Patañjali, 84–85; rejection of, 76, 77–80, 158; in Śaiva-Siddhanta, 158–59; in Śaivism, 158–59; and Yoga, 76, 80, 85, 105

Sphoṭa-Siddhi (Miśra), 63, 72

Sphoṭavāda, 49, 53 (*see also* Grammarians; Sphoṭa); meaning in sentences in, 52, 60, 67–68, 71–72, 126, 160; as monistic, 54; and Nāda-Yoga, 208; and Nāth Yoga, 100; Paśyanti in, 76; rejection of, 76, 77–80, 102, 158, 163, 190, 193, 197, 206, 210–11, and Vaiṣṇavism, 172; and Varṇavāda, 7, 17, 19, 62, 205, 208

Srī. *See* Lakṣmi

Śrī-Cakra, 140–41

Śrīdhara Swami, 187, 196–97

Śrī-kula. *See* Tripurasundarī

Śrī-Sūkta, 137, 180

Śrī-Vaiṣṇavism, 54, 172, 189–92, 197, 210

Śrī-Vidyā, 126, 136–44, 178; cakras in, 139–41, 143; Goddess in, 18, 121; mantras in, 18, 137–41; *nāda* in, 140, 141–42, 143; Nāda-Brahman in, 18, 121, 141–42, 143–44; Om in, 18

Śrī-Vidyā-Mantra, 137–40, 198

Staal, Frits, 5, 10, 30, 32–33, 37

Steiner, George, 31, 217, 218

Subramania Iyer, K. A., 62, 64, 74–75

Śuddhādvaita-Vedānta, 194

Suparṇī, 29

Sūta Goswami, 184–85, 200

Śvetāśvatara-Upaniṣad, 47–48, 185, 191–92

Swami, Pūrṇānanda, 129–30

Taber, John, 33–34

Taittirīya-Prātiśākhya, 39–40

Tamil Veda, 156

Tantra, 18, 92 (*see also* Śākta-Tantra); and the Āgamas, 149, 150; Brahman in, 18, 123–24, 131, 145; cakras in, 97; defined, 121–22; gender polarization in, 101–2, 208; and Indian classical music, 96, 109; and Kālī, 144–47; mantras in (*see* Mantras, and Tantra); and the Mīmāṁsās, 125–

Tantra, *contnued*
26, 160; *nāda* in, 82, 123, 154, 158; Nāda-Brahman in, 9, 48, 124–25; Om in, 206, 208; *śabda* in, 123, 126; sacred sound in, 9, 48, 122, 123, 124–25, 126, 172; Śakti in (*see* Śakti, in Tantra); Śiva in (*see* Śiva, in Tantra); studies on, 122–23; and Vaiṣṇavism, 184, 186, 198; word mysticism in, 76
Tantrāloka (Abhinavagupta), 130, 161, 168, 169
Thākur, Śrīla Bhaktivinode, 202
Theology, 12–13, 14–15, 76
Tillich, Paul, 16, 60
Torah, 24, 151
Trimūrti, 153, 154
Tripurā. *See* Tripurasundarī
Tripurasundarī, 137, 139, 143; and Śrī-Vidyā, 18, 121, 136, 138, 142, 144
Tripurā-tāpinī-Upaniṣad, 137, 138

Udgītha, 48, 205
Upaniṣads, 105, 137 (*see also* Vedas); Brahman in, 8, 42, 43–48, 89–90, 96, 185; *cakras* in, 94–96; Indian classical music in, 107, 108, 110; Indra in, 27; mantras in, 95, 134, 179, 199–200; *nāda* in, 94, 96; and Nāda-Brahman, 8, 92, 93, 99, 206, 211; Om in, 16–17, 42–48, 82, 89, 90, 92, 95, 110, 118, 178, 179, 185, 205–6; *praṇava* in, 205, 206; *śabda* in, 96; Śabda-Brahman in (*see* Śabda-Brahman, in the Upaniṣads); and Vaiṣṇavism, 184, 185
Upavarṣa, 61, 78, 80
Utpala, 126, 164

Vācaspati, 208, 212; commentary of, on *Vyāsa-Bhāṣya*, 82, 83, 85, 87, 88, 89, 91
Vaikhānasa, 173
Vaikharī, 7, 11, 205; and the Grammarians, 96, 207; in Kashmiri-Śaivism, 162, 169; in Śākta-Tantra, 143; in Vaiṣṇavism, 177, 178, 180, 182, 186
Vaiśesika school, 38, 52–53, 54
Vaiṣṇava. *See* Vaiṣṇavism
Vaiṣṇava Sampradāyas, 19, 172, 192, 194, 209; influence of *Bhāgavata-Purāna* on, 184, 187, 189 (*see also* Caitanya; Madhva; Nimbārka; Rāmānuja; Śrī-Vaiṣṇava; Vallabha)
Vaiṣṇava-Āgamas, 150, 173–83 (*see also* Pāncarātra texts)
Vaiṣṇavism, 8, 103, 144, 147, 160; Bhakti in, 201, 202; dualism in, 149, 189, 192; and the Grammarians, 192, 210; Krishna in (*see* Krishna, in Vaiṣṇavism); literature of, 150; mantras in (*see* Mantras, in Vaiṣṇavism); and Mīmāṁsā, 190–91, 192; monism of, 189, *nāda* in (*see Nāda*, in Vaiṣṇavism); and Nāda-Brahman (*see* Nāda-Brahman, in Vaiṣṇavism); *nāma-japa* in, 188–89, 199; Om in (*see* Om, in Vaiṣṇavism); origins of, 172; and the Pāncarātra texts, 19, 148, 184, 189, 192, 198, 210; rosary used in, 194, 202; and sacred sound, 16, 19, 52, 121, 148, 172–73, 176, 187, 201, 203; and Śākta-Tantra, 178, 195, 198; Śatki in (*see* Śakti, in Vaiṣṇavism); Sanskrit in, 175, 176, 177, 182–83, 185, 192–93; sects of, 172, 184, 187, 189, 209; soteriology of, 187–88, 201; Sphoṭavāda rejected by, 80, 193, 197; Viṣṇu in (*see* Viṣṇu, worshipped in Vaiṣṇavism)

Vāk, 7, 11, 20, 80; and Brahman, 7, 18, 29, 41; in Brāhmaṇas, 18, 28–29, 41; and creation, 73, 205; as feminine, 8, 25, 27–29, 35, 36, 51, 96; and Gorakhnāth, 100; and the Grammarians, 68, 73, 76; and the language of nature, 25–27; mantras as applied, 8, 23, 29, 51, 182, 205; and Nāda-Brahman, 46, 97; and Om, 205; and Prajāpati, 29, 41; and Śabda-Brahman, 16, 17, 42, 46, 52, 205; in Śākta-Tantra, 135, 143; and Śakti, 175; and speech, 16, 25, 35, 36; stages of, 97, 100–101; in Vaiṣṇavism, 175, 182; in the Vedas, 8, 16–17, 18, 25–29, 35, 36, 41, 42, 48, 51–52, 76, 205; in Yoga, 94

Vākyapadīya (Bhartṛhari), 65, 163; consciousness in, 73; grammar in, 72, 73; mantra recitation and cognition in, 71–72; *śabdapurva-yoga* in, 74, 75; sound in, 70; words and meaning in, 63, 66

Vallabha, 172, 184, 189, 194–96, 210

Vallabhācārya. *See* Vallabha

Vallabha-Sampradāya, 194–96

Van Buitenen, J. A. B., 13

Van der Leeuw, Gerardus, 34

Varenne, Jean, 97

Varivasyā-Rahasya (Rāya), 141–42

Varṇavāda, 49, 102, 197, 206 (*see also* Mīmāṁsās); adopted by Hindu sectarian traditions, 207, 210, 211; language in, 125–26; and Nāth Yoga, 100; refutation of, 205, 208 (*see also* Sphoṭavāda); and Sphoṭavāda, 7, 17, 19, 62, 205, 208; and Tantra, 160; and Vaiṣṇavism, 172, 182, 192; *varṇa* in, 8, 18, 52, 60, 130, 210; and the Vedas, 53, 206; word and meaning in, 54, 60–62

Vasugupta, 164, 169

Vāyu, 26–27

Vedāṅgas, 23, 65

Vedānta, 13, 52, 65, 90, 97; Brahman in, 18, 190, 194; Om in, 135; Sphoṭavāda rejected by, 76, 206

Vedānta-Sūtra, 79, 92; commentaries on, 190, 193, 194, 199

Vedas, 20, 74, 87, 186 (*see also* Āraṇyakas; *Atharva-Veda;* Brāhmaṇas; *Ṛg-Veda; Sama-Veda;* Upaniṣads; Vedāṅgas; *Yajur-Veda*); and the Advaita-Vedāntas, 79; and the Āgamas, 150, 153; as authorless and eternal, 13, 30, 33, 53, 57, 58, 59, 77, 78, 79, 190, 197, 211; Brahman in, 44, 66; Indian classical music in, 107–8; and India's living religion, 10, 151–52; injunctions in, 33–34, 55, 57, 59; language of, 31–33, 50, 58–59, 63; mantras in, 23, 29, 30–41, 47, 134, 136, 185; meter in, 40–41, 47, 51; and the Mīmāṁsā (*see* Mīmāṁsās, and the Vedas); *nāda* in, 107; Om in, 29, 64, 66, 69, 128, 138, 153, 205; oral character of, 2, 30; origin of, 23–24, 185; and phonetics, 16, 35–36, 216; relationship of word to meaning in, 31–32, 35, 49; revelatory character of, 10, 23–24, 37, 52–53; and ritual, 23, 30, 51, 59, 61, 62, 205 (*see also* Mantras); and Śabda-Brahman, 54, 81; and the Sāṁkhya doctrine, 77; sound in, 16, 23–24, 35, 37–38, 46, 51, 53, 59, 81, 204, 205, 218; and Vaiṣṇavism, 183, 185, 191–92, 197; Vāk in, 8, 16–17, 18, 25–29, 35, 36, 41, 42, 48, 51–52, 76, 205

Vikyābhūṣaṇa, Baladeva, 199

Vidyāranya, 126

Viṣṇu (*see also* Brahman; Krishna); and Brahman, 9, 45, 48, 96, 153, 154; and Lakṣmi, 175, 178; and mantras, 175, 183; and Nāda-Brahman, 48, 109, 203, 209, 210; and Om, 9, 46, 175, 179, 187, 191; and Pāncarātra, 151; personal role of, 18, 187, 209, 211; in Śaivism, 19, 157; Śakti of, 176, 178, 179, 183; and Sanskrit, 175, 176; and Tantra, 184; and the Vedas, 44, 46, 172, 184; worshipped in Vaiṣṇavism, 13, 19, 103, 148, 172, 174–75, 176, 178, 179, 183, 184, 185, 187, 189, 191, 192, 193, 203, 210
Viṣṇuswamin, 194
Vṛtra, 26–27, 40
Vyāsa, 208; commentary of, on the *Yoga-Sūtra*, 83, 85, 86–87, 88–89, 91

West, 6; Hinduism studied in, 3, 4, 5, 6; intellectual colonialism of, 12; language in, 62–63; Nāda-Yoga techniques in, 111; positivist prejudice in, toward non-Western mysticism, 10; and the relationship between word and meaning, 54, 58; rosary beads known in, 134; and Tantra, 122–23; terminology of, 12–13; visual orientation of, 1–2, 10; word mysticism in, 217–18
Wheelock, Wade, 33, 136
Whitney, W. D., 51
Woodroffe, Sir John, 122, 129
Woods, James H., 83, 84

Yajur-Veda, 23, 33, 40, 44
Yāska, 59, 80
Yoga, 23, 83, 166; academic study of, 83; *bindu* in, 93, 99, 104, 105, 206, 208; and Brahman, 89–90, 91, 94, 95, 96; cakras in, 94, 98–99; divinity in, 87, 94, 98, 102; and the Grammarians, 83–85, 105; and Indian classical music, 96, 109, 110; and Īśvara, 82, 86; and mantras (*see* Mantras, in Yoga); *nāda* in (*see Nāda*, in Yoga); *Nāda-Brahman* in (*see Nāda-Brahman*, in Yoga); and Om (*see* Om, in Yoga); origins of, 82; in the Pāncarātra texts, 174; and Patañjali, 82, 97; *śabda* in, 52; and Śabda-Brahman, 35, 52–53; and sacred sound, 16, 17–18, 20, 35, 48, 52, 81, 83, 85–86, 91, 92; and Śaivism, 159, 161, 165; and Sāṁkhya, 77, 84; and Śiva-Śakti, 101, 102; sonic meditation in, 17, 46, 73, 83, 85–86, 89–90, 91, 92, 93, 99–100, 211; soteriology in, 97; *sphoṭa* supported in, 76, 80, 85, 105; in Vaiṣṇavism, 176, 183, 184; word mysticism in, 76
Yoga-Bhāṣya (Vyāsa), 85, 88
Yogacūḍāmaṇi-Upaniṣad, 95–96, 99
Yogarāja, 164
Yogaśikha-Upaniṣad, 92, 94–95, 96
Yoga-Sūtra (Patañjali), 83–92; authorship of, 82, 83–85; commentaries on, 83, 85, 86–87, 88, 208, 212; and Grammarian doctrine, 84–85; meditation on sacred sound in, 85–88; Om in, 86; and *sphoṭa*, 84–85
Yoga-Sūtra tradition, 17, 81
Yoga-Upaniṣads, 81, 91–97, 98, 99, 118; *nāda* in, 92–97, 208; Nāda-Brahman in, 17, 92–97, 99–100, 208; and Nāda-Yoga, 112; and nonlinguistic sound, 46; *praṇava* in, 82
Yoga-Vārttika (Bhikṣu), 83, 85
Yoginī-hṛdaya-Tantra, 139, 141, 142